An

invitation

to

teach

the

young

and

participate

in

the

unfinished

work

of

the

schools

Kevin Ryan

University of Chicago

James M. Cooper

University of Houston

HOUGHTON MIFFLIN COMPANY

BOSTON New York Atlanta
Geneva, Illinois Dallas
Palo Alto

Spare the rod
and spoil the child.

Education
is power!

Geometry teaches
you how to think.

Teach the whole
child.

Open a school
and you'll close a prison.

This will all make
sense to you
later on.

What these kids
need is motivation.

There is no such thing
as a bad question—
only bad answers.

Those

who

can,

teach

Printed in the U.S.A.

Library of Congress Catalog Card Number: 74-169893

ISBN: 0-395-12666-5

To

the

human

potential

of

the

young

Contents

Editor's Introduction

Not so long ago, the introductory course in Education (capital E) was on most campuses a pretty dull experience. In all probability the professor was a good guy (or gal), and no doubt there were some high spots along the way; but the typical textbook was less than exciting, and the typical student— let's face it—was justifiably skeptical about the course and what he might expect to gain from it. Education (capital E) just wasn't a reputable discipline, and especially at the introductory level its content seemed thin.

Well, things are a little different now. Education (capital E) hasn't yet attained full respectability, and there remain some thin spots. But it seems that everyone in the country is all steamed up about education (small e), one way or another, and both the introductory course and its literature now seem more important. The business of becoming a teacher is now taken much more seriously, and those who would write textbooks for prospective teachers have to meet much higher expectations than before.

Kevin Ryan and Jim Cooper have responded to this challenge with remarkable skill. They're experienced enough to know what teaching is all about, but they're young and rebellious enough to feel that at this stage teaching poses many more questions than answers. Their approach to education is fresh and lively, and they've worked hard to bring the reader with them into the experience of the book. Every so often, for example, they stop to talk to each other within earshot—or should I say eyeshot?—of the reader (see the Dialogues). Frequently they ask the reader himself to stop and talk at least to himself about an issue or problem. The chapters are full of illustrative material and authentic cases or examples. Even the end-of-chapter questions and suggestions, which in most textbooks are mere busywork, play a strong part in helping the reader to become very much involved in examining teaching as a career.

Also helpful to the reader is the rather unusual format for introducing each of the eleven chapters. Not only a brief outline of contents but also a review of "key points" is furnished, with references to classifications, concepts, theories, facts, sequences, and methodology.

In each chapter there is a brief biographical sketch of a teacher of note. The sketches include some of the all-time greats who are no longer with us (Montessori, Dewey, Thoreau, Mann and Pestallozi), some luminaries on the current scene (Ashton-Warner, Bruner, Bettelheim and Illich), and two lesser-known teachers—the late Ray Fleming and twenty-seven-year-old Anselmo Garza—whose experiences exemplify what many teachers are up against today.

Although historical and background information is not neglected, the main emphasis in the book is on current problems and questions. In the opening chapter, for example, the student examines the unfinished work of the schools. Next, in the curriculum chapter, he looks at emerging alternatives. Chapter Seven addresses problems teachers face, and following a review in Chapter Eight of the ways schools are governed are three concluding chapters that deal with the role and status of teachers, the tension points in education, and some of the new developments in organization, instruction, and school design.

For readers whose commitment to the teaching role may be tentative, there are three chapters of special significance. In the fourth chapter—which, by the way, includes some good case material—the student is challenged to examine both the nature and the legitimacy of his interest in a teaching career. Chapter Five discusses various factors in the makeup of a teacher, and Chapter Six tells how people become teachers. In this chapter, I found the section on "learning how not to be a teacher" particularly intriguing.

As Chapter Nine shows, the future of teaching is quite uncertain. "You've come a long way, Teach," a theme that is developed in this provocative chapter, is not the same as saying that Teach has "arrived." On the other hand, a survey book of this sort helps us to appreciate that education (small e) is a varied and complex enterprise and that the young man or woman who enters its ranks must necessarily be intelligent, well prepared, and highly motivated.

Certainly the two young authors have these qualities, and their work should be well received by kindred spirits. We might even expect that the introductory course in Education (capital E), with this book and its companion reader[1] as resources, will be anything but dull.

Robert H. Anderson
Harvard University

---

[1] *Kaleidoscope* (Boston: Houghton Mifflin, 1972), edited by Kevin and Jim, is a collection of recent, nontechnical thoughts on teaching and education from diverse sources and people.

Preface

This is a book of questions. In fact, it was written in the first place to answer the question, "What are the things people beginning their formal study of education should do?" We think the answer is questions—questions which are keys to the central issues and problems of education—and we have organized the book around such questions. We must warn you, though: the questions look deceptively simple, like an innocent packet of fishhooks. We have embellished these question-hooks with lures and baited them with dainty morsels. And, like good fishermen, all we want you to do is swallow them. We believe that, once that happens, the hooks will stick in your vitals and our work will be done. Putting aside this discomfiting metaphor, we hope that these questions provide direction and focus to your study well beyond the time you spend with this book. For those of you who are contemplating careers in teaching, we believe that pursuing answers to these questions will help you clarify your career goals.

In writing this book, we put aside many cherished rules of textbook writing: "Authors should be distant and remote"; we have tried not to be. "The authors' bias should be suppressed or at least well-hidden"; our biases are all too evident. "Textbooks should be deadly serious, especially about such a sacred matter as education"; we genuinely enjoyed writing our book and hope we can provide an occasional smile. "Textbooks should be free of distracting materials"; ours is filled with distractions, as a flip through the pages will prove. "Textbooks should be uncontroversial and safe"; we would be disappointed if ours did not provoke controversy. "Textbooks should treat the reader as a passive recipient of their wisdom"; we have written a book for active, responsive readers. "Textbooks are written for the authors' professional colleagues"; this book was written for students. "Textbooks should cover everything, at least once-over-lightly"; we have sacrificed comprehensive treatment in order to highlight what we consider most critical in education today.

Perhaps our most serious departure from the rules is that, when discussing the schools and the teaching profession, we occasionally lack the appropriate reverent tone. The reason is simple. We don't have the appropriate reverence. While we are truly proud of many of the accomplishments of our schools and of the dedication of so many teachers, we are nevertheless

convinced that schools should be much more effective. We need a curriculum not for the past but for the future. We need better-trained, more skillful teachers. We need teachers with a clearer grasp of why and how they are
developing the human potential of their students. We can do much better.

We wrote this book because we couldn't find the kind of textbook our
students and the students of many of our colleagues needed and wanted.
We wrote it in the particular manner we did because it felt more honest to
write it this way and because it was certainly more fun. We hope our sense
of the kind of book satisfying to today's students is correct. If we were wrong,
please tell us (see page 487).

A final word about the title. George Bernard Shaw, the great English play-
wright with the razor tongue, had many unpleasant things to say about
schools and education, but one of his cruelest remarks was reserved for
teachers: "He who can, does. He who cannot, teaches." The world has taken
a lot of turns since Shaw wrote that line. Education is no longer a luxury of
the leisure class. The teacher can no longer be a silly, foppish pedant.
Teaching is a much more demanding and crucial occupation than it ever
was before. Developing man's human potential is serious work. Now those
who can, teach.

Kevin Ryan
University of Chicago

James M. Cooper
University of Houston

ACKNOWLEDGMENTS

Whenever any of us put pen to paper, we are indebted to many people. However, in the writing of this book we were especially conscious of the help given by the following people: William MacDonald, who talked us into the project and supported us all the way; Robert H. Anderson for his excellent critical readings and suggestions; Myra Sadker, whose help in gathering data was invaluable; Ernie Lundquist for sharing with us the secrets of the Cosmic Apple and for running out for coffee and sandwiches; Ann Lebowitz for her sensitive editing and general good sportsmanship; Libby Scanlon for keeping the editing going; Penny Hull for taking us down the home stretch and across the finish line; Roberta Osler for her work on the annotated list of audiovisual materials; Marge Coffing for her editorial assistance on the first drafts; William Geulcher for his aid in developing the case materials in Chapter Four; Martin Haberman, Alice Carnes, Fred Wilhelms, Wilford Weber, Pearlie Dove, E. C. Powell, Bruce Appleby, Richard L. Hopkins, Jonathan Ball and G. W. Ford for their helpful readings of our first draft; David R. Helmstadter for overseeing the finishing touches; Marion Crowley and Kathy Carey for their assistance in typing the several drafts of this book; and our colleagues and students for their many good ideas and continuing support. Very special acknowledgment is due to our wives, Marilyn and Sue, for the substantial intellectual and psychological contributions they made to this book.

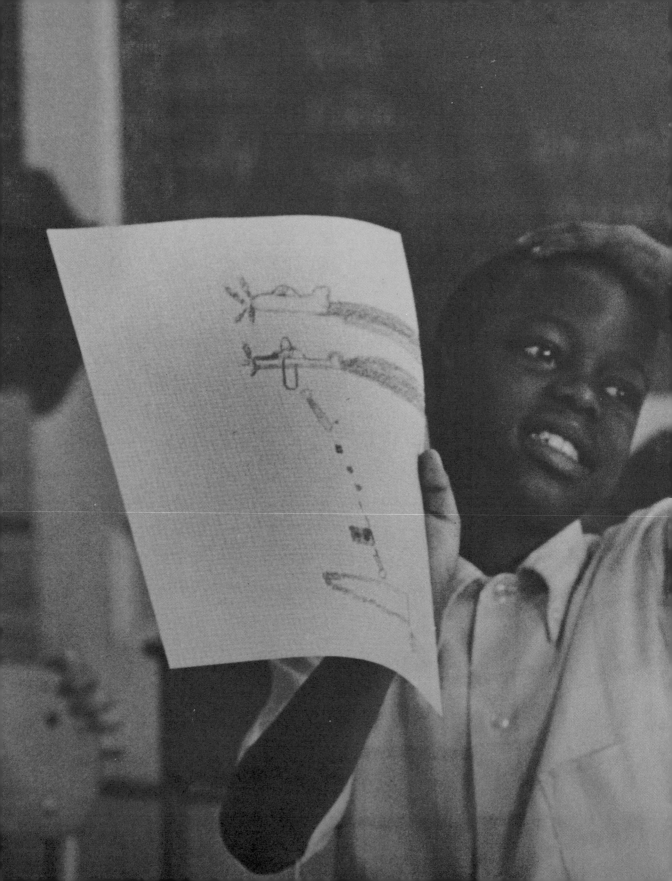

SCHOOLS

1 What Is a School?

"What is a school?" This may not strike you as a particularly profound question. In fact, it probably seems rather tame. School is an everyday thing. We have all spent vast stretches of our time there. Much of what we are—intellectually, socially and emotionally—can be traced to our experiences in school. School is just . . . school. However, behind the familiar words and images lie thorny issues which have baffled theoreticians and practitioners of education for years. Quiet communities have been split into warring camps because of their inability to agree on an answer to this question. Let us see if you can answer the question, "What is a school?" In the space provided below, jot down a definition or two of school.

_____

_____

_____

_____

_____

If you did not stop reading to think about the question or commit yourself to writing an answer—well, you're probably like a majority of readers. What kept you from doing so? The answer to this question may tell you a good deal about yourself as a learner and about the educational system of which you are a product. Have you been trained to devour pages without really confronting the issues conveyed by the words? Have you been conditioned to think that other people's—experts', authors', teachers'—answers are more important or more "right" than yours? Are you the product of an educational system which claims it wants you to think independently but functions by forcing answers on you and requiring you to spit them back? Probably you are. If so, it is our hope that this will be a different kind of book and a different type of reading-questioning-thinking experience for you.[1] We want it to be unlike so much else we read: things we pick up, spend time with and put down again without having been moved or changed in any way. Being teachers ourselves, we want this book to have an impact on you and to help you make a good decision about whether or not to be a teacher. We want you

---

[1] We are violating a time-honored textbook convention by switching voices. We find that in writing this book we sometimes speak to the reader in the third person, such as "the reader will note" or "one might argue." At other times we use the more intimate second person, as in "you may not agree" or "we would like you to . . ." We are inconsistent in this matter because our mood is inconsistent. We wish to speak more directly to the reader at some times than others. We also find that we use "you" when we feel more urgency about an issue.

It is also conventional to refer to the teacher as "he." Since teaching is an occupation with large numbers of both men and women, we have chosen to refer to the teacher sometimes as "she" and sometimes as "he." We also do this because we do not want to be accused of being male chauvinist pigs.

to be seeking answers to the questions which can lead you to be a good teacher. For these reasons, you need to read this book in a different way. Encounter it. Participate in it. Fight with it. Laugh with it. Laugh at it. Improve it by adding yourself to it. You will be asked and nudged to do things which are not in keeping with your natural style of learning. Doing them, however, may help you identify more clearly how you learn best and give you a sense of the various ways one can learn and can know something.

We're asking you to invest something of yourself in this book. That old tired cliché, "you get out of it what you put into it," applies here. So, again, if you didn't think about and write down an answer to "What is a school?" go back and have a try at it.

Your answer to the question, "What is a school?" reflects who you are and what your experience with school has been. Perhaps you responded in one of the following ways:

A school is an agency which weans the child from the protective warmth of the family and gets him ready to contribute to the world of work.

A school is a bunch of bricks and mortar, chalkboards and water fountains (usually with wadded gum in them) arranged in a predictable way.

A school is a place where they fix your head so you think like everyone else.

A school is where children fall in love with learning.

Photo by William Simmons for Educational Facilities Laboratories.

SCHOOLS

A school is a place where young savages become citizens.

A school is where we learn how good or bad we are compared with a lot of people our own age at a lot of different skills and tasks.

A school is a place where we explore who we are and how we can become full, creative human beings.

A school is where children learn to be virtuous.

A school is a place where the children of one generation come together to unite against the generation in power.

A school is a fun palace.

A school is a fact factory.

A school is a tax-supported institution where the dead wisdom and worn-out skills of the past are force-fed to the young.

A school is where education takes place.

Each of these descriptions says a great deal about the school experience of the person who formulated it. What does your definition say about you and your experience?

EDUCATION AND SCHOOLING

It is commonly believed that school is where people go to get an education. On the other hand, Marshall McLuhan, one of the sages of the Sixties, has quipped that today children interrupt their educations to go to school. The distinction between ''schooling'' and ''education'' implied by this remark is important. Like ''school,'' ''education'' has myriad definitions. We have sprinkled a few such definitions here and there throughout the book for you to sample. For the moment, however, let us say that education is a process of human growth by which an individual gains greater understanding and control over himself and his world. It involves our minds, our bodies and our relations with the people and the world around us. Education, while taking many institutional and sometimes rigid forms, is strictly speaking a process, an activity characterized by continuous development and changes. The end product of the process of education is learning.

If a school is a physical location, schooling is the specific process which takes place there. It is a formalized process, and its basic pattern varies little from one setting to the next. Throughout the country, children arrive at school at approximately the same time, take assigned seats, are taught by an adult, use the same textbooks, do homework, take exams and so on. The slices of reality which are to be learned, whether the alphabet or an understanding of English metrics, have usually been specified in advance. What is learned as a result of schooling is also limited by subject: if a little boy wants to learn what a girl *really* looks like, he just knows that school is not the place to make his investigations. In the same way, the high school student knows she is not likely to find out in her classes how practical politics really operates or what contemporary *avant garde* writers are up to. Finally, schooling tends to be limited to the young. There are, then, definite conditions surrounding the formalized process of schooling.

Education is much more open-ended and all-inclusive than schooling. Education knows few bounds. It can take place anywhere, whether in a tavern or on a tractor. It includes both the formal learning which takes place in schools and the whole universe of informal learning, from hooking a worm on a line to burping a baby. The agents of education can range from a revered granddad to the guests on a late-night TV talk show, from a retarded child to an acorn. While schooling has a certain predictability, education takes us by surprise. We go to the movies to relax and come home with a vivid sense of poverty's corrupting influence on the human spirit. We get into a casual conversation with a stranger and discover how little we know about other religions. People are engaged in education from the cradle to the grave. The child learns how to satisfy himself by putting his thumb into his mouth. A retired businessman picks up a book on prison life and goes on to become involved in penal reform. In its all-inclusiveness, education, as a term or label for human activities, is similar to the word "life." In the same unspecified way everything is part of life, almost everything can be called education.

WHAT IS THE RELATIONSHIP BETWEEN EDUCATION
AND SCHOOLING?

The relationship between education and schooling is not always a positive one. While education is essentially a process of growth, schooling can provoke growth, stagnation or even deformation. Another related issue has to do with the teacher's place in the schooling–education relationship.

Schools are created for the express purpose of providing a certain type of educational experience, which we call the curriculum. Teachers are trained and hired to fulfill the purposes of the curriculum. In simpler societies, when a boy could learn to be a man by following his father around and imitating the men of the village, schools were not necessary. Formal schooling became a social necessity when the home and the community were no longer effective or competent at training the young for adulthood through informal contacts. Societies have realized that education is too important to be left to chance. While important things are sometimes learned on street corners and grandfathers are excellent teachers, they are simply not as reliable as the formal educative process. There is an excellent possibility that if education is randomly acquired the young will grow up with a lopsided understanding of the world and poor preparation for adult life. The chance schooling of the street has educated many in such skills as how to exploit one's fellow man, and produced many a champion penny-pitcher who can't read. Occasionally we see families with the intellectual resources, skills and time to

SCHOOLS

. . . if we divorce schools and their curriculum from the guts and hopes of human beings, we can expect students to find them gutless and hopeless. Dr. Mark Shedd, Philadelphia Bulletin, December 15, 1970.

educate their own young, but this is all too rare amid the complexities of modern life. Also, for each individual set of parents to educate their children, even with the help of older children, grandparents and neighbors, is wasteful and socially inefficient. So schools are established.

The distinction between education and schooling is often blurred because the two concepts are undifferentiated in most people's minds. Keeping the differences between these two concepts clearly in mind is often particularly difficult for the people who should be most sensitive to them, teachers who "do" education "in" schools. People enter teaching because they wish to educate. However, the everyday experience of working in a school inevitably causes their allegiances to shift from abstract educational ideals to the network of personalities and ideas surrounding the particular schools where they teach. Often teachers find themselves doing things that are contrary to their ideals, such as behaving in extremely authoritarian ways, because such practices suit the institutional demands of their school. This is a particularly dangerous tendency at times like the present when many of society's institutions need to be changed or adjusted to new cultural realities. Teachers almost inevitably invest themselves in what the school *is* rather than what it should be. Much of the unrest on faculties can be traced to their confusion about the relationship of education to schooling.

DISCOVERING THE PURPOSES OF SCHOOL

By distinguishing between education and schooling we may have clarified the question, "What is a school?", but we have not yet answered it. We need to think further about the goals of a school. What follows are some means of searching out its purposes and functions.

FORMAL STATEMENTS

The most direct method is to read official statements of purpose. Like most institutions, our schools have occasioned many official attempts to explain what they are all about. A few illustrations may suffice. In 1960 John Gardner contributed the chapter on education to the report of the President's Commission on National Goals. Discussing the purposes behind our society's support for schools, he wrote, "Our deepest convictions impel us to foster individual fulfillment. We wish each one to achieve the promise that is in him. We wish each one to be worthy of a free society, and capable of strengthening a free society."[2]

A year later, The Educational Policies Commission of the National Education Association issued a statement entitled "The Central Purpose of American Education," whose last paragraph reads:

The purpose which runs through and strengthens all educational purposes—the common thread of education—is the development of the ability to think. This is the central purpose to which the school must be oriented if it is to accomplish either its traditional task or those newly accentuated by recent changes in the world. To say that it is central is not to say that it is the sole purpose or in all circumstances the most important purpose, but that it must be a pervasive concern in the work of the school. Many agencies contribute to achieving educational objectives, but this particular objective may not be generally attained unless the school focuses on it. In this context, therefore, the development of every student's rational powers must be recognized as centrally important.[3]

Both these statements by high-level groups are representative of official views of the purposes of the schools. They are eloquent, but they are also highly abstract. They may point a teacher in the general direction he should be traveling, but such statements have little value in the fast-moving world of the classroom. When a teacher is struggling to come up with an approach to a map-reading lesson, statements of purpose such as "to foster individual fulfillment" and "to develop the ability to think" are not especially helpful. However, expecting that kind of relevance may be asking for too much.

There is, however, the question of accuracy. To what degree do these statements reflect the real purposes and functions of school? Terry Borton, a Philadelphia teacher, doesn't think they are very accurate. He writes:

There are two sections to almost every school's statement of educational objectives: one for real and one for show. The first, the real one, talks about the academic excellence, subject mastery, getting into college or a job. The other discusses the human purpose of school: values, feelings, personal growth, the full and happy life. It is included because everyone knows that is important, and that it ought to be central in the life of every school. But it is only for show. Everyone knows how little schools have done about it.[4]

Another factor limiting the value of statements of purpose is their after-the-fact quality. Purposes and goals are determined for public consumption, not as guides to moment-by-moment behavior. They are not intellectual

---

[2] American Assembly, *Goals for Americans: Programs of Action in the Sixties,* ed. President's Commission on National Goals (Englewood Cliffs, N.J.: Prentice-Hall, 1960), p. 81.

[3] Educational Policies Commission, *The Central Purpose of American Education* (Washington, D.C.: National Education Association, 1961), p. 15.

[4] Terry Borton, "Reach, Touch, and Teach," *Saturday Review* 52 (January 18, 1969): 56.

Miss Peach by Mell Lazarus. Courtesy of Publishers-Hall Syndicate.

cornerstones for real curricular decisions about what should be taught and how it should be taught. They do not affect a school's decision to teach the children to read or not to push other children or not to talk while the teacher is talking. These lessons will be taught in schools that have opposing goals, and in schools that have no written statements of purpose at all. In other words, schools do not come into existence to fulfill their stated purposes. The educational psychologist, J. M. Stephens, speculates that "the very existence of schooling may stem not from a deliberate decision of groups or societies, but from blind, spontaneous tendencies which are developed by evolutionary demand and which are found to be prevalent in human beings, although more pronounced in some people than in others."[5]

A final point about statements of purpose is that they may mask completely contradictory practices. For instance, it is common for schools to espouse in their charters the idea, also proposed in the Educational Policies Commission's statement, that the schools should develop the child's ability to think. The painful fact is, however, that much of our schooling teaches children that they cannot think. Many children, as a result of what they are made to learn and how they are taught, leave school believing they are "dumb-dumbs" and that the life of the mind is not for them. For them, school is an intellectually discouraging place where they learn what they are not capable of rather than what they can do. But these schools, too, repeat noble phrases attesting to their dedication to teaching children to think.

PERSONAL EXPERIENCE

If the formal statements by commissions and individuals can be misleading, why cannot we simply rely on our own experience? We have all spent a large percentage of our lives in schools, and each of us has a rich store of ideas and impressions to draw on. Personal experience is undeniably a very im-

---

[5] J. M. Stephens, *The Process of Schooling, A Psychological Examination* (New York: Holt, Rinehart & Winston, 1967), p. 8.

REPRODUCE YOUR SCHOOL IN WORDS

Spend a few minutes reflecting on one of the schools you attended before coming to college. Recall its physical characteristics, the dominant colors, how it smelled, the architectural imagination it reflected. Think of the moods you associate with this school. Then write down all of the descriptive words and phrases that have come to your mind. Don't be concerned with order or form, but try to write at least twenty such phrases.

Now that you have recorded these bits of description, pick out the five you feel to be most important. Write them below in order of importance.

portant source of data to help us come to know what a school is. Understanding the school from personal experience has, however, two limitations. One is the angle from which we have seen our own schools; the other is the narrowness of that angle. The position from which the student observes, experiences and comes to know the school is just one of several vantage points. Teachers have another very different point of view. Administrators another. Parents another. Militant student groups another. And foreign visitors to our schools another. For instance, the students in a seventh-grade American history class finish the year confused and upset because their teacher has raised serious and unanswered questions about the administration of justice in our country. But the teacher feels that unsettling the students, and goading them to asking new questions, is exactly what he is trying to accomplish. The principal, on the other hand, is worried about all the calls he has received from the children's parents, some challenging what the teacher is doing and threatening to withdraw their support of the school. Many of the parents think their children are too young to deal with complex social issues. One community group has condemned the teacher as un-American, unprofessional and a troublemaker. Another organization has come to his defense for making education socially relevant and for personifying American idealism. A foreign visitor may be confused by all the uproar, shocked by the lack of respect afforded the teacher and disturbed that the teacher told the students so little and asked them so many questions. The angle from which we perceive, then, affects what we see of school and the judgment we make about it. We have somehow to make up for the limitations of our angle of vision if we are really to know what a school is.

The angle of perception is not the only limitation of personal experience: so is the narrowness of the slice of experience we observe. You have just composed a word picture of a school you have attended. Contrast your word picture with these two:

strong smell of disinfectant and human sweat in the air   gritty sound of chalk scrapping blackboard   fear of getting beat up on way home   drab, greenish paint everywhere   hundreds of broken windows

bright colors and sunny rooms   same alphabet cards as grade school on top of board   knowing everyone—all 105—in the school   bonfire prep rally for whole community before regional football championships   two-year-old desks with carved up tops!

Certainly, the two word pictures differ immensely. It is doubtful that their authors went to the same school, and, if both portraits are accurate, it is evident that their high schools were quite different. The first sounds like a rather run-down school in a slum. The second could be a relatively new school in a rural area. The point is that the same word, "school," conjures very different images in two minds. This is because schools, and the experience of going to school, vary radically within this country. The public school in a small cattle town along the Rio Grande River, serving mainly Mexican-American children, is worlds away from the private boys' preparatory school on the outskirts of New Haven, Connecticut. The newly-integrated elementary school in a tense working-class neighborhood can be profoundly different from the busy, innovative elementary school in a quiet suburb just 15 freeway minutes away. When we call on our own experience to answer the question, "What is a school?" we must remember that each of us has had quite limited experience. A great variety of people, motives, activities and outcomes are covered by the simple word "school." Nevertheless, there *are*

The school is an old, dark, brick, two-story contraption, a Norman fortress, built as if learning and virtue needed a stronghold, one defended by old-fashioned weapons, in place of turrets and parapets, with narrow slits in the bricks through which scholars with crossbows can peep out at an atomic age. John Hersey.

many points of commonality in the school experiences of people in this country, which we will explore throughout this volume.

MODELS OF SCHOOLS

A model is a representation of reality. All of us create mental models to help us sort out the hundreds of thousands of sounds and sights we encounter daily and to organize them into sensible patterns. Scientists, in particular, use theoretical models in their efforts to predict events and to explain why certain things have occurred. Models can be similarly useful to us as we attempt to answer the question, "What is a school?" A number of descriptive models have been developed to explain the purposes and functions of a

Cartoon by Joseph Farris, copyright ©
1968, Saturday Review, Inc.

"The main thing is not to take it personal."

school. A few such models are briefly described below.[6] As you read, think about how well each one describes the schools you know.

The School as an Acculturator.   The school brings together people of divergent backgrounds to accommodate themselves to and share one culture. The school's role is to teach "the American Way of Life," and to pass on the customs, values and social patterns of the dominant group to immigrants and others who have been excluded from full participation in this society. According to this view, the school is a melting pot, whose function is to minimize the influence of minority ethnic, racial and religious influences and to teach "Americanism."

The School as a Factory.   The school prepares children for industrial work. The modern school, which was in fact designed during the Industrial Revolution, preadapts children to the world of work by immersing them in a crowded, noisy environment ruled by a time clock and dominated by the production mentality. Large numbers of students (raw material) are brought together to be processed by teachers (workers) who are overseen, in turn, by administrators (foremen). As in a factory, regimentation, lack of individualization and systemization (seating, grouping, grading) are the major operating principles. The final product of the school is "a good worker."

The School as a Preparer for College.   The school prepares the student for more schooling. The goal of the school is to ready the boy or girl for admission to college. As a result, the here and now is not nearly as important as the future. Using this model, the curriculum of the secondary school is justified to the degree it prepares students to do college-level work. Likewise, the elementary school curriculum is justified to the degree it prepares students for success in secondary school. In this model, the "prestige" of a school as a stepping-stone to a "good college" is an important consideration.

The School as a Bureaucracy.   The school is a training ground for life in a bureaucratized society. According to this model, the school is a set of experiences which wean the child from the protective and highly personalized care of his family so that he can deal with the governmental and economic bureaucracies he will encounter in later life. School teaches us how to cooperate and interact easily with large numbers of people we do not know well. We learn how to live by rules in whose formulation we had little or no voice. According to this model, the school helps to modify the individual so that he will not oppose the bureaucracy, thus assuring the safety of the system.

---

[6] Several of the models described below are adapted from Bernard Spodek's "Early Learning for What?" *Phi Delta Kappan* 50 (March 1969): 394–396.

The School as Babysitter.   The school relieves the parents of full-time responsibility for their children. The school is valued as a repository or "dumping ground" which enables parents, particularly mothers, to pursue new alternatives. In an industrial state such as ours, releasing women from extended childrearing frees them for other work. A variant of this is the mean babysitter model: the parents are free to be continually loving and permissive to the child, while the school dispenses discipline and, sometimes, punishment.

A phenomenon as varied and widespread as a school cannot be explained by a single model. And a model is only as good as its ability to explain reality to us. Therefore, a model of a school has value to the degree that it helps us understand what we already know about schools and to make sense of the new information we receive.

THE NEED FOR OBJECTIVITY

Our attempt to find out what a school is can be greatly aided by the objectivity that characterizes scientific investigation. We can avail ourselves of such objectivity in two ways: we can acquire it ourselves by studying and using the scientific method and we can familiarize ourselves with the work of scientists from various disciplines who have studied education and the schools.

Throughout this book we call upon a large number of sources to further understanding or, at least, to strengthen our grasp on the questions we have posed. Besides teachers and children, and an occasional novelist and poet, we have selected from the research and theories of philosophers, psychologists, economists, computer scientists and scholars from several disciplines. Since we have borrowed rather heavily from psychology, sociology and anthropology, a page or two of introduction may be helpful to readers who have not yet studied these disciplines. Let it be understood, however, that these are very abbreviated and thus potentially deceptive descriptions. Readers familiar with the intellectual approaches of these disciplines are urged to skip ahead to the section entitled, "The Function of the School: An Anthropologist's Analysis."

The Psychologist's View.   A psychologist studies the mind and human behavior. An educational psychologist specializes in the relationship between the human mind and education. There are several types of educational psychologists, and different schools of thought within the discipline, but broadly speaking they all concern themselves with human development and the conditions that foster it. Among the areas on which they focus are the development of concepts, the formation of attitudes, stimulation of creative behavior, the use of instructional strategies in the classroom and the motivation of the learner. Because of the nature of his field and the questions with which he is dealing, the educational psychologist is especially interested in the question, "What is a school?" He is not satisfied to regard the school simply as the setting where the activities that interest him happen to take place. The school and its characteristics have a pronounced effect on the phenomena he studies. In attempting to answer our

Photo by Eileen Ahrenholz.

Maria Montessori (1870–1952)

Maria Montessori became a proponent of preschool education, an urban educational reformer and a believer in equal opportunities for women sixty years before any of these issues were matters of widespread concern.

As a child, Maria Montessori excelled in mathematics and thought of becoming an engineer. Later she developed an interest in medicine, and overcame tremendous criticism to become the first woman to enroll in the University of Rome's medical school. After graduating, she lectured on anthropology at the university, and became associated with the psychiatric clinic. She developed an interest in retarded children and, suspecting that they were far more capable of learning than was commonly believed, founded and headed the Orthophrenic School, where she achieved remarkable results with mentally defective children.

But it was not until she was 36 years old that Madame Montessori found her lifework. Believing her methods could be even more effective with normal children, she opened her first school, the Casa dei Bambini (Children's House), to the preschool-age street urchins of Rome. Madame Montessori's school was run on the principle of allowing children freedom within a carefully-designed environment and under the sensitive guidance of a trained directress. The materials and toys available in the school were prescribed, but the children were allowed freedom to handle or ignore them as they wished. Self-learning and individualization were stressed, but there were definite limits on freedom: students were required to come to school clean, and even their free play was structured. However, a child was never forced either to play or to learn. The teachers were instructed simply to wait until the child became interested in a particular game or project. A child who was concentrating deeply on a ritual with a toy was not aided or corrected by a teacher unless he asked for help.

Madame Montessori discovered that certain simple and precise educational materials evoked sustained interest and attention in the young child. Children under five years old would concentrate on a single task, oblivious to distraction, for periods of from 15 minutes to an hour,

and afterward seem refreshed rather than tired. Madame Montessori's close observations of children led her to conclude that, from birth to age six, every child possesses an "absorbent mind" which equips him to learn more quickly and easily than at any subsequent period in his life. Throughout these years, she found, the child experiences periods of specialized sensitivity, during which his interest and mental capacity are particularly suited to the acquisition of particular knowledge, such as colors, language and textures. Montessori recognized that small children learn through their senses, and developed methods of stimulating the child's senses in ways that would enhance learning. For instance, children were taught the alphabet with sandpaper letters which they could manipulate with their fingers. Montessori was the first to use flashcards as a sensory stimulus, and she even introduced the hula hoop, which became a fad in the U.S. in the fifties. She was severely criticized for ignoring discipline; she replied that, in the conventional schools she had visited, children were "not disciplined, but annihilated."

Madame Montessori's teaching methods have aroused considerable interest in the U.S. as a result of recent psychological research verifying many of her theories. Psychologists and educators have come to agree with her that the period of early childhood is critical in determining a person's intellectual potential.

Before her death, Madame Montessori travelled widely, establishing schools, teaching teachers and promoting her still unconventional ideas. A typical Montessori classroom today is a beehive of activity, each child pursuing an independent task at his own speed. A two-and-a-half-year-old carries a tray holding a jug of water and two glasses across the room. On reaching the other side he begins to fill the glasses with dry grains of rice. He is joined by a little girl who sweeps the spilled rice into a pile. A third child appears with a brush and dustpan to collect the deposit. A group of children is busy using colored pencils to shade designs they have made themselves using geometric forms cut out of metal. The teacher dictates words to some boys who compose them on a mat with large moveable letters.

New Montessori schools have recently sprung up in this country in response to the demands of parents. Teachers of underprivileged or minority children, in particular, claim great success with Montessori techniques, and the day-care center movement and the Head Start program have both been significantly influenced by her views and methodology.

question, the trained psychologist would ask such questions as the following: What changes is the school attempting to make in the child? How is it known whether these changes have been made? How are the components of the school—teachers, learning materials and physical phenomena like heat and light—organized to help the student learn, and thus achieve the goals of the school? What principles of learning pervade the school's activities. In what ways is the school hindering learning? What unconscious or incidental learnings are acquired by children who attend school? And then there is the overriding question: is the school experience nurturing the intellectual, social and emotional potential of the children?

Before a psychologist would attempt to answer such questions, he would observe and record much of the behavior that takes place in the school. He would also administer tests to ascertain the students' capacity to learn and how well they are actually learning. The educational psychologist does not try to explain all the phenomena of the school, but only those that bear directly on the mind and its development.

The Sociologist's View.   Sociologists investigate how people live together in groups—how groups are formed and how they function, how individuals behave collectively and how they organize themselves to get things done. The educational sociologist looks at the school as a specialized agency for the socialization—that is, the adaptation to society—of the young. The educational sociologist perceives the school as one of society's institutions, like the family, the church or the occupational group, and studies the school as purposeful collections of human and nonhuman resources.

Trying to understand the school on these terms, the educational sociologist asks such questions as: What does the school provide a society? Do the schools furnish the same services to the lower and the upper classes? If not, what are the effects of these discrepancies on individuals and on the society? What are the characteristics of a school as an institution? If an institution is defined as a network of rewards and punishments, how does this definition apply to the school? How are teachers rewarded? How are they punished? How do they reward and punish students? How do students reward and punish teachers? Does the culture of the school reflect the multi-racial, pluralistic nature of American society, or is one set of values predominant? How does the school impose this culture on the young? If every institution has a social structure, what is the school's structure? What is the flow of authority in a school? Who has power? Under what circumstances? What are the various student subcultures? How do teachers and administrators react to these subcultures?

Sociologists have been called people with a compulsion for organizing common sense. While this is a left-handed and unfair definition, it is true that sociologists examine what is right around us. Frequently, however, when sociologists organize common sense observations, we are startled by a new insight. An example is the great sociologist Talcott Parsons' assertion that the primary concern of the school is motivating the child to *achieve*. While some were arguing that the school teaches the 3 R's, and others that it trains children for American citizenship, Parsons pointed out that a school is a social agency which teaches achievement and competition, virtues which are highly prized in an industrial society.

The Anthropologist's View. The popular image of an anthropologist is someone who spends time on South Seas islands taking detailed notes on the behavior of the exotic inhabitants. This is a dated notion, since the anthropologist is increasingly applying his trained powers of observation to urban society. Essentially, the anthropologist is a student of man, and focuses on man's customs, social relations and culture. He normally lives among the people he is studying so that he can observe firsthand and in intimate detail their manner of life. From this immersion in the flux and flow of everyday life, and analysis of the data he has collected, the anthropologist is frequently able to identify and explain the complex patterns inherent in the behavior of a group of people.

Anthropologists are bringing a fresh perspective to the study of the school. By training, anthropologists are equipped to observe and study relatively small communities of people, and their methods are proving effective in the investigation of classroom procedures and cultures. They have the added advantage of a cross-cultural perspective, which enables them to compare and contrast the ways education is conducted in different societies. Most of us are hyperopic—that is, unable to see clearly what is nearby—about our own culture, and particularly so about schools. For instance, schools are characterized by rituals, in which we have all engaged more or less unquestioningly. Here are just a handful:

We had to stand when we recited, even though sometimes neither visibility nor audibility were relevant factors.

We had to be ready to account for our behavior to the teacher, but were not allowed to ask the teacher to account for his behavior.

We had to do homework that no one ever examined, for reasons never made clear to us.

We had to bring notes from home if we needed anything or wanted anything that was different from what the others generally needed.

When bells rang, we had to stop what we were doing and what we were thinking and go to other places.

We had to participate in air raid drills that everyone knew were absolutely worthless.

We had to refrain from talking in class, in the halls, in the lavatory, and in the auditorium.[7]

---

[7] Adapted from Robert Goldhammer, *Clinical Supervision* (New York: Holt, Rinehart & Winston, 1969), pp. 26–29.

There is nothing on earth intended for innocent people so horrible as a school. To begin with, it is a prison. But it is in some respects more cruel than a prison. In a prison, for instance, you are not forced to read books written by the wardens and the governor. G. B. Shaw, Parents and Children.

Many schools are still storage bins, twelve year warehouses for the young where, ideally, very little is supposed to happen and where all events are subject to intensive control. Organized from the outside in, they were created on the basis of buildings, budgets, administrative efficiency, pupil head counts, accounting procedures and rigid structures. Variety, flexibility and originality are untolerable because they make administration difficult, they ruin normal accounting and scheduling systems, and they make the citizens suspicious. Thus the textbook and syllabus become the academic analogs of fenders, or tail-lights and spray paint on the assembly line: they are added to the kids as they move through on the curricular belt. It is easy to teach 'facts' not only because the culture is fact-ridden, but because it is easy to test for learning when 'facts' are to be regurgitated. Peter Schrag, Voices in the Classroom, p. 276.

To the anthropologist, with his ability to discern patterns and meanings beneath the surface of events, a culture reveals itself in its treatment and training of the young. Therefore, he has many questions to ask about the schools: What are the culture's core values and how are they modified by the schools? Does the school reinforce the traditions of the culture? What is the meaning and importance of school rituals (the fall weekend football pageant, graduation ceremonies) and customs (pre-holiday assemblies and school dances)? How do they prepare people to fit into the larger culture? What is the language of the classroom and how does it differ from the language of the street?

The anthropologist is then, a "culture watcher," and as such he can help us analyze the schools to overcome our blindness to what is most familiar.

THE FUNCTION OF THE SCHOOL: AN ANTHROPOLOGIST'S ANALYSIS

The reason for disciplined inquiry into the nature of the school and other issues raised in this book is to transcend commonplace, and frequently faulty, conclusions. To illustrate, let us examine a particularly penetrating analysis of the function of the school, one which surpasses common sense. Earlier we claimed that it is a task of the school to interpret the world to the young. This assertion is faulty on two counts. First, obviously, the world in all its variety—people, anteaters, floods, eggplants, newspapers, logarithms—is just too much with which to deal. Schools have to be selective. They must choose fragments from the universe of knowledge. The goal, of course, is to select those bits and pieces which can be used by people to discover more and more. The second error is more subtle: while educators may think they are interpreting the world to the young, what they are ordinarily doing is transmitting their own culture and its values.

By "culture," we mean the system of norms and standards which a people develops over the course of many generations and which profoundly influences their everyday behavior. More simply, culture is as people do. The implication, clearly, is that American public schools teach the American way of looking at the world and the American way of doing things. By and large this is not a conscious process. It was not consciously introduced into the curriculum. If we ask educators what, broadly speaking, they are trying to do, they are likely to reply that they are teaching reality and how to deal with it. But, in fact, our schools teach our version of reality and our way of handling the real world. And so, too, do the schools of other countries. Schools in Northern India differ markedly from those in Ghana, and neither have much in common with American public schools. However, the schools of each country are attempting to perform a similar function: to transmit the unique culture of the country to its newest members, the young. This desire to insure that the young share the common culture may explain why we teach American history in the third grade, the seventh grade and again in the eleventh grade, and why we give very little attention to the history of China. China is the most populous nation in the world, with one of the oldest and richest cultural heritages. China may have introduced the first formal schooling. Most scholars and foreign policy experts are sure that China will loom large in the future of this country. Nevertheless, until recently the American people had developed the habit of ignoring China, and as a result its existence is hardly acknowledged in schools.

There is danger inherent in this tendency of schools to concentrate on transmitting the dominant culture. Just a few decades ago there was little apparent need for different cultures to understand and appreciate one another, but electronic communications, nuclear weapons and jet travel have changed all that. If schools offer the young an understanding only of the prevailing culture, the result may be an attitude of smug cultural superiority, a phenomenon which frequently leads nations to foolish actions. In cultural terms, what we do not know we frequently do not respect. Without mutual respect people easily become enemies.

This tendency of the schools—of all schools everywhere—to modify reality by filtering it through the lens of a particular culture is not all bad. A society's culture is, perhaps, its most precious gift to its young. A culture is a structure for ordering the chaos of raw existence. It provides a framework —a language system, rules for interacting with other people, ways of solving problems—within which to know oneself and the world. It assures the individual that life is worthwhile and defines for him what constitutes the good life. A person's culture, whether he is an Australian bushman or a Swiss

School days, school days!
Good old, golden rule days.
   Ernie Lundquist, The Millard Fillmore Junior High School Marching Band
   and Fight Song (*an original composition*)

The object of the common school system is to give every child a free,
straight, solid pathway by which he can walk directly up from the ignorance
of an infant to a knowledge of the primary duties of a man, and can acquire
a power and an invincible will to discharge them. Horace Mann, 1837.

banker, is his compass and anchor in the storm of life. According to the anthropologist's analysis, then, the school's major function is to transmit this precious and necessary heritage to the young.

THE UNFINISHED WORK OF THE SCHOOLS

It is probably clear by now that there is no single satisfactory answer to our question, "What is a school?" This and many other questions we will ask in this book are too large and complex to be adequately answered here—if, indeed, they can be answered at all. We pose them and talk about them anyway to aid you in your investigations into the issues behind the questions. People contemplating a career in education, in particular, must commit themselves to working out answers to these questions. It seems unlikely that you can make a good career choice lacking an understanding of the institution you are considering entering. And if you hope to survive and be happy within an institution, you will need to know how it works. You need to know what the institution says it is doing ("we are training future citizens," or "we are educating well-rounded citizens prepared to excel in college") and what it actually does. You need to know what a particular school's expectations of you, as teacher, will be, so you can decide how to respond or if you wish to respond at all. Finally, if you hope to improve the schools, that is, make them better because of your involvement with them, you need a realistic view of what is presently going on in the schools and a vision of what the schools can become.

   Schools are a human invention. As we established earlier, people bring schools into being for social purposes. The overall purposes of school are to advance the common good and to help people live better and happier lives. However, if schools are to serve society, they must at least keep pace with the society. Many people who are concerned about our schools feel that they are moving very slowly while the rest of society experiences dynamic change. In effect, the schools are out of phase with and lagging behind the society they are supposed to be serving. The result is tension. As happens frequently in times of tension, views polarize in the manner suggested by John Gardner's statement on page 25. Nevertheless, the purposes for which schools are brought into being are still vital. People still desire good schools for their children. And, as you will see later in this book, many excellent ideas are being generated and movements are underway for the renewal of our schools.

Some readers may be uncomfortable with the idea that it is their job to renew the schools. Many may feel that becoming a good classroom teacher is enough. The teacher, however, is more than a worker. As professional people he and his colleagues *must* have a voice in deciding how their services are rendered. It follows that the teacher is not responsible simply for his own performance, but bears responsibility for the total educational enterprise. To live up to this responsibility requires a deep understanding of the schools and much hard work, but it is the very critical nature of the problems confronting the schools that makes teaching such an exciting occupation today. Schools are becoming increasingly important in the life of each individual and in the health of the society. Pressures are building for changes in public education. In the immediate future, education is where the action will be. Society is inviting us to complete the unfinished work of the schools.

DISCUSSION QUESTIONS

1. Can you think of some pieces of information you picked up on the street that you later "unlearned" in school? Can you think of some things you learned in school that your experience later taught you were untrue? Which has happened more often? How do you react to this?

2. To what extent did the schools you attended serve the purposes suggested by the various models we described? Can you suggest any models we have overlooked?

3. Which of the models of the school we have discussed is illustrated by the cartoon on page 14? Is it inappropriate to any of the models we have discussed? Does it seem to you an apt comment on your own education?

4. How do you react to the remark, "Children enter school as question marks and leave as periods"? Is this desirable? Is it necessary? How would its meaning be changed if the statement were changed to, "Six-year-olds are question marks and seventeen-year-olds are periods." Would that statement be equally true?

5. What are the dangers inherent in the schools' tendency to transmit their own culture? What gaps did this tendency leave in your own schooling? What purpose does this tendency serve?

6. Think about Marshall McLuhan's statement that children interrupt their education to go to school. What kinds of things does the school expect children to learn on their own, outside of school? What kinds of things

The 23rd Century scholars made another exceptionally interesting observation. They pointed out that 20th Century institutions were caught in a savage crossfire between uncritical lovers and unloving critics. On the one side, those who loved their institutions tended to smother them in an embrace of death, loving their rigidities more than their promise, shielding them from life-giving criticism. On the other side, there arose a breed of critics without love, skilled in demolition but untutored in the arts by which human institutions are nurtured and strengthened and made to flourish. Between the two, the institutions perished. John W. Gardner, from a speech entitled "Fall of the Twentieth Century," Chicago Sun-Times, June 16, 1968.

Education is man's oldest and best means of shaping future generations and perpetuating his past society. Bruno Bettelheim, "Psychoanalysis and Education," School Review (June 1969): 73.

does society expect children to learn in school and makes no effort to teach elsewhere?

FOR FURTHER READING

Broudy, Harry Samuel. *Paradox and Promise: Essays on American Life and Education.* Englewood Cliffs, N.J.: Prentice-Hall, 1961. A collection of fifteen essays by one of America's leading educational philosophers on major issues confronting the schools.

Cremin, Lawrence A. *The Transformation of the School.* New York: Alfred A. Knopf, 1961. An award-winning history of the progressive education movement from 1876 to 1954. The book carefully traces the origins, development and finally the effect of the progressive education movement on our schools.

Dewey, John. *Democracy in Education.* New York: Macmillan, 1916. The key work, and certainly the most widely read book on education, by America's foremost philosopher and contributor to educational thought. (See also biography on p. 155.)

Gardner, John W. *Excellence: Can We Be Equal and Excellent Too?* New York: Harper and Row, 1961. A challenging analysis of the problem of fostering both excellence and equality. Major attention is given to the role of the schools.

Grannis, Joseph. "The School as a Model of Society." *Harvard Graduate School of Education Association Bulletin* 21 (Fall 1967): 14–27. In this article the author describes three different models of schools and their effect on children. The major point is that the hidden curriculum of the school is the structure of the school and the way human beings are organized within it.

Henry, Jules. *Culture Against Man.* New York: Random House, 1963. A distinguished cultural anthropologist writes vividly of the weaknesses of complex urban and industrial cultures. This book contains some withering analyses of what goes on in the American schools.

Hutchins, Robert M. *Education for Freedom.* Baton Rouge, La.: Louisiana State University Press, 1943. A distinguished American educator argues the case for a conservative approach to education if we are to preserve and extend freedom.

Mayer, Martin. *The Schools.* New York: Harper and Row, 1961. A provocative, stimulating description of life in American classrooms and the controversies affecting them, by a literate and sophisticated journalist. The book is extremely well-written and filled with interesting anecdotes and personal impressions.

Peddiwell, J. Abner [Harold Benjamin]. *The Saber-Tooth Curriculum.* New York: McGraw-Hill, 1939. A satirical spoof on the origin of schools, the inadequacies of the curriculum and the reluctance of educators to keep the curriculum relevant to societal needs. Humorous and entertaining reading.

Schaefer, Robert J. *The School as a Center of Inquiry.* New York: Harper and Row, 1967. A short, highly readable description of how the schools might more adequately serve children by returning to their central task of stimulating inquiry.

Spindler, George D., *ed., Education and Culture: Anthropological Approaches.* New York: Holt, Rinehart & Winston, 1963. This book was written by anthropologists and social scientists whose studies relate to education. The tools and techniques used by anthropologists offer the reader a number of fascinating insights into American education.

Thelen, Herbert A. *Education and the Human Quest.* New York: Harper and Row, 1960. An insightful book which addresses major questions about the relationship between man's development and education. Many questionable practices are analyzed by a writer of immense sensitivity and wisdom.

FILMS

Abraham Kaplan (Indiana University Audio-Visual Center, 16mm, b & w, 59 min.) One of a series of five films about "Men Who Teach." Abraham Kaplan, professor of philosophy at the University of Michigan, explains his beliefs and attitudes toward teaching, as well as the differences he sees between instruction and education.

No Little Hope (Center for Urban Education, 16mm, color, 28 min.) Documents the meaning of education to various people in New York City.

Through the words of the people interviewed, many of them parents, it becomes clear that "the process of education" cannot be fully understood without taking into account parents, the community, mass media—and, of course, the schools.

Rubin on Schools (American Documentary Films, 16mm, 15 min.) Jerry Rubin speaks on the antihuman institutional oppression of modern educational systems.

Summerhill (Contemporary / McGraw-Hill, 16mm, color, 28 min.) A visit to a coeducational English boarding scnool founded by A. S. Neill forty-five years ago. The school's objectives are explained by filming the students and faculty in various activities.

AUDIOTAPES

Education: For What and For Whom? (The Center for the Study of Democratic Institutions, 3.75 ips, $\frac{1}{2}$ track, 30:15 min.) This tape of a talk given at the Tenth Anniversary Convocation of the Fund for the Republic, presents Robert Hutchins, head of the Center for the Study of Democratic Institutions; Rosemary Park, former president of Barnard College, and Admiral Hyman Rickover in an analysis of educational problems.

The School an Empire Transmitting Technological Verities. (Noumedia #N7004, 3.75 ips, $\frac{1}{4}$ track, mono or stereo, 1 hour, 1970) In the second of three lectures given at Yale University in 1970, Ivan Illich discusses in depth the inhibition and perversion of human growth by institutionalized schooling, as well as the high costs and illusory goals of schools.

Schooling Today (Noumedia #N7003, 3.75 ips, $\frac{1}{4}$ track, mono or stereo, 1 hour, 1970) In the first of the Yale lectures, Illich discusses what he considers to be the problems of schooling today. The sound is poor, but audible.

Schooling vs. Education: Rx for Junior Colleges (The Center for the Study of Democratic Institutions, 3.75 ips, $\frac{1}{2}$ track, 56:20 min.) W. H. Ferry of the Center for the Study of Democratic Institutions and James D. Finn of the University of Southern California School of Education argue about the gap between schooling and education. Using the California schools as his model, Ferry offers a prescription for junior colleges to correct the gap. Finn follows with a dissent.

Yesterday I Could Not Sleep Because Yesterday I Wrote My Name . . . (The Center for the Study of Democratic Institutions, 3.75 ips, $\frac{1}{2}$ track, 42:09 min.) Ivan Illich tells John Cogley, editor of *The Center* magazine, "in the name of education, we must get rid of the school." Illich goes on to claim that instead of liberating people, school reinforces and widens the gap between rich and poor.

Refer to Appendix for distributors' addresses.

What Did You Do In School Today?

How many times did your mother or father ask that? And how many times did you answer, "Oh, the same old things"? In school you meet your friends, grab a smoke in the john, daydream a lot. Lunch and band are the most fun, but somehow you learn to read and write, too.

2   What Is Life in Schools Like?

KEY POINTS

CLASSIFICATIONS
Direct and indirect verbal behavior

EXPERIMENTS AND STUDIES
Krech's deprivation and enrichment of rats
Jackson's study of classroom routine
Flanders' study of classroom verbal behavior
Bellack's study of language moves
Gallagher's study of teachers' questions
Galloway's study of nonverbal communication
Parsons' study of the school as an agency of differentiation
Neugarten's study of social status and friendship
Coleman's study of the adolescent subculture
Henry's study of intragroup aggression

CONCEPTS
Heredity vs. environment
Deprivation
Interactive environment
Delay, denial, interruption, social distraction
Teaching cycles
Cognitive-memory, convergent, divergent and evaluative questions
Nonverbal communication

Identification

Cognition

Incidental learning

Teaching patterns or behaviors

THEORIES

School-induced failure (Glasser)

Precedence of nonverbal over verbal messages

FACTS

The "rule of two-thirds"

SEQUENCES

Structuring, soliciting, responding, reacting

METHODOLOGY

Flanders' Interaction Analysis

Bellack's language moves

Note-taking, analysis, interviews, video- and audiotapes

Sociometry

CHAPTER CONTENTS

You cannot make children learn music or anything else without to some degree converting them into will-less adults. You fashion them into acceptors of the status quo—a good thing for a society that needs obedient sitters at dreary desks, standers in shops, mechanical catchers of the 8:30 suburban train—a society, in short, that is carried on the shabby shoulders of the scared little man—the scared-to-death conformist. A. S. Neill, Summerhill.

Teachers are overworked and underpaid. True. It is an exacting and exhausting business, this damming up the flood of human potentialities. What energy it takes to make a torrent into a trickle, to train that trickle along narrow, well-marked channels! Teachers are often tired. In the teachers' lounge, they sigh their relief into stained cups of instant coffee and offer gratitude to whoever makes them laugh at the day's disasters. This laughter permits a momentary, sanity-saving acknowledgement, shared by all, that what passes for humdrum or routine or boring is, in truth, tragic. (An hour, of which some fifty minutes are given up to "classroom control." One child's question unanswered, a hundred unasked. A smart student ridiculed: "He'll learn better." He learns.) Sweet laughter, shooting up like artesian water, breaks through encrusted perceptions and leaves a tear in a teacher's eye. A little triumph.[1]

Is this an accurate portrayal of classrooms and teachers? Many observers of American education—and many teachers and students—would insist that it is. Others might not recognize much truth in it. Generalizations of this sort are necessarily inexact, for no single observer has seen more than a tiny fraction of American schools, let alone tried to concoct a description which does equal justice to every school. As a result, some characterizations of the schools are criticized on the grounds that the schools sampled are not representative—but in what sense can one school really be representative of another? Different socioeconomic groups, different communities and different sections of the country produce schools that are dissimilar in certain respects. Even two schools in contiguous neighborhoods may be markedly different, and a single school can change radically in a few years' time. It is also important to remember that observers are no more interchangeable than schools are. Each of us perceives reality differently. As you read this chapter, for example, you will undoubtedly react to particular passages by thinking, "That's just what life in my school was like," or "It wasn't like that at all." Someone else who attended the same school, but whose background and experiences differ from yours, may remember the school in an entirely different light. There is no certified version of reality.

---

[1] From p. 1 of *Education and Ecstasy* by George B. Leonard. Copyright © 1968 by George B. Leonard. Reprinted by permission of the publisher, Delacorte Press.

But, despite these important qualifications, the authors—and other observers—believe that certain conditions are more typical of schools than they are idiosyncratic and that some observations are authentically generalizable. Let's look at life in the schools, and see what we can find out about the school as an environment.

THE SCHOOL AS AN ENVIRONMENT

The relative importance of heredity and environment is an old issue among philosophers and educators, and one that seems unlikely to be resolved in the near future. Perhaps it's insoluble. But one thing seems clear—both heredity and environment deeply influence an individual's capacity to learn. We all feel intuitively, though we'd probably have trouble proving it, the crucial importance of environment in shaping who we are. John Dewey, the American educational philosopher, contended that environment

leads [an individual] to see and feel one thing rather than another; . . . it strengthens some beliefs and weakens others . . . it gradually produces in him a certain system of behavior . . . . In brief, the environment consists of those conditions that promote or hinder, stimulate or inhibit, the characteristic activities of a living being.[2]

ENVIRONMENT AND LEARNING

If school represents a major aspect of the environment of every child, how important is the school environment in facilitating or impeding learning? The work of psychologist David Krech[3] may give us some clues.

Environmental Richness.   To determine the effect of environment on rats, Krech is rearing matched sets of rats in sharply contrasting environments. One set of rats is kept in a sealed room, where each animal lives in a separate cage, in darkness and silence. The second set of rats, littermates of the first, lives together in a large cage with an abundance of playthings. They are taken out each day and handled; they learn to explore mazes; their environment is rich.

Krech has discovered that the enriched rats develop a higher concentration of an important brain enzyme than do the deprived rats. As a result of the lives they live, the brains of the enriched rats become larger and heavier, particularly the cortex or outer bark, associated with higher learning. The deprived rats are markedly inferior to the enriched rats in learning ability; they are mentally crippled.

It is dangerous to equate the deprived condition of the rats in the experi-

---

[2] John Dewey, *Democracy and Education* (New York: Macmillan, 1916), p. 13.

[3] As reported in Leonard, *Education and Ecstasy,* pp. 36–37.

ment with the deprivations of children in certain of our schools and communities. And yet it is almost impossible not to draw inferences about schoolchildren who are deprived of affectionate physical contact, denied playthings, strictly regimented and not allowed freedom to interact with other children and with their own environment. What kind of brain atrophy might be occurring in this situation?

Interactive Environment. The environment of the advanced rats has two distinct characteristics: it is rich in physical objects and it is interactive. That is, it allows the individual rat involvement with other rats, with playthings and mazes and with human beings. It is highly unlikely that the rats would show comparable advancement if they were allowed only to look from a distance at a rich and varied environment. In this respect, the setup of the experiment is undeniably relevant to human beings: mere physical proximity to a stimulating environment does not stimulate; interaction must occur for the learning process to be affected. This is why taking a group of children from an inner-city ghetto to an art museum to "expose" them to cultural riches usually has little or no impact. As Leonard states:

No environment can strongly affect a person unless it is strongly interactive. To be interactive, the environment must be responsive, that is, must provide relevant feedback to the learner. For the feedback to be relevant, it must meet the learner *where he is,* then program (that is, change in appropriate steps at appropriate times) as he changes. The learner changes (that is, is educated) through his responses to the environment.

Within these constraints, the human organism is incredibly flexible. If there are limits on the human ability to respond to learning environments, we are so far away from the limits as to make them inconsequential. Throughout human history to date, it has been the environments, not the human beings, that have run up against limitations.[4]

An environment must, then, be interactive in order to exert a strong influence. A teacher-dominated classroom in which lecturing is the standard mode of instruction obviously does not encourage or permit effective interaction. Yet, as we will see later in this chapter, teacher dominance and teacher talk are the rule rather than the exception. Consider, for example, these observations of school environments:

What a bore school is nowadays, the same as it has been for hundred of years. What we get is the same old thing—teacher, outdated textbooks, and a class fed up to the teeth with the teacher and the school. What we need is one vast change in the educational system of this country. Children do not want to be taught at, but want to find out things for themselves. If a child is interested in the way a dogfish's heart works, let him go and find out, by cutting one up. *Robin, 16*

---

[4] *Ibid.,* pp. 39–40.

. . . the basic premise is that the teacher and the school have unlimited faith in the capabilities of the pupil. The children must exist in an atmosphere where they can fully and entirely respond to the people and objects around them. A child who is blandly presented with a difficult English text to precis, or who has to copy a mass of fact concerning fossils covering a blackboard, will in the majority of cases react unfavorably. How much better it would be to let this child write a vivid description of some deep and moving experience, or to go out and discover for himself some interesting rock or fossil.[5] *Kenneth, 17*

The room in which I taught my Fourth Grade was not a room at all, but the corner of an auditorium. The first time I approached that corner, I noticed only a huge torn stage curtain, a couple of broken windows, a badly listing blackboard and about thirty-five bewildered-looking children, most of whom were Negro. White was overcome in black among them, but white and black together were overcome in chaos. They had desks and a teacher, but they did not really have a class. What they had was about one quarter of the auditorium. Three or four blackboards, two of them broken, made them seem a little bit set apart. Over at the other end of the auditorium there was another Fourth Grade class. Not much was happening at the other side at that minute so that for the moment the noise did not seem so bad. But it became a real nightmare of conflicting noises a little later on. Generally, it was not until ten o'clock that the bad crossfire started. By ten-thirty it would have attained such a crescendo that the children in the back rows of my section often couldn't hear my questions and I could not hear their answers. There were no carpetings or sound-absorbers of any kind. The room, being large, and echoing, and wooden, added resonance to every sound. Sometimes the other teacher and I would stagger the lessons in which our classes would have to speak aloud, but this was the makeshift method and it also meant that our classes had to be induced to maintain an unnatural and otherwise unnecessary rule of silence during the rest of the time.[6]

The environments described above are clearly not designed to stimulate the learner, to meet him where he is, to interact with him or to provide relevant feedback as he responds to his surroundings. But it did not take a long and arduous search to find such descriptions; these are situations in which millions of students find themselves daily. Is it any wonder that so many students fail to learn when the environment specifically intended to facilitate learning—the school—has the opposite effect on many who spend time there? While there may be millions of other students whose classroom experiences do stimulate learning, we suspect that they represent a minority of school

---

[5] The schools described here are not American. These are reports by English children which appear in a fascinating book, *The School That I'd Like,* edited by Edward Blishen (Harmondsworth, England: Penguin Books, 1969), pp. 59, 64. Copyright © Penguin Books and the contributors, 1969. Reprinted by permission of the publisher.

[6] Jonathan Kozol, *Death At An Early Age* (Boston: Houghton Mifflin, 1967), pp. 29–30. Reprinted by permission of the publisher.

Neighborhood centers could be bridges between home and school environments—relaxed, unpressured places to talk to an understanding adult, learn new games, learn how to make things—and places to watch the television programs you can't watch at home because you're always overruled.

Photo by James Foote for VISTA.

environments. Dr. Kenneth Clark, after examining I.Q. and achievement scores of youngsters in Harlem, commented:

It is an ironic and tragic inversion of the purpose of education that Negro children in ghetto schools tend to lose ground in I.Q. as they proceed through the schools and to fall further and further behind the standard for their grade level in academic performance. The schools are presently damaging the children they exist to help.[7]

Conflicting Environments. It is often argued, in defense of the schools, that they are not the children's sole environment. In fact, the home and the street are ordinarily more influential in a child's life. This is of particular concern when the school environment is in direct conflict with the rest of the child's experience. The value system of the school is likely to honor work for its own sake and to stress obeying rules and preparing for the future by delaying gratification. The culture of the neighborhood, on the other hand, may regard work as exploitation or as a necessary evil, hold the law in low regard and value action and excitement above order. The child's parents may have adopted a philosophy of "eat, drink and be merry" as a defense against despair. How fully are neighborhood values assimilated before the child

----

[7] Kenneth B. Clark, *Dark Ghetto* (New York: Harper & Row, 1965), p. 124.

STUDENTS TALK ABOUT SCHOOLS

Schools usually have one thing in common—they are institutions of today run on the principles of yesterday. 15-year-old girl

I am tired of hearing that the hope of my country lies in my generation. If you give me the same indoctrination as a child, how can you expect me to be any different from you? 15-year-old girl

Give me the school where discipline, regimentation and good manners are not everything. We would rather have a school where we can talk on equal terms with our teachers on sex, morals, ethics, royalty, religion, etc. We want the school where teaching will be equated with a perpetual quest for truth, beauty, integrity. A school where personality and brain-building come first and diplomas or certificates last. After all, a diploma or degree is not the perfect vaccine against stupidity. Cosette, 17

In my view, the sooner we all get out of the stuffy classroom, the better it will be for everybody. Life is much more interesting if you can go out and see something instead of just sitting in a desk and being loaded with in-formation about it. Lynne, 15

A school where the teacher is regarded as a friend and yet respected;
Where the barrier of the desk is overcome,
And learning is a series of discussions and experiments;
Where the formidable word 'lesson' is incomprehensible,
For there are no lessons as such,
And yet we learn more willingly than before. Susy, 17

History and geography are dealt with adequately, but psychology and poli-tics, drug-taking and smoking and love and death are not mentioned in the school syllabus at all. Kari, 13

A teacher can be very rude and cruel to a child, but any objection on his part is treated as impertinence. Education is a search after the truth, and to find the truth one must be humble. This is impossible if teachers are too proud to admit when they are wrong. Janet, 16 even begins school? How are children affected by inconsistency in their environments?

Nevertheless, psychiatrist William Glasser argues that when children do not learn it is the school, not the parents or the neighborhood, that has failed; the students have not been taught in school to gain and to maintain a sense of identity and self-worth through social responsibility. The student, Glasser maintains, has learned a lot about the world by the time he enters school and has, within the limits of his age, learned to cope with it; whatever his environment, he is optimistic about the future.

Very few children come to school failures, none come labeled failures; *it is school and school alone which pins the label of failure on children....* Whatever their background, children come to school highly receptive to learning. If they then fail to continue to learn at their rapid preschool rate, we may if we wish blame it on their families, their environment, or their poverty, but we would be much wiser to blame it on their experience in school.[8]

STUDIES OF LIFE IN CLASSROOMS

While the total environment of a school is highly significant, some educators are more concerned with specific dimensions of life there. An excellent perspective on how time is typically spent in the elementary classroom is provided by Philip W. Jackson's *Life in Classrooms.*[9] Before describing Jackson's findings, let's try an experiment. Listed below is a series of words representing the opposite extremes of a continuum, each pair connected by a row of boxes. Place a check in the box which you think best represents the child's experience of life in an elementary classroom. Do this quickly, giving your immediate responses rather than thoughtful consideration.

distraction	□	□	□	□	□	□	□	□	□	□	concentration
delay	□	□	□	□	□	□	□	□	□	□	promptness
boredom	□	□	□	□	□	□	□	□	□	□	excitement
postponing	□	□	□	□	□	□	□	□	□	□	doing
unexpressive	□	□	□	□	□	□	□	□	□	□	talkative
confusion	□	□	□	□	□	□	□	□	□	□	order
restriction	□	□	□	□	□	□	□	□	□	□	freedom
interruption	□	□	□	□	□	□	□	□	□	□	continuity
denial	□	□	□	□	□	□	□	□	□	□	satisfaction
repetition	□	□	□	□	□	□	□	□	□	□	freshness

Check back later to see how your responses compare with Jackson's findings. Do your perceptions of life in an elementary classroom agree with his?

---

[8] William Glasser, *Schools Without Failure* (New York: Harper & Row, 1969), p. 26.

[9] Philip W. Jackson, *Life in Classrooms* (New York: Harper & Row, 1969).

He's dumb just like his brother.

We'll do that later.

Wait! I only call on people who have their hands raised.

The kids were just great; not a sound out of them.

This will all make sense to you later on.

In my class, you earn what you get.

What these kids need is motivation.

Grammar was good enough for me; it ought to be good enough for them.

The Significance of Routine. Anthropologists have taught us that the humdrum aspects of human existence have cultural significance, and Jackson asserts that we must look at the most routine events in an elementary classroom if we are to understand what happens there. Are certain trivial acts repeated innumerable times? How frequently do they occur? What is their cumulative effect on the child? What do they teach him? Jackson's observations of elementary school classrooms demonstrate how revealing the answers to these questions can be.

Have you ever figured out how many hours a child spends in school? In most states the school year is 180 days. The day typically begins at nine and ends at three, a total of six hours. Thus, if a child doesn't miss a day of school, he spends over a thousand hours in school each year. Including kindergarten, the average child will spend over seven thousand hours in elementary school. How are those hours typically spent?

You may think first of the curriculum—so many hours of reading and language arts, so many hours of mathematics, science, play, social studies, music, art, and so on. But what do students really *do* when they are studying these subjects? They talk individually, to the teacher and to one another. They read silently and aloud. They yawn. They look out the window. They raise their hands. They line up. They stand up. They sit down. In short, they do a number of different things, many of them commonplace and trivial.

And what about the teacher? Jackson has observed that the elementary teacher engages in as many as a thousand interpersonal interchanges each day. What is the nature of these interchanges? The teaching-learning process consists, for the most part, of talking, and the teacher controls and directs discussion. The teacher acts as a gatekeeper, deciding who shall and who shall not speak. (One may debate whether or not this *should* be the teacher's role, but clearly most teachers function this way.)

The teacher also acts as a dispenser of supplies. Since space and resources are both limited, and the number of students wishing to use them at any one time is likely to be greater than the supply, the teacher must dole them out. A related function is the granting of special privileges to deserving students—passing out the milk, sharpening the pencils, taking the roll or operating the movie projector. Although little teacher time is involved in the awarding of these special jobs, they are important because they help structure the classroom socially as a system of rewards and punishments.

Time-keeping is another teacher responsibility. It is the teacher who decides when a certain activity ends and another begins, when it is time to stop science and begin spelling and when to go outside for recess. In some schools the teacher is assisted in time-keeping by bells and buzzers which signal when a "period" is over. As Jackson observes, things happen because it is time for them to occur and not because students want them to.

These teacher functions can all be seen as responses to the crowded conditions in the classroom. If the teacher were dealing with one student at a time in a tutorial situation, gatekeeping, granting special privileges, dispensing supplies and time-keeping would become superfluous. But since this is not feasible, much time and energy are spent keeping order. The resulting atmosphere has unavoidable effects on the students. What are some of the consequences for students of crowded classroom conditions?

WHAT STUDENTS EXPERIENCE.   One of the inevitable outcomes for the student as a result of what Jackson calls these "traffic–management" functions performed by the teacher is the experience of delay. Since a student's actions are limited by space, material resources and the amount of teacher attention he can command, there are definite limits on his freedom in the class. In addition, since the class ordinarily moves toward a goal as a group rather than as individuals, the pace of progress is often determined by its slowest members. Waiting is a familiar activity for elementary school children—waiting in line to get a drink of water; waiting with arm propped at the elbow to be called upon to answer a question; waiting to use the paper cutter; waiting until others have finished their work to go on to the next activity, waiting until four other students have finished reading aloud for his chance to do so.

Denial of desire is another common experience for elementary students. His question goes unanswered, his raised hand is ignored, talking out of turn is not permitted, relief of bodily functions is allowed only at specified times. Some denial is necessary, and some is probably beneficial, but one thing is certain—delayed gratification and denied desire are learned in school. Though you as a teacher will invariably be kept busy, it is important to recognize that this is not the case for your students and that a certain amount of student frustration is bound to develop as a result of delay and denial.

Students also experience frequent interruption and social distraction. Interruptions are of many sorts—interruptions of seatwork by the teacher to give additional instructions or to clarify one student's question, mechanical interruptions when the motion picture film starts to flicker, interruptions when messages from the principal's office are read aloud to the class, interruptions for fire drills, interruptions when the teacher is working with one student and another student misbehaves, and so on. Students are expected either to ignore these intrusions or quickly to resume their activities. The emphasis on an inflexible schedule contributes to the sense of interruption by frequently making students begin activities before their interest has been aroused and stop at the height of their interest when the schedule dictates that they must begin another task.

A related phenomenon is social distraction. Students are often asked to behave as if they were in solitude when in fact they are surrounded by thirty or so other people. At certain times during the day students are assigned seatwork and required to work on their own. At such times communication among students is often discouraged if not forbidden. To be surrounded by friends, sometimes seated across from them at a table, and not allowed to talk is a difficult and tempting situation. As Jackson remarks, "These young people, if they are to become successful students, must learn how to be alone in a crowd."[10]

Delay, denial, interruption and *social distraction,* then, are characteristic of life in elementary classrooms. How are children affected by these classroom facts of life? It is difficult to measure their effect, because they are present to a greater or lesser degree in every classroom. Also, different students have different levels of tolerance for these phenomena. It would seem, however, that the student who either possesses or quickly develops patience will find school more tolerable than the student who lacks it. The ability to control desires, delay rewards and stifle impulses seems to be necessary to the "mature" student. Jackson explains:

Thus, the personal quality commonly described as patience—an essential quality when responding to the demands of the classroom—represents a balance, and sometimes a precarious one, between two opposed tendencies. On the one hand is the impulse to act on desire, to blurt out the answer, to push to the front of the line, or to express anger when interrupted. On the other hand, is the impulse to give up the desire itself, to stop participating in the discussion, to go without a drink when the line is long, or to abandon an interrupted activity.[11]

The necessary balance is achieved by the majority of students. Others may respond in either of the two ways described above, or in still another manner. If you as a teacher are to understand why children act as they do, an understanding of the dynamics of the classroom is a necessity. Jackson's book offers considerable insight into life in elementary classrooms.

---

[10] *Ibid.,* p. 18.

[11] *Loc. cit.*

DIALOGUE

Kevin: *Do you think we're drawing an overly depressing portrait of American schools?*

Jim: *Well, yes and no. I can think of scores of good schools that I have visited or taught in. I hope we're not giving the impression that such schools don't exist or are so few and far between that they're inconsequential.*

Kevin: *I'm afraid we may be giving that impression.*

Jim: *Then I hope we've clarified that point—there are hundreds or thousands of excellent classrooms and schools in this country. But, on the other hand, I think our descriptions are far more typical of the majority of schools. So many schools are what Charles E. Silberman has described in the Carnegie Report, ". . . grim, joyless places . . . oppressive . . . intellectually sterile and aesthetically barren."*

Kevin: *Jim, you're lapsing into gloom again! I think we should emphasize, however, that what is, is not what should be or necessarily what will be. There are many efforts being made by people both within and outside the educational system to change the picture.*

Jim: *We ought to say, also, that if we didn't think the new people entering education could have a meaningful impact in changing the system, then we wouldn't have made the effort to write this book.*

Kevin: *Amen.*

The Language of the Classroom. In any elementary, junior or senior high school classroom, at any given moment, the chances are very good that someone will be talking. Who will it be? Will he be talking about something related to instruction, or to management of the classroom, or about something extraneous to the lesson? These kinds of questions have been asked by researchers for years, but only recently have effective techniques and instruments for analyzing the language of the classroom been developed.

INTERACTION ANALYSIS. One of these instruments, developed by Ned Flanders and called Flanders' Interaction Analysis, enables the observer to categorize both teacher and student verbal behavior. Developed to facilitate extensive research into teacher influence on student attitudes and achievement, Flanders' system measures a primary component of teacher influence: verbal directness or indirectness. The amount of intellectual freedom the teacher grants to students can be estimated by determining the proportion of directness and indirectness in the teaching. Direct verbal behavior on the part of the teacher—lecturing, giving directions, reciting facts, criticizing—tends to minimize the variety of possible student responses. Indirect behavior—eliciting student statements, accepting and making use of student ideas, praising, encouraging, varying strategies in response to the situation—increases the freedom of the student.

Flanders' initial research project involved 147 teachers, representing all grade levels, six different school districts and two counties.[12] In summarizing his findings, Flanders discovered the "rule of two-thirds": during about two-thirds of classroom time, someone is talking. About two-thirds of the time, the person talking is the teacher. Two-thirds of the teacher's talk is spent giving directions, expressing opinions and facts and occasionally criticizing students. Flanders also discovered that superior classes—those that scored above average on constructive attitudes toward the teacher and the classwork—also scored higher on content achievement tests, after test results were adjusted for initial ability.

In studies of seventh-grade social studies and eighth-grade mathematics classes, Flanders found that the teachers in superior classes talked only slightly less than the teachers in the other classes, 50 to 60 percent of the time, but that only 40 to 50 percent of their teaching was directive. In other words, the teachers whose classes had constructive attitudes and scored higher on content achievement were more flexible than other teachers in the quality of their verbal influence.

By contrast, the analysis of classes below average in constructive student attitudes and in content achievement showed that their teachers spoke over 75 percent of the time, and that over 75 percent of their talk was devoted to giving directions, expressing opinions and facts and, occasionally, criticizing students. For these teachers, the rule of two-thirds becomes the rule of three-fourths plus.

The implications of Flanders' research are that much teaching is directive, and that directive teaching tends to make students dependent on the teacher. Interestingly enough, Flanders has found that pre-service and in-service teachers trained in the use of Interaction Analysis have been able to become more indirect, to accept more student ideas and to criticize less than teachers not so trained.[13]

LANGUAGE MOVES. In another study Arno Bellack used a totally different conceptual framework to study classroom language patterns. Utilizing 15 teachers and 345 pupils in "Problems of Democracy" classes in high school,

---

[12] Ned A. Flanders, "Intent, Action and Feedback: A Preparation for Teaching," *The Journal of Teacher Education* 14 (September 1963): 251–60.

[13] Edmund J. Amidon and Evan Powell, "Interaction Analysis as a Feedback System in Teacher Preparation," in *The Nature of Teaching,* ed. Lois N. Nelson (Waltham, Mass.: Blaisdell, 1969), p. 82.

Bellack viewed classroom discourse as a game played with language.[14] He found that the statements made by pupils and teachers could be divided into four major categories:

1. *Structuring.* Structuring moves serve to focus attention on subject matter or classroom procedures and launch interaction between students and teachers. An example of a structuring move would be: "Students, yesterday on our field trip to the river we saw how dirty the water was. Today, let's look at this map of the river and the descriptions of the plants located on the river to try to determine how the river has become so dirty, and what exactly is going into it."

2. *Soliciting.* Soliciting moves are designed to elicit a verbal or physical response—questions, commands and requests are soliciting moves. "Johnny, why do you suppose the temperature of the water below this point on the map is 5 degrees warmer than the water above this point?"

3. *Responding.* Responding moves are the reciprocals of soliciting moves. They fulfill the expectations of soliciting moves. Johnny—"Because the waste material that the nuclear plant puts into the water is hot and raises the temperature of the water at that point and for several miles downstream."

4. *Reacting.* Reacting moves are occasioned by a structuring, soliciting, responding or other reacting move, but are not directly elicited by them. Reacting moves modify, accept, reject or expand on what has been said previously. Susan—"Yes, and because the water is so much warmer many of the fish are dying."

A structuring move or a soliciting move begins the process, and subsequent moves occur in cyclical patterns called *teaching cycles.* Bellack's analysis of classroom language yielded several valuable insights:

1. Teachers dominate verbal activities. The teacher-pupil ratio in terms of lines spoken is 3:1; in terms of moves, the ratio is about 3:2.

2. Appropriate teacher and pupil moves are implicitly but clearly defined— the teacher is responsible for structuring, soliciting and reacting, while the student is ordinarily limited to responding. (This evidence corroborates Flanders' finding that teachers dominate classrooms in such a way as to make the students dependent.)

3. Teachers initiate about 85 percent of the cycles. The basic unit of verbal interchange is the *soliciting-responding* pattern. Verbal interchanges take place at a rate of slightly less than two cycles per minute.

---

[14] Arno Bellack, *The Language of the Classroom* (New York: Teacher's College Press, 1965).

4. In approximately two-thirds of the moves and three-fourths of the lines, talk is content-oriented.

5. Fact-stating and explaining account for between 50 and 60 percent of the total discourse in most classrooms.

Bellack's empirical evidence suggests that the classroom is teacher-dominated, subject-matter-centered and fact-oriented. The student's primary responsibility seems to be to respond to the teacher's soliciting moves. Thus, student initiative does not seem to be characteristic of the high school social studies classes sampled. It is, once again, dangerous to generalize from a limited sample. Yet evidence from studies such as Bellack's indicates that, for a large number of classes if not the majority, this is the case.

QUESTIONING. In a third study of classroom language, James Gallagher investigated the kinds of questions that teachers ask. His study involved 235 boys and girls in ten different classes for gifted children at the junior and senior high school level.[15] Gallagher differentiated between four categories of questions:

1. *Cognitive-Memory* questions require the student to reproduce facts or other remembered content through the use of such processes as recognition, rote memory and selective recall. An example of a cognitive-memory question would be: "Can you tell me where Christopher Columbus first landed in the Americas?"

2. *Convergent* questions require the student to generate new information which leads to the correct or conventionally accepted answer. Given or known information usually determines the correct response. An example of a convergent question might be: "Could you summarize for us the author's major point?"

3. *Divergent* questions require the student to generate his own data independently in a data-poor situation, or to take a new perspective on a given topic. Divergent questions have no "right" answer. An example of a divergent question is, "How might the history of the United States have been different if the Pilgrims had landed on the west coast instead of the east coast?"

4. *Evaluative* questions require the student to make value judgments and decisions regarding the goodness, correctness or adequacy of information, based on a criterion usually set by the student. For example, the evaluative question, "Which president did more to enhance the office of

---

[15] James J. Gallagher, "Expressive Thought by Gifted Children in the Classroom," *Language and the Higher Thought Processes* (Champaign, Ill.: National Council of Teachers of English, 1965), pp. 56–65.

the Presidency, Jefferson or Jackson?'' requires the student to decide on criteria to judge what enhancing the office of the Presidency means, and then to compare Jefferson and Jackson with respect to those criteria.

The results of Gallagher's study show that in practically all class sessions, Cognitive-Memory questions comprise 50 percent or more of the total questions asked. The more the class tended toward a lecture mode rather than a discussion mode, the more often teacher questions and student responses fell into the Cognitive-Memory category. Convergent questions were the second most frequent category, with very few Divergent or Evaluative questions and responses. In fact, Gallagher surmises that class discussion could operate normally if only the first two categories of question were available.

Gallagher also found an extremely close relationship between the type of teacher questions and the pattern of thought expression observed in the students' responses. To a large extent, he observed, the teacher controls the expressive thought patterns of the class.

NONVERBAL COMMUNICATION. When we think of language we ordinarily think of words. A number of researchers have recently become interested in another kind of language—the silent language of gestures, facial expressions, bodily movements and other means of nonverbal communication. In his book *The Silent Language*,[16] anthropologist Edward Hall maintains that much of the content of a culture is communicated nonverbally. Hall has helped train American diplomats to understand how gestures and expressions which communicate one thing in our culture may be interpreted quite differently in another culture. He uses as an example the differences between American and Arab culture regarding the appropriate distance between two conversing people. If two Americans are carrying on a conversation at a distance of twenty feet, they will consider the distance unacceptable and will move closer together until both are more comfortable. The exact distance they choose will vary, depending on how well they know each other, but about three feet is the norm. However, in Arab cultures the appropriate distance is less than three feet. Therefore, when an American and an Arab are conversing, the Arab is trying to get closer while the American is trying to move backwards in order to establish the "appropriate" distance. Hall reports that he has seen this situation occur with the result that the Arab wonders what is wrong with him since the American seems repelled, while the American *is* repelled by what he considers pushy behavior.

An interesting story, but what does it have to do with teaching? The answer: a great deal. Most teachers are totally unaware of their nonverbal communication patterns. That they may be saying one thing verbally and communicating the opposite nonverbally does not even occur to most

---

[16] Edward T. Hall, *The Silent Language* (Garden City, N.Y.: Doubleday, 1959).

At their ages, these Navajo children probably don't have a good enough command of English to make the spoken dialogue of the puppet show warrant their obviously rapt attention. What does make them so attentive?

Photo by Paul Conklin.

teachers. For instance, the third-grade teacher who puts her arm around the white students in her class, or pats their heads fondly, yet maintains a certain distance with the black students, is definitely communicating a message. Yet, if asked if she discriminates between her students, she would be likely to reply indignantly in the negative. In fact, research indicates that lower-class youngsters rely heavily on nonverbal communication to understand meanings in the classroom.[17] The authors maintain that, if there is a discrepancy, the message a teacher communicates nonverbally is probably more valid and truthful than the verbal message, because it is much easier to conceal real feelings in words than in actions.

Since nonverbal communication is more difficult to conceptualize, define, interpret, and measure than verbal communication, very little work has been done to date in this area. Charles Galloway has, however, developed guidelines for observing a teacher's use of *space, time* and the *body.*[18]

Space. A teacher's use of space can convey meaning to the students. For example, when and where a teacher chooses to travel in a classroom has significance. A teacher who never ventures far from her desk at the front of the room may convey insecurity to the students—she seems reluctant to

---

[17] Basil Bernstein, "Social Structure, Language and Learning," *Educational Research* 3 (1961): 163–176.

[18] Charles Galloway, "Nonverbal Communication," *Theory Into Practice* 7 (December 1968): 172–175.

leave "home base." Some teachers rarely venture into the students' territory except to monitor their seatwork. A teacher's unwillingness to mingle with students will certainly be detected by them.

Time. How a teacher uses classroom time is often an indication of the value he places upon certain activities. The elementary school teacher who spends a great deal of class time on social studies but very little on mathematics is conveying a message to the students that they will almost surely detect.

Body Maneuvers. Teachers frequently use nonverbal tactics to control students' behavior. The raised eyebrow, the finger to the lips indicating silence, the hands on hips and the silent stare all communicate unmistakeable meanings. Galloway notes that when the teacher's verbal and nonverbal communications are in contradiction, the students read the nonverbal cues as a truer reflection of the teacher's real feelings and act accordingly. You can see this happening when a teacher verbally reprimands a student for talking but acts in such a way that the student knows the teacher doesn't really feel strongly about it. Shortly thereafter, the student begins talking again.

How can a teacher analyze or become more aware of his nonverbal communication? Perhaps the best and most accessible cue the teacher receives is feedback from students, though teachers vary considerably in their ability to recognize student responses and to utilize this information to analyze their own behavior. You can also make a videotape of yourself teaching and analyze the tape to pick out inconsistencies between your verbal and nonverbal behavior. The videotape recorder is a tremendous boon to teachers in that it allows them to criticize their own performances relatively objectively.

Still another means of analyzing nonverbal communication is by using Galloway's nonverbal analysis instrument (see Table 2.1). Modifying Flanders' instrument, Galloway concentrates on two major categories of nonverbal communication—encouragement and restriction.[19] His instrument classifies the teachers' or students' verbal behavior, and then categorizes the teacher's accompanying nonverbal behavior in terms of whether it en-

---

[19] Sue S. Lail, "The Model in Use," *Theory Into Practice* 7 (December 1968): 176–180.

courages or restricts interaction. Unlike Flanders' system, which encompasses all verbal communication, Galloway's does not purport to describe all kinds of nonverbal communication. You might want to try analyzing the nonverbal behavior of one of your friends using Galloway's system.

We have seen in our brief survey that decoding language of the classroom can shed considerable light on what happens there. The techniques and systems that Flanders, Bellack, Gallagher and Galloway have developed to look at the language of the classroom can also be used by teachers to analyze their own communication processes and messages. How much do you want to dominate discussion when you become a teacher? Do you want to have a direct or indirect influence on students? Do you want the students to become dependent on you, or do you want to foster independence? Do you know when you are communicating one message verbally and another nonverbally? What kinds of thinking do you want your students to practice— recall and recognition, or analysis and evaluation? The kind of thinking they do is in part a product of the kinds of questions that you ask them. If you feel it is important to understand your experience, it would make sense for you to develop competency in one or more of these language evaluation systems during your teacher education program.

The School as a Social System. One way to view life in schools is to look at it as a social system to be analyzed. One sociologist, Talcott Parsons, has done an extensive examination of both elementary and secondary classes as social systems.[20] The two main questions he sought to answer were: 1) How does the school class instill in each pupil the commitment to a future adult role and make him capable of performing successfully in that role? and 2) How does the school help allocate the human resources of the students within the role structure of adult society? Since completion of high school—and, increasingly, college—is the minimum educational level which allows much freedom of occupational selection, Parsons also tried to discover how it is determined who goes to college and who does not.

Studying a sample of 3,348 Boston high school boys, Parsons found that the factor which determines whether a student enters college is his prior enrollment in the college preparatory program. With very few exceptions, this course of action is determined by the ninth grade, and the most important element in the decision seems to be the boy's performance in elementary school. The student's record is evaluated by teachers and principals who advise him for or against enrolling in the college preparatory program, and few students act against their advice. Thus, Parsons concludes, the primary selective process for college occurs in elementary school and the "seal" is put on it in junior high school.

---

[20] Talcott Parsons, "The School Class as a Social System: Some of its Functions in American Society," in *Society and Education,* ed. R. Havighurst, B. Neugarten, and J. Falk (Boston: Allyn & Bacon, 1967), pp. 122–134.

Table 2.1. *Summary of categories for interaction analysis using nonverbal categories*

	VERBAL (FLANDERS)	NONVERBAL (GALLOWAY)	
		Encouraging	*Restricting*
TEACHER TALK	1. ACCEPTS FEELINGS	1.	11.
	2. PRAISES OR ENCOURAGES	2. CONGRUENT: non-verbal cues reinforce and further clarify the credibility of a verbal message.	12. INCONGRUENT: contradiction occurs between verbal and non-verbal cues.
	3. ACCEPTS OR USES IDEAS OF STUDENT	3. IMPLEMENT: implementation occurs when the teacher actually uses student's idea either by discussing it, reflecting on it, or turning it to the class for consideration.	13. PERFUNCTORY: perfunctory use occurs when the teacher merely recognizes or acknowledges student's idea by automatically repeating or restating it.
	4. ASKS QUESTIONS	4. PERSONAL: face-to-face confrontation.	14. IMPERSONAL: avoidance of verbal interchange in which mutual glances are exchanged.
	5. LECTURES	5. RESPONSIVE: change in teacher's pace or direction of talk in response to student behavior, i.e., bored, disinterested, or inattentive.	15. UNRESPONSIVE: inability or unwillingness to alter the pace or direction of lecture disregarding pupil cues.
	6. GIVES DIRECTIONS	6. INVOLVE: students are involved in a clarification or maintenance of learning tasks.	16. DISMISS: teacher dismisses or controls student behavior.
	7. CRITICISMS OR JUSTIFIED AUTHORITY	7. FIRM: criticisms which evaluate a situation cleanly and crisply and clarify expectations for the situation.	17. HARSH: criticisms which are hostile, severe, and often denote aggressive or defensive behavior.

	VERBAL (FLANDERS)	NONVERBAL (GALLOWAY)	
		Encouraging	*Restricting*
STUDENT TALK	8. STUDENT TALK-RESPONSE	8. & 9. RECEPTIVE: involves attitude of listening and interest, facial involvement, and eye contact.	18. & 19. INATTENTIVE: involves a lack of attending eye contact and teacher travel or movement.
	9. STUDENT TALK-INITIATION		
	10. SILENCE OR CONFUSION	10. COMFORT: silences characterized by times of reflection, thought, or work.	20. DISTRESS: instances of embarrassment or tension-filled moments, usually reflecting disorganization and disorientation.

Source: Sue S. Vail, "The Model in Use," *Theory Into Practice* 7 (December 1968): 177.

Except for sex differences, there is initially no formal basis for differentiation of student status within the elementary school class. Differentiation develops gradually in the elementary school along lines of achievement, and extends through high school, where it distinguishes the college-goers from the non-college-goers. As Parsons says:

The essential point, then, seems to be that the elementary school, regarded in the light of its socialization function, is an agency which differentiates the school class broadly along a single continuum of achievement, the content of which is relative excellence in living up to the expectations imposed by the teacher as an agent of the adult society.[21]

In addition to the school class, there are two primary social structures in which the student participates: the family and the informal peer group. Because the school functions as a socializing agency for society, both of these groups have an impact on the child which may either complement or coun-

---

[21] *Ibid.*, p. 126.

teract the school's socializing function. We will look at the influence of peer groups later in the chapter. Parsons asserts that the child's learning of achievement motivation is, psychologically, a process of identification with the teacher, and hypothesizes that those students who identify with the teacher will probably go on to college, while those who identify with their peer group instead will probably not go to college.

While the teacher thus plays a role in the child's development similar to that of the parent, there are some important differences between them. The teacher is more concerned with performance than with solicitude for children's emotional needs. A mother, on the other hand, must give first priority to the needs of her child, regardless of his capacity to achieve. A child has only one mother, but many teachers; thus, unlike mothers, teachers are in a sense interchangeable. Parsons sees this as an important distinction, for it means that the child must internalize his relation to the teacher's *role* rather than to her particular personality.

Thus, Parsons sees the socialization and selection process in the elementary school as involving: 1) an emancipation of the child from primary emotional attachment to his family; 2) an internalization of societal values greater than he can learn from his family alone; 3) a differentiation of the school class along the lines both of actual achievement and of the value placed by the child upon achievement, and 4) the selection and allocation of human resources by the school, acting as an agent of society, with respect to the adult role system.

Contrasting the roles of elementary and secondary schools, Parsons states that the elementary school phase is concerned with the child's internalization of motivation to achieve and the selection of persons on the basis of their achievement, while the secondary school phase focuses on the differentiation of *qualitative* types of achievement. Those secondary school students who are relatively high in what Parsons calls "cognitive" achievement but who are not college-bound will seek more or less technical roles as electricians, mechanics and the like; whereas those students who are relatively high in what Parsons calls "moral" achievement (generally known as citizenship) and who are not college-bound will seek more diffuse, "social" or "humanly" occupations as, for example, salesmen and insurance agents. For those students who are college-bound this distinction will evidence itself in emphasis on intellectual curricular work for the "cognitive" types, and, for the "moral" types, leadership roles in student government and extracurricular activities.

What Parsons has shown us is a way to conceptualize how the school, particularly the elementary school class, serves as a socializing and selection agency for society. How fully the student identifies with the teacher's role and, in so doing, accepts the values of the school as personified by the teacher, is, Parsons maintains, the factor which determines his future adult roles in society. The students who reject these values, do not identify with the teacher's role and favor peer-group identification will be non-college-

PEANUTS

Panel 1: DO YOU KNOW WHY ENGLISH TEACHERS GO TO COLLEGE FOR FOUR YEARS?

Panel 2: NO, I DON'T KNOW WHY ENGLISH TEACHERS GO TO COLLEGE FOR FOUR YEARS..

Panel 3: WELL, THEN I'LL TELL YOU WHY ENGLISH TEACHERS GO TO COLLEGE FOR FOUR YEARS....

Panel 4: SO THEY CAN MAKE STUPID LITTLE KIDS WRITE STUPID ESSAYS ON WHAT THEY DID ALL STUPID SUMMER!!

goers, thus determining to a large extent what roles they will play in society. The crucial criterion in determining future adult roles is student achievement in the elementary school. If Parsons' thesis is correct (remember that his study was limited to boys), the elementary school years are the crucial period in a student's development.

Peer Relationships and Social Class.   In this country virtually all children receive some public education, and children from different socioeconomic levels frequently attend the same schools. When children go to school, they make friends of their classmates and form friendship groups. An interesting question might be: "Is the social-class position of the family a contributing factor in determining either a child's choice of friends or his reputation? In other words, do children tend to make friends with children from similar social-class backgrounds, or are the schools a melting-pot where children from different social classes meet and become friends?" Another pertinent question might be: "Is the relationship between friendship groups and social class the same in the elementary schools as it is in the high schools?"

These questions were the subject of a study by sociologist Bernice Neugarten conducted in 1946.[22] She selected a community whose status structure was divisible into five social classes. Group A consisted of the "upper crust," the "money crowd," and comprised only 2 percent of the town's population. Group B consisted of professionals, members of the school board and active community leaders. This group was highly educated, lived in big houses, and had higher-than-average incomes. Group C consisted of the "average man," and constituted the bulk of the population. Group D was the lower income group—poor but honest blue-collar workers. Group E was distinctive primarily on the basis of nonrespectability. This group—all Caucasian—was considered dirty, dishonest and both biologically and morally inferior by other community members.

---

[22] Bernice L. Neugarten, "Social Class and Friendship Among School Children," in *Society and Education,* ed. R. Havighurst *et al.,* pp. 102–108.

The subjects of the study were children enrolled in grades 5, 6, 10 and 11. Since hardly any children from Group A were enrolled in the public schools, this category was eliminated. Neugarten administered to the students a sociometric test consisting of a series of short statements or descriptions, each followed by a blank space in which the children were instructed to write the name of the child who, in their opinion, best fitted the description. To gather data regarding friendship status, the children were asked for the names of the other children whom they would and would not want to play with or be friends with, and with whom their mothers would not want them to associate.

At the elementary school level, the results showed that children are selected as friends by children from their own social level more often than by children of other social levels. This is not surprising since neighborhood friendships carry over to the schools, and children from the same neighborhoods are likely to belong to the same social class.

Neugarten found a mutual rejection between groups B (professional background) and E (nonrespectability) greater than that between any other two groups. It might be expected that the greatest divergence of views and values would exist between the two groups at opposite ends of the class axis. The lower the social class of the child, the less often he was mentioned as a best friend. With the exception of the group of lowest status, children tend to select as friends, first, the children of higher status than their own and, second, children of their own status level.

The data on reputation follow the same pattern as the data on friendship. In fact, there is even less variation. All children, regardless of their own social class, agreed that the Group B subjects were well-dressed, good-looking, good in school and leaders. By grade 5, the child of the lower class faces a different problem of adjustment in school life than does the child from the middle class, since membership in the lower class is almost certain to result in an unfavorable reputation among his peers.

When the data from the elementary school children is compared with that from the secondary students, some important differences emerge. While both age groups discriminated by class in their selection of friends, high school students did not adhere to class lines in rejecting individuals as friends. While at the elementary school level members of Group E tended to be rejected as friends, particularly by Group B, in high school this rejection did not occur. Neugarten hypothesizes that not being mentioned at the high school level may be indicative of an even greater degree of rejection than unfavorable mention at the elementary level. Whereas in elementary school Group E children may still be potential playmates, at the high-school level Group B may be so distant psychologically from Group E that students from the latter group do not enter their minds as potential friends. Another possible explanation is that differences in social status may be less recognizable at the high school age, due partially to the dropping-out of the "most objectionable" members of Group E. A final possibility is that high school students are more democratic than elementary school students.

Group B students were found to have the most positive reputations at the high-school level. Groups C and D students were not singled out as having either positive or negative reputations. Group B students were in the lime-light, while Group E students were isolated and ignored.

Neugarten summarizes her findings in the following manner:

The finding that social-class differences in friendship and reputation are so well established by the time children reach the fifth grade may be of some importance to the psychologist. The child of eleven or twelve soon becomes aware of his reputation and desirability as a friend, and he must make his adjustment in the light of what others think of him. Perhaps one of the reasons that the child of lower class is so often a "behavior problem" in school is that he finds himself rejected by his classmates and enjoys such an unenviable reputation. This may also be one of the reasons why lower-class children often find school unpleasant and unrewarding and why the child of lower class so often welcomes the first opportunity to leave school altogether.

From one point of view the data also raise the general question of the extent to which the school, in communities like Hometown [the site of the study], is encouraging democratic living on the part of its children. It is undoubtedly true that the teacher plays a central role in influencing the opinions of one child toward another. While there is no systematic research on the topic, anecdotes and observations suggest that teachers' behavior toward children of lower class is different from their behavior toward those of middle or upper class and that this discrimination follows the differences in reputation among the social groups.[23]

Peer Relationships and Values. The studies by another sociologist, James Coleman, of peer relationships among adolescents have resulted in some very interesting observations.[24] Coleman believes that industrial society, by shifting much of the responsiblity for the training of a child from his parents to the school and by extending the necessary period of training, has made of high school a social system of adolescents. The values and activities of this adolescent subculture are quite different from those of adult society, and its members' most important associations are with one another rather than with adults. Society has created for adolescents a separate institution of their own; home is merely a dormitory while "real" living consists of activities unique to the peer group.

Coleman asserts that society has not yet recognized the existence of this adolescent subculture; education continues to focus on individuals. Teachers exhort individuals to concentrate on scholarship while the community of adolescents diverts these energies in other directions. If educational goals are to be realized in today's society, Coleman argues, the power of the ad-

---

[23] *Ibid.,* p. 108.

[24] James S. Coleman, "The Adolescent Subculture and Academic Achievement," in *Society and Education,* ed. R. Havighurst *et al.,* pp. 109–115.

olescent community must be taken into account. At present, adults establish goals and create institutions to help students reach those goals. If the adolescent community were allowed to formulate its own educational goals, its very structure would reinforce those goals, rather than hindering them, as is now the case.

Coleman studied ten high schools, all located in the Midwest. To gather his data, Coleman asked the students to respond to a questionnaire. Among the questions asked the boys was, "How would you most like to be remembered in school: as an athletic star, a brilliant student or the most popular?" In every school the boys showed a greater tendency to select "star athlete" than either of the other choices. In almost every case the leading crowd tended to choose the athlete image, and in all cases they rejected the ideal of the brilliant student. Boys were also asked to name the best athlete, the best student and the boy most popular with the girls. Boys named as best athlete were identified as members of the leading crowd twice as often as were those named as best students.

Each girl was asked how she would like to be remembered: as a brilliant student, a leader in extracurricular activities or the most popular. The girls tended slightly less than boys to want to be remembered as brilliant students. The girl who was most often named as best student had fewer friends and was less often in the leading crowd than was the boy most often named as best student—which, remember, was less than half as often as best athlete. The girls in the ten schools were split as to whether the image of activities leader or of most popular girl was more desirable.

Coleman points out that in every social context certain activities are highly rewarded, while others are not. Those activities that are rewarded will attract nearly everyone with some ability to compete. Conversely, those activities for which there are few rewards will not attract the potentially most talented. Interscholastic athletics attract academically talented boys because of the social rewards. Athletes are rewarded because they bring glory to the school and community, whereas the rewards for high grades are usually individual and personal. Good students force their classmates to keep up with them and frequently bring upon themselves such derisive labels as "curve raisers" and a few others we think it safer not to print.

In a school where academic achievement brings few social rewards, few students will excel in scholarship and those who get good grades will tend not to be those of greatest ability but those of mediocre ability. The academically gifted will be concentrating their efforts in areas which bring social rewards. Coleman's study thus indicates that the adolescent subculture generally acts as a deterrent to academic achievement, and that high schools actually encourage a diversion of academic talent into other channels.

The adolescent subculture's values and norms thus supersede the school's stated objective of academic excellence. The authors do not agree with Coleman that the adolescent subculture's values differ markedly from those of adult society; we think that adult society also values athletics and popularity over intellectual attainments (witness the huge audiences sporting events attract on television and the use of professional athletes to endorse commercial products). It may be that the high schools accurately reflect not just the adolescent subculture, but a large subculture of adult America. In any case, it is obvious that peer relationships and values exert a tremendous effect on the behavior of adolescents in high school—an effect that teachers frequently forget in the daily instruction of kids.

Teaching Patterns, Incidental Learnings and Ritualism. Just as there is a difference between the scholastic objectives of a school and the behavioral preferences of students, there may also be a disparity between what a teacher thinks she is teaching and what the students are actually learning.

In a provocative book on the supervision of teachers Robert Goldhammer proposes a thesis with very significant implications for anyone preparing to teach.[25] Goldhammer observes that a kind of learning entirely unrelated to the teacher's intended objectives takes place in the classroom. This learning, which he calls "incidental learning," is not measured or evaluated by the teacher, and the teacher is rarely even aware that it occurs. Incidental learning can facilitate intended learning, impede it or have very little effect upon it. Goldhammer's thesis is that if a teacher continually repeats certain behaviors, the implications of these "teaching patterns" will be grasped and digested by the students. Isolated teaching behaviors will not have this effect, but behaviors repeated day after day for an entire school year will produce incidental learnings that the teacher may not even recognize. Let's look at some examples of teaching patterns and make some guesses about what the students may be learning in response to them:

All directions are given by the teacher.

All questions originate from the teacher.

All evaluations are performed by the teacher.

The pace of instruction and all sequences of instruction are determined by the teacher.

The teacher asserts that he will not call on people who call out, out of turn, but he often does.

The teacher uses school work as an instrument of punishment:
   a. Pupils who have committed a disturbance are required to copy the "W" pages from the dictionary for homework.

The teacher takes the entire class to the bathroom at the same time every day.

The teacher assigns extra work, that is, more of the same thing, to children who finish their assignments quickly.

A reward pattern: When a pupil has finished reciting, the teacher generally responds, "Yes, but . . ."

---

[25] Robert Goldhammer, *Clinical Supervision: Special Methods for the Supervision of Teachers* (New York: Holt, Rinehart and Winston, 1969), pp. 11–32.

Discipline Code from a High School Student Handbook

OFFENSE	DISCIPLINARY ACTION
1. late to detention	1 hour detention
2. disturbance in detention	1 hour detention
3. food thrown in cafeteria (M)	1 hour detention
4. trays left in cafeteria (M)	1 hour detention
5. cutting in cafeteria line (M)	Monitor asks student to take his proper place in line; if student refuses, a 1 hour detention.

6. tardiness because of the following:
  a. doctor's appointment
  b. funeral
  c. college interview
	No penalty when student shows appointment card for doctor's appointment or note for funeral excuse.
	Student must bring in note, sign log in office, and return the attendance verification by 2:30.

7. any other tardiness	Each term a student is allowed to be tardy twice without penalty. The third un-excused tardiness and those following will result in a 1 hour detention.
8. no note or doctor's appt. card when tardy	1 hour detention
9. truancy	1 hour detention for each period cut, served consecutively
10. failure to return absentee note	a. If not returned the day following absence, student is marked NO NOTE by the nurse. This list is sent to the office. b. The second day, the student goes to the office with his note. c. If he does not have the note on the second day, 1 hour detention for each day not returned.
11. cutting detention	detention is served plus 1 more hour
12. failure to return office forms and documents such as report cards, insurance forms, library notices after 3rd notice, etc. when the student is allowed more than 1 day	1 hour detention for each day not returned

13. smoking or suspicion of (M)
  a. first offense
  b. second offense
	a. 2 hour detention period
	b. internal suspension

_____

(M) refers to Monitor

The teacher corrects papers, figures attendance, and so on, while, at the teacher's direction, a pupil is reciting.[26]

These practices are illustrations of negative teaching patterns; that is, they distract pupils from the intended object of study and teach the children perceptions of themselves, of school or of learning that can lead to distrust, self-deprecation, confusion or insecurity. What incidental learning might result from the first four examples given above? The students are probably learning that the teacher is the director and that they are dependent on her for their learning. What about the teacher who assigns extra work to those who finish early? Perhaps the students learn to dawdle to avoid extra work. And how about the teacher who responds, "Yes, but . . ." to students' answers? Perhaps the students learn that the teacher has all the correct answers, or maybe they learn not to volunteer answers, since no matter what they say it is never right.

Needless to say, there are many positive teaching patterns as well. For example, the teacher who listens intently to student comments and then builds upon them, without interjecting her own thoughts, may be teaching students that she values their ideas and their participation. Undoubtedly many teaching patterns have positive connotations for some students and negative meanings for other members of the class. The point to remember about teaching patterns and incidental learnings is that the teacher is usually unaware of them and of the power that they possess. In many cases incidental learnings have a far greater impact on classroom environment and overall learning than do the intended learnings—so be on the alert for incidental learnings that may result from your teaching patterns.

Robert Goldhammer is also critical of school practices which he believes foster student dependence on the teacher and a condition of docility. One of the practices which contributes to this condition he labels "ritualism." He has observed that students are required to behave in certain ways to conform to school rituals without knowing why they should do so and without being permitted to question the practice. He further contends that these ritualistic practices serve to infantilize the student, produce conformity and reduce the student to a state of blind acceptance. A democracy depends on enlightened citizens, Goldhammer argues, and these ritualistic practices subvert the development of the kind of questioning behavior necessary to citizens who think and act for themselves. (See the newspaper article on this page as an example of a ritual which students are not permitted to question.) Goldhammer also offers some good examples of ritualistic practices:

I must regularly participate in various patriotic litanies, for example ". . . for Richard stands, one naked individual . . ."

---

[26] From *Clinical Supervision: Special Methods for the Supervision of Teachers* by Robert Goldhammer (p. 15). Copyright © 1969 by Holt, Rinehart and Winston, Inc. Reprinted by permission of Holt, Rinehart and Winston, Inc.

Girl With Midi-Dress Refused Her Diploma

MOUNT VERNON, N.Y., June 19 (AP)—A girl was refused her diploma from Nichols Junior High School here Friday because she was wearing a midi-length dress.

Anthony Solodano, the principal, said he gave the girl, Joan Capra, the option of pinning up the hem or changing clothes with her mother, who was wearing a mini. The teen-ager declined.

Mr. Solodano said he refused to give Miss Capra a diploma because they are awarded not only for academic achievement "but for good behavior and a cooperative spirit."

School authorities said Miss Capra would be admitted to high school in the fall on the basis of her academic record even without the diploma.

All the other girl graduates wore mid-thigh minis.

When bells ring, I must stop what I am doing and what I am thinking and go to other places.

I must follow lines and arrows painted on the floors when going through the halls, even when I am the only student in the hall.

I must go up certain stairs and down others.

Although I have nothing to do during large chunks of class time, I am not allowed to do my homework during that time.

I must prove my points by citing evidence (that is, by quoting authorities), even though the teacher never does.

I must study what I am told to study, whether or not that represents something I would like to study.

I may not wear my shirt out.

I may not chew gum.

I am taught to value freedom, but have little opportunity to experience it.[27]

[27] From *Clinical Supervision: Special Methods for the Supervision of Teachers* by Robert Gold-hammer (pp. 26–29). Copyright © 1969 by Holt, Rinehart and Winston, Inc. Reprinted by permission of Holt, Rinehart and Winston, Inc.

Dress Code from a High School Student Handbook

Appearance requirements at _____ High School encourage the student body to follow current acceptable standards of appearance. The following are not considered acceptable:

Men's jeans if stained, bleach spotted, torn or ragged.

Men's T-shirts reminiscent of underwear; differentiation to be made by color, style, and thickness of material.

Flapping shirts--men's shirts designed to be tucked in the trousers should be worn that way, not left flapping outside.

Any clothing which is too tight or too short.

Students must wear socks or stockings with all shoes except sandals. Safety rules dictate, however, that sandals must not be worn in the shop area.

Gym garments are to be worn only in the physical education area where they are required.

At evening and away from school functions, where the school is being represented, students shall dress in current business attire.

In school, appearance (hair, clothing, footwear, accessories, and make-up) of students should be neat, clean and appropriate.

Goldhammer's point is that school is for many students a place where they must obey certain rules, ask or not ask certain questions, do certain assignments and take part in certain ceremonies—for reasons which are mysterious to them. They do certain things because they have been told to do so or "because they're rules," without knowing why. The result is tragic when the students no longer even question why they do something; they do it simply because they have been told to do it. Certainly blind obedience to authority and an unquestioning attitude are antithetical to the principles of democratic citizenship. Our schools are charged with the task of preparing citizens for participation in a democracy, but those that emphasize obedience, blind deference to authority and ritualistic behavior cannot possibly produce enlightened citizens. In such cases, the means surely will not achieve the desired ends.

The Witch-Hunt Syndrome. According to anthropologist Jules Henry, intragroup aggression is characteristic of American culture. In his observations of classrooms Henry has occasionally seen what he identifies as "the witch-hunt syndrome,"[28] a pattern of feelings and actions involving hostile criticism of others, docility, feelings of vulnerability, fear of internal aggression, confession of evil deeds and boredom. Flagrant examples of this syndrome appear to occur somewhat rarely, although Henry asserts that the syndrome exists in mild or partial form in many American classrooms.

In one elementary classroom, Henry reports, the teacher had organized a Vigilance Club whose members, in order to learn to become better citizens, reported to the class and teacher the good and bad deeds of their classmates. When misdemeanors were reported, the guilty children were sent to the "bull pen," an area behind the teacher's desk. Henry cites an example of witch-hunting that he observed during a game of spelling baseball. One child raised her hand and reported to the teacher that Alice and John had been talking to each other. This occurred when neither child was "at bat," and thus not really cheating. The teacher asked Alice if the report was true and Alice replied that it was, but John denied having spoken to Alice. The teacher said that John must have listened to Alice, but he denied this too. Then the teacher questioned some children seated on the far side of the room, and who could not have seen Alice and John, about the incident. All those testifying said they had seen Alice talking but denied John's guilt. Alice was sent to the "bull pen," which meant that she had to sit on the floor behind the teacher's desk and could no longer participate in the game.

Typically, teachers engaged in the witch-hunt syndrome think they are encouraging good citizenship and the ability to receive criticism and justified punishment. Instead, they frequently encourage intragroup hostility and a feeling of distrust in the classroom. Henry cites five components of this syndrome:

---

[28] Jules Henry, *Culture Against Man* (New York: Random House, 1963).

1. Destructive criticism—the phenomenon of carping destructive criticism is encouraged. The teacher criticizes the child or encourages classmates in their criticism of him.
2. Competition—the students attempt to best out their peers for the attention of the powerful adult figure, the teacher, as in this example from a fifth-grade class:

Teacher: Which one of you nice polite boys would like to take (observer's) coat and hang it up (Observer notes: from the waving hands it would seem that all would like to claim the title.) Teacher chooses one child . . . who takes observer's coat. . . .
Teacher: Now children, who will tell (observer) what we have been doing?
Usual forest of hands . . . and a girl is chosen to tell. . . .
Teacher conducted the arithmetic lesson mostly by asking, "Who would like to tell . . . the answer to the next problem?"
This question was usually followed by the appearance of a large and *agitated* forest of hands; apparently *much competition to answer.*[29]

3. Docility—the teacher encourages student docility and the students respond by giving the teacher what she wants. An incident cited by Henry took place in a second-grade class. The children had just seen a movie of birds, which ended with a picture of a baby bluebird:

Teacher: Did the last bird ever look as if he would be blue?
The children did not seem to understand the "slant" of the question and answered somewhat hesitantly, yes.
Teacher: I think he looked more like a robin, didn't he?
Children, in chorus: Yes.[30]

4. Confession—the teacher encourages students to confess to weaknesses or evil ways and then to repent. The other children seem to take pleasure in hearing someone else confess to evil deeds that they themselves would like to commit.

5. Boredom—the witch-hunt syndrome helps to allay boredom. The implicit feeling seems to be it is better to hunt than be bored.

Henry summarizes the witch-hunt syndrome as follows:

We see in the organization of the components of the witch-hunt syndrome an important phase in the formation of American national character, for tendencies to docility, competitiveness, confession, intragroup aggression, and feelings of vulnerability the children may bring with them to school, are reinforced in the classroom. This means that independence and courage to challenge are observably played *down* in these classrooms. . . . It means, further, that while many teachers do stress helping others they may inadvertently develop in the children the precise opposite, and thus undermine children's feelings of security.[31]

---

[29] *Ibid.,* p. 200.

[30] *Ibid.,* p. 203.

[31] *Ibid.,* p. 213.

THE SCHOOL AS POTENTIALITY

It appears that life in schools is not the exciting experience it should be for students. The difference between eager first-graders and blasé teenagers, or even between first-graders and fifth-graders, is an object lesson on the effects of schooling. As students spend time—or do time—in school they are inevitably shaped by it. They become docile, they question authority less, they learn to think of themselves as successes or failures, they perform rituals without knowing why, they are asked to memorize things they do not care about—and this is called learning. Let us look at some exceptions to the picture we have painted, keeping in mind that exceptions are just that—deviations from the norm.

THE PARKWAY PROGRAM

What are the alternatives? Can the school environment be humanized and made conducive to learning, or is there something about schools which enforces rigidity, conformity and boredom? The Parkway Program, an interesting experiment currently being undertaken in Philadelphia and imitated in other cities across the country, is based on the premise that students do not need to be isolated in a special building from the larger community in order to learn. Parkway has no school building. It is a high school without walls which makes use of the city of Philadelphia as its classroom and learning environment. With 500 students, 30 faculty members and 30 university interns, this unique school allows students to direct their own learning experiences, in the belief that a student learns best if he is self-reliant, self-defining and self-directed.

Students are organized into tutorial groups of 15, and one full-time faculty member and one university intern are assigned to each group. The tutorial group is responsible for the acquisition of basic skills in language and mathematics, and provides support, encouragement and counseling to students.

The formal curriculum is a combination of institutional offerings, basic skills offerings and electives. The graduation requirements are the same as those of any other high school in Philadelphia. The institutional offerings are courses provided by the nearly 200 participating institutions, such as service stations and leather-making shops, usually at the request of the students. The basic skills offerings in language and mathematics, and the elective offerings in the humanities, physical sciences and social studies, are taught by the Parkway staff. Each student is also encouraged to offer a special problems course in an area of his own interest and to participate in work programs at the participating institutions as an extra noncredit component.

Classes are often mixed, allowing freshmen and seniors to exchange ideas. No marks are given; a student is simply given credit or denied it. Informality and responsibility are emphasized. For the most part, attendance is not com-

Sylvia Ashton-Warner

A visitor to Sylvia Ashton-Warner's New Zealand classroom finds it very different from the traditional American school. The Maori children make noise and run around; raw emotion is an integral part of classroom life.

The Maori five-year-old comes to school with unbridled aggressive impulses: he expresses himself in taking, breaking and dominating. In Miss Ashton-Warner's classroom, however, the destructive child is neither punished nor suppressed, but allowed to vent his frustrations. Having come to believe from her work with the Maori that violent and destructive tendencies can be channelled toward creative ends, Miss Ashton-Warner encourages the children to express themselves in art. She subscribes to Eric Fromm's idea that adult destructiveness is the outcome of an unlived life, and argues that people should be allowed to work out aggressive feelings when they are children. The children in her classes often draw pictures of houses engulfed in flames, make bombs out of clay and destroy clay figures as soon as they are made.

Twenty-four years of teaching Maori and white New Zealanders have contributed to Miss Ashton-Warner's theory of organic teaching, which she describes as

the preservation of inner resources,
the exercise of the inner eye and
the protraction of the true personality.

Specifically, she uses the children's own work as the basis for teaching. They write their own readers and draw up their own vocabulary and spelling lists. According to Miss Ashton-Warner, learning should progress from the known—one's own inner feelings—to the unknown—the outer world. Young children are ready for and respond to this kind of learning as they do not to lessons arbitrarily chosen by the teacher. Describing New Zealand as a society in which people's inner resources have atrophied because everything they want is available readymade, she declares, "I think that we already have so much pressure towards sameness through radio, film and comics outside the school, that we can't afford to do a thing inside that is not toward individual development."

Miss Ashton-Warner believes that her method of teaching can make the human

being naturally and spontaneously peaceable. In brief, she argues that education must deal with aggression—the name we give to the expressions of the child's frustrated drives toward self-preservation and sexual gratification. By recognizing and even welcoming their presence in the child, and making them the foundation for "organic learning," these drives can be diverted to constructive and creative ends.

In theory, Miss Ashton-Warner would have children do nothing but creative artwork in school until they are seven. She admits, however, to a gap between theory and practice which requires her to teach some things during this period. Miss Ashton-Warner identifies two "enemies of traditional education": the children's interest in each other and their desire to make things. Instead of telling the children to "be quiet" and "work by yourselves," the traditional refrains in American schools, she has them do all their work in pairs. Each checks the other's mistakes and hurries him up if he is too slow. The children sit cross-legged on mats, fighting, arguing, correcting and helping each other. As a result, learning becomes an integral part of their relationships with each other.

Miss Ashton-Warner's encouragement of the children to make things can be hard on the visitor's—and the teacher's—ears. If you don't like noise, she warns, don't be a teacher—at least not one like her.

Miss Ashton-Warner is presently co-director of the Aspen Community School in Colorado.

pulsory. Students share in planning their curriculum and are free to choose most of their courses; if they want to learn about something not formally offered, they are encouraged to seek experts from the community to assist them. Since a school for 500 pupils costs about a million dollars to build, and since Parkway's capital costs were practically nothing, the potential savings from a school of this nature is tremendous.

How do the students and teachers like this alternative to the traditional high school? The response has been overwhelmingly positive. In 1969 there were 10,000 applications for the 500 student places. Personal interviews with the students and teachers indicate a remarkable exuberance. Problems exist, of course—some students find it difficult to assume so much responsibility for their own learning. Time is wasted. But the process of solving these problems is viewed by most participants as an important aspect of the learning process.

The Parkway Program's basic philosophy is that if schools are to help students grow up and live in the world, they do their students a disservice by isolating them from that world in monolithic school buildings.[32]

THE BELOIT-TURNER MIDDLE SCHOOL

Although the Parkway Program is an exciting alternative to the traditional school, it is unlikely that many of our readers will find themselves teaching in a school without walls. But there is no reason why an interactive, responsive environment cannot exist within a school building. Consider, for example, the Beloit-Turner Middle School in Wisconsin, a school specifically designed for young adolescents rather than for miniature adults.[33] The school consists of three large open classrooms or pods, each serving as a homeroom for 125–150 students, and as a classroom for varying numbers of students throughout the day. These pods are arranged around a central core of administrative and special service offices and a large open instructional materials center. Carpeting covers the floors of all the building, including the cafeteria.

The program is based on the assumption that sixth-, seventh- and eighth-graders have special needs, interests and objectives—and that the school should take these factors into account rather than working against them. It recognizes that early adolescents are in the process of discovering themselves and of defining their relationships with everything and everyone. They are in a questioning stage and need to draw upon various disciplines to explore social issues and problems and to develop individual interests, values and attitudes.

---

[32] James D. Greenberg and Robert E. Roush, "A Visit to the 'School Without Walls': Two Impressions," *Phi Delta Kappan* 51 (May 1970): 482.

[33] James Cass, "A School Designed for Kids," *Saturday Review* 53 (March 21, 1970): 65–67, 75.

The school day is divided into three large blocks of time, each of which is spent in the pursuit of a different major objective. One-half of the day is devoted to "Developing Social Sensitivity and Understanding" (which draws on the social studies, English and foreign languages); one-fourth of the day is spent on "The Physical Environment" (which focuses on science and math), and the rest of the day is given to "Developing Creative Interests and Abilities" (which allows students freedom to develop their own interests in art, music, home economics and industrial arts). Each pod has a team of teachers, assistants, student teachers and interns, and the instructional program is not predetermined but is planned on a day-to-day, week-to-week basis by the instructional team and the students. The part of the day devoted to creative interests is totally controlled by the students and subject to change as they see fit.

'The teachers don't push you into learning,' a diminutive sixth-grader explains. 'They let you come in by yourself and do it the way you want. We learn more because we want to—and it's so great because after you've done your work nobody cares if you visit with your friends.'

'You can't help but learn more, there are so many things to do—and in the afternoon (during the time allotted to creative interests) you can do anything you want.'[34]

A final point: as a result of student demand, the school is open seven days a week!

CLASSROOM OBSERVATION

You will probably benefit most by reading the rest of this chapter rather quickly now and rereading it before you observe schools and classrooms. The material on the following pages is somewhat technical in nature, and is probably best assimilated when you know that you will be making use of it soon.

A school is a complicated social environment in which many different people play roles—students, teachers, counselors, teacher aides, clerks, librarians, nurses, administrators, kitchen personnel, custodians and, in some schools, policemen. Even if we focus exclusively on the classroom, and particularly on the teacher and students, it is extremely difficult to sort out and make sense of everything that happens within its four walls. A classroom is an extremely busy place. Remember Jackson's finding that the elementary teacher engages in as many as 1000 interpersonal interchanges each day (and his study did not even attempt to record pupil-to-pupil interchanges, activities or movements). How then can an observer hope to filter

---

[34] *Ibid.,* p. 75.

Jim: It's becoming clear to me that one of the most significant movements in education today, and one that's particularly attractive to today's youth, is the movement toward informal education.

Kevin: The term "informal education" is being kicked around a good deal these days. What exactly do you mean by it?

Jim: I mean the rejection of the notion that learning occurs only as a result of formal teaching. I think today's students believe that the most significant learning occurs as a result of self-discovery and that truth can be acquired only through personal involvement and experience that is self-directed. Since most formal instruction is definitely not self-directed, many people are seeking alternatives outside the formal educational establishment.

Kevin: Do you mean such things as the free schools and the human potential movement?

Jim: Yes. These and other educational alternatives that allow individuals to shape their own learning, based on what is meaningful to them are, it seems to me, what kids are seeking. They want education to help them answer such questions as, "Who am I?" "What do I want to do with my life?" "How can people relate more honestly to one another?" "How can prejudice, dishonesty and injustice be overcome in our society?"

Kevin: Do you really think formal educational institutions are incapable of allowing this type of human exploration to occur? Or do you think this can be accomplished only through the informal education movement because of the restrictions placed on conventional schools?

Jim: I think there's enough discontent now within the educational establishment that we'll see many more public schools revise their curricula to deal with questions like "Who am I?" If we don't change in this direction, I think we're in trouble.

out the important happenings from the unimportant ones in order to make sense of an extremely complicated environment?

Virtually all teacher education programs provide opportunities for the prospective teacher to observe experienced teachers. Observation may take place "live," or it may involve viewing videotape recordings of classroom sessions. Either alternative can be extremely valuable if it offers an opportunity for insight into how a classroom is organized, how the teacher relates to different students or how different forms of instruction can be used. On the other hand, observation of a classroom can be boring, tedious and educationally irrelevant. What is it that makes observation valuable or worthless? The difference is a matter of knowing specifically what you are attempting to observe and why, being able to gather information accurately and interpreting your data in order to learn from it. Thus, to really benefit from observing an actual classroom you must have some training in observational techniques.

It is physically and mechanically impossible to record *everything* that occurs in a classroom, let alone an entire school. Thus any technique used to gather data about the classroom environment must of necessity be selective. This is a built-in and unavoidable limitation of all recording instruments and techniques of observation.

Furthermore, the background and training of the observer influence the classroom phenomena he chooses to focus on and the ways in which he interprets them. If the variable in question is aggressive behavior among students, for example, an educational psychologist may interpret a classroom outbreak as a result of the teacher's inconsistent reward pattern. An anthropologist might view it as a normal event within the youth subculture. A student teacher, because of her own needs and anxieties, might assume that the students are misbehaving because they don't really like her. For this reason, objective interpretation is as much of an impossibility as is comprehensive observation. But knowing the limitations of observational techniques will help the observer interpret her data better, and being aware of her particular perceptual habits will help her exert caution in interpretation.

DATA-GATHERING TECHNIQUES

The observational methods used in education were developed by the behavioral and social sciences to gather data about and interpret complex environments and later found to be appropriate for use in schools as well. This section will introduce you to some of these tools and approaches, and to the kinds of preliminary decisions and subsequent interpretation which give meaning to observation. The scrupulous observer must ask certain questions: What specifically will be observed? Which method of gathering data will be most effective? What do these data mean? To learn from observation, then, the observer needs 1) objectives, 2) a way to record observations, and 3) a way to interpret observations with respect to objectives.

Observation should not be aimless. If you are to find out what life in the classroom is like you must decide which aspects you wish to focus on. Your objective may be very broad, such as, "What does the teacher do and say during a class period?" Or it may be as narrow as, "How many times does a particular student speak to another student?"

From the data that you collect you can form a hypothesis about why certain things occur, and can test this hypothesis by making predictions about what should happen if it is correct. If your prediction is not validated, you can reexamine your data and try to develop another explanation. If your prediction is repeatedly validated, you will know that you are moving in the direction of understanding what is happening in the classroom and, possibly, why. For example, suppose your objective is to examine the teacher's verbal interaction with each individual student. After performing frequency counts—recording how many times the teacher calls on each student, or how many times each student volunteers information or asks the teacher a question—over a period of a week, you might hypothesize about the frequency distribution for the following week. If your predictions are validated you should then try to interpret your findings. Was the teacher displaying a bias against certain students? Did the teacher systematically ignore the students seated in a particular part of the room? Were certain groups of students treated in particular ways, e.g. girls, certain socioeconomic groups? Caution must be exercised in drawing conclusions, however, because rival hypotheses may explain the same phenomena.

The point to be emphasized is that, in order to understand the happenings in a classroom, you must select objectives which provide you with a focus. Since you can't see, hear and interpret everything, you must be selective. To be selective you must establish the purpose of your observation.

You may find one of the following techniques of data-gathering particularly appropriate, given your objectives, the equipment available and the degree of access you have to a school. All have been used profitably by classroom observers.

Note-taking. Probably the most common means of gathering data in the school is note-taking. The method is borrowed from cultural anthropologists, who take copious notes of their observations while living with the natives of an unfamiliar culture. You can use the same approach to accumulate information about the interpersonal relationships, values or social status of individuals in a class.

If you choose the note-taking approach, certain preliminary decisions will have to be made. First, how comprehensive should your notes be? You will be attempting to record everything you see that relates to your objective. Thus the broader your objective the more you will have to record. In many instances it will be difficult for you to decide quickly on the relevance of a specific event. A handy rule of thumb: when in doubt, write it down. Too much information is better than not enough, for insufficient data can lead to frustration and to erroneous conclusions.

Second, should you write a description of what you see and hear or should you simply record what is said verbatim? Should you write down your impressions of incidents or should you be as objective as possible? We recommend that, whenever possible, data be recorded verbatim. In trying

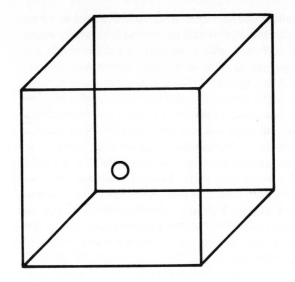

Figure 2.1 An "ambiguous" figure—the Necker cube—which we perceive as spontaneously alternating in depth. In describing the figure verbally you would be right if you called the plane with the small circle in it either the back or the front. Does this literal analogy help show why classroom observations should be factual, not impressionistic?

to summarize or describe what takes place you are likely to substitute your own perceptions of what took place for what was actually happening. If you wish also to record your impressions, insights, inferences and comments, keep them in the margin or draw brackets around them in order to distinguish them from the raw data. This distinction is crucial, because of the tendency to make inferences based on selected perceptions or personal biases. If we are happy, we tend to see happy people; if tired, we see the teacher's and students' behavior through the filter of fatigue and interpret it accordingly. We may see relationships that don't actually exist and miss ones that do. Therefore, recognizing that complete objectivity is impossible, we should still aim to achieve it rather than relying on our own interpretations of events.

You will find that recording nonverbal behavior tends to be much more impressionistic than recording verbal behavior. If we observe a student fidgeting in his seat, picking his nose and looking out the window, it is tempting to assert that he is bored; yet that is an inference. Keep checking on yourself to make sure you are distinguishing between actual behavior and inferences drawn from behavior.

It is much easier to be comprehensive in your note-taking if you establish a standard format and abbreviations. For example, indenting student comments will help you distinguish them from teacher comments and will save you from repeatedly having to indicate who is talking. Abbreviating words by omitting vowels, employing homonyms and using phonetic representations will also allow you to record more efficiently.

Note-taking has a number of advantages as a means of gathering data about classroom actions. It is relatively simple and very economical. You can flip back and forth in your notes easily when you begin to interpret the data. The notes can be cut up and juxtaposed in whatever fashion you want to help you discern patterns or repeated themes. Ideas and events can be assimilated rapidly by scanning written notes. The notes constitute a permanent record, which you can keep to compare with other observations and to develop, support or reject hypotheses.

A major disadvantage of note-taking is the difficulty of recording everything you see and hear. Even though you have selected limited objectives to guide your observations, action often develops so fast that you fall behind and miss some of what is said or done. Taking notes forces you to keep your eyes on the paper in front of you, and prevents you from observing the class uninterruptedly. In other words, your observation system tends to become overloaded with stimuli. Nevertheless, note-taking is probably the most frequently-used method of gathering data in the classroom.

Standardized Observation Systems. Standardized observation systems make use of lists of categories—as minuscule as sneezes or smiles or as broad as teacher-student rapport—to record the verbal or nonverbal interaction in the classroom.

Although many observation systems have been developed, only a few are in general use. Probably the best-known category system for observing teachers and pupils is Flanders' Interaction Analysis, described earlier in the chapter. You will remember that Interaction Analysis is a technique for categorizing direct and indirect verbal behavior in the classroom.

Flanders identified ten different categories of verbal behavior; the first seven apply to teacher talk, the next two to student talk, and the final category records silence or confusion. The categories are: 1) accepting student feelings; 2) giving praise; 3) accepting, clarifying or making use of a student's ideas; 4) asking a question; 5) lecturing, giving facts or opinions; 6) giving directions; 7) giving criticism; 8) student response; 9) student initiation; and 10) confusion or silence. Categories 1–4 represent indirect teacher influence, while categories 5–7 represent direct teacher influence. An observer using Flanders' system records every three seconds the category of verbal behavior occurring that instant; then an analysis is made of verbal interaction during the entire class period. Thus a profile of the teacher's direct or indirect influence can be obtained.

Flanders' system has limitations, but it can be a helpful and informative tool in analyzing a certain kind of verbal behavior in the classroom. It has been used extensively and considerable research data has been collected. Instructional booklets and audiotapes are available to students interested in learning to use the system and interpret data. Many universities and colleges, as well as public schools, are using Interaction Analysis to help teachers analyze their teaching.

What could this girl have heard to delight her so? Thanks to tape, she could be experiencing music or other sounds otherwise unavailable in a school; perhaps she is listening to her own voice for the first time.

Photo by Eileen Ahrenholz.

Analysis of Artifacts.   Much can be learned about life in the classroom without directly observing teachers and students. The textbooks and supplementary materials in use can reveal a lot to the careful observer. Similarly the tests given, the placement of chairs and desks, the materials displayed on the bulletin board and the audiovisual equipment used (or neglected) are clues about what activities take place and what kind of learning is valued. What kinds of questions are on the examinations? Do they emphasize the acquisition of facts to the exclusion of problem-solving, analyzing or synthesizing ideas, making evaluations, comparing or contrasting different points of view, drawing inferences from limited data or forming generalizations? Do the chairs and desks always face the teacher, the dominant person in the classroom? Or are they frequently grouped in small circles, indicating opportunities for pupil-pupil interaction? Is a multimedia approach used so that students may learn from a variety of sources?

You probably have the idea by now—clues about what a teacher thinks is important, whether students are involved in instruction as well as learning and how the teacher views his role can be garnered by a careful analysis of materials used and produced in the classroom. Valuable inferences may be made from data available to the naked eye; it is crucial to remember that such inferences are hypotheses only and that additional data must be gathered to confirm or invalidate them.

Interviews. Interviewing teachers, students, administrators, counselors, librarians and other school personnel is an excellent way to gather data about life in school. People who play different roles in the school, and thus see it from different vantage points, often have highly disparate views of it. The cook in the school kitchen may have a very different opinion of the food's quality than do the students or the teachers, and the administrator's view of detention hall is probably very unlike the students'. Questioning the students about what occupies most of their time in the classroom, what they think the school's purpose is, why they go to school or how their good teachers differ from the poor ones can produce fascinating and highly valuable data. Some sample questions, the answers to which should help you better understand life in a particular school, are listed below:

1. Where is the school located in the community?
2. How old is the school?
3. Is it a parent-, teacher-, administration-, or student-centered school? What evidence leads you to your conclusion?
4. Does the school have an adjoining playground or recreational area? When is it used most—before, after or during school?
5. Is there a school library? Where is it? How does a student gain access to it? What are the library procedures?
6. Where is the nurse's office? What are the major concerns of the health administrator in this school? What are the major complaints (types of illnesses)? What are the procedures for being sent home or remaining in the health office?
7. Where does physical education take place? What is the usual activity? Who participates? What do students do if they are not participating?
8. What is the procedure for tardy students?
9. Who administers this procedure?
10. Do students move from one classroom to another during the school day? How is this accomplished?
11. Is there a dress code? Who decided on its standards? How are infractions handled?
12. What are some frequent causes of disciplinary action against students?
13. What is the system for reinstating a student who has been suspended or expelled?

14. Is there a teachers' lounge? What is the function of this lounge?
15. Are teachers allowed to make educational decisions? If so, what kind?
16. How does a student make an appointment to see the principal or a counselor? What is the usual waiting period?
17. Does the student council have any real power to promote change in the school? If the answer is yes, ask for some examples.
18. Does the student council represent the entire student body or is it a select group?
19. Do parents come to the school? If so, when and for what reasons?
20. Is there a lunchroom in the school? Describe the facility. Do students congregate in identifiable patterns during lunch?
21. Are there extracurricular activities? Music, sports, clubs, meetings?
22. Does the school empty faster at the end of the day or during a fire drill?
23. If you are investigating a secondary school, does it have a newspaper? Ask the editor or a staffer what its function is and how much freedom students have to print what they wish.
24. Is there an auditorium? How often is it used? Why?
25. Are students bussed to school? Ride a school bus one day to see what it's like. Is it different in the morning than in the afternoon?
26. Listen to the students' language, in class and out. Any difference?
27. Ask an administrator, secretary, custodian, teacher, librarian and nurse to describe the student population.
28. Are students trusted? What evidence can you find one way or the other?
29. Are teachers trusted? Must they sign in and out? In what areas of school life do they have decision-making power?
30. What is unusual about this school?
31. Which students are most popular with their peers? Which most respected? If there is a difference, why?
32. Which teachers are most popular with students? Which most respected? If there is a difference, why?
33. What do the school's administrators do? What are their major areas of responsibility? What are the major pressures on them?[35]

The Sociometric Method. The sociometric method—briefly described earlier in connection with Bernice Neugarten's study of children's friendship choices—is used to gather data about patterns of acceptance and rejection, or affection and dislike, among members of a particular group. The method involves asking each member of the group privately to name the persons he would most and least like to work with on a project, sit next to in class, or otherwise associate with. Usually the teacher distributes to each student a sheet of paper carrying a description of an activity, and instructs the students to write down the names of three classmates with whom they

---

[35] The authors are indebted to Professor Emma Cappelluzzo of the University of Massachusetts for many of these questions.

would like to share that activity. When the teacher tallies the students' responses (Figure 2.2), certain students are found to have been chosen more often than others. The distribution of choices can be plotted on a diagram called a *sociogram* (see Figure 2.3). A common pattern is that a relatively small number of group members receives a large number of choices, while others receive few or none; few are sociometrically wealthy but many are sociometrically poor.

CHOOSERS \ CHOSEN	Pam	John	David	Steve	George	Brian G.	Paul	Scott J.	Scott K.	Jeff	Ruth	Marc	Libby	Sherman	Sharon	Tony	Judy	Alan	Brian S.	Jane	Wayne	Bill	Keith	Sandy	Lane
Pam											1				2	3									
John *																									
David				3		2										1									
Steve					1													3				2			
George											1				2				3						
Brian G.		1													2						3				
Paul											1	2							3						
Scott J.							2		1										3						
Scott K.							2								3							1			
Jeff				3														2				1			
Ruth												1							3						2
Marc							1									2	3								
Libby	3						2																1		
Sherman							2									1			3						
Sharon	3									1						2									
Tony			1																		3				
Judy	3													1											2
Alan							1										2		3						
Brian S.							2											1			3				
Jane				3						1	2														
Wayne							2				1						3								
Bill						2	3																1		
Keith		2	3																					1	
Sandy						2									1				3						
Lane										1						2							3		
CHOSEN 1.		1	1		1	2			1	3	4	2			1	2	1				3	1	1		
2.	1			2			7			1	1	1				2	2	1			2			1	2
3.	3			3	1							1			1	1	1	2			9	1	1		
TOTALS	3	2	1	3	1	3	9	0	1	1	3	5	3	0	2	5	3	3	4	0	9	4	2	2	2

\# John absent

Figure 2.2 Chart of seating preferences in a sixth-grade class. Each child was to list three children he would like to sit next to, in order of preference. The choices are entered on the chart on the horizontal dimension.

From *Educational Psychology,* Second Edition, by Frederick J. McDonald (p. 634). © 1959, 1965 by Wadsworth Publishing Company, Inc., Belmont, California 94002. Reprinted by permission of the publisher.

WHAT IS LIFE IN SCHOOLS LIKE?

The sociometric method can be used to determine which students will benefit most from help in improving social relations. The sociogram allows the teacher to identify the *isolates* (those students whom no one chooses) and the *neglectees* (those receiving only one choice). This information can help the teacher to understand the feelings of these students, and to interpret their behavior in class more sensitively. For example, a student whom the teacher considered the class showoff may be found to be an isolate. Thus, he may be showing off in a desperate attempt to attract attention and affection from the teacher and the students.

In sociometric choosing, boys tend to choose boys and girls to choose girls. The percentage of cross-sex choices increases slightly at the secon-

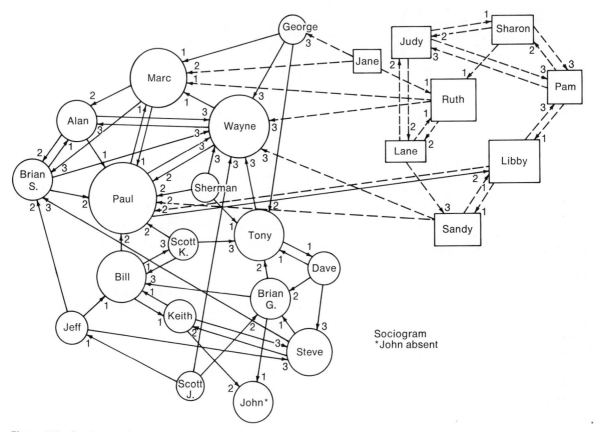

Figure 2.3 *Sociogram based on seating preferences charted in Figure 2.2. The arrows point from chooser to chosen; the numbers beside the arrowheads indicate order of preference.*

dary school level. Also, the percentage of cross-sex choices depends on the sociometric criterion: children choose members of the opposite sex more often as seating or work companions than as play companions.

The number of mutual choices—two group members' choices of each other on the same sociometric criterion—in a group is a general indication of the degree of socialization among group members. A relatively high percentage of pupils makes mutual choices at all grade levels.[36] Pupils whose choices are not reciprocated tend to be those in low sociometric status categories, that is, unpopular; low status-group members tend to choose high status-group members and high status-group members tend to choose each other. A relatively small percentage of mutual choices occurs between members of the opposite sex. The sociometric data suggest that the average boy or girl has two mutual friends among his or her classmates at all grade levels. Girls tend to have more mutual friendships than boys, possibly indicating greater socialization.

The sociometric method is a useful technique for gathering data about patterns of likes and dislikes among students. However, because the information collected by this technique is highly personal it must be kept in strict confidence and extreme caution exercised in drawing conclusions.

Video- and Audiotapes.   Public schools and colleges are making increasing use of mechanical recording devices as analytical and training tools. Audiotape recorders have been available for quite a while, but portable videotape recorders are a relatively recent innovation. Both devices, particularly videotape recorders, have enabled teachers and researchers to analyze what happens in the classroom more completely and objectively. Videotape recorders can register both the image and the sound of classroom interaction, and the resulting record is more accurate and comprehensive than either notes or an observation schedule. Videotapes have many other advantages: the tapes can be replayed without limit; they are reusable after erasing; the Fast Forward and Rewind components make it possible to locate or repeat a particular passage quickly, and the data can be stored almost indefinitely.

The same criteria or objectives may be applied to taped data as to live observation. The advantage, of course, is that something that is missed in the first viewing can be repeated until the viewer has absorbed it—a luxury unavailable in live observation. You might wish to analyze verbal interactions using Flanders' Interaction Analysis, or to watch the behavior of a particular child or to count the number of encouraging gestures the teacher makes toward students. The possibilities are endless.

Many teacher education programs are collecting videotapes to demonstrate particular classroom phenomena to prospective teachers, some showing only a single "critical incident." The tape can be stopped to allow

---

[36] Norman Gronlund, "Typical Sociometric Patterns," in *Society and Education,* ed. R. Havighurst, B. Neugarten, and J. Falk (Boston: Allyn & Bacon, 1967), pp. 320–328.

speculation about how the teacher will or should respond, started again to view the actual teacher's actions and stopped for further discussion.

We have not attempted to train you in the techniques, methods and tools of classroom observation, believing that this is better and more appropriately accomplished as part of your teacher education program. Instead, we have tried to acquaint you with methods that have been and are currently being used by educators to gain a greater understanding of school environments.

DISCUSSION QUESTIONS

1. Is the deprivation of David Krech's rats comparable to that of disadvantaged children? Why or why not?
2. Krech found that rats learn best when they live in a cage with other rats; Jackson found that schoolchildren experience continual frustration and distraction as a result of their proximity to many other people in the classroom. How do you reconcile these findings?
3. William Glasser says that the school alone must bear responsibility for children's failure to learn. What does his statement imply about the causes of failure? In order to eliminate such failure, do you think the school should draw more heavily on the culture of the neighborhood, or should it try to counteract the neighborhood's influence? Why?
4. Talcott Parsons found that children who identify with the role of the teacher, rather than with peers, tend to go on to college. Taking into account the findings we report in this chapter about teachers' behavior and about peer relationships, what do you think would be the effect on a child's personality of identification with the teacher? with peers? How do you think Parsons' finding would be affected if teachers taught more indirectly, asked more divergent questions and performed fewer "gatekeeping" functions?
5. Did you identify with teachers more than with peers when you were in elementary school? If so, are the behaviors you developed as a result useful to you in college? If not, how do you reconcile your presence in college with Parsons' finding?
6. Which of the hypothetical explanations for the discrepancies between elementary and secondary students in Neugarten's study seems most convincing to you? Why? What are the implications of this discrepancy and of your explanation for it?
7. Do you agree with James Coleman that an adolescent subculture exists and that its values are different than those of the dominant culture? of the school? What effect did peer pressure have on your behavior in high school? Is its effect different now? If so, how? And how do you explain this difference?
8. What additional incidental learnings might result from the teacher

behaviors described on pages 61–62? How do school rituals relate to incidental learnings?

9. Analyze the sociogram on page 80. Who are the isolates? the neglect-ees? the stars (most popular)? If you were the teacher in this class, what information would you consider particularly important? What might you do in response?

10. Many people maintain that the school should develop disciplined minds, and should therefore emphasize high academic standards and mastery of subject matter. Do you agree? If so, how would you recon-cile your views with the findings about teacher behavior in this chapter? If not, what findings would you draw on to support your views?

FOR FURTHER READING

Adams, Raymond S., and Biddle, Bruce. *Realities of Teaching: Explorations with Video Tape.* New York: Holt, Rinehart & Winston, 1970. An examina-tion and analysis of classroom life using videotape recordings. It provides a number of concepts that can be used in classroom observation and is very useful for gaining insight into teaching practices.

Barker, Roger G., and Wright, Herbert F. *One Boy's Day.* New York: Harper and Brothers, 1951. A minute-by-minute account of the events and activi-ties of an elementary school boy during one school day. The reader is struck by the boredom that characterizes much of the day.

Bellack, Arno, *et al. The Language of the Classroom.* New York: Teachers College Press, 1966. An attempt to describe the linguistic behavior of teachers and pupils in selected high-school social studies classes. Class-room discourse is viewed as a language game, and the characteristic verbal moves of pupils and teachers are classified and analyzed.

Blishen, Edward, ed. *The School That I'd Like.* Middlesex, England: Penguin Books, 1969. A compilation of British secondary school children's descrip-tions of the kinds of schools they would like. The book is fascinating reading and amounts to a passionate and sustained attack upon the Brit-ish educational system, which might appropriately be applied to our own schools.

Coleman, James S. *The Adolescent Society.* New York: Free Press, 1961. A sociological study of the high school as an adolescent social system. Coleman's major thesis is that, due to peer influence and the reward system of the high school, academically talented students seek to become not scholars but athletes and social leaders.

Cuban, Larry. *To Make A Difference.* New York: Free Press, 1970. A candid view of the problems faced by teachers in inner-city schools. The book's major thesis is that the individual teacher must match the methods and materials of instruction to the student. The author discusses different learning styles, the teacher as liaison with the community and as curriculum developer and specific problems such as race, discipline and expectations.

Dennison, George. *The Lives of Children.* New York: Random House, 1969. The story of the First Street School in New York City, an alternative school which saw itself as an environment for growth and treated relations between the children and the teachers as the very heart of the school. A fascinating account of an alternative school based on freedom for children and teachers alike.

Galloway, Charles. "Nonverbal Communication." *Theory Into Practice* 7 (December 1968): 172–175. This article describes a system for observing nonverbal communication in the classroom.

Glasser, William. *Schools Without Failure.* New York: Harper & Row, 1969. A psychiatrist details the shortcomings of current education, contending that it is failure-oriented. Glasser advocates the use of the class as a counseling group which spends time daily developing the social responsibility necessary to solve behavioral and educational problems within the class.

Goldhammer, Robert. *Clinical Supervision.* New York: Holt, Rinehart & Winston, 1969. This book on supervision is also most appropriate for beginning teachers, particularly Chapter I. Goldhammer's major thesis is that teaching tends to follow patterns, from which students may learn lessons not intended by the teacher.

Grannis, Joseph. "The School as a Model of Society." *Harvard Graduate School of Education Association Bulletin* 21 (Fall 1967): 14–27. Grannis argues that every school presents its students a model of society. He believes that it is not subject-matter content but the structure of the school which instructs most systematically. Grannis describes three models of school which he has observed: the family, the factory and the corporation.

Greenberg, James D., and Roush, Robert E. "A Visit to the 'School Without Walls': Two Impressions." *Phi Delta Kappan* 51 (May 1970): 480–484. Two outside observers record their impressions of Philadelphia's Parkway Program. One observer is extremely enthusiastic, while the other is somewhat more reserved.

Havighurst, Robert J.; Neugarten, Bernice L.; and Falk, Jacqueline M., eds. *Society and Education.* Boston: Allyn & Bacon, 1967. A collection of readings on the sociology of education, which treats such issues as: the school in the social status structure; the school as a socializing agent; the school in the local community; the school in the wider society, and the teacher. The number and variety of articles is vast.

Henry, Jules. "Attitude Organization in Elementary School Classrooms." In *Education and Culture,* edited by George Spindler, pp. 192–214. New York: Holt, Rinehart & Winston, 1963. An anthropologist discusses what he believes to be one characteristic of American culture—intragroup aggression in the classroom. Henry analyzes with examples a phenomenon he describes as the "witch-hunt syndrome."

Jackson, Philip W. *Life in Classrooms.* New York: Holt, Rinehart & Winston, 1968. Using anthropological methods, Jackson analyzes and categorizes everyday occurrences in classrooms. To understand life in elementary school classrooms, Jackson believes we have to appreciate the cultural significance of its humdrum elements, such as repetition, waiting, interruptions, frustration and constant rapid-fire interchanges between teacher and students.

Kaufman, Bel. *Up the Down Staircase.* Englewood Cliffs, N.J.: Prentice-Hall, 1965. An easy-to-read, humorous and poignant semi-fictionalized account of a beginning teacher's experience in a New York City high school. A thoroughly enjoyable book.

Kohl, Herbert. *36 Children.* New York: New American Library, 1968. A popular account of a Harvard graduate teacher's first year in a ghetto school in Harlem. Describes the students' initial hostility and the ways Kohl overcame it. The book also describes vividly the difficult conditions under which teaching is practiced in some sections of New York City.

Kozol, Jonathan. *Death At An Early Age.* Boston: Houghton Mifflin, 1967. A first-year teacher's account of life in a Boston ghetto school. Tyrannization of the children, cynicism, condescension, racism and anti-intellectualism are dominant themes in Kozol's account. The book has become a rallying-point for critics and educational reformers.

Leonard, George. *Education and Ecstasy.* New York: Dell, 1968. Based upon the work of advanced innovative schools, brain-research laboratories and experimental communities, this book urges that education become an ecstatic unity of learning and living.

Postman, Neil, and Weingartner, Charles. *Teaching as a Subversive Activity.* New York: Dell, 1969. A direct, no-nonsense book which urges teachers to adopt the inquiry approach to teaching in their classrooms. Provocative, to say the least.

Schrag, Peter. *Voices in the Classroom.* Boston: Beacon Press, 1965. A description of schools in various areas of the United States. Schrag attempts to look at the culture of the schools and how they differ from one another.

Silberman, Charles E. *Crisis in the Classroom.* New York: Random House, 1970. Sponsored by the Carnegie Foundation, Silberman's book argues that American schools are grim, joyless places—oppressive, intellectually sterile and aesthetically barren. This condition, Silberman argues, is due primarily to the mindlessness of American education. However, he finds hope in the implementation of concepts borrowed from British primary schools.

Smith, Louis M. and Geoffrey, William. *The Complexities of an Urban Classroom.* New York: Holt, Rinehart & Winston, 1968. An intensive analysis of a single seventh-grade classroom with a middle-class teacher in a slum school. Beginning with a description of the behavior of the teacher and pupil as the school term starts, the authors use these data to develop a framework of initial social structure and process in the classroom.

Spindler, George, ed. *Education and Culture.* New York: Holt, Rinehart &

Winston, 1963. A collection of readings by anthropologists whose studies relate to education. The tools and techniques used by anthropologists offer the reader a number of fascinating insights into education in America.

FILMS

Alice—A High School Junior (Indiana University Audio-Visual Center, 16mm, b&w, 22 min., 1967)

A candid view of eleventh-grade students in a number of normally scheduled school activities. There is no plot and no narration, for the film's intention is to provide behavioral data for observation and analysis. Other films in the same series are *Keith—A Second-Grader, Dick—A Fifth-Grader* and *Greg—an Eighth-Grader.*

Anything You Want To Be (Liane Brandon, 16mm, b&w, 8 min.)

A tragicomedy about a high-school girl who finds that her life has been too well-defined by others' expectations: she should be class secretary, not president; a nurse and not a doctor; a housewife and not an intellectual. She is primed by her guidance counselor, her parents, her boyfriend and others for the roles she must fulfill as a "successful woman."

End of a Morning (EDC Film Library, 16mm, b&w, 16 min.)

Documents a classroom of four-year-olds at the Hilltop Head Start Center in Roxbury, Massachusetts. Attention is focused on the completion of their morning's activities.

Football (Time-Life Films, 16mm, b&w, 1 hour)

Documents the ritualism surrounding the annual football game between two high schools in Miami.

Gum (Liane Brandon, 16mm, b&w, 6 min., 1968)

A film by the Theatre Arts and Filmmaking class at Quincy High School (Quincy, Massachusetts). They describe it as "a tragicomic student view of the double standard, a wicked teacher, a role-reversing fantasy, and an ironic conclusion."

High School (Zipporah Films, 16mm or 35mm, b&w, 74 min.)

Frederick Wiseman's *High School,* filmed at an upper-middle-class public high school in Philadelphia, depicts episodes in student life, with particular attention to acts of repression on the part of faculty and administrators.

High School Rising (Boston Newsreel, 16mm, 15 min.)

High school students analyze how the schools exploit, oppress and manipulate them through the tracking system, reinforcement of sex roles and lies in the classroom.

The Kindergarten Child, Part II (Massachusetts Department of Education, 16mm, b&w, 48 min., 1968–70)

This film was produced to stimulate interest in early childhood education and to help school systems and schools of education prepare kindergarten staff and curricula. Although this film depicts a single morning in a kindergarten classroom, it has been divided into six separate episodes, with blank film inserted between sections, for convenience in stopping the projector for discussion.

No Reason To Stay (Contemporary/McGraw-Hill, 16mm, b&w, 27 min.)

A look at the school dropout and what he drops out *from.* Through the eyes of Christopher Wood, we are shown both real incidents and fantasies about teachers who "bore to death thousands of innocent students." The film takes a deliberately biased look at the educational system and how it fails.

Le Sujet C'est Nous (Liane Brandon, 16mm, b&w, 13 min., French dialogue, 1969)

An extremely interesting film made by members of a fourth-year French class at Quincy High School (Quincy, Massachusetts) for "cultural exchange." By depicting a variety of life styles in their high school, and narrating in French, the group hoped to communicate their ideas about school and "life in general."

They Can Do It (EDC Film Library, 16mm, b&w, 35 min.)

This film, made in the Pastorius Public School in Philadelphia, documents the school experiences of 26 six-year-old first-graders who have never been in school before. Starting with the second day of school, the film records the class on six separate occasions throughout the school year.

VIDEOTAPES

A Day at Pacific High School (Raindance, 1/2" videotape, Sony, 30 min.)

A "youth rap" with students from Pacific High School in Los Gatos, California.

Hanging Out in the School Playground (Raindance, 1/2" videotape, Sony, 30 min.)

An edited videotape of kids hanging out in the school playground in Berkeley, California, and the West Village, New York City.

Refer to Appendix for distributors' addresses.

3   What Is Taught?

Baseball, debating, reading, science. . . . Yes, along with love, tolerance and independence. Frustration as well as mathematics and dramatics. Values and ceramics, woodshop and poise, history and boredom, auto mechanics and leadership—all are learned in school, some intentionally, and others in reaction to or in spite of the teacher's intentions.

We define the curriculum as all of the organized and intended experiences of the child for which the school accepts responsibility. In other words, the curriculum is not just the intellectual content of the subjects taught, but also the methods used to teach it, the interactions that occur between people and the school-sponsored activities which contribute to "life experience."

THE CURRENT CURRICULUM

During your high school years, many daily activities organized under the auspices of the school were probably considered "extracurricular." The formal courses of study—history, science, mathematics, English—were curricular, while participation on the football team, cheerleading, Future Teachers club or the band belonged to another, lesser, category. But, we ask, shouldn't all activities which are school-sponsored and contribute to the growth and development of the students be considered part of the curriculum? There is little doubt that informal learning experiences are at least as important to intellectual and social development as are the formal courses of study. Consider, for example, the following list of objectives.[1] Choose the three or four you consider most important and decide whether each is best achieved in a context of formal courses, informal school experiences or a combination of the two:

1. Cultivation of talents, capabilities and potentialities
2. Understanding of self
3. Development of character and moral responsibility
4. Wholesome use of leisure time
5. Enjoyment of beauty
6. Ability to work and associate with other persons on a mutually satisfying basis
7. Discharge of civic responsibilities
8. Success in a vocation
9. Enrichment of family life
10. Good health

A strong argument could be made that each of these goals is best attained by a combination of formal and informal learning experiences. Some, certainly, cannot be achieved through formal educational channels alone.

---

[1] Adapted from J. Galen Saylor and William M. Alexander, *Curriculum Planning for Modern Schools* (New York: Holt, Rinehart & Winston, 1966), p. 146.

Nevertheless, most of the efforts that go into curriculum development are still concentrated on traditional subject matter. The typical elementary or high school is organized according to subject-matter divisions, despite the efforts of some educators to replace them with an experience-based curriculum. Some historical background may help to explain the current strong emphasis on traditional subject-matter areas.

WHERE DOES THE EXISTING CURRICULUM COME FROM?

Curricula are always changing in one way or another. Nevertheless, we can distinguish between sweeping changes which represent new philosophies of learning and teaching and minor adjustments which leave the overall curriculum relatively intact. What follows is not a thorough history of American curriculum revision, but a brief overview of the educational philosophies which have prompted major curriculum change, to help you better understand the motives which molded today's curriculum.

Shifting Motives. Two curriculum writers have identified five major motives which have held sway more or less consecutively and have dominated the development of the curriculum in American schools: 1) religious, 2) political, 3) utilitarian, 4) the movement for mass education and 5) the movement for excellence in education.[2]

The religious motive held sway from approximately 1635 to 1770, when the schools were expected to promulgate the religious beliefs of the community. The period 1770–1860 was characterized by a politically-motivated desire to produce a literate populace in order to ensure the preservation of liberty and the new democratic form of government. Utilitarian goals 1860–1920 resulted from the pressure of a rapidly-expanding economy for educated people to fill the new jobs that were being created. The mass education motive (1920 to the present) is a product of the belief that all children are entitled to equal educational opportunities. Although this principle is widely espoused, it has yet to be achieved. The movement for excellence in education (1957 to the mid-1960's) was prepared for by the discovery during World War II that many high-school graduates were virtually illiterate in mathematics and science, but concern and action lagged until 1957, when Sputnik focused upon the public schools the most critical attention they had received in decades.

Sputnik and the Reaction to Progressivism. When the Russians launched Sputnik, the American public—which had complacently believed American schools to be far superior to any other country's—reacted against what they considered the "softness" of the curriculum and demanded a return to

---

[2] J. Minor Gwynn and John Chase, Jr., eds., *Curriculum Principles and Social Trends* (New York: Macmillan, 1969), pp. 1–29.

the "meat and potatoes" of learning—the academic disciplines, with particular emphasis on science and mathematics. More students were competing for college entrance, middle-class parents wanted to make sure their children were prepared for the increased competition. During the so-called "progressive education" era of the Twenties, Thirties and Forties, the schools had emphasized citizenship and self-adjustment. If the progressive curriculum can be seen as child-centered or society-centered, curriculum development during the Fifties and Sixties must be considered discipline-centered; this approach was characterized at the time as a return to excellence in education, though many critics today question the superiority of such a disciplinary approach.

Prosperity was a major factor in the extensive curricular change of the Fifties and Sixties. The middle class saw education as the path to a good life for their children. The more education one received, the more likely one was to earn a good income and enjoy the comforts of life. As a result, the public was willing to spend increasing amounts of money for education. As is so often the case, however, action lagged behind intentions until Sputnik's launching triggered intense awareness of the public school curriculum. Because of its concern for national defense and worldwide prestige, the federal government poured huge amounts of money into curriculum development projects, teacher training workshops and research. The influence of the federal government on the development of new curricula cannot be underestimated. Prior to this period the federal government had played a limited role in education, which was considered the exclusive responsibility of the individual states. During the Fifties the role of the federal government in public education was a hotly debated issue; the outcome is obvious in the fact that federal involvement in education is taken for granted today.

Another contributory factor was the tremendous postwar knowledge explosion, which was forcing new approaches to curriculum planning by making many areas of the existing curricula obsolete. In addition, a combination of social and political factors encouraged a new approach to the educational needs of the country; the 1954 Supreme Court decision outlawing "separate but equal" education meant that school and educators had to rethink their approaches to time-honored traditions.

Jerome Bruner *(1915–   )*

Jerome Bruner has achieved a certain fame among Harvard psychology students for his imitations of babies, baboons and slow lorises and his sparkling enthusiasm for knowledge and discovery. Outside the Harvard community, however, he is better known for his studies of child development and his important work in educational psychology and curricular reform.

Bruner grew up in Lawrence, Long Island, where he spent his childhood fishing, sailing and reading voraciously. He remembers that school was no challenge —it was too easy—and that he was always looking for something new to read. His father, a German-Jewish watch manufacturer, died when Bruner was 12. After high school, Bruner went to Duke University for his B.A., and received a Ph.D. in psychology from Harvard in 1941. He served in the Office of War Information and then returned to Harvard, where he remained until moving to Oxford University in England in 1972 to be the Watts professor of psychology.

Bruner joined the critics of American education ten years ago, when he served as chairman of a conference of scientists, scholars and educators at Woods Hole, Massachusetts, on the teaching of science. For years there had been a gulf between "serious" psychology and such mundane matters as pedagogy; scholars looked down their noses as what they considered the province of teachers' colleges. The only exception was B. F. Skinner, the renowned behaviorist, who has done pioneering work on teaching machines and programmed instruction. Bruner's report on the Woods Hole conference, *The Process of Education,* was hailed as a major contribution to curriculum reform and won him instant fame. It has since been translated into 22 languages and is studied by teachers all over the world. The most memorable statement in the report, and the gist of Bruner's argument, is quoted widely: "Any subject can be taught effectively in some intellectually honest form to any child at any stage of development." According to Bruner, a school subject is not something one "knows about," but something one "knows how to do." It is a way of thinking and doing, rather than a collection of facts.

In keeping with his famous statement of a decade ago, Bruner has developed a fifth-grade social studies curriculum called *Man: A Course of Study,* which provides ten-year-olds with materials like those social scientists use and encourages them to investigate what is human about human beings. The course, which includes units on the life cycle of the salmon, on baboons and on the Netsilik Eskimos, has been adopted by more than 1500 schools.

In 1960 Bruner and psychologist George Miller organized Harvard's Center for Cognitive Studies, where they investigated the instinctive acts of the infant—sucking, looking, reaching, grasping—as if they were observing the behavior of an unknown species. From these simple, innate activities the baby develops four crucial abilities: voluntary control of his behavior; internal control of his attention; the power to carry out several actions simultaneously, and the use of reciprocal codes which pave the way for speech. By studying infants long before they learn to talk, Bruner and others have concluded that language competence is just one aspect of the infant's ability to systematize learning. They suggest that the human mind possesses innate programs of learning, discernible immediately after birth, not only for language but also for the use of hands, eyes and tools. If Bruner and his co-workers succeed in decoding these mysteries of the mind, the implications for education will be immediate and massive.

Bruner advocates more problem-seeking and problem-solving for all learners, from infants to college students. He has proposed a dual curriculum for colleges which could satisfy both traditionalists and innovators. On Mondays, Wednesdays and Fridays, students would continue to take traditional courses; on Tuesdays and Thursdays they would be free to govern their learning in experimental ways. This experimentation might include taking part in university budget decisions and teacher evaluation and, most important, learning to deal rationally with their own problems.

One way to implement such a dual curriculum is to make basic changes in student living arrangements. Bruner acted on his interest in extracurricular learning by becoming Master of Currier House, a new Harvard-Radcliffe coed residence. He helped solicit private funds for a day-care center at the House, and invited people from many spheres of life to dine with students. He and his students wanted Currier House to serve as an example of how a community can encourage and make use of its members' initiative to deal with its own problems, both simple ones like the care of babies and large ones like drug abuse. Rather than limiting the curriculum to course work, Bruner sees the dual curriculum as an opportunity for students to put knowledge to work in their own lives.

The Discovery Method. The curriculum reform movement was crystallized by the publication in 1960 of *The Process of Education*,[3] a short book by Jerome Bruner, a Harvard psychologist. Bruner's ideas, though by no means entirely original with him, were the most profound and elegant expression of the spirit and convictions behind the movement for curriculum change. Bruner's basic thesis was that any discipline could be and should be studied, at any level of complexity, in terms of its "structure." The structure of a discipline Bruner defined as the concepts and methods of inquiry which are its most basic components. Instead of studying random facts or incidental phenomena, students should learn the principles which constitute the heart of a discipline. A knowledge of fundamentals would enable the student to inquire into and solve problems in the discipline independently. Learning the structure of a discipline would equip the student to transfer useful concepts from one situation to another, or, in other words, to learn how to learn. This Bruner considered crucial, because the totality of knowledge in any discipline is too massive for anyone to acquire, and because knowledge changes so rapidly that what is current one year might be out-of-date the next. Bruner urged that students be provided opportunities to become problem-solvers through direct and prolonged experience with objects or raw data, in the same way that a historian studies history or a biologist biology. Teachers were encouraged to let students discover meanings for themselves. This "discovery" or "inquiry" method, Bruner asserted, would make it possible to teach young children complex concepts in language they could understand. Having learned a concept on a simplified level, they could later return to it at a somewhat more advanced level. Thus, the concepts fundamental to the discipline's structure would be studied over and over throughout the school years, but each time from an increasingly complex point of view. The curriculum of the discipline would resemble a spiral; as the student moved along the spiral, he would reencounter familiar concepts in more complex forms.

Bruner's ideas alone did not cause the tremendous curriculum reforms of the Fifties and Sixties; many forces for change were already in motion prior to the publication of *The Process of Education*. However, Bruner's concept of the structure of disciplines catalyzed the already-widespread reaction to the fusion of disciplines which had occurred in the schools, and it was implemented in numerous curriculum development projects. These projects have had considerable impact on the public schools' curricula, particularly in the areas of mathematics, biology, chemistry, physics and foreign languages. Their influence on social studies and English has not been as great, because there have been so many different social studies projects that their impact has been diffused, and because little agreement has been reached regarding objectives and methods for teaching English.

The new projects have generally had less impact at the elementary level

---

[3] Jerome S. Bruner, *The Process of Education* (New York: Random House, 1960).

than at the secondary level, with the notable exception of mathematics and, possibly, science. Many elementary educators considered the study of distinct disciplines inappropriate to the elementary school. They felt that the significant problems of mankind could not be studied through the disciplinary approach, and called instead for a "holistic" curriculum which would treat life as something whole rather than piecemeal. They also were concerned that emphasis on underlying concepts, abstractions and intuitive behavior would lead to neglect of practical operations and applications. Since the new curricula were designed to reform disciplines already well-established in the schools, it appeared to many that they would leave no room for emerging fields. But probably more than anything else, the elementary educators objected to planning from the top down, from the secondary to the elementary, which failed to take into account sufficiently the developmental processes of young children as learners—their interests, their individual differences and the irregularity of their growth. To them, curriculum reform seemed to be putting the discipline before the child.

Not surprisingly, the feeling that the curriculum unwisely stresses the subject above the learner is shared by many secondary educators as well; they question the relevance of such a curriculum. So do we.

Photo courtesy of Education Development Center.

Photo by William Simmons for the
Ford Foundation.

WHAT IS THE CURRENT CURRICULUM?

Looking at the courses of study prescribed by the fifty states, one discovers that the similarities far outweigh the differences. We will discuss some of the reasons for this phenomenon later, but in the meantime let's examine what is presently taught in elementary and secondary schools across the country.

At both levels the curriculum is organized into subject-matter areas, which ordinarily are science, mathematics, social studies, foreign languages, English, reading and language arts, the fine arts and physical education; the latter three areas tend to emphasize developing skills rather than mastery of a particular body of knowledge.

In some elementary schools all subjects are taught by one teacher; other schools bring in specialists to teach the fine arts and physical education, and still others hire specialists to teach reading, science and mathematics.

Science. Science instruction in elementary schools is in, to put it simply, a state of flux. Many schools still base their science programs on the notion of social utility; what is taught must be of practical use in solving problems which people face every day. This approach is out of favor with leaders in science education because the knowledge explosion may make presently "practical" information quickly obsolete. Science educators are proposing that students learn the conceptual schemes upon which each branch of science is based, and the processes by which scientists acquire new knowledge, in order to keep pace with the rapid expansion of knowledge.

In an effort to "catch up with the Russians," a number of science curriculum revision projects were funded by the National Science Foundation, and other federal agencies, after the launching of Sputnik in 1957. These projects—which were developed by people of diverse backgrounds, including leading scientists, science educators, teachers, psychologists, educational evaluators and artists—differed in format and intention, but each called for new teaching roles. The teacher can no longer be considered the fount of knowledge. Instead of dominating the learner, the teacher must create an open, nonthreatening atmosphere which offers the child numerous opportunities to manipulate scientific objects and materials. In addition, the teacher is discouraged from simply *telling* the students answers and encouraged to allow them to ask questions, face problems and pose tentative solutions; she should foster an environment that encourages an inquiry approach. Since these teacher skills differ fundamentally from those demanded by more traditional programs in science, a number of workshops have been funded by the National Science Foundation to train teachers in the new approaches.

Among the most widely adopted elementary science curriculum projects are the Science Curriculum Improvement Study (SCIS), a project developed at the University of California, Berkeley; *Science—A Process Approach,* a project developed by the American Association for the Advancement of Science (AAAS), Washington, D.C.; the Elementary Science Study (EES), a project developed by Education Development Center, Inc., Newton, Massachusetts; and the Minnesota Mathematics and Science Teaching Project (MINNEMAST), a project developed at the University of Minnesota, Minneapolis.

Similar projects were developed for secondary schools in the biological and physical sciences, particularly biology, chemistry and physics. Most notable of these efforts are the Biological Sciences Curriculum Study (BSCS), the Chemical Bond Approach Project (CBA), the Chemical Education Material Study (CHEM Study) and the Physical Science Study Committee (PSSC).

Mathematics. Mathematics education was equally affected by Sputnik. As a matter of fact, mathematics was the first area in which curriculum builders undertook the revision process. Since math is taught on a K-12 basis, most of the new projects incorporated all grade levels to insure continuity.

Mathematics today is viewed as a language which both communicates ideas about numbers and describes the quantitative aspects of ideas, ob-

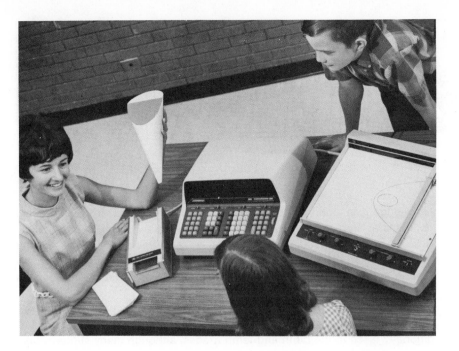

jects. At the elementary school level, mathematics instruction attempts to help children assign meaning to numbers. A distinction is made between *number,* which is a mental concept, and *numeral,* the physical symbol which represents that concept. That a child can count from one to one hundred does not necessarily mean that he possesses an understanding of number concepts. As a result, mathematics today stresses *structure* rather than drill and computational skills.

Among the foremost mathematics projects are the School Mathematics Study Group (SMSG), the Greater Cleveland Mathematics Program, the Madison Project of Syracuse University and Webster College, the University of Illinois Committee on School Mathematics (UICSM) and the University of Maryland Mathematics Project; the most widely adopted of these is the SMSG project.

Social Studies. Social studies—the study of man, his ideas, actions and relationships—is not a discipline in the same sense as are mathematics or science, although it draws on the various social science disciplines for its content and methods of inquiry. (A discipline has been defined as an area of inquiry containing a distinctive body of concepts and principles, with techniques for exploring the area and for correcting and expanding the body of

knowledge.)[4] In contrast to the sciences and mathematics, fundamental concepts and processes have not been identified and agreed upon by curriculum builders in social studies. History has traditionally been the king of the social studies, at both the elementary and secondary levels, and, although some inroads have been made by other disciplines, it still remains dominant.

The pattern of courses taken in high school has also remained relatively standard for the past twenty-five years. Civics and world history are traditionally taken in the ninth and tenth grades, although many students take no social studies courses then. American history is usually taken in the eleventh grade. Problems of democracy and elective courses such as economics, American government and sociology are taken in the twelfth grade.

The most common approach to social studies at the elementary level focuses on the "widening horizons" of a child's environment. In the primary grades, children study the family, the home and the school; as their scope of attention expands, they study the neighborhood, the local community and other types of communities, the state, the nation and other parts of the world. Thus, the social studies curriculum is conceptualized as a series of concentric circles, with the child at the center, and each grade level focuses on a particular ring of the circle. History and geography dominate the social studies in the elementary school, as does the use of a single textbook. There is heavy emphasis on learning to interpret graphs, charts and maps and on the development of communication skills.

Some of the new curriculum projects take an interdisciplinary approach, while others focus on individual disciplines, such as anthropology, geography, economics, political science and sociology. No single social studies project has gained the general acceptance and wide distribution that SMSG has in mathematics and BSCS in biology. However, over fifty new social studies projects have been developed since 1960, making it highly unlikely that any one of them could dominate the field.

---

[4] Arthur W. Foshay, "Knowledge and the Structure of the Disciplines," in *The Nature of Knowledge: Implications for the Education of Teachers,* ed. William A. Jenkins (Milwaukee: University of Wisconsin, 1961).

Language Arts. The language arts program seeks to develop in children the skills of reading, writing, speaking and listening. The importance of language arts cannot be overemphasized, since no subject can be successfully studied without language skills. Most elementary language arts programs share the common goal of developing in the student the following capacities:

1. intelligent use of common modes of communication
2. the ability to talk formally and informally with and to a group and individuals, and to listen effectively and courteously
3. the ability to read analytically and critically for information
4. enthusiasm for continued learning through communication
5. facility with the English language through awareness of language patterns and structure, and effective skills in writing including spelling and handwriting
6. ability to use the tools of the language arts, particularly the dictionary, encyclopedias, and other reference and resource materials[5]

Language arts curricula must be organized to foster continuous growth and increasing sophistication in the four major skill areas during the elementary years, and graded elementary schools ordinarily employ sequential curricula.

A number of curriculum reform projects in language arts on the secondary level have been developed in recent years, supported by the federal government. In 1961 the U.S. Office of Education launched Project English—now known as the English Program of the U.S. Office of Education—in an attempt to improve instruction at all levels in English literature, reading and writing; to coordinate the efforts of teachers, school administrators and university professors in improving the quality of English teaching; to sponsor research, experimentation and dissemination; and to assist universities to establish centers for the development of new curriculum materials and teaching methods.

An investigation of the various projects which have emerged from these new curriculum centers reveals that they have several characteristics in common.[6] 1) Student activities involve listening and speaking to each other in natural settings. The stress is on informal discussion rather than platform presentations. 2) Traditionally, the schools have tried to standardize the language of the students and to purify it of ungrammatical patterns. Rather than attempting to extinguish "bad" language patterns, the new projects concentrate on exploring acceptable alternative possibilities and testing their effects. In other words, the new language instruction explores grammatical structures and linguistic units to see how they work, without prescribing proper and improper usage. 3) At one time literature was regarded

---

[5] William Vernon Hicks, W. Robert Houston, Bruce Cheney and Richard Marguard, *The New Elementary School Curriculum* (New York: Van Nostrand, 1970), p. 158.

[6] Robert Hogan, "What's New in Curriculum—English," *Nation's Schools* 84 (July 1969): 37–38.

as a means to teach reading skills and as an instrument for moral education. More recently it has been used to portray our cultural heritage and to illustrate style, technique and character development. The use of contemporary literature, paperbacks and individualized reading programs is growing in popularity, and increasing effort is being made to find literature that involves students, elicits intense personal response and motivates the students to further reading. 4) English classes are taking advantage of the increasing interest in new media, particularly by studying and discussing serious films. Some schools offer film-making and multimedia presentations as part of the English program. 5) The new curricula are emphasizing interdisciplinary study, in conjunction with other areas of the humanities such as music, art and, occasionally, history.

A second major influence on the English curriculum was the Anglo-American Seminar on the Teaching of English held at Dartmouth, England in 1966. The participants in the seminar—leading scholars, teachers of English and English education—came to the conclusion that the traditional content-centered curriculum is sterile and that treating English as a "discipline" is restrictive as well as unworkable. The participants agreed that English is more than the structural "tripod" of literature, language study and composition it had been considered for more than a decade.

One new approach to English is outlined in James Moffett's *A Student-Centered Language Arts Curriculum, Grades K–13.*[7] Taking human discourse as the central unifying concept, Moffett offers a series of activities intended to develop logically and cumulatively the student's own language powers. In effect, each student produces his own language texts by experimenting with narrative, dialogue, improvisation and biography and recording the results. This approach rejects explicit instruction in rhetoric or literary data and instead emphasizes the validity of oral language as a basis for all other activities in English.

However, such new approaches have met strong resistance, partially because of widespread philosophical controversy about the nature of English itself. Despite the work of the curriculum centers and of individual spokesmen, the majority of teachers and scholars of English maintain that the "discipline" approach to English is the only viable one; they acknowledge that its implementation needs revision, but find no fault with the concept itself. They regard only written literature as valid, to the exclusion of oral composition, and insist that some form of grammar study be maintained. Thus, as in social studies, change is slow to come to the English classroom. One survey indicates that few of the curricular innovations advocated by the new curriculum centers are being implemented in the classroom.[8]

---

[7] James Moffett, *A Student-Centered Language Arts Curriculum, Grades K–13: A Handbook for Teachers* (Boston: Houghton Mifflin, 1968).

[8] Fred I. Godshalk, "A Survey of the Teaching of English in Secondary Schools," *School and Society* 98 (April 1970): 249–250.

Foreign Languages. The foreign language programs of our public schools have changed considerably over the last twenty years. Prior to World War II, most foreign language instruction stressed reading and writing, to the virtual exclusion of listening and speaking. Furthermore, foreign language instruction was almost exclusively the domain of the secondary schools. Since the Fifties a new kind of foreign language instruction has been introduced into elementary as well as high schools. The new audio-lingual approach is designed to develop competence in speaking and listening to others speak a foreign language. As evidence of this dramatic change, the number of language laboratories—rooms equipped with listening tapes, headsets and machines which can monitor the pace of the student and allow him to respond to the tapes—in public schools nationwide has grown from several dozen in 1957 to at least 8,000 by 1966. There is, however, some evidence that their use is not as widespread as was once believed.

Photo by Patricia Hollander Gross through Stock, Boston.

Photos by S. Jacobs.

The adoption of the audiolingual approach necessitated the retraining of many foreign language teachers and, with support from the National Defense Education Act and the U.S. Office of Education, hundreds of summer workshops have been held. In addition to French, German, Spanish, Italian and Russian, new materials have been developed for the study of Arabic, Chinese, Japanese, Portuguese, Greek and Hebrew.

The Arts.　Teachers of the fine and applied arts have been fighting an uphill battle to maintain a secure position in the regular school curriculum. During the post-Sputnik era, budgetary cutbacks were made in the arts to finance enriched programs in mathematics and the sciences. Recently, however, many public school art programs have become sources of pride.

Art and music in the elementary school are ordinarily taught by regular classroom teachers, although some schools hire specialist teachers in one or both areas. Dance and drama are by and large ignored in the elementary school, though children of this age are less inhibited and seem to enjoy these activities more than do students in the secondary schools. The small amount of instruction in the arts provided for elementary students is replaced in high school by drama clubs, orchestras, bands and dance groups. In most instances, instruction in music or dance during a child's elementary-school years takes the form of private instruction, outside the public school.

Elective and Vocational Courses.　Most high schools today offer their students a number of options regarding the courses they take. While the average high-school student graduates with sixteen to twenty units—a year-long course representing one unit—large high schools may offer as many as one hundred courses. The average student, then, will probably choose among optional courses according to his interests or academic ambitions.

Although college preparation has been the major goal of many high schools, increased effort has been made recently to provide well-balanced programs for students not planning to attend college. This trend is especially evident in rural areas where small local high schools are being replaced by comprehensive regional high schools. Some of the new courses, such as

industrial education, distributive education, home economics, business education and agriculture, are specifically vocational in nature. Others, such as driver education, consumer education and conservation, have been added to the curriculum because of an obvious societal need or in response to student interest.

Activities and Other Aspects of the Curriculum. At the beginning of this chapter we defined curriculum as all the experiences for which the school accepts responsibility, including activities pursued outside the formal course of study. Such organized non-credit activities are the primary vehicle by which the schools promote one of their main stated objectives, individual growth and development. For example, most high schools offer a program of varsity and intramural sports, as well as civic, social and hobby clubs. Many schools have active student government organizations (which are more often regarded as a means to promote cooperation among students than as real decision-making bodies with the power to affect life in the schools).

IS THE EXISTING CURRICULUM RELEVANT TO TODAY'S SOCIETY?

Perhaps the most basic function of all education is to increase the survival chances of the group. When educational systems have not fulfilled this function, whole civilizations have been known to disappear. What happened in those civilizations is that environmental conditions changed, requiring the development of new skills, new ideas and new concepts to survive, but the more conservative elements of society insisted on maintaining the traditional educational forms. As long as the environment remained stable or changed very slowly, the skills necessary for survival also remained constant. In such times, when the culture of the past has proven able to insure the survival of the group, education can be content to transmit that culture. If, however, the dominant characteristic of the environment is change, concepts and skills useful for survival must be separated from what is useless or outmoded, the former retained and the latter discarded. In addition, new concepts and skills appropriate to the new demands of the environment have to be developed to replace those that are discarded.

Our society and our environment are presently undergoing change at a rate unprecedented in mankind's history. The population of the world is expanding at an almost geometric rate, and exerting severe pressure on the environment. We are consuming natural resources at such a rate that it is only a matter of time before many will be depleted. We are polluting the air we breathe and, at the same time, destroying huge tracts of plants which provide us with oxygen. We are fouling the water we drink and, as a consequence, must spend billions of dollars to try (not very successfully) to purify it. Racial and ethnic prejudices which have gone unchallenged for decades are no longer being endured by their victims. Nations now possess the power to annihilate one another at the push of a button. In short, we have reached a point at which many leading thinkers are questioning man's (note: not the United States' or the U.S.S.R.'s, but *man's*) ability to survive another century on this planet.

If we are to rely on education to increase our chances of survival, education must turn its attention to the concepts and skills—that is, survival strategies—necessary to cope with or control such environmental change. Our ability to recognize and to discard concepts and approaches that have been rendered irrelevant, and to substitute new ones in their places, may indeed determine our survival. We must question the relevance of our curriculum.

The Saber-Tooth Curriculum. In his classic satire on curriculum irrelevance, *The Saber-Tooth Curriculum*,[9] Harold Benjamin—using the pseudonym Abner J. Peddiwell—describes how the first school curriculum was developed in the Stone Age. The earliest educational theorist, according to Benjamin's book, was a man named New Fist, who hit upon the idea of deliberate, systematic education.

Watching children at play, New Fist wondered how he could get them to do the things which would gain them more and better food, shelter, clothing and security. He analyzed the activities that adults engaged in to maintain life and came up with three subjects for his curriculum: 1) fish-grabbing-with-the-bare-hands, 2) woolly-horse-clubbing and 3) saber-tooth-tiger-scaring-with-fire. Although the children trained in these subjects enjoyed obvious material benefits as a result, some conservative members of the tribe resisted the introduction of these new subjects on religious grounds. But, in due time, many people began to train their children in New Fist's curriculum and the tribe grew increasingly prosperous and secure.

Then conditions changed. An ice age began, and a glacier crept down over the land. The glacier brought with it dirt and gravel which muddied the creeks, and the waters became so dirty that no one could see the fish well

---

[9] Abner J. Peddiwell [Harold Benjamin], *The Saber-Tooth Curriculum* (New York: McGraw-Hill, 1939).

enough to grab them. The melting waters from the approaching ice sheet also made the country wetter, and the little woolly horses migrated to drier land. They were replaced by antelopes who were so shy and speedy that no one could get close enough to club them. Finally, the new dampness in the air caused the saber-tooth tigers to catch pneumonia and die. And the ferocious glacial bears who came down with the advancing ice sheet were not afraid of fire.

The thinkers of the tribe, descendants of New Fist, found a way out of the dilemma. One figured out how to catch fish with a net made from vines. Another invented traps for the antelopes and a third discovered how to dig pits to catch the bears.

Some thoughtful men began to wonder why these new activities couldn't be taught in the schools. But the wise old men who controlled the schools claimed that the new skills did not qualify as *education*—they were merely a matter of *training*. Besides, the curriculum was too full of fish-grabbing, horse-clubbing and tiger-scaring, the standard cultural subjects, to admit new ones. When some radicals argued that the traditional subjects were foolish, the wise old men said that they taught fish-grabbing not to catch fish but to develop agility; horse-clubbing to develop strength, and tiger-scaring to develop courage. "The essence of true education is timelessness," they announced. "It is something that endures through changing conditions like a solid rock standing squarely and firmly in the middle of a raging torrent. You must know that there are some eternal verities and the saber-tooth curriculum is one of them!"[10]

The Saber-Tooth Curriculum was written in 1939, but its continuing applicability seems to be one of the true "eternal verities."

What's Relevance? Before one can determine whether a particular curriculum is relevant, some difficult questions must be asked: relevant to what? To life in society as it is now, as it probably will be in the future or as it ideally should be? Relevant for whom? For the individual learner, or for society and its needs? And who determines social needs—the adults who represent the "establishment," or some other group? The question of curriculum relevance is very complicated, for it draws upon one's entire philosophy of education. Is education's primary purpose to help students develop their minds by exploring ideas of the past that have proven to have enduring meaning? Or is education's primary purpose to help students experience growth through interaction with their environment? Is there a particular body of knowledge or repertoire of skills that all members of our society should possess? Or should students be free to explore many different areas in accordance with their own needs, curiosities and interests? Should education give priority to the study of immediate problems and to developing the processes, understandings and skills necessary for their solution? Or should education concentrate on guiding behavior according to agreed-

---

[10] *Ibid.,* pp. 43–44.

We don't acquire our really important learning in packages. As interested explorers we are not concerned about boundaries which mark those august empire states called disciplines—separating literature from history, sociology from psychology, chemistry from biology, and so on. But as educators we begin to be concerned about passports, visas, and entry and exit permits, failing to realize that the student wants to explore life in its mysterious wholeness, rather than in the exclusive little principalities of subject areas. Walter R. Coppedge, "What the World is Coming To," Phi Delta Kappan 52 (October 1970): 77.

upon standards, and on study of the past as a way of preparing for the future?

In a society as large and pluralistic as the United States, all of these philosophical positions, and more, have committed supporters. How can the schools incorporate in their curricula such diverse philosophies? Obviously, they cannot. If a certain philosophy is dominant within a given community, the curriculum of its schools is likely to reflect that set of beliefs, and those who don't agree will remain dissatisfied. More often than not inertia keeps traditional programs ensconced in the schools until a catalytic event, such as Sputnik's launching or rioting in white neighborhoods, or an intellectual force, such as the progressive education movement, arouses enough momentum to bring about change. It is only reasonable to expect that the philosophies which have molded the present school curriculum will dominate until an opposing point of view gains enough support to supplant them.

Mortimer Smith argues that all educational philosophies, however various, fall into two basic categories and characterizes them as follows:

On this matter of priorities in education, the picture seems clear: One group believes that the school must maintain its historic role as the chief institution in charge of intellectual training; another group—and perhaps the dominant one in public education—maintains that intellectual training is only a part of the school's total program, and not necessarily the most important part.[11]

If one considers the school's primary objective to be the intellectual training of students, any curriculum which does not emphasize scholarship will be judged irrelevant. Conversely, if one believes that the school should emphasize the development of the "whole child"—his emotional and social, as well as intellectual, growth—curriculum devoted exclusively to English, history, the sciences, mathematics and foreign languages will be considered inappropriate for many students and thus irrelevant.

---

[11] Mortimer Smith, "Fundamental Differences Do Exist," *American Education Today,* ed. Paul Woodring and John Scanlon (New York: McGraw-Hill, 1964), p. 29.

The main charge of the public schools' critics is that the curriculum is irrelevant to the needs of many children and of society. They accuse it of emphasizing knowledge and skills for which many students have no use. They argue that unless a student is preparing for college, teaching him to bisect an angle or to recite facts about the ancient Egyptians is a poor use of his time (and perhaps of the college-bound students' time too). They charge that the traditional subject-matter approach to the curriculum ignores the learner's needs and interests.

A corollary criticism is that studying unrelated subjects, each by a different method and according to a unique logic, begs the question of integration of knowledge. The problems we encounter in life do not come neatly organized

BERRY'S WORLD

© 1969 by NEA, Inc.

"Now, then—just which part of the kindergarten curriculum needs to be more relevant?"

Cartoon by Berry, copyright © 1970 by The New York Times Company Reprinted by permission.

according to subject matter; such distinctions are arbitrarily imposed on them by people.

The arbitrariness of the boundaries between disciplines is evident in the emergence of fields of study with names such as biochemistry, psycholinguistics, operations research, biophysics and ecology—to name only a few. These fields have come into being in response to problems which could not be solved within the limits of any one discipline; they demanded a multidisciplinary approach. If problems do not come prepackaged in distinct disciplines, why does the public school impose on students a curriculum made up of discrete subjects, each of which must be studied at an assigned time? If high school students apply in one class ideas learned in another, it is more a matter of chance than of planning. To the extent that we allow the school curriculum to be dominated by the disciplines, we deny students the opportunity to become more than superficially acquainted with profound public problems. The fascinating story of the discovery of DNA, the heredity molecule, by James D. Watson and Francis Crick, is a beautiful example of the arbitrariness of the disciplines. Watson, a biologist, recounts in *The Double Helix*[12] that, though untrained in chemistry, he brought to the project something more valuable, a different perspective and a fresh viewpoint; the solution won him and Crick the Nobel Prize.

The arbitrary selection of disciplines is another serious weakness of the curriculum. Most of the subjects offered—history, English, foreign languages, mathematics and science—are required today because they were required yesterday, and the day before and . . . . They are not the sole survivors of a careful appraisal of what subjects are most worth knowing. They can, in fact, be seen as vestiges of an era when man's knowledge was much more limited; these subjects encompassed much of what was then known. But that is hardly the case today—what about cybernetics, anthropology, sociology, psycholinguistics, ecology and psychology? Or computer sciences, operations research, statistics, black studies, aesthetics and human relations? Or philosophy, theology, semantics, logic and group dynamics? Do you think any of these subjects should be represented in the public school curriculum?

But even if new subjects replace traditional ones, our prime objection would still stand: subject-matter fields should not be studied simply because someone says so. The importance of studying ecology, for example, does not lie in its inherent value as a system of thought, but in the use that can be made of the knowledge gained in its study. By and large, the more importance a particular field has for society, the more relevance it will have for the student as an emerging member of that society. Education will be irrelevant to students' development, or even undermine it, if it does not address itself to crucial social issues and the problems of growing up.

---

[12] James D. Watson, *The Double Helix* (New York: Atheneum, 1968).

Now that you know our position on the issue of curriculum irrelevance, how do you feel about it? The discipline approach is very appropriate for some students, but many others find it so restrictive and limiting that they are literally "turned off." If the discipline-oriented curriculum cannot respond effectively to the criticisms which have been leveled against it by students and educators, protest is likely to take other forms. Arthur Foshay predicts that many students will simply refuse to enroll in discipline-oriented courses, and cites as evidence a 10 percent drop in physics enrollment throughout the country in the last ten years.[13]

Many students are currently insisting that their education become more personally involving. Nevertheless, most disciplines continue to emphasize objectivity and logic, which students who lack prior interest in a subject tend to interpret as impersonality. We are not arguing against logic; we are observing that an exclusively objective approach may permanently discourage a student from ever developing an interest in a subject. It makes more sense to us to start with the students' interests, concerns and needs, and then demonstrate the value of objectivity in situations which demand it. Many school dropouts, when asked why they left school, offer as a primary reason the meaninglessness and irrelevance of what they were taught. Consider, for instance, this statement by a young black high school dropout:

Now, from almost the beginning in school all they've been teaching was math, science, social study, history and English. Ever since I have been in school, that's all I heard.
Then they repeated it the next year and over and over.
What do you want to hear about the Romans for? They're dead. Like history—you get the same thing over and over.[14]

We don't need to sacrifice the intellectual quality of the best of the new curricula in order to find ways of allowing real problems a place in the curriculum. We must develop new syntheses of the actual and the conceptual suitable for students to study.

ALTERNATIVES TO THE CURRENT CURRICULUM

Studying Values and Social Policies. Let us look at some alternatives to the present curriculum approach. Metcalf and Hunt, defining the curriculum as "the formal coursework taken by students," believe that the curriculum acquires relevance whenever it impinges upon what students believe and whenever it has the effect of producing a pattern of belief that

---

[13] Arthur Foshay, "How Fare the Disciplines?" *Phi Delta Kappan* 51 (March 1970): 349–352.

[14] Quoted in George H. Weber and Annabelle B. Motz, "School as Perceived by the Dropout," *Journal of Negro Education* 37 (Spring 1968): 131.

is well-grounded and internally consistent.[15] Their position is that youth's rejection of adult culture is a significant social movement and that any school which has not made it a subject of serious study is guilty of irrelevance. Metcalf and Hunt suggest that the schools make the study of this movement a part of the curriculum, with emphasis on examining, testing and appraising the beliefs it represents. Such a curriculum would help young people examine their basic assumptions about society and its improvement by studying values and social policies, subjects almost totally foreign to existing public school curricula. Metcalf and Hunt do not, however, believe that addressing the personal problems of youth in itself makes a curriculum relevant. It is crucial to engage young people in a study of the problems of the larger culture in which many of their personal problems originate. The problematic aspects of the culture—that is, the large conflicts and confusions which translate into the conflicts and confusions of individuals—are of crucial significance to the young and should be dealt with honestly and thoroughly at the school level.

The Moving Wheel.   Theodore Brameld calls his model of an alternate curriculum "The Moving Wheel."[16] He visualizes the curriculum as a moving wheel whose rim is the unifying theme of mankind's predicaments and aspirations. The hub of the wheel is the central question at issue during any given period of learning—as short as a week or as long as a semester—while the spokes are the areas of inquiry that contribute to understanding the central issue. The spokes, in other words, represent courses, but not in the usual sense of the term, for each course is regarded as a component of a whole. Brameld makes a number of suppositions which he considers necessary to a valid curriculum. Among these are:

1. The prime responsibility of the curriculum is the confrontation of young people with the array of disturbances that beset man.
2. These disturbances are not the exclusive concern of the social studies, but pervade every aspect of human life.
3. We must recognize the universality of the critical period through which we are passing, and create new models of the curriculum that illustrate this universality.
4. These new models must repudiate the conventional structure of subjects and subdivisions of knowledge which are now outmoded.

---

[15] Lawrence D. Metcalf and Maurice P. Hunt, "Relevance and the Curriculum," *Phi Delta Kappan* 51 (March 1970): 358–361.

[16] Theodore Brameld, "A Cross-Cutting Approach to the Curriculum: The Moving Wheel," *Phi Delta Kappan* 51 (March 1970): 346–348.

Examples of the kinds of issues that might form the hub of Brameld's "moving wheel" curriculum are:

1. Can the ordinary human being fulfill his capacities in face of technological and depersonalized forces?
2. Can one form deep relationships with others amidst chronic instabilities?
3. Can human conflicts—between sexes, generations, classes—be ameliorated?
4. Can a converging awareness and unity of mankind as one species be achieved?
5. Can economic and political establishments be rebuilt so that people all over the earth have access to physical and human resources?

Brameld suggests that a minimum of one-half the entire time devoted to the curriculum be spent outside the classroom, allowing learning to occur directly through travel and vicariously through films, the fine arts, visits from experts and other resources. In this respect his proposal resembles the Parkway Program described in Chapter Two. He also suggests that the teaching be done by teacher-consultants in flexible partnerships of interdisciplinary study, research and field involvement, and that students share in the planning and implementation of each year's program.

The Survival Curriculum. In a paper entitled "Education for Survival,"[17] philosophy professor Michael Scriven submits that our educational system is severely mismatched with our current needs. Education today prepares the child to survive in society *as long as it remains stable,* and even this it accomplishes rather inefficiently. Students, he argues, must be educated to create and adjust to revolutionary change. "The survival of a society whose citizens are not *directly* educated to instigate and handle radical change, and in particular a society whose citizens are educated in a way that depends on the absence of radical change, is simply a temporary accident of evolution."[18] Since the one thing that we can be sure of is change, the intermediate aims of Scriven's survival curriculum are to create in people the capacities to a) produce, and b) rationally evaluate and relate to socially and intellectually revolutionary *suggestions, candidates, threats* and *actions.*

The curriculum of any high school can be examined to determine whether it is educating students for survival. Scriven asserts that students should derive from the curriculum a general familiarity with the arguments for and against abortion, censorship, incest taboos, the graduated income tax, dependents' exemptions, contraception, the Fifth Amendment, local control

---

[17] Michael Scriven, "Education for Survival" (Paper prepared for the Ideal School Conference Series, Elk Grove Training and Development Center, April 9, 1968).

[18] *Ibid,* p. 2.

of schools, liberal education, police review boards, pacifism, charity, states' rights, the United Nations, the need for police, euthanasia, nationalization of foreign-owned industry, jury trials, excise taxes, war, automation, unionism, *de facto* school segregation, sumptuary laws (especially those regulating the use of drugs, alcohol and nicotine), equal time rules for TV, "mental illness," violent revolution, monasticism, legalized prostitution, a guaranteed income, the death penalty, segregated private clubs, premarital chastity, egocentric hedonism, suicide, subsidized art, environmental contamination and conservation, compulsory schooling, voting, labor arbitration, blood tests and military service. How many of these topics received attention when you were in high school?

Each of these topics impinges on several academic disciplines, but Scriven argues against spending a single moment of class time studying disciplines for their own sake. This he considers an academic luxury. "[Although] some points from game-theory, welfare economics, and functional anthropology need to be made and discussed in explaining the role of an ethical system, it is mere professional conceit to suppose they cannot be appreciated without a *course* in each subject."[19] What is needed is to extract relevant concepts and data from many subjects. "Education is giving us cake today when we need bread."[20]

Scriven defines the Survival Curriculum in terms of three areas of learning: *knowledge, skills* and *motivation.* The *knowledge* necessary to survival has several sources. We need, first, knowledge of man as an individual, including information on sex, drugs, insanity, neuroses, birth defects and diseases.

We need basic familiarity with the nonhuman world, including information on food production potentialities, radioactive and industrial waste contamination, the magnitude of the pest and parasite problem in food production and storage, the size of our coal and oil reserves, the knowledge explosion and the data storage problem it creates. Scriven urges that we structure the curriculum around real problems, introducing theoretical concepts whenever necessary, rather than starting with academic fundamentals and working gradually toward practical application.

Survival education also requires knowledge of the government, economics, anthropology and sociology of major current and past cultures and of deviant civilizations. This area of the Survival Curriculum would emphasize the problems, failures and mistakes, as well as the achievements, of our culture. Theories of the nature and foundations of government, law, economics and ethics would be studied, not at an academic level of abstraction but for awareness of the practical and easily-comprehensible issues involved.

The Survival Curriculum would enhance sensitivity without making value judgments. "Instead of legislating the course of aesthetic education, for

---

[19] *Ibid.,* p. 16.

[20] *Ibid.,* p. 17.

example, education should modify itself to develop the appreciations that children naturally discover. The high school and college male finds cars and girls beautiful, *MAD* funny, rock music, science-fiction and some TV serials exciting—a marvelous basis for providing the facts and contrasts that refine such appreciations and increase the enjoyment they produce."[21]

Scriven lists the following cognitive and social skills as necessary to the curriculum:

1. the super-R's: speed reading, shorthand/typing, calculating/programing, memory training
2. analytical reasoning
3. interpretive skills
4. scientific method
5. people study
6. skills of appreciation: art appreciation, sensory awareness training courses

The *motivational* aspect of the Survival Curriculum is designed to reinforce motives which Scriven believes necessary to survival. These include physical motives such as the desire to exercise, cognitive motives such as the desire to solve problems and moral motives such as the desire to help others.

Proposals such as Brameld's and Scriven's make sense to the authors. The world is changing at a fantastic rate—physically, psychologically and socially. Because the discipline approach fails to meet the needs and concerns of students in specific and of society in general, and because the transfer of knowledge from study to the solution of real problems is not made explicit, we submit that the discipline approach is no longer fruitful. The curriculum of the public schools cannot continue to deal with reality obliquely. It must concern itself directly with mankind's problems. It *is* a matter of survival.

HOW IS A NEW CURRICULUM DEVELOPED?

When you begin to teach, it is likely that the curriculum you use will already have been formulated. It may have been developed by a large national curriculum project such as SMSG or BSCS, or it may be the work of teachers within the school district. Your school may provide a curriculum guide—a compilation of objectives and activities for a particular course—whose purpose is to aid the teacher in planning and organizing the course for the year. These curriculum guides range in quality from being nearly worthless to acting as a source of helpful ideas, particularly for beginning teachers. When you begin to immerse yourself in the curriculum, you are likely to ask such questions as, "How does one develop a curriculum? Are there any

---

[21] *Ibid.*, p. 29.

guidelines? How do you choose what should be included and what should be omitted? Is it purely a matter of choice on the part of the developers? Is the curriculum based on any particular philosophical position? Will people with different philosophies of education develop different curricula, or will they be basically the same?"

These kinds of questions have been posed for years by curriculum developers, and the result has been a number of curriculum development models.[22] However, the unembellished facts of life about curriculum development are that very few curricula are developed according to clearly-articulated principles. Much of what is taught in the schools today is developed by teachers, either individually or in groups, and tends inevitably to be influenced by such factors as what's available in texts, what other teachers are doing, guidelines established by the school district or the state, what the department has done in the past, the teachers' own preferences, seat-of-the-pants intuition, how past students have responded to certain topics and learning experiences, what's happening in the media and what college courses the teachers have taken—the proportion differing for each teacher according to the phase of the moon and the number of days until Christmas.

We do not mean to put down teacher-developed curricula. The important thing to remember is that *the curriculum is what happens to the kids, not what is in the curriculum guides or the resource units.* Any number of factors influence this "final" or "received" curriculum. It is also not our purpose to describe in detail how to go about developing curriculum in a systematic and orderly way. We do want to discuss, however, a number of principles or guidelines which we believe to be basic to the development of a relevant and meaningful curriculum.[23]

First, *a curriculum should not be prepackaged, rigidly scheduled or uniform throughout a school system. Instead, it should be flexible and geared to the unique needs of the students.* A prepackaged curriculum says, in effect, "Whether you're black, white, brown or yellow, whether your parents earn $30,000 or $1,500 per year, whether you can read well or just barely, whether you're secure and have developed a good self-concept or not, here is what you need to learn!"

A flexible curriculum geared to the unique needs of the students says, in effect, "This curriculum is designed to help you deal in personal terms with the problems of human conduct, rather than with the requirements of various subject disciplines. We start with you, the learner, not with the content, because you are more important than the subject matter."

---

[22] Two of the most recognized books on curriculum development are Ralph W. Tyler, *Basic Principles of Curriculum and Instruction* (Chicago: University of Chicago Press, 1950) and Hilda Taba, *Curriculum Development: Theory and Practice* (New York: Harcourt, Brace & World, 1962).

[23] The authors are indebted to Mario Fantini and Gerald Weinstein for elucidating these principles in their pamphlet, *Toward a Contact Curriculum* (New York: Anti-Defamation League of B'nai B'rith, 1969).

Second, *a curriculum should start from an "experience" base, rather than a "symbol" base.* Because symbols are abstract, they are not appropriate starting-points for instruction. It is not that symbols and abstractions are unimportant—in fact, they are crucial in our society—but abstraction must be grounded in the concrete reality of the individual student's life if it is to have meaning for him. As the "Cone of Experiences" on this page illustrates, the kinds of experiences that can be provided the student vary on a continuum from the most direct to the highly abstract. When direct experience is impossible, contrived or dramatized experiences are often good substitutes. For example, a study of government might be initiated by having the students role-play individuals on a desert island with an ample supply of food, clothing and shelter. The only rule is that they are not permitted to make up *any* rules! In one classroom, the students concluded after about three sessions that they could not function without rules to protect individuals' rights. They then proceeded to develop basic rules and a village

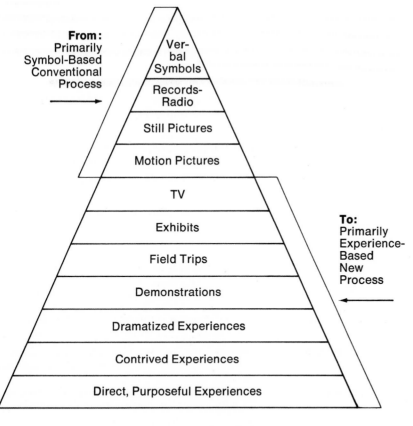

From: Primarily Symbol-Based Conventional Process

To: Primarily Experience-Based New Process

Ver-bal Symbols
Records-Radio
Still Pictures
Motion Pictures
TV
Exhibits
Field Trips
Demonstrations
Dramatized Experiences
Contrived Experiences
Direct, Purposeful Experiences

CONE OF EXPERIENCES

Source: Edgar Dale, *Audio-Visual Methods in Teaching,* rev. ed. (New York: Dryden Press, 1954), p. 43.

government. After that, they were eager to compare their village rules with an actual small community's laws. As Fantini and Weinstein put it, the cardinal rule of this approach is, "Experience first, we'll talk later!"

Third, *a curriculum should be immediate-oriented rather than past-and-future-oriented.* "You need to study this because it will help you get a good job." "Studying the Romans will help us understand and appreciate our lives today." "When you get to college you will be glad you studied this." Phony! While middle-class children may be better able to accept long-range goals (and even this is a dubious assumption), lower-class children have difficulty understanding time as a continuum.[24] As a result, justifications of past-oriented study alluding to its future value seem phony to many students.

Because most of what we currently teach is either future- or past-oriented, it lacks relevance for present-oriented students. Or, as Fantini and Weinstein argue, "To a child who has not been socialized in such a way as to make specific connections between present events or activities and future goals a process which emphasizes long-term goals becomes discriminatory. The disadvantaged child is a kind of existentialist—to him, the present moment is absolute and relevant, all else is meaningless verbiage."[25] A curriculum, to be truly meaningful, must use the present as a starting-point for learning. This is not to say that the study of past- or future-oriented material should be discarded, but that it must follow upon and be integrated with present-oriented material and experiences.

Fourth, *a curriculum should emphasize* why *rather than* what.

"On what date did Columbus discover America?" "What's the specific gravity of iron?" "What are the major exports of Japan?" "What were the major causes of the Civil War?"

If you were to conduct a systematic study, or even a random sampling, the chances are that you would find the majority of curriculum guides, examination questions and classroom discussions to be *what*-oriented rather than *why*-oriented.

"What" questions can be useful, but they have limited transferability. Compare the potential usefulness of these two pieces of information:

Alaska is the largest of the fifty states.

If two persons have had different experiences with words, or if they view the communication situation differently, the meaning of what is said will differ for them.

The first statement can be looked up in a reference book; it is an isolated piece of information which has limited value. The second statement cannot be derived from any convenient source, but its meaning can be applied to

---

[24] Basil Bernstein, "Social Class and Linguistic Development: A Theory of Social Learning," in *Education, Economy, and Society,* ed. Halsey, Floud and Anderson (New York: Free Press, 1961), p. 297.

[25] Fantini and Weinstein, *Toward a Contact Curriculum,* p. 22.

PHONY CURRICULUM

Imagine a unit of study, somewhere in the primary grades, on "The Family . . . ." How is "family" generally represented in the early grades?

The houses in which families live never, as far as we are told, include toilets. Members of the family never scratch themselves, utter obscenities, cheat on their wives, fix traffic tickets, drink beer, play the horses, falsify their tax returns, strike one another, make love, use deodorants, gossip on the telephone, buy on credit, have ulcers, or manifest a million other signs of life that even the most culturally deprived child knows about in the most intimate detail . . . .

Certainly, at their dinner tables, no textbook fathers talk about having outbargained that New York Jew, about the niggers who are trying to take over the neighborhood, the cops, the Birchers, the hippies, the war, and so on. On the contrary, one may safely expect the textbook family to be disembodied, apolitical, generally without a specific ethnic identity or religious affiliation, free of social prejudice, innocent of grief, economically secure, vocationally stable, antiseptic and law-abiding straight down the middle. It occupies a universe from which disaffection, divorce, cynicism, loneliness, neurosis, bastardy, atheism, tension, self-doubt, wrecked cars, and cockroaches are inevitably absent.

Unless he is downright dull, it is impossible to imagine that at some level of experience the child is not aware of the thundering disparity between the real world and the school's priggish, distorted, emasculated representations of that world. It seems reasonable to suspect that the child's knowledge almost certainly includes the realization that, in plain language, the curriculum is phony, at least in relation to the example we have considered.
From Clinical Supervision: Special Methods for the Supervision of Teachers *by Robert Goldhammer. Copyright © 1969 by Holt, Rinehart and Winston, Inc. Reprinted by permission of Holt, Rinehart and Winston, Inc.*

many situations and can help an individual understand why failures of communication occur.

Since students cannot be taught everything that is known, the curriculum must incorporate concepts and ideas that can be widely applied, both within and outside the classroom.

Fifth, *a curriculum must be based on reality rather than fantasy or sterility.* Dick, Jane and Spot live in a white house in the country; a smiling Mexican boy sits atop a burro; Mr. Adams, the butcher shop owner, is always smiling, and the clean, well-dressed, middle-class children are always alert and responsive to the teacher—and the whole thing is as unreal and antiseptic as a cartoon. It would be surprising if any child recognized himself in Dick or

Jane, but children who live in urban areas and have never been to the country cannot possibly identify with them. And if the smiling Mexican boy is an accurate representation of his country, why is there so much poverty and hunger in Mexico?

One of the most serious deficiencies of our present curriculum is its stereotyped, middle-class, all's-right-with-the-world approach. When junior high school students study other countries, accurate glimpses of the lifestyles are conspicuously absent from their textbooks. As Jean Grambs states, "The school demands of children that they deny what their own sense experiences tell them and accept instead the school's version of reality."[26] It is almost as if many schools are afraid to deal with real life problems and prefer to whitewash them. The school must not only acknowledge reality in the curriculum, but also must help the student to interpret it and his relationship to it. Merely to expose the child to the harshness of reality without equipping him to interpret it is potentially harmful. But if children are to relate to the curriculum, they must perceive it as real and personally meaningful instead of artificial and unrelated to their experience.

Sixth, *a curriculum must give equal emphasis to affective and cognitive content.* For years the school's role has been primarily to dispense knowledge, packaged according to subject-matter. If you ask a high school instructor what he does for a living, he is likely to reply, "I'm an English (social studies, science, French) teacher." Accordingly, we tend to view the role of the teacher in terms of the subject-matter dispensed. Questions such as "Why do I feel the way I do?" "What do others think of me?" "Do I care?" "Why do I want to do that?" "Who am I?" and "What can I do about things I don't like?" are legitimate in a curriculum concerned with the whole child. But rarely has the curriculum formally recognized the importance of the learner's feelings, concerns or fears. Yet there is considerable psychological evidence that unless feelings are acknowledged they may impede learning.

We would argue, however, that an affective curriculum is legitimate in its own right, irrespective of its tie to cognitions. Unless a person has learned to recognize his fears, wants, anxieties, concerns, needs and pleasures, and has either accepted them or learned to cope with them, he will be incomplete as a human being. One of the major reasons for the current popularity of the "human potential" movement is that our schools have virtually ignored this area of life. As a result, many college students and adults are attempting to compensate for a need that should have been fulfilled many years earlier.

CURRICULUM CHANGE—WHO'S RESPONSIBLE?

How does the school curriculum get changed? Who makes changes occur? These are important questions, for their answers will tell us a great deal about how schools operate and to what social forces they respond.

---

[26] Jean Grambs, *Schools, Scholars, and Society* (New York: Prentice-Hall, 1965), p. 80.

Ronald C. Doll, a curriculum developer, has identified four major forces affecting curriculum change: 1) the drive for power, 2) the appeal of the dollar, 3) growth in knowledge, and 4) the needs and concerns of people in schools.[27]

The Drive for Power. Doll identifies a number of groups and organizations which are vying for power to change the curriculum: scholars in various disciplines, who have in recent years had tremendous impact on the public school curriculum; groups on the far left of the political spectrum promoting certain kinds of political education, and groups on the far right militating against sex education and sensitivity training; militant teacher organizations; local community groups seeking school control at the expense of centralized control of schools; militant youth; regional or national agencies, such as the Education Commission of the States; the United States Office of Education, at the expense of state and local control, and minority groups seeking recognition of their heritage in the curriculum. Doll sees the power of curricular decision-making shifting from teachers, administrators and school board members to scholars in subject-matter fields, the citizens who complain most vehemently, people with special programs to promote, the inner councils of teachers' unions and associations, sponsors of summer in-service institutes, designers and reviewers of project proposals, bureaucrats at the state and federal level of government and self-appointed community leaders.

It might be interesting to examine in detail how some of the above-named groups have already influenced curriculum change. Let's look first at the effect minority groups have exerted on the curriculum.

One of the most shocking facts of school life is that the longer black children of low socioeconomic status remain in school, the further behind grade-level achievement they tend to fall in reading and mathematics.[28] Educational experts attribute this phenomenon to a number of factors, among them teachers' lack of understanding of the children's subculture and its reward system; the lack of appropriate learning materials which allow the children to identify with the people they read about, and the discriminatory attitude of many teachers toward these children and their values. As a result, many poor black parents are exerting pressure on school boards to improve the education of their children. They are demanding more local control of the schools, including the right to change the curriculum to make it more appropriate for their children and the right to include more community personnel in the instructional process. As a result of such pressures, some school districts, most notably in New York City, have experimented

---

[27] Ronald C. Doll, "The Multiple Forces Affecting Curriculum Change," *Phi Delta Kappan* 51 (March 1970): 382–384.

[28] James S. Coleman, *et al. Equality of Educational Opportunity* (Washington, D.C.: U.S. Department of Health, Education, and Welfare, 1966).

with decentralized control of certain areas within the city and have allowed local communities considerable freedom to reconstruct the curriculum, employ indigenous personnel to assist teachers and hire new teachers. One of the major innovations to result from the community demands is the inclusion of black studies in the curriculum.

It is too early to measure the success of these attempts at community control within large urban areas. It is tragic, however, that the public schools have failed the children of several minority groups so severely that their parents feel they must gain control of the schools in order to insure that their children are properly educated.

An example of a pressure group exerting its influence to *prevent* curriculum change involves the issue of sex education. Teenage marriages, the growing rate of venereal disease and changing attitudes toward sex have led many people to believe that sex education is necessary in the public schools, particularly because most parents are apparently unqualified or unwilling to teach their children about sex. However, there is tremendous opposition to such courses. Groups such as the John Birch Society have denounced sex education as a violation of the First Amendment on the grounds that it usurps a privilege and right which belongs to parents. Despite surveys indicating that students and teachers see a need for it, organized opposition has kept sex education out of the curriculum in many communities.

Students themselves are becoming increasingly vocal about the curriculum and instruction. Demands for "student power," once exclusive to college campuses, are now being voiced in the secondary schools of America. Students are refusing to be treated as if they had neither rights nor freedom, personally or politically. Many schools treat their students as captives, making them adhere rigidly to disciplinary rules and curriculum requirements. Often the students and educators distrust each other. The guidance process, according to many students, is used to make students conform to the school's standards, rather than a means of helping students personally and educationally.

A recent task force of the National Education Association charged many public schools with failing to comprehend and protect their pupils' rights as citizens and as "clients" of the educational system. The task force's report predicts that student government will gain more effective control over student affairs, "due process" will replace administrative fiat, options for independent study and less standardized academic requirements will be developed and students will have more of a voice in the process of reform.[29]

As student demands escalate, conflict will undoubtedly continue between students and teachers, on the one hand, and between teachers and administrators on the other. It is likely that if high school students insist on co-

---

[29] Fred Hechinger, "N.E.A. Foresees Greater Student Power," *New York Times,* July 12, 1970.

DIALOGUE

Kevin: *If I were to rank man's achievements in order of their impact on the world, I'd put media and communications very high on my list.*

Jim: *So what? This is a book about education, not media.*

Kevin: *The point I'd make is that despite the availability of films, television, satellite communication and videotape, the formal educational process makes very little use of media.*

Jim: *That's undeniably true, but you have to remember that informal education depends heavily on these media.*

Kevin: *That's exactly my point. Elementary and secondary school students grow up in a culture that uses the world's most advanced technology to sell them commercial products and to show them historic events the very days they happen, and the students interact intellectually and emotionally with the medium. But our schools don't begin to compete in the degree of sophistication they use to communicate with students.*

Jim: *What effect do you think this has?*

Kevin: *The major effect, I think, is that the schools bore young people used to learning from television. I think programs like* Sesame Street *have shown that they can be educational and entertaining at the same time. But so many schools still rely on lecturing, textbooks and dull drills to teach students.*

Jim: *Kevin, if that's so, how come we wrote this textbook?*

Kevin: *Because we're hoping NBC will buy the rights and do a one-hour special on it.*

Jim: *OK, wise guy—back to work.*

operative decision-making, school administrators will reject their demands as beyond students' prerogatives. Yet what better way is there of allowing students to experience and learn about participatory democracy? It is inevitable that, as such conflicts occur, we will see student strikes and other militant measures employed by students.

Another institution affecting the curriculum is television. In 1969 a television series called *Sesame Street* was introduced, funded by the U.S. Office of Education, the Ford Foundation, the Carnegie Foundation, the Markle Foundation and Operation Head Start. The series uses commercial television programming techniques to teach preschool youngsters reading and arithmetic readiness skills prior to the time they enter school, and as a result children who are not normally exposed to this kind of preparation in their homes may enter first grade at parity with middle-class children whose homes provide them ample opportunity to learn to count and recognize letters of the alphabet. Originally geared to urban children, particularly black youngsters, the series proved to be an overwhelming hit with preschoolers from all ethnic, racial and socioeconomic groups. Nielsen audience ratings indicated that during its first year the series was seen each day by over six million children.

Mrs. Joan Cooney, creator of the series, hopes *Sesame Street* will make kindergarten and first-grade teachers take a harder look at their curricula and possibly decide to start teaching reading earlier. Initial research on children in Maine, New York and Tennessee indicates that poor children who viewed the program regularly during its first six weeks of broadcasting made achievement gains two-and-a-half times as great as a control group of children who did not watch the program.[30] If similar results continue, the children's accelerated skill may force primary teachers to revise the curriculum.

Sesame Street may also succeed in transmitting to children new positive images of black people. Exposure to the two black stars of the program may, in the long run, prove to be its most lasting benefit to both black and white children.

The Appeal of the Dollar. The appeal of the dollar is, according to Doll, a major factor in curriculum change. School personnel seeking new sources of funds to supplement their budgets turn to the federal government and private foundations, both of which maintain strict guidelines regulating the scope and direction of curriculum changes in districts receiving funds. Thus, the pursuit of additional funding often forces a school district to make changes specified by bureaucrats unfamiliar with the district. The available dollar, in effect, realigns curriculum priorities.

The textbook industry is another source of financial pressure on the public school curriculum. The textbook continues to be one of the prime determinants of what is taught in schools. In many classrooms, in fact, the textbook *is* the curriculum.

How appropriate is the textbook as the major teaching tool in the public school? Gwynn and Chase cite a number of the advantages and disadvantages of the textbook.[31] Among its advantages are:

1. it may be the underprivileged child's only reading matter;

2. it serves as a source of final authority for the child;

---

[30] "'Sesame Street' Series Wins Acclaim of Public," *Phi Delta Kappan,* 51 (March, 1970): 409.

[31] Gwynn and Chase, *Curriculum Principles,* pp. 194–195.

3. its vocabulary and learning sequences are tailored to the child's level of mastery;

4. it helps the beginning teacher by giving him a sense of security and confidence;

5. many schools and communities do not have extensive library facilities to provide supplemental learning materials if the textbook were not used;

6. the text has many illustrations which can add interest and help the student better understand difficult concepts; and

7. the teacher's manual offers many suggestions to the teacher for more effective teaching approaches.

Among the textbook's disadvantages are:

1. it is out-of-date when it comes off the press by from one to four years;

2. the illustrations also are frequently out of date (hair and clothing styles are among the first to change);

3. one text cannot give a full picture of society, its customs and its history;

4. the authors of textbooks disagree tremendously about the aims, content and sequence of materials;

5. the textbook frequently limits the growth of the teacher, for it tends to arbitrate what the teacher is supposed to know and what the pupils are supposed to learn; and

6. textbooks handle controversial topics poorly; they are usually bland and wishy-washy.

We can expect that publishers will continue to support textbook development and distribution, since sales to schools represent a major portion of their income. And local school districts comply in this situation by encouraging full use of the textbooks they buy in order to "get their money's worth."

How then do textbooks affect curriculum change? In many states, textbooks from various publishers vie with one another for statewide adoption. State departments of education provide the textbooks they select free-of-charge to school districts within the state. A statewide adoption means a great deal of money for the author and publisher of a textbook. As a consequence, both author and publisher are customarily reluctant to include material in the book which might jeopardize the book's chances of adoption. In practice, this means that the opinions of certain powerful groups must be considered when writing textbooks. The Daughters of the American Revolution, the American Legion, the John Birch Society, the Veterans of Foreign Wars and the United Daughters of the Confederacy have sufficient power in many states to prevent adoption of texts they disapprove. The result, particularly in areas such as history and social studies, is bland textbooks. Thus, lively and exciting issues are made dull and lifeless for the student.

However, the development of new texts representing various viewpoints and approaches to problems can have an impact on the curriculum. Since the textbook plays a major role in many classrooms, texts with unusual approaches can influence teachers to alter not only what is taught, but also the way it is taught.

Growth in Knowledge and Personal Needs.   Growth in knowledge forces curriculum change. As Doll says, "The teacher is no longer able to 'cover the book.' Instead, many books now cover the teachers."[32] As we have seen, the expansion of knowledge has also spawned new curriculum projects, some of which are deeply affecting what is taught in the schools.

The fourth major force affecting curriculum change is the needs and concerns of pupils, teachers, administrators and parents. Attempts to relate the curriculum to the students' life outside the school fall into this category.

Doll emphasizes the interaction of these four forces to produce curriculum change; it is very rare that change can be attributed to a single cause. Ideas advocated by power-seeking groups may be accepted by teachers concerned about students' needs and implemented with the aid of commercially-developed materials. Thus change in the curriculum is ordinarily the result of multiple causation.

THE TEACHER'S ROLE IN CURRICULUM CHANGE

Many school districts sponsor summer workshops for teachers to develop new courses. Experienced teachers are ordinarily entrusted with curriculum development, for which they are compensated. A team of teachers may develop an entirely new course, which is offered the following year on an experimental basis, or they may revise the content of a currently-offered

---

[32] *Ibid.*, p. 383.

course. Locally-developed curricula range from extremely exciting, innovative approaches to tired rehashes of the same old thing. Most local efforts suffer from a lack of the resources, personnel, money, time and materials necessary to do the kind of job the teachers would like to do. National curriculum projects have millions of dollars to work with, and it is impossible for local curriculum efforts to compete. As a result, more and more local curriculum efforts are being limited to individual units within a course.

Experimental "mini-courses" have been very successful in some high schools. Mini-courses are short—usually about two weeks in length—and intensive, and are usually offered at the end of the school year. Students are free to select any course they wish to take, and often initiate new mini-courses themselves. Teachers often bring to them an enthusiasm unmatched in the regular classroom. Typical courses might be "The Battle of Gettysburg," "Long Distance Bicycling," "Auto Mechanics for Women," "Chess Playing," "Selected Works of Mark Twain," "Scuba-Diving," "History of the Blues," "Communal Living," "Drugs," "Plastics," "Income Tax," "Test-Taking," "The Moon," "Statistics," "Sound and Light" or "Theatre of the Absurd."

EPILOGUE

Though the public school curriculum is never entirely static, most changes are of a low order of magnitude. The subject-matter approach introduced in the nineteenth century to teach science, mathematics, English or language arts, history and foreign languages is still intact. We have obviously argued in this chapter that the discipline approach to the curriculum is outmoded. Though the content itself is not necessarily obsolete, studying subjects separately, unrelated to the pupils' lives and interests or to mankind's problems, is an organizational arrangement subject to charges of "irrelevancy."

An even more serious issue is the schools' responsibility to contribute to man's ability to survive. How are the schools educating students to eliminate air pollution, purify polluted waters, control the population explosion, increase food production without the use of harmful pesticides or dispose of our waste products without fouling our environment? Most don't even acknowledge that such problems exist! Lest you think we exaggerate, let us quote from Dr. Paul Ehrlich, author of *The Population Bomb,* and a professor of biology at Stanford University:

Many of the creatures of the earth have seniority over us. They made it this far by remaining compatible with their environment, by adapting and adjusting to the natural circumstances of their existence. There are many species that have vanished because they could not adapt. It's not at all inconceivable that man will follow these creatures into extinction. If he continues to reproduce at the present soaring rate, continues to tamper with the biosphere, continues to toy around with apocalyptic weapons, he will probably share the fate of the dinosaur. If he learns to adapt to the finitude of the planet, to the changed character of his existence, he may survive. If not, nothing like him is likely to evolve ever again. The world will be inherited by a creature more adaptable and tenacious than he.[33]

Who is that creature? The cockroach.

In the face of the potential holocaust predicted by Ehrlich and many other frightened scientists, it is almost inconceivable that our public schools can continue to teach mathematics and science and social studies without relating them to the real problems of the human race.

The children of today cannot afford to grow up ignorant of these problems and unequipped to cope with them, but well-versed in quadratic equations and the problems of the Jamestown colony in 1607. It is time that our teachers began educating students to face the issues of today rather than yesterday. The world has changed. We must rid ourselves of our own saber-tooth curriculum.

DISCUSSION QUESTIONS

1. Which of the five motives identified by Gwynn and Chase as influencing curriculum development since 1635 do you think are still operative? What evidence can you marshal to support your views?
2. How well do you think the public schools are increasing the survival chances of Americans? What parallels, if any, do you see between the Saber-Tooth Curriculum and the curriculum you were offered in high school? With which of the two basic philosophical stands summarized on page 106 are you most in sympathy? What evidence can you muster to support your position?
3. "To the extent that we allow the school curriculum to be dominated by the discipline approach to learning, we fail to offer students the opportunity to become more than superficially acquainted with great public problems" (page 108). If you do not agree with our assessment of the relevance of current curricula (and many people do not), what arguments can you advance to support your view? If you agree, what arguments can you add?
4. Would you feel more comfortable teaching a traditional curriculum or one of those proposed by Metcalf and Hunt, Brameld or Scriven? Why? What are the similarities and differences between these three hypothetical curricula?
5. Weigh the relative advantages and disadvantages of textbooks. If you were to begin teaching now and had the choice, would you choose to use textbooks? What factors would you consider before deciding? What are the

---

[33] Interview with Dr. Paul Ehrlich, *Playboy* 17 (August 1970): 154.

advantages and disadvantages of allowing every teacher to use textbooks and materials of her own choice?

6. Should a teacher be allowed to teach a curriculum of her own design? Where does professional autonomy and the teacher's freedom of choice come in? What should be its limits?

7. Do you believe every discipline has an inherent structure? What might be a convincing argument against this view?

FOR FURTHER READING

Birnbaum, Norman. "The Arbitrary Disciplines." *Change* 1 (July-August, 1969): 10–21. This article raises some fundamental questions regarding the arbitrariness of the scholarly disciplines. Birnbaum asserts that recent changes in society necessitate the creation of new systems for codifying knowledge.

Bruner, Jerome. *The Process of Education.* New York: Random House, 1960. In this influential volume, Bruner advocates studying the structure of each discipline in order to develop learners with a true understanding of the discipline. Many of the concepts explicated in this volume undergirded the curriculum reform movement of the late Fifties and early Sixties.

Chinn, William. "What's New in Curriculum—Mathematics." *Nation's Schools* 84 (July 1969): 29–31. A brief summary of recent developments in the field of mathematics.

Fantini, Mario, and Weinstein, Gerald. *The Disadvantaged: Challenge to Education.* New York: Harper and Row, 1968. While focusing on the disadvantaged, this book addresses the education of all children by reexamining and reevaluating traditional modes of education, and proposing the beginnings of a new, more adequate process of education. Current educational processes are described, analyzed and diagnosed with respect to the cultural norms of several subcultures. Both theoretical and practical.

Fraser, Dorothy. "What's New in Curriculum—Social Sciences." *Nation's Schools* 84 (July 1969): 31–35. A brief overview of recent developments in the social sciences curriculum.

Goodlad, John. *The Changing School Curriculum.* New York: Fund for the Advancement of Education, 1966. An easy-to-read account of the major curriculum development projects of the Fifties and Sixties and their outstanding characteristics.

Goodman, Kenneth. "What's New in Curriculum—Reading." *Nation's Schools* 84 (August 1969): 38–40. A brief review of new curriculum developments in the field of reading.

Gwynn, Minor J., and Chase, John. *Curriculum Principles and Social Trends,* 4th ed. New York: Macmillan, 1969. A major curriculum source book which treats the history of curriculum development in both elementary and secondary schools, as well as major influences in curriculum development. The modern curriculum movement of the Sixties, influences on curriculum change and models for curriculum revision are discussed.

Haven, Elizabeth W., *et al.* "High School Curriculum Survey." *School and Society* 98 (April 1970): 239–254. A report by the Educational Testing Service which attempted to assess the impact of the major curriculum projects on the public schools. A brief but very enlightening survey of what is actually being taught in the public schools.

Hicks, William Vernon; Houston, W. Robert; Cheney, Bruce; and Marquard, Richard. *The New Elementary School Curriculum.* Princeton: D. Van Nostrand, 1970. A description of the major curriculum areas currently being taught in the elementary schools.

Hogan, Robert. "What's New in Curriculum—English." *Nation's Schools* 84 (July 1969): 37–38. A brief overview of recent curriculum developments in the field of English.

Karplus, Robert. "What's New in Curriculum: Physical Sciences." *Nation's Schools* 84 (July 1969): 35–36. A brief overview of recent curriculum developments in the physical sciences.

Peddiwell, Abner J. [Harold Benjamin]. *The Saber-Tooth Curriculum.* New York: McGraw-Hill, 1939. A satirical spoof on the origins of schools, the inadequacies of the curriculum and the reluctance of educators to keep the curriculum relevant to societal needs. Humorous and entertaining reading.

Pillet, Roger. "What's New in Curriculum—Foreign Language." *Nation's Schools* 84 (August 1969): 41–42. A brief review of recent curriculum developments in the field of foreign languages.

Sanders, Norris, and Tanck, Marlin. "A Critical Appraisal of Twenty-Six National Social Studies Projects." *Social Education* 34 (April 1970): 383–446. Analyzes and appraises 26 national social studies curriculum development projects. Various projects emphasize anthropological, economic and interdisciplinary approaches in both elementary and secondary curricula.

Saylor, J. Galen, and Alexander, William M. *Curriculum Planning for Modern Schools.* New York: Holt, Rinehart & Winston, 1966. Attempts to analyze the process of curriculum planning, to define the basic elements which should constitute the determinants of an educational program and to describe the principles and procedures that should guide curriculum change.

Tyler, Ralph W. *Basic Principles of Curriculum and Instruction.* Chicago: University of Chicago Press, 1950. This little booklet is the classic rationale for curriculum development. Tyler stresses the need to use several data sources, including the learners' needs, in order to develop an adequate curriculum. Although developed in the Fifties, Tyler's principles for curriculum development are still held to be valid.

Van Til, William, ed. *Curriculum: Quest for Relevance.* Boston: Houghton Mifflin, 1971. Focuses on curriculum development for the Seventies. Contains a series of widely-diversified positions, including the entire contents of an issue of the *Phi Delta Kappan* (March 1970) edited by Dr. Van Til and devoted to elementary and secondary school curriculum.

FILM

Build Yourself a City (Philadelphia Board of Education, 16mm, b&w, 15 min., 1967) The Philadelphia Cooperative Schools Program was a six-week summer project in which 100 junior-high and senior high-school students, representing diverse educational backgrounds, contributed their own points of view to the study of communications, urban affairs and drama. This film documents the urban affairs course, which "presented an alternative to crises becoming the form of change." The narration is from three perspectives: that of a curriculum developer, a social studies teacher and a city resident who helped to teach the course.

Classrooms in Transition (EDC Film Library, 16mm, b&w, 30 min.) This film documents the use of Elementary Science Study materials in the Cardozo Model School District in Washington, D.C.

Eastern District High School Students View the World (The Moving Image, 16mm [kinescope made from a television program], b&w) Several students appear with their film teacher, Linda Bastian, to discuss the way films are made in their school. The films shown cover many different themes and use various film techniques.

Hello Darwin (University-at-Large, 16mm, color, 48 min.) A fifth grade Boston public school class studies Darwin's theories of evolution by means of *Man: A Course of Study.* The film attempts to show what Bruner means by "Education is a process, not a product."

It's Between the Lines: Drama for the Classroom (Philadelphia Board of Education, 16mm, b&w, 15 min., 1967) This film also documents a portion of the 1967 Philadelphia Cooperative Schools Program: a course in which both improvisational and formal drama are explored with students of middle-school age.

The Kindergarten Child, Part II (Massachusetts Department of Education, 16mm, b&w, 48 min., 1968–70) This series of short episodes ("Did you forget I'm five?") presents various teaching methods, materials and curricula which can be used effectively in the kindergarten classroom.

Making Sense: Inside and Out There (Philadelphia Board of Education, 16mm, b&w, 10 min., 1967) This film is also about the 1967 Philadelphia Cooperative Schools Program. It shows how the communications course combined a multimedia approach with a series of metaphors to teach basic communications skills and understanding.

My Name is Children (Indiana University Audio-Visual Center, 16mm, b&w, 60 min., 1967, NET) This film presents scenes of children and teachers at Nova Elementary School in Fort Lauderdale, Florida, to show how one school uses an "inquiry approach" to motivate students. A montage of activities is accompanied by natural, spontaneous dialogue by students and teachers.

A Time for Learning (University-at-Large, 16mm, color, 38 min.) One of a series of three films on Jerome Bruner's fifth-grade curriculum, *Man: A Course of Study.* This film shows a portion of the curriculum being used in four Boston suburban and central-city classrooms.

VIDEOTAPE

System of Teaching Reading by Color Coding Words (Electric Eye, $\frac{1}{2}$" videotape, several hours) This tape, produced by a group whose motto is "Tell a vision, not sell a vision," presents the work of Dr. Caleb Gattegno at San Jose State.

AUDIOTAPE

The Parkway Program: The Curriculum (National Education Association, 7" reel, 3.75 ips, 8:40 min.) This sound segment is part of a longer tape on *The Curriculum,* intended to serve as a discussion starter. Demonstrates how the entire Philadelphia community has become the school's campus.

Refer to Appendix for distributors' addresses.

TEACHERS

4   Why Teach?

If you teach, it is very likely that by the end of your second year of teaching you will have had both of the following experiences:

1. You will be at a party, or some other social gathering, and be asked what you do. One of the guests will express interest in the fact that you are a teacher and will ask you questions about how you like teaching. Shortly, the person will tell you that he (or she) has always wanted to be a teacher, and regrets the day he (or she) became a stockbroker/housewife/bookkeeper/ salesman/airline stewardess/sanitary engineer. He (or she) may just give it all up and become a teacher yet.

2. You will get to know an experienced teacher who confides in you that she deeply regrets having become a teacher. In college she felt sure that she was cut out for teaching, and she actually enjoyed it in the beginning. But gradually she became bored with the whole thing—bratty kids, pushy administrators, the same old faces in the teachers' lounge, the instant-expert parents and the boring curriculum. Now she feels trapped in teaching and can't see any satisfying way to get out.

The purpose of this chapter is to keep you from becoming "the other person" in either of these two scenes. It is to help you make a good decision about what to do with your life, particularly if you are undecided about becoming a teacher.

Centuries ago, Francis Bacon told us that "knowledge is power." Much earlier still, Socrates recognized the special power of self-knowledge when he urged, "Know thyself." An understanding of one's motives in something as important as a career choice can help prevent faulty decision-making. A superficial motivation to teach can, and frequently does, lead to failure and disappointment. For instance, you may admire and want to emulate a former teacher. And you may, out of respect for this person, decide to teach without ever analyzing whether or not you have the necessary capacities or the drive to attain them. Or you may think it is admirable to like and help children. But, in the process of actually working with, say, sixth-graders, you may discover that you can't stand sixth-graders, or that you're not even particularly interested in children.

Clarifying your motives helps you both identify your strengths as a prospective teacher and cope with your shortcomings. Someone whose desire to teach grows out of a passion for art history has to know how to guard against hostility toward students who don't share his love of art. More than a few frustrated teachers have been heard to mutter, "Those ungrateful little monsters aren't worthy of Shakespeare" [or French infinitives, or Victorian poetry, or the niceties of quadratic equations].

PITFALLS IN CHOOSING TO TEACH

The most common difficulty facing someone trying to decide on a career is not having enough data. The young person who decides to be a business

I refuse to accept the idea that the 'isness' of man's present nature makes him morally incapable of reaching up for the 'oughtness' that forever confronts him! Martin Luther King, Jr.

executive or a physical therapist or an interior decorator usually does so without a deep understanding of what his future occupation entails. Rarely do prospective workers know the daily demands of the job or the kinds and degree of expertise needed. Nor do they know enough about the satisfactions they may take from performing well in a particular career. As a result, a career choice is frequently a response to fragmentary information or to a highly romanticized view of an occupation. The choice of a teaching career, however, usually involves a somewhat different set of problems. One of the pitfalls, in fact, is *over*familiarity.

OVERFAMILIARITY

A college student contemplating a career in teaching usually has far too much data at his disposal; in other words, he has been overexposed to teachers and schools. A major portion of his life since he was five or six has been spent in schools and around teachers. Schools, he thinks, can hold no more surprises for him. Becoming a teacher seems to him like marrying the girl next door. (Anyone who *is* married to the girl next door could alert him to some of the surprises he is in for!)

Most of the 200,000 or so new teachers who enter American schools each year receive a rude awakening. Although the routines—homeroom, clubs, bells, books and ball games—are all familiar to the new teacher, there is much about life in school he doesn't fully appreciate. Most new teachers, for example, have had relatively pleasant experiences as students. If they had not succeeded in school, they probably would not be in a position to become teachers. As a result, new teachers are frequently astounded by how difficult learning is for some children and by how unhappy many children are in school. Many students are difficult to reach and apparently unconcerned about learning. Beginning teachers are surprised at the amount of administrative and clerical work that goes with the job. Nor did they realize that good teaching takes so much time-consuming preparation. Another shock for many is the amount of energy, both physical and emotional, teaching requires. Somehow these facets of teaching rarely get communicated to the audience of students. We will examine this topic in more detail in a later chapter.

It may be erroneous and misleading to say that the problem is overfamiliarity. Too much data is usually not a problem in itself. Applying prior information to the solution of a problem is the sticky part. What each of us knows about teaching needs to be evaluated for accuracy and supplanted, if necessary, by new information and, especially, new perspectives.

PERSONAL MISCALCULATIONS

Knowledge about teaching and schools is only half the prerequisite to a sound career choice, and probably not the most important half. Knowing your own capabilities and limitations is the other half. Do you really like children? What age groups do you enjoy most? Do you consider a particular age group particularly stimulating and compatible? Do you really enjoy helping people learn new skills and knowledge? How do you know this? Can you take satisfaction from work which frequently offers few tangible results? How is your stamina? Are you comfortable dealing with and having to manage twenty-five or thirty people at once? Can you live satisfactorily on the salary currently earned by teachers? Do you have status hang-ups which could get in your way? Are you confident that you can teach different ethnic groups and social classes? With which would you be most and least successful? How do you know this? These are only a few of the questions you should be asking about yourself.

BEING A CAPTIVE OF EXPERIENCE

In recent years the country has become increasingly concerned about the schools serving the urban poor. Report after report has chronicled the ineffectiveness and human waste of so many large city schools. Large numbers of idealistic young people responded to the plight of the urban schools by seeking teaching positions in them. Although they did so for the very best reasons, many failed miserably. Their backgrounds and educational experiences had not only not prepared them for the encounter but, in fact, served as stumbling blocks. These young teachers wanted their pupils to be like the children they had known in their own suburban schools. They went into urban schools with the idea of totally replacing the culture of the children with the culture they brought with them from white, suburban America. This story is sad for both the children and the teachers. It goes without saying that we are all deeply influenced by our past experience. Occasionally, however, we need to transcend our own personal experience to avoid becoming its slave. Personal experience can exert too strong an influence on our career choice. For example, some people choose teaching because their own school years were pleasant and carefree, and they hope by becoming teachers to recapture past happiness. The opposite also occurs. In the same way that some people become psychiatrists in an attempt to solve their own problems, people who have had particularly troubling or frustrating experiences in school may become teachers in an unconscious quest to resolve their early problems. By "returning to the scene," they are seeking an

Photo by Anna Kaufman Moon.

opportunity to work out unresolved conflicts. We must, therefore, draw on our experience, but must use it in a thoughtful, balanced way.

We should add that being a captive of one's experience can have the opposite outcome. Many potentially creative and inspiring teachers reject careers in education because of the drabness of their own school experience. They see in teaching very little opportunity to express their imagination and creativity and so never seriously consider it as a career. This is particularly disappointing as education is beginning to change and there is a greater opportunity than ever for dynamic, creative teachers.

THE CASUAL CHOICE

Many people make the decision to teach in a careless, unreflective manner. Compared to professions like architecture or medicine, which require long and arduous training periods, the "entrance dues" for teaching are relatively low. Candidates for teaching certificates are subjected to relatively little pressure or competition. Most do not have to make heavy sacrifices of time or effort, which might prompt them to think long and hard about whether or not they really want to teach. Many people, in fact, can get teaching certificates while they are pursuing a bachelor's degree. As a result, the decision to become a teacher is frequently casual and unexamined. Although this state of affairs is not always harmful, it can contribute to disastrous mistakes.

SOURCES OF USEFUL EXPERIENCE

There is no single foolproof method of making an intelligent career choice. Individuals learn in such various ways, and differ so much in what they already know and need to learn, that we can only suggest sketchy guidelines. We recognize four categories of experience which are potentially fruitful in the quest for an answer to "Should I teach?"

REAL ENCOUNTERS

Anyone who plans to be a teacher should test himself against "the real world" often and in as many situations as possible. "The real world" for a prospective teacher is real people—children or adolescents who are seeking some kind of help. Many teaching candidates avoid real contacts with the young until they begin student teaching, only to find the young considerably different from the romantic images they had been manufacturing. "Those nasty little fifth graders are so disgustingly . . . human!" as one shocked student teacher put it. Frequently, too, teaching candidates limit their encounters to normal elementary- and secondary-school students. They never consider teaching mentally-retarded children or the physically handicapped or the imprisoned, or even becoming a specialist such as a reading teacher. They have exposed themselves to only a segment of the real world.

Increasingly, school districts are employing students as teacher aides and assistant teachers, both during the regular school year and in summer school. And many teacher education programs have cooperative arrangements with schools which allow college students opportunities to play a variety of roles within the school, often as part of their coursework in education. Even some high schools now encourage their students to work with younger children as part of their educational experience. Schools, however, do not define the limits of the "real world." There is much to be said for non-school contact with children, such as camp counseling, playground work, after-school recreation projects, working in orphanages and settlement houses and youth-related church work. Other possibilities are coaching a team or sponsoring a club. The opportunities are many. The important thing, however, is to get your feet wet—to get the feel of working with children in a helping relationship.

Hence cometh all the need and fame of teachers, men of inborn nobility, call'd Prophets of God ... the sainted pioneers of civilization, unto whom all wisdom won and all man's future hope is due. Robert Bridges "Testament of Beauty," IV, 232–9

VICARIOUS EXPERIENCES

Not all learning has to take place at "the school of hard knocks." In fact, civilization itself requires that we be able to capitalize on the experience of others. Artists and other talented people can make the experience of others accessible to us for enjoyment, edification or both. One result of the widespread interest in the schools over the last few years is that accounts and dramatizations of school-related experiences are becoming increasingly available. There are great fictional classics about teachers and schools such as *Goodbye, Mr. Chips* by James Hilton and *The Corn is Green* by Emlyn Williams, and more recent novels like Bel Kaufman's *Up the Down Staircase* and Evan Hunter's *Blackboard Jungle.* Within the last few years we have also seen a spate of realistic accounts by teachers of their own experiences, including *The Way It Spozed To Be* by James Herndon, *36 Children* by Herbert Kohl, *Death at an Early Age* by Jonathan Kozol, *The Lives of Children* by George Dennison and *Hassling* by Sylvia Williams. Prospective teachers may prefer these books to fiction because they present children, schools and teachers as they are in the raw, instead of transforming reality for heightened effect.

Films and television are another source of vicarious experience. Although there have always been great films about teaching in the schools, such as "In the Early World" and "Near Home," it has not been until recently that

LAST DAY

The last bell rang.
The building filled with shouts and cheers
And emptied soon. Yet one still sat.
He looked at me, and I could see in that thin face
An awful realization no other child had known:
The year was gone.

I knew, but I was older. I could bear
The lost and sickish feeling of farewell
From simple familiarity with it.
I went back to where he sat;
I said there would be other years.
I said that I would write him letters in the summer.
Somehow he knew, this child who had never had a letter in his life,
That warm words are always somehow cold on paper,
And never take the place of being close.

Slowly he gathered up his books.
Walking toward the door, he looked around the room.
What did he see? What had this been to him?
I knew, and yet I could not know.
It was the end
Of a year.

Reese Danley Kilgo, Phi Delta Kappan 51 (May 1970): 475. Reprinted by permission of the author and publisher.

there has been so much attention to school life in films. Films such as "Kes," "If," "The Prime of Miss Jean Brodie" and "The Strawberry Statement" center on the student, while "To Sir, With Love" and "Up the Down Staircase" focus on the teacher. Recently television has begun to deal with school life, most notably in two series, "Room 222" and "The Bill Cosby Show".

These vicarious experiences can be a valuable source of learning and testing for prospective teachers, particularly if they approach the experience somewhat more critically than does the ordinary viewer or reader. We need to remember that books, films and TV portray school life as a much more intense, dramatic set of human encounters than the normal teacher faces. Also, the media school seems to have a much higher concentration of attractive sex symbols than does the normal school. Then, too, the flux and flow of life in a real school is just not visible. The drama of teaching is quiet, long-term and terribly real.

GUIDANCE

Another aid is the advice and counsel of those who know you; besides parents and friends (who may be too close to you to be objective), there are former teachers, career placement counselors, people you have worked for and education professors. The latter group, your professors of education, will have the added perspective of familiarity with the demands of teaching. Some cautions should be exercised here, however, First of all, pick people who know you fully rather than those who have just seen you at your better moments. Second, do not expect an IBM printout of hard data with a firm decision at the end. If you get a few glimpses of insight from the person whose advice you are seeking, be satisfied. Third, be cautious, since many of us are compulsive advice-givers. Frequently people generalize on too little knowledge, and they are often just plain wrong. Receive advice openly, but follow it cautiously.[1]

REFLECTION

As we said earlier, decision-making about a career in teaching is difficult because we are overfamiliar with schools. Even making use of all the data-gathering methods mentioned above does not in itself insure good decision-making. The most important aspect of the real school encounters, guidance and vicarious experiences we collect is that they provide us with data for reflection. By "reflection" we simply mean sitting down and trying to under-stand fully our experience and its implications for us. We are often so busy experiencing things, or getting ready to experience them, that we fail to reflect on what we have done in a manner that would assure getting the most from it.

We cannot stress this point about reflection enough. It goes to the very heart of the reasons why we wrote this book. Both of us are convinced that many people make very sloppy decisions about becoming teachers. They have not asked fundamental questions about themselves and about schools. This is precisely the reason why we have organized this book around a series of questions, such as "Why teach?" and "What is a school?" It is also the reason why we periodically ask you to stop and reflect on a particular question. Occasionally, we ask you to commit yourself in writing since doing so can be helpful in clarifying exactly what you mean. We have also included case studies, anecdotal material and actual accounts by teachers. We hope that you will regard them as vicarious experience to stimulate your own reflection. In effect, we are much less interested in telling you something than in presenting you with some tough questions. Although the questions, like what makes a teacher a teacher, may sound simple, their answers are

---

[1] Although Ernie Lundquist has tried to claim credit for this thought, we feel that Polonius beat him to it.

DIALOGUE

Jim: Are we giving the impression that once you make the decision to go into education, you're stuck with it?

Kevin: Perhaps we are, but I hope not.

Jim: In our effort to get the reader to take these matters seriously, we may have made it sound like a do-or-die lifetime commitment.

Kevin: This is a tricky issue, Jim. Both of us agree that the high dropout rate of teachers is a serious problem in the schools. It's hard to establish a stable profession with 12 percent of all teachers leaving the field each year.

Jim: I can imagine how medical services would decline if 12 percent of the nation's doctors dropped out each year.

Kevin: Putting the stability of the teaching profession aside for a moment, it ought to be acknowledged that not all people are temperamentally suited to or interested in a lifetime career in the classroom. A lot of college graduates would like to spend three or four years as teachers and then do something else. Teaching or other youth-related work could be a form of service performed by young adults.

Jim: Somewhere in his writings Bertrand Russell suggests that very few people are suited to teach children after they reach age thirty.

Kevin: Hmmm. That could explain a lot of things that happened to me in school. Seriously though, if you had a hard core of highly-trained career teachers and a lot of well-educated, energetic beginners, you could really change the character of schooling.

frequently quite complex—if they are answerable at all. It is our hope that you will use these questions not only to guide your career choice, but to reflect on the whole phenomenon of teaching and learning.

THERE'S MORE TO EDUCATION THAN TEACHING

Our tendency throughout this book is to write as if education offered only a single career pattern—elementary or secondary teaching. Although convenient for the authors, this is misleading. There is great diversity within the career labeled "teaching," from nursery school to graduate school and from remedial reading to astrophysics. Also, there are countless careers in education other than teaching. Some of these occupations, such as school librarian, are closely related to schools and children, while others, like project officer for the U. S. Office of Education, are physically quite remote from children.

In the same vein, we don't mean to give the impression that there is one, and only one, appropriate career in education for any given person. On the contrary, education is a field which offers many opportunities to move from one type of work to another. The traditional progression is from classroom teaching to a vice-principalship or principalship. Besides becoming department or grade-level chairmen, many experienced teachers choose to become guidance counselors. Still others go into teacher education or a related field like educational publishing.

We are outlining below, for three reasons, the careers available in education. First, most people think of education as a field composed of teachers and principals, and we frankly want to expand public awareness of the wealth of careers in education. Second, we want to point out, to students who find they are not interested in teaching, the variety of non-classroom jobs available in education. Third, we want to illustrate the variety of opportunities open to people once they have embarked on a career in education. What follows, then, is a list of some of the positions available in education.

CAREER OPPORTUNITIES IN EDUCATION

Rapid change is characteristic of modern existence. More people, more problems, more technological advances and more of everything are causing the rate of change to accelerate geometrically. The repercussions have been pronounced in almost all careers, but especially so in the professions. Until recently, though, education has been very slow to change. Many of us were taught in the same manner as were our parents, because traditional ideas and approaches seemed perfectly adequate. Those quiet days seem to be over, though; the pace of change is catching up with the schools. Social philosophers and future-watchers are anticipating massive changes in the ways children learn, teachers teach and schools operate. New shifting patterns, revised decisions about what should be learned in schools, instruction by computers and other new media, learning drugs, manipulation of the genetic code—all will have an explosive impact on education in the decades ahead.

Education has been characterized as a "growth industry." It has become enmeshed in the social and economic goals of the nation. Once a relatively stable occupational area, it is now becoming subject to pressures and fluctuations. The Sixties were characterized by a serious teacher shortage, which experts expected to continue through the Seventies. But on the first day of school in September 1970, there were 88,000 newly-trained and certified teachers who could not find teaching positions. Suddenly teaching has again become a competitive career. If a teacher does not perform well, others are waiting in the wings to take his place. However, while the demand for classroom teachers has decreased, new opportunities are continually arising. Presently, there is a serious need for trained people to direct and work in day-care centers. We are becoming an educating society and there will always be a place for skilled and dedicated people.

It is nice to know that there will continue to be important, attractive careers in education, but right now your career choice is what matters most. Your personal happiness will depend in large measure upon the decision you make. We see a direct relationship between the number of unsuited and unsatisfied people in education and the casualness which characterizes career choices in education. We urge you, then, to use the resources available to you—your experience, the counsel of others and, most important, your own thoughtful reflection—in planning your future.

1. Precollegiate education (public and private)
   a. Paraprofessional (assistant teacher, educational technician, teacher aide)
   b. Teacher
      Nursery school and preschool, kindergarten, elementary, junior and senior high school
   c. Supervisor (most supervisory positions are combined with teaching responsibilities)
      grade-level chairman, department chairman, critic teacher, master teacher
   d. Consultant
      curriculum, teaching process, specialized areas, affective education
   e. Guidance
      academic counseling, personal counseling, career guidance, college placement
   f. Administration
      assistant or vice-principal, principal, special project director, associate superintendent (business, maintenance, personnel, curriculum), superintendent
   g. School specialist
      librarian, school psychologist, nurse, dietician, coach, research director, attendance officer

2. Junior college, college and university education
   a. Teacher
      teaching assistant; instructor; lecturer; assistant, associate and full professor
   b. Department chairman
   c. Administration
      (1) dean (of the faculty, of students, of instruction, etc.)
      (2) vice president
      (3) provost
      (4) president

d. Special services
   (1) registrar
   (2) career guidance and placement
   (3) admissions officer
   (4) research director
   (5) librarian
   (6) health service personnel

3. Government
   a. State department of education (curriculum, instruction, certification, research, etc.)
   b. Federal agencies
      (1) Office of Education (Washington, D.C. and regional offices)
      (2) Research and development centers
      (3) Regional laboratories
      (4) Overseas schools sponsored by the State and Defense Departments for dependents
      (5) UNESCO and other international education agencies

4. Foundations
   a. Executive
   b. Program officer and staff
   c. Researcher or writer

5. Business
   a. Communications industry
      (1) TV or radio reporter
      (2) newspaper educational reporter
      (3) freelance or magazine writer on education, or writer for professional journals (i.e., *English Journal,* or *Today's Schools*)
   b. Publishing
      (1) textbook editor or writer
      (2) curriculum materials developer
      (3) salesman of educational materials
   c. Private consulting firms providing specialized expertise to schools, i.e., computers, new technology, inservice training, research services

6. Professional organizations
   a. NEA and United Federation of Teachers
      (1) executive and staff positions
      (2) researcher or writer
      (3) field worker
   b. Specialized teacher associations, i.e., National Association of Mathematics Teachers, National Association of Secondary School Principals
   c. Educational fraternities, i.e., Phi Delta Kappa

Photo by George Zimbel.

MOTIVES FOR TEACHING

We would like you to take a moment to write down what you feel are your motives for wanting to be a teacher. If you are unsure whether or not you want to be a teacher (this probably applies to the majority of readers), list your motives both for and against becoming a teacher. A space is provided below. You may not wish to use it, but we suggest that you write down your list someplace permanent. Although the purpose of this list is to help you think about yourself and analyze your career choice, you may wish to save it for future reference.

We referred to your motives, in the plural, for a reason. Most of us have mixed motives, some altruistic and some selfish, about most of the things that are important to us. Our motives often conflict and occasionally they are incompatible. In any event, one motive is rarely sufficient to explain a choice as complex as how we plan to spend a portion of our lives.

_____

_____

_____

_____

_____

There must be a nearly infinite number of answers to the question, "What are my motives for wanting to become a teacher?" Here are a few examples you might check against your own list:

I really like the idea of having control over and influence on 30 (or 150) kids every day.

Teachers are my favorite people, and I want to stay among them.

I can't think of anything else to do with my major.

Teaching seems to be a fairly safe, low-risk occupation with a lot of attractive benefits.

The instruction I had in school was just incredibly bad, and I want to correct that situation.

I don't know what I want to do. So I'll teach for a while until I make up my mind.

My parents would really be pleased if I were a teacher.

I just love children—especially the scruffy, unattractive ones everyone else ignores.

I would rather be a big fish in a little pond than a little fish in that great big world out there.

One of my students might become a famous painter, or the president of a major corporation or who knows what. It would be nice to strongly influence just one significant life.

I've never wanted to do anything else. As far back as I can remember, I've always wanted to teach.

I really want to become a principal (or a coach, or a guidance counselor, or a college professor or an educational researcher) and this seems to be the way one has to start.

CASE STUDIES IN MOTIVATION TO TEACH

The rest of this chapter is composed of five case studies illustrating some common motives for going into teaching. Each case study is followed by a set of questions and a comment by the authors. The cases are intended as examples of how particular abstract motives take shape in the lives of teachers. We offer these case studies to you as vicarious experiences to use in testing your own motivations. You may also want to discuss the cases and the accompanying questions with other people. The shared experience of reading the cases and responding to the questions should aid in probing and understanding your own motivations. And, finally, the cases and accompanying comments raise important issues about the nature of teaching.

The five motives we have chosen are:

DIALOGUE

Jim: I'm having a little trouble with this list.

Kevin: What's the matter? Can't you find your motive on it?

Jim: Seriously, it could be confusing to the reader. For instance this one: "the desire to work out one's own problems." This seems much more likely to be an unconscious motive than the others do.

Kevin: I agree, but some of the other motives can be hidden, too, like the desire for respect and prestige. On the other hand, some people go into teaching to relieve the anxiety and discomfort they feel about particular social wrongs. They are consciously seeking to work out something that is a problem to them.

Jim: All right, but I'm troubled about another thing. The way we've separated out these motives and the way we've written the cases make it appear that individuals are driven by a single motive. Life just isn't that way. We are driven by many motives, some of which contradict each other.

Kevin: You're right. The way we've done it makes a very complex phenomenon seem quite simplistic. But if we tried to portray the full range of human motivations in each case, we'd have five novels instead of five brief episodes. But you bring up a good point, and I hope the reader is forewarned.

Jim: One final point. This reads like THE list. We don't mean to give this impression, do we?

Kevin: Oh, no, we've left out all sorts of motives. For instance, men who go into teaching because they want to coach a state championship athletic team; girls who become teachers because they want an occupational "insurance policy" in case something happens to their husbands or their marriages; people who use teaching as a second job so they can support themselves in what they really want to do, like writing; and people who espouse a particular religious doctrine or economic system and are seeking converts. No, this list doesn't scratch the surface. We're just trying to get people to begin thinking about why they want to teach.

1. The desire to work out one's own problems
2. The desire to aid in the renewal of society
3. The desire for respect and prestige
4. The desire to help children prepare for life
5. The desire to teach a particular subject

CASE NUMBER ONE
The desire to work out one's own problems

Jean was a new teaching intern in a Chicago high school whose student population was fairly evenly mixed between black and white. As a white teacher, Jean worried a lot about her ability to "relate to" black children. On one visit from her college supervisor, she told him that she was pleased with the way things were going. The supervisor asked what particular aspects of the class pleased her, and she replied that she had achieved a good relationship with her black students. The supervisor asked how she had accomplished this, and Jean answered that she had spent a great deal of time talking with them as a group and that, under her sponsorship, the students had formed a Black Student Union and an activist committee. She felt that her black students were "really getting themselves together!" The supervisor, a youngish man with a great deal of experience in urban situations, was not as pleased with her well-being and apparent success as Jean was.

"Jean," he said, facing her, "What do you really want to do here? Is it your goal to organize the black students into a power coalition? Is that what you feel you're getting paid to do?"

"Well," she replied, "these kids just have to get organized. The only answer to the social oppression they've been living under is to organize and begin making their weight felt as a group."

"That may or may not be true," said the supervisor, "but that's not the point at issue. You have a mixed class of children, and you're here to help them acquire some understanding of each other along with skills, knowledge and outlooks which will help them survive and excel in society. But you wanted the black students to like you, so you identified with their feelings of separateness and their prejudices about whites. And, if you will, you have created two factions in your class and you treat each differently."

"*I* didn't do that!" Jean contested hotly. "Society did."

"No, Jean, you did," said the supervisor. "Instead of encouraging your students to confront and understand their prejudices, and creating an atmosphere which would allow them to emerge as individuals capable of solving their own human problems, you encouraged them to value their prejudices and to think that they were right to maintain those prejudices. As a white teacher teaching blacks and whites, you have a tremendous opportunity to help the black understand the white. You say you understand these kids, and that's important, but it's equally important that they understand you and other people like you. Is it your goal for black students to come to you whenever they have a problem with the whites and have you solve it for them? What happens when you are no longer around and those kids run into that problem? Do you think they're going to love you and respect you for not teaching them how to work with whites? Not on your life. They're going to hate you for using them and failing to teach them what they need to know to get along."

"I honestly feel that I owe them something," Jean said. "And I just can't work it out that easily. What are you telling me to do? To ignore their problems and go back to 'business as usual' with the workbooks and all that?''

"You *do* owe them something, but '*them*' means all of those kids. You've got a rare opportunity here to help both the black kids and the white kids learn how to master themselves and to handle their prejudices so that they can settle the problems of living together without being dependent on you and the other white liberals for help. You can get these kids to confront their fears, bring them out in the open and deal honestly and rationally with them in class. You can deal with it through the subject matter, through composition, through general class discussion. These kids may discover that they are much more alike than different, regardless of their color.''

"I really don't think it will work," said Jean. "The black kids are angry and they've heard too much discussion and too much bull to take more of it from a white teacher.''

"Look," the supervisor replied, "I taught psychology in a junior college before coming to the University. I had white kids from Cicero and back of the stockyards who weren't exactly thrilled at having a black teacher. But I knew that this class was ok when one of those white kids said that he had thrown a stone at Martin Luther King on his march into Cicero, and that he was amazed at his own ignorance in doing such a thing. Then a black got up and said that he had attacked white people on the street for no good reason, and he too was amazed at his own prejudice. Here was a bunch of kids who were learning to see people as people. It can be done if the teacher has a clear sense of how his subject matter can help people understand themselves.

"When a student in the class began talking about 'whitey' or 'niggers,' as they did in the early meetings, we'd ask the class to stop and consider their feelings in view of the reading we'd done on fears and aggression. In that way each member of the class was forced to come face to face with his own doubts and fears. I'm a teacher, Jean, and I tried to use my subject matter and my objectivity to help people see themselves as they are. The more they understood themselves, the more they understood others in the class as people. That's why they could admit their failings in front of a whole class of people like themselves. I really feel, Jean, that teaching English gives you a good opportunity to do some of the same things. There seems to be one lesson that you have to learn from your teaching, and that is . . .''

"Yes?''

"That teaching is a relationship to be ended, not to be continued.''

"I don't understand what you mean by that," Jean said, with a puzzled look. "Would you explain?''

"Sure," said the supervisor. "A mature teacher prepares his students for independence, not dependence. He tries to get them to the point where they are able to fend for themselves. And I guess that's what I'm questioning about your relationship with your students. Are you really doing that for them?''

"I don't know," said Jean, softly. "I honestly don't know.''

1. How would you characterize the personal problems Jean seems to be working out in her teaching?
2. Have you had experience with teachers who seemed to be working out personal problems in their classes? What kinds of problems? What was the effect on the class?
3. Have you ever known personal problems to be used effectively in a classroom? If not, can you imagine circumstances in which they might be made use of effectively?
4. How do you evaluate the advice Jean received from her supervisor?
5. What are some of the implications of the supervisor's statement that a "mature teacher prepares his students for independence, not dependence"? What are some ways that elementary and secondary school teachers can stimulate independence?
6. Did the supervisor think that organizing a·union of black students would have a bad effect on the school?
7. Was the supervisor simply telling Jean to teach the subject matter in which she had been trained? What instructional technique did Jean's supervisor use in dealing with the problems of his students?

COMMENT

Insecurity is endemic to the beginning teacher. She wants assurance. As a result, some teachers seek to be popular with their students. There is a difference, however, between popularity and a genuine helping relationship. Popularity may make a real helping relationship impossible. In a sense, this is what Jean did with her black students. She achieved quick popularity by organizing their political aspirations, and that was why, as her supervisor pointed out, she thought she understood their needs. But she had really given the students not what they needed but only what she thought they needed. Had Jean better understood what she herself *needed,* as well as what she wanted, then her relationship with the students would have been more mature. Jean's experience illustrates the importance of examining one's own motives before attempting to motivate others. Perhaps if Jean had examined her own motives a bit more deeply, she would have realized that she had to overcome fear of rejection by her black students before she could teach effectively. The very fact that Jean spent much of her time worrying about relating to black students, rather than relating to Roger and Mark, Frances and Lucy Ann, tells us that she had not grasped the importance of teaching at a personal level; she had, in truth, not yet acknowledged the individuality of her black students.

One characteristic of a mature person is the ability to work out one's own problems in an objective way. If Jean could have realized that her own fears of rejection and of confronting explosive feelings were detrimental to her, she would have seen that the purpose of mature teaching is to help children discover that they can face and handle their own fears. The supervisor tried to show her that she was forcing students to need her support rather than making them independent of her. He was trying to tell her that her popularity may have been gained at the cost of her integrity as a teacher.

CASE NUMBER TWO
The desire to aid in the renewal of society

Fred was in his late thirties. His disposition was so pleasant, and a smile came so readily to his face, that one of his fellow teachers in the large metropolitan high school referred to him as "everybody's father." Fred was remarkable for his ability to remain relaxed when everyone else was tense, and he frequently broke up emotionally-charged situations with an appropriate quip or question.

Each year Fred asked to teach the slow freshman history class and, of course, his request was always granted, for the slow or "basic" classes were regarded by the other teachers as "punishment." Year after year, Fred happily worked with children nobody else really wanted.

Fred's freshman history class was one of the most active in the whole school; he took his students beyond the walls of the school on expeditions to day court, the police station and jail, through industrial plants in the area—and he even snuck in a baseball game one day. Yet his classes were not characterized by fun and games. The students worked very hard on long and involved homework assignments, intricate discussions of problems and searching tests.

At one point in a particular academic year, Fred invited another teacher to give a talk to his class on shipbuilding in the eighteenth century. The talk went well, and after the session the other teacher, Mr. Dixon, commented to Fred that the temper of the discussion following his talk had been very different than he had anticipated; the questions were thoughtful and displayed observation of detail which the guest speaker had not expected from a "bunch of basics."

Fred greeted Mr. Dixon's remarks with a chuckle. "You know, Earl," he said, "they really amaze me too sometimes. Most of these kids really have behavior problems, not intellectual ones. If you looked at their case histories, you'd find that the majority of them were 'dropped through the ranks'!"

"What do you mean?" asked Mr. Dixon.

"I mean that they were in regular classes a good bit of their scholastic lives. But, when they became problems in class, their teachers decided that the cause of their poor behavior was that the work was too hard for them. So, the majority of children in this class really represent the rebels, the nonconformists, the 'anti-socials'!" They're the kids about whom teachers say,

'I don't care if they learn any history at all as long as they become good citizens.'"

"Yes, but you must admit that very few of them will go to college. Most basics just drop out," said Mr. Dixon.

"Maybe you're missing my point," said Fred. "I guess I'm saying that a person can't be a 'good citizen' unless he is a contributing member of society, and that he should contribute something that he thinks is worth contributing. If he can't get the basic tools that make a person productive, how can he be a good citizen? It's a lot more than getting a job or making a decent living. If that were the case, we could put these kids through an industrial arts program and that would be the end of it. No, in some ways, I feel that these kids are much more capable than the kids we send to the university."

"In what sense?"

"In the sense that they are the least accepting of society as it exists now," replied Fred. "If you talked to some of them for an hour or so, you'd find that they really feel the school is hypocritical in many ways, and they aren't afraid to point out the hypocrisies. They'll tell you, for instance, that there are two sets of rules in the school, two sets of discipline procedures, two sets of privileges, and all the rest."

"But I hear the same thing from my 'honors' classes," protested Mr. Dixon. "Those kids know about the double system too. They often tell me that an honor student here can get away with anything from cutting class to smoking in the john. The 'double system' isn't any secret in this school."

"You've got me wrong again, Earl. I know about that, but that wasn't what I was talking about. What these kids are saying is not that we expect too much of them, but too little. For instance, if a kid dropped from an A to a C in your honors history course, what would happen to him?"

"He'd probably go in and see the counselor—by request."

Fred replied, "That's right. When he does poorly, people get concerned. They try to help him take a look at what's wrong. If one of these kids goes from a C to an F, though, everyone says, 'Well, what more do you expect? He's only a basic and doesn't have the ability to sustain a C.' And they get all the inexperienced teachers and martinets in the school. Oh, they know that if they become real problems, they'll get counseling and possibly even better teaching. But that isn't their complaint. They know that the system isn't out to punish them. It just doesn't care enough about them to want to punish them. They know that the system would rather they just go away and not bother anyone. That's the double standard in this school—those that are cared about and those that aren't: that's what these kids will tell you. It's not injustice, it's no justice at all."

"Is this why you request basic classes every year?" asked Mr. Dixon.

"That's part of it," said Fred. "But it's not the whole reason. I'm not quite that altruistic. No, I see in these kids something that frightens me. They have capability, but if it isn't developed it can become capability for hate, a hate based on fear. They're a mark for anyone who comes along with a good strong 'hate' message; I know it and it frightens me. They can rant and 'bitch,' but they have to be taught to analyze critically, to think through problems and to care about other people. In my mind, that is what a good citizen does. He has a developed capability for understanding, and that is what I am trying to do—develop that capability. I think these kids need that capability developed even more than the kids in the honors classes do, because that attention the honors children get in the course of their day here will pull them through. Plenty of people challenge them, listen to them and chastise them when they need it. But with these kids it's a different story."

"You know," said Mr. Dixon, "you're just not talking about the basic classes. I think the same thing is generally true of average classes. It seems that a kid who's really bright gets a lot of attention, and so does the kid who is really slow, but it's that kid in the middle . . ."

"You're right," said Fred. "The kids in this class are the bottom of that middle group in terms of the concern they arouse from the system. And they know it. Yet, as you saw today, they are capable. We owe them a decent set of expectations. I've maintained high expectations from the kids. I would prefer to slightly overmatch them intellectually than undermatch them, because no development is possible when you're being undermatched constantly."

"You know," said Mr. Dixon, "you make a pretty strong argument for your way of teaching, but someone could use the same argument to justify a very academic college prep course which would really be irrelevant for those kids."

"Only if his aim was to teach a very academic college-prep course. The course is a means to an end, in my mind, not an end in itself. My course is somewhat scholarly and academic, but it's not a waste of time for the kids. When we study the court system, for instance, we confront the problem of giving each man his due. We talk about the difficulties of guaranteeing the individual his rights and the group its rights. I like to feel, Earl, that the goal of schooling is not more schooling, but rather an ability to push back against the society in a constructive way."

"Fred," Mr. Dixon said, "I'd like you to come to my class in American history and make the same points with them that you've made with me. You seem to be talking about several problems that have come up in our class. I just wonder how you'd fare with those kids. They have some very strong opinions of their own."

"I'll take my chances any time after next week, Earl. We're going down to the legislative session at the Capitol next week."

QUESTIONS

1. How is Fred's commitment to social renewal specifically manifested out in his classroom teaching?

John Dewey *(1859–1952)*

John Dewey, the father of progressivism, is widely considered the single most influential figure in the history of American education thought.

No prodigy as a child, Dewey attended public schools and the University of Vermont. As a graduate student in philosophy at Johns Hopkins University, he met and was deeply influenced by William James, the philosophical pragmatist. Dewey recognized the implications for education of James's argument that ideas are valuable only insofar as they help to solve human problems. Calling his own philosophy *instrumentalism*, to emphasize the principle that ideas are instruments, Dewey argued that philosophy and education are identical, both involving the practical, experimental attempt to improve the human condition.

The public school curriculum in the nineteenth century was scholarly and classical, designed to improve the mind by filling it with large doses of approved culture. Dewey denounced this curriculum as the invention of a parasitical leisure class, totally unsuited to the demands of industrialized society. He claimed that the schools were divorced from life, and that they failed to teach children how to *use* knowledge. The schools, he said, should teach children not what to think but how to think through "continuous reconstruction of experience." In *Democracy and Education*, published in 1916, Dewey pointed out that Americans were being called upon to make crucial political decisions unprecedented in history, and that the schools offered no preparation for the responsibility of citizenship in a democracy. Dewey called for concentrated study of democratic processes as they are manifested in the units of political organization with which the child is familiar—the school, the local community and the state government—in ascending order of complexity. But his most radical suggestion was that students be given the power to make decisions affecting life in the school in a democratic way. Participation in life, rather than preparation for it, he considered the watchword of an effective education.

In 1893 Dewey established an elementary school at the University of Chicago which was experimental in two senses: in its use of experiment and inquiry as the method by which the children learned, and in its role as a laboratory for the transformation of the schools. The activities and occupations of adult life served as the core of the curriculum and the model teaching method. Children began by studying and imitating simple domestic and industrial tasks; in subsequent years they studied the historical development of industry, invention, group living and nature. This curriculum was in keeping with Dewey's argument, espoused in *The School and Society*, that we must "make each one of our schools an embryonic community life, active with types of occupations that reflect the life of the larger society and permeated with the spirit of art, history, and science." Dewey also believed it to be the absence of cooperative intellectual relations among teachers which had caused young children's learning to be directed by a single teacher and older children's learning to be compartmentalized.

From the late Twenties to the early Forties—the era of progressive education—a massive attempt was made to implement Dewey's ideas, but the rigid manner in which they were interpreted led to remarkable extravagances in some progressive schools. Some considered it useless to teach geography because maps changed so rapidly. Some would encourage a student who, when his teacher asked why he was not studying for an exam, replied that he wanted to come to it fresh! The role of subject matter was gradually played down in progressive schools; the method and process were regarded as more important. The rationale was that it was more important to produce a "good citizen" than a person who was "educated" in the classical sense. Dewey fought vehemently against these corruptions of his views well into his nineties.

Throughout his long life, Dewey was a social activist, marching for women's right to vote, heading a commission to investigate the assassination of Trotsky, organizing a protest against the dismissal of a colleague at the City College of New York and the like. Though he had enormous influence on the schools and on American intellectual life, his advocacy of a socialist economy and welfare state caused him to be characterized by some as an archfoe of the American way of life. In recent years, Dewey has once again been championed by educational critics and practitioners who consider his ideas a blueprint for more relevant and humanistic schooling, even in our own times.

2. According to Fred, what is the criterion for assignment to basic classes in his school? Was this true of your high school?
3. What is the double standard of which Earl Dixon spoke, and how do you explain it? What is the double standard of which Fred spoke, and how do you explain it? Did either of these double standards exist in your school?
4. In what sense are Fred's basic students more capable than the college prep students? In what sense are they a more dangerous element in society? Do you agree with Fred's analysis here?
5. In what ways is Fred different from most of the teachers you have known? How are his expectations for his students different?
6. What does Fred see as the role of academic disciplines in education? If you had to, how would you argue against his position?

COMMENT

John Dewey, the American teacher and philosopher, called attention to our need to educate the young in the entire range of skills necessary for citizenship in a complex technological society. Many of Dewey's ideas were misapplied or corrupted. What Fred was reacting against is a case in point. In Fred's school as in many others, Dewey's concept of citizenship has been completely perverted.

During the Thirties many schools adopted the policy of awarding a grade for citizenship. This grade was originally intended as a measure of the student's ability to use the processes of democracy in a profitable, efficient way. However, as the democratic processes Dewey had introduced to the classroom degenerated into empty forms, the citizenship grade became more and more a judgment of conduct. As long as the student "played the game" of democracy in the classroom, displaying a compliant attitude and voting for class officers who were officers in name only, he was given a high grade in citizenship. Citizenship became a code word among teachers. A teacher who was given a class of "low achievers" or "discipline problems" was sometimes told, "Don't worry about the academics with these children. Just make them 'good citizens.'" This meant that the teacher would not be expected to teach the students anything, for they were not capable of learning, but that he had better keep them docile and out of everyone else's way. Parents were told that their son wasn't a very good student but that he was "an excellent citizen." This meant that though he didn't learn anything, he did everything that students were supposed to do without question.

The use of the word "citizenship" as synonymous with "docile conduct" was a travesty of Dewey's intention. He envisioned training for citizenship as a process of working out in class actual problems that arise in a democracy. Dewey valued informed dissent, and wanted children to develop the intellectual wherewithal to make reasonable decisions based on the disciplined study of alternatives. He would have considered the use of a citizenship grade as a conduct mark an absolute travesty of the system he had designed, for good citizens were not docile sheep who could be "conned" with impunity. They were men and women who could make the tough decisions that democracy needs in order to function as a system. He realized that the schools were an appropriate place to teach students about the nature of such decisions and to give them "low risk" but real practice in decision-making in a context where mistakes were not "for keeps."

The long-term effect of the misinterpretation of Dewey was to discredit citizenship as an appropriate goal for schooling. Citizenship became too closely associated with conformity and "following orders." Yet, in the case of Fred, we see a person consciously attempting to develop educated citizens. Fred's convictions are very close to Dewey's idea of citizenship in many ways. His visits to courthouses, legislative sessions and factories, and the classroom study of major social problems, are very much in keeping with what Dewey had in mind when he spoke of "educating for freedom."

CASE NUMBER THREE
The desire for respect and prestige

Miss Karen Woodbury had been teaching for two years, in a Seattle elementary school where she had a reputation for being prim and aloof. Because she was young, Karen felt it necessary to hold herself somewhat apart from her students in order to gain the respect she thought a teacher should be accorded. But lately some of her students were becoming bothersome—to be more precise, they were rude and impudent. Karen was finding it increasingly difficult to control her sixth-grade class. In fact, she occasionally found herself having to shout to compete with the roar of the classroom. These incidents were not frequent, but she admitted to herself that they were increasing as her frustration mounted.

One day Karen went to a fellow teacher hoping to find out what impression she made on students and why she was getting such mixed signals from them. Some unknown boys from down the hall at times yelled out, "Hey Teach!" or "Hey, Babe!" to her considerable embarrassment. They had even started hanging around her classroom before school in the morning, and she didn't know how to handle them. Then there was the day the principal had called her attention to complaints from the book room that dictionaries used in her room were defaced by four-letter words. That was even more upsetting, since she thought she had conveyed her distaste for improper language; when swear words were muttered in class she tried to show that she was not going to make an issue over utterances she wished she hadn't heard.

After describing these occurrences to Joyce, who was in her fourth year of teaching, Karen added, "My teachers were respected. In fact, one reason I went into teaching was that I admired one of my teachers very much. Why do I have trouble getting students to respect me? Other teachers aren't having the same problems, are they? What do you think I should do?"

After a pause, Joyce replied, "Karen, you're young and attractive, which might explain some of the four-letter words. Part of this is just body chemistry. These kids want attention and affection from their teacher. And sometimes they react oddly to a young teacher. Kids will do things like writing or saying dirty words to shock an innocent teacher and therefore get attention, or at least to get attention directed at their handiwork and maybe some recognition from their friends."

"But what should I do?" Karen interrupted.

"I'm no expert," came the reply, "but try dealing with dirty words in a direct, unembarrassed way. Let them know where you stand and that you demand respect, but keep your cool. If you find yourself losing control of them, try to go back to dealing with each one as an individual. Give the annoying ones attention, too—don't just ignore them because they don't behave the way you think a student should."

"What can I do about the kids I don't even know?" Karen asked.

"Well, those kids who call you 'Teach' aren't committing a crime. They're probably just trying to make you talk to them so they can find out what you're like. Tell them your name and get to know theirs. Once they stop being anonymous, they won't seem a threat to you either. . . . But, if you want my opinion there is a more important problem. The kids in your *own* classes probably don't know you, Karen. You don't seem to be involved with them in a personal way at all."

"I try to be friendly, but a teacher has to maintain distance, too."

"Karen, I don't want to sound harsh, but are you sure you aren't just marking time? Isn't teaching a haven for you while you wait to get married?"

Karen reddened a little and protested, "I can't help wanting to get married and have a family of my own someday."

"Kids have a way of knowing if teaching is just a job for you. They don't know you as a member of their community, just as an adult who comes to school each day and leaves again. Any young teacher gets tested by students who are really trying to find out how deeply you're committed to them. For these kids the teacher has to be willing to grapple with their problems or they'll consider her a distant stranger unable to touch them. . . . Do you like being in the classroom with them, Karen?"

"Well, I thought I did, until these incidents made me wonder what was going wrong," she replied a little heatedly.

"Karen, you're an interesting person. In the teacher's lounge you talk about women's lib, election reform and other things that matter to you, but in your teacher role you project a less interesting personality. Maybe you have some idealized view of a prim teacher who follows the syllabus and keeps herself aloof. The kids deserve some of your mirth and charm, too, not just the modest reserve of your image of the 'teacher'."

"Do I really do that?" came the shocked question.

"I'm only guessing," said Joyce, "but I suspect your students would respect you more if they sensed you really cared about them. Decide for yourself the extent of your commitment to this career. Ask yourself if you took this job to be detached and reflective or if you're prepared to get your feet wet, to get involved with the kids' interests and problems—which may not

Photo by Paul Conklin.

seem so trivial after a while. Those thirty kids in your class demand that you interact with them. Teaching is more than transfer of knowledge—it's a commitment to being involved with their lives. Students admire the teacher who is open about her own natural interests and instincts, and open to theirs. They're as preoccupied with mating, ideas and activities as you are. But you haven't let them see your real self alive and stimulated by the world around you. Try letting them see the real you and see what happens. . . . Wow, I didn't mean to make a speech. That will teach you to ask advice!"

"Thanks, Joyce," said Karen with a genuine smile, "this has been hard to hear but I'll see what I can do."

QUESTIONS

1. Do you agree with Joyce's analysis of the problem and her advice to Karen? If not, how would you analyze the problem and what advice would you offer?
2. Do you feel that being a teacher insures respect and prestige? What is the difference between respect for a role and respect for an individual?
3. Joyce accused Karen of using teaching as a haven while she waited to get married. What do you think about young women doing this? What do you think of young men who use teaching as a stepping-stone to school administration?
4. How could her desire for respect and prestige be used to strengthen Karen's effectiveness as a teacher?
5. Other than those suggested in the case, what are some ways in which the desire for prestige and respect can inhibit effectiveness?
6. As motives, how would you distinguish between prestige and respect?
7. Do you feel that the desire for prestige and respect is satisfied equally for men and women teachers?
8. What did Joyce mean when she said, "Your students don't know you as a member of their community."

COMMENT

Of all the professions and so-called "middle class" occupations, teaching probably has the least prestige. Yet the individual teacher often commands a great deal of respect. Almost everyone, during the course of his life, has felt the influence of a teacher in making a watershed decision. Often a businessman, receiving a service award, will thank "dear old Mrs. Swanson," the fifth-grade teacher who made him sit down and master grammar, thereby proving to himself that he could indeed succeed at things that at first seemed difficult to him. If you asked that man to diagram a complex sentence or define a dangling participle, his answer would probably be little better than guesswork. For what he learned from "dear old Mrs. Swanson" was perhaps not so much grammar as a certain respect for the language. She may have been a person who believed in what she taught and did her best to communicate the richness her study and experience had added to her own life. In doing so, she earned for herself the kind of respect that only teachers can merit—a grudging respect that is by no means earned by everyone who occupies a classroom. And teachers themselves usually know who among their colleagues is a real teacher and who is simply doing a job. While the desire for prestige and respect are motivating factors for many teachers, others associate teaching with a genteel uninvolved life, strict routine and prescribed methods: the proper old schoolmarm who never uttered a "damn" or adjusted her stocking in front of a man. Today a person who embodies the "Genteel Ideal" of the teacher would do well to get into some nice related career like Educational Paleontology.

In Western history the teacher has traditionally been regarded as a more or less passive person, philanthropically untempted by power or fortune, and interested in solving problems through reflection rather than action. The teacher has traditionally been a person who loved knowledge for its own sake, and pursued it in that spirit. The same tradition, however, has contributed to the passive image of the teacher reflected in the popular refrain, "Those who can't do, teach." The teacher, with his short workday and long vacations, is expected to spend much of his leisure time preparing himself to teach by reading and studying. It may be that this expectation—the image of the teacher as scholar—motivates some people to enter teaching. Society seems to consider it a necessity for certain people to remove themselves sufficiently from the struggle of life so as to maintain a dispassionate view of it, and society is willing to sustain them (at not too high a level) and even reward them (but with praise rather than things). For many young people who reject the values of corporate life, teaching seems a good alternative. Like Chaucer's scholar in *The Canterbury Tales,* they prefer being "poor but honest" to being rich but corrupt. They may believe that their rejection of affluence and power allows them to maintain an innocence and incorruptibility which frees them from the guilts of living, as if powerlessness were an atonement or penance for the collective guilt of society. The walls of the classroom may seem to keep out the world, so that contemplation and reflection can reign and one can view it with detachment. This attitude, considered as a motive for entering teaching, has positive and negative aspects.

On the positive side, the classroom has the potential to be a reflective haven where things proceed according to an orderly pattern and children learn to think rationally. Routines, ground rules and control of self probably do, in some fashion, pervade most constructive teaching-learning experiences. A teacher whose classroom is built on respect, self-control, restraint and rational problem-solving will develop many commendable qualities in her students (provided that these phenomena are reciprocal, i.e., that the teacher respects the student and has good self-control herself). Students in her class will come to feel that the world can be an orderly place where people can develop by giving and taking in an orderly way.

On the negative side, however, are the specters of irrelevance and of tyranny by an adult among children. The classroom is not hermetically sealed from the outside world; the skills and values developed there are not an end in themselves but simply a means to an end outside the classroom. Scholarship is not the end of scholarship, for the student is not compelled to live the life or accept the values of the teacher. He has a right to demand that the skills of the classroom be transferable to his present or future life. Therefore, the teacher who thinks of the classroom as his little refuge from the world, where scholarship, rationality and peace prevail, is thinking not of a school but of a medieval monastery where monks spent their lives copying and illuminating the works of others.

Years ago, Edgar Allen Poe wrote a popular short story called "The Masque of the Red Death" about a group of nobles who thought they could avoid the plagues raging across the countryside by gathering behind high castle walls and indulging in merriment with no thought of what lay beyond the castle moat. But, Poe's story tells us, they could not sustain their abandon. The striking clock and red shadows gave witness to a presence that could not be ignored. The Red Death was already among them, and no amount of carousing could hold him off past the stroke of midnight. This situation parallels the notion of a classroom as a haven from life's problems and stresses; the specter of life is already inside the door when the children enter. They bring it with them. The best the teacher can do is to show the child that life is not frightening to her, that she can consider it rationally and even with pleasure, preparing herself for it even as she prepares the children.

The individual considering a career in teaching should realize that, unlike sore feet, prestige and respect don't come with the job. You will not find anything but the most surface respect and prestige as a beginning teacher. Although there is potential for considerable respect and prestige, they must be earned.

CASE NUMBER FOUR
The desire to help children prepare for life

Jerry joined a Florida high school teaching staff after graduating from college with a fine academic record, and the intensity with which he took on students' problems soon won him the respect of the rest of the faculty. He made himself constantly available to students, both during and after school. Students from many different classes brought their most personal problems to him, and Jerry often would spend his evenings at home discussing personal crises in the lives of his students. His office and his home were always open to the students, and it wasn't long before he was constantly busy with such problems.

In the late winter of his first year, some students in Jerry's sophomore

English class asked to be transferred. Jerry had sensed that something was wrong from the apparent hostility of some of his students, but when he heard that students wanted to transfer out, he was deeply hurt.

After a few days of brooding, Jerry approached one of the senior teachers and related his problem. The older teacher told Jerry that he would "check around," and during the next week he stopped some of Jerry's students to find out what was going on. Then he reported back to Jerry.

"Jerry, a fairly consistent picture is beginning to emerge."

"Fire away. And remember, I'm a big boy, so don't feel you have to be kind."

"Don't worry. Tact isn't my long suit. First, the good news—a lot of those sophomores love you. They think you're the best teacher they ever had."

"And?"

"There seems to be an equally large number in that class who are really put out with you."

"I know that, but why?"

"They claim that all they do in your class is waste time. As one kid told me, 'All we do in here is discuss stupid stuff like drugs, pollution, boy-girl relationships and civil rights.' Another said, 'It ain't English. It's sumpin' else!'"

"Is that all of it?"

"No. There seems to be a deeper problem. A lot of your kids feel like second-class citizens in your class."

"What's that mean?"

"They claim that you've got a very close relationship with about half the members of the class, that you see them after class and they feel free to call you up. The complainers feel that they are frozen out. They feel that in terms of your affection there's a definite in-group and out-group."

"Well I guess there is, but it really isn't my fault."

"That's your view, but not theirs. They feel excluded and they think that success in your class is no longer determined impartially or on the ability to handle English assignments. They feel the insiders have a distinct advantage. From my sampling it seems that the in-group, the ones who are involved in the discussions, are the naturally verbal ones; the others, who probably need the verbal training, sense they aren't getting any and that you don't really care about them as much."

"I can't believe I'm hearing this! You mean to say those kids want to diagram sentences and all that old-fashioned bit? Those kids have *really* missed the whole point!"

"Listen, Jerry, I've heard both sides. If you want my opinion it's you who's missed the boat."

"What do you mean?"

"You've got to make a decision. Either you set yourself up as a therapist-counselor and assume an entirely new role or you start becoming an English teacher and help all your students gain understanding of their lives and problems through literary and composition experiences. What do you want to be, Jerry? A counselor or an English teacher?"

1. If Jerry had come to you for advice, what advice would you have given him? And why?
2. How do Jerry and the older teacher differ in their views on helping children prepare themselves for life? Which of the two would you side with?
3. Do you feel that Jerry's disgruntled students were fair to him? If you were a parent of one of those students, how would you feel?
4. If you agree with the statement "Human problems are more important than subject matter," what was wrong with Jerry's approach?
5. If teachers are to help children prepare themselves for life, who decides what kind of life they should prepare for?
6. What are some of the problems involved in teaching a "more relevant" curriculum?

COMMENT

One of Jerry's problems was that, while he probably saw clearly what kinds of behavior should be encouraged in particular students, he lost sight of the goals of the class as a group. In administering to the individual problems of certain pupils, he neglected the needs of others. He forgot that students in his class were under pressure to achieve, and that they expected these needs to be met in Jerry's class. Perhaps Jerry, to whom high achievement came easily, had a tendency to play down the importance of academic successes, even though they formed the foundation of his own life style and career. The children, however, could not afford to play his game. When he lost sight of the need to pursue certain predetermined goals, such as learning to write well, Jerry became increasingly blind to the reasons why he was teaching English and to the students' expectations of him as their English teacher.

Most primary teachers are aware that their students need to *do,* as well as to talk and listen, but, as pupils advance to the upper grades, verbal skills are increasingly emphasized, often at the expense of action. Secondary teachers sometimes lose sight of the relationship between performance and learning; Jerry, with the best intentions, frustrated his students by neglecting to define goals in his class. The class lost its sense of performance and accomplishment. Jerry was no longer a teacher, but was becoming a counselor, a therapist or, at worst, a babysitter.

In the same way that we investigate our own motives to answer the question, "Why teach?", children demand to know, "Why learn?" In one way or another, they ask teachers this question every day. When the child asks the teacher, "Why are we doing this?" he is really asking, "So what??" "So what if I can't define causes of the Civil War?" "So what if I can't recognize a lyric poem?" The child needs to understand the function that underlies the form. He wants to know what this task or information does for him as a person attempting to solve his own life problems. About the best the teacher can do is to tell the child, as candidly as possible, what these particular tasks have meant to him in his own life. Perhaps they have enabled the teacher to think of himself as an educated man, or to explain reality to himself more effectively. If the tasks the teacher assigns have had no real meaning in his own life, perhaps he had better not teach them; if he is obligated to do so, he would do well to ask someone to whom these learning exercises "make sense" to "teach" him about their value.

As knowledge proliferates and there is more and more to learn, people are beginning to feel overwhelmed. Learning any particular segment of knowledge may appear rather arbitrary. As a result, students are more frequently asking "So what?" about what is taught in schools. These questions will not go away. No matter how tired we become of the word "relevant," it will remain a pivotal idea for teachers for many years.

For a little exercise in relevance testing, open a textbook in your major subject to one of the chapter openings. Read the first two pages or so of the chapter and then ask yourself, "So what?" If you can come up with two or three defenses of its relevance, approach one of your friends in another field of study and try to explain to him why it is vitally important that he be familiar with the content of these two pages.[2] You may find yourself feeling like a used-car salesman attempting to sell an old wreck to a minister. If your friend remains unconvinced, it may not necessarily mean that the information in the book is worthless; it may have implications you are unaware of. But try it and see, remembering that students in your future classes who ask you "So what?" have less vested interests in education than does your friend. The issue here is quite clear: if you can't answer when you're asked "So what?" you may spend your career trying to force people to do what they really don't want to do. If you do develop a rationale for what you teach, you'll spend your time helping people do things which you and they value and like to do.

---

[2] It is unfair and therefore not allowable to use our book in this test.

CASE NUMBER FIVE
The desire to teach a particular subject

Sarah was a veteran of thirty-three years in a fifth-grade classroom. She had spent the last fifteen years in a moderately large Pittsburgh elementary school. This particular year had not been pleasant for her, though, because of a young male teacher who had been added to the staff and who was also a fifth-grade teacher. The language-composition program had for a good many years been considered by the other teachers in the school as Sarah's private domain, but the young teacher, Mr. Walker, had shown signs of what Sarah termed "uncooperation." When she received a note from the principal asking her to drop by, she knew that it had something to do with Mr. Walker.

When Sarah walked into the principal's office, she did not feel particularly uncomfortable; she had been there a thousand times before, and the principal, Mr. Paul, was an old hand at the game. As he said, they had "soldiered" together for more years than either wanted to remember.

After a cordial exchange of amenities, Mr. Paul got right down to business. "Sarah," he said, "you know why I asked you here. It's this business with Mr. Walker. I can't help hearing the static between you two, and knowing you so well, I thought that, well, maybe we could see what the problem was."

"David," Sarah began, "you know me, probably as well as anyone around here knows me. I've spent a good deal of time putting together that language-composition program, and it's a good one. You know that I want only the very best for the children, and that I consider in detail each of the offerings that we bring into the comp program."

"Yes, I know that's true."

"Well," Sarah continued, "this young man comes into the school and just plain refuses to use the program which I spent so long developing with the other people on the staff."

"Doesn't he use it at all?" asked Mr. Paul.

"Not for the important things. One of the areas which I've always really stressed has been outlining and notetaking. When I suggested—rather pleasantly, I may add—that he work on these skills with the children, he said that he preferred not to use the guide with the book. He said that he would rather teach these skills through the science program. Then do you know what he said when I asked him why?"

"What?"

"He said that the way we taught outlining taught the children to organize other people's thinking, but not their own. He said that he considered it better for the children to learn to organize their own thinking by observing phenomena and then deciding upon the appropriate logic for schematizing, whatever that means. I pointed out to him the importance of organizing other people's thinking as a prerequisite to organizing their own, so that they could take a sensible set of notes on the reading or the lesson. He said that life experiences weren't that way, that they didn't come neatly organized for us. All these years, I've tried to show children something about how great minds work, and I've produced kids that could think with the best, David.''

"Yes, Sarah," said Mr. Paul. "But it seems to me that his point is valid. Now look. You're a real teacher. You've been at the game long enough to see some real changes in the way people live, and in how people think. Children today are thinking differently, and I guess in some ways better, than they did when you and I were in grammar school, and we've never particularly thought that the way we learned was the best anyway. Now, why does this guy scare you so much? He's only another young teacher, and you've seen 'em come and go for a long time."

"David, I don't know. I'm not sure," responded Sarah. "It's just that he seems so sure he's right. He seems so well-prepared, so creative, and he seems to be telling me that I've been wrong all of these years in the way I've tried to send children out of my class. I was very good in college, David— Phi Beta Kappa from Cornell, and in English, too."

"I know you, Sarah, and you're certainly as well qualified for this job as anyone I've seen. Yet here's a guy who's trying to bring in a skill that we really haven't developed before. I don't think that outlining is a formal skill; I think it's a functional skill, a life skill as opposed to a literary exercise, and I know that you agree with me. Now, as an administrator, I would like to see both ends of this skill spectrum be taught. We have two people admirably qualified to do a job for these kids like kids seldom get. My question to you is why you two have to work at cross-purposes? Perhaps I miss the nuances of the situation, but I feel that you could learn a great deal from each other."

"Do you want me to make him the director of literature and composition for fifth grade?" Sarah asked testily.

"Did I say that, Sarah? You were teaching children before he could button his own pants. I'm not so sold on youth that I think we should all genuflect to it. No, that's not at all what I want. Do you know what I really want?"

"No," Sarah answered. "What do you want me to do?"

"I just want you to say to yourself, and mean it, that this guy is a good teacher and that he could be one of the very fine ones; that's all I want you to do, because once you recognize that, I know you're enough of a pro to figure out how to take advantage of his ability and how to bring him along."

After a long pause, Sarah sighed deeply and replied, "Perhaps you're right David. I guess I've been feeling threatened . . . and unnecessarily. I don't have to apologize for my career. He's not asking me to, either, is he?"

"No, he's not. As a matter of fact, he requested transfer here from Bradley so he could work with you in the language program. It says so right in his file."

"Why didn't you tell me that? I had a right to know."

"Maybe I should have told you, Sarah, but there's only one empire-builder around here, and that's me. All you need is a few disciples and the other teachers wouldn't see a dollar of the budget. No thanks."

"Dave," said Sarah, as she arranged her purse on her arm, "you've just reconfirmed my prejudices. You've got to be some sort of a sneaky devil to be a good principal."

QUESTIONS

1. What was there about Sarah's personality and about her motive for teaching that led her into conflict with Mr. Walker?
2. From the information available, how would you characterize Mr. Walker's motivation to teach?
3. How would you respond to the judgment that the principal, David Paul, manipulates his teachers?
4. In what ways can the decision to teach a particular subject or grade level reflect an individual's personality and character?

COMMENT

Teaching style is directly related to the personality of the teacher. Sarah and Mr. Walker chose different approaches to the teaching of English because of their differing personalities and values. Sarah had taught for many years and was more tradition-minded. She organized the curriculum around a formal approach to the structure of learning. Students were explicitly instructed in notetaking and outlining, rather than acquiring those skills in the process of organizing their own ideas. Sarah's Great Ideas approach reflected her respect for learning what others have accomplished, while Mr. Walker thought it more important to allow children to develop their own personalities through more independent and individual instruction. The disagreement between the two, though it had other ramifications, reflected the conflict between traditional and experimental approaches.

Understanding why a person prefers one pattern of reality to another provides an excellent key to personality. Two people watch the same event; one sees a problem being solved while the other sees a problem being created. Sarah viewed Mr. Walker as a problem because of the method he used to teach children; the principal thought Walker was an asset for children.

Once Sarah saw that there was more than one approach to a single problem, she began to fear it less. If she had been dissatisfied with the language program, or felt reservations about her own ability to handle it, the problem would have been seriously magnified. This case illustrates how people reveal themselves by the problems to which they are drawn.

If you ever watch passengers on a train or bus attack the daily newspaper, you will get some real, if incomplete, insights into the values of the different readers. The man in the dark grey is likely to turn to the business section first to check the stock quotations. Another will begin by studying the hands set out in the daily bridge lesson. A college student with books on the seat beside him might turn directly to the second page, where world news is reported and interpreted in depth. A high school girl may turn directly to Ann Landers. Each of these people has identified himself with a problem area which can serve as a rough index to his personality, motives and behavior patterns.

A college student's choice of major is a more reliable guide to personality than are his newspaper reading habits. In choosing a study program, a person is selecting an "arena" or environment whose problems, methods and materials are tailored to his abilities and his interests. Some fields are highly logical and exacting. Others demand less methodology and logic, but more human emotion, involvement and even physical labor. Every prospective teacher owes it to himself to understand the requirements of teaching, and the kinds of commitment which it requires, for these are the factors which determine the rewards and challenges of the job. Society is generally miserly in its formal rewards for a job well done, and this is true in teaching. For this reason, it is particularly important to choose a subject matter and grade level which are rewarding in themselves to the young teacher. Commitment to the goals and methodology of a particular subject or level, and enjoyment of the problems it poses, are among the major rewards of teaching.

In choosing one subject-matter field over another, a person is deciding to highlight one aspect of his life over another. To choose to become a teacher, and to teach a particular program, can mean that the person is attempting to illustrate those things in his own life which he feels must be worked out or solved, or, perhaps, those things which are worth solving and which he is competent to solve.

DISCUSSION QUESTIONS

1. Can you draw any conclusions about the relationship between your personal experience and your expectations of teaching? At what age were you happiest in school? unhappiest? (Compare your answers with your friends'. Did many of you like or dislike the same grade? If so, how do you explain this?) What subjects did you like best? What grade or subject do you imagine yourself teaching? With what kinds of educational experiences are you totally unfamiliar?
2. What are you doing right now in an effort to answer the question, "Should I teach?" What could you do? What will you do? What "real world" opportunities are available to you?
3. Reflect on the list of careers in education on pp. 143–144. If you were to

graduate today, what position would you choose? What position might you eventually aim for? Are there any positions listed that you have never considered before but might be interested in? What effect might an oversupply of teachers have on your decision?

4. What is the present and projected teacher supply in the field that currently interests you most? in the geographic area?

5. Can you see the influence of John Dewey, or of the corrupted versions of Dewey's ideas, in your own education? How relevant do you think his ideas are today?

6. Which of the case studies do you identify with most strongly? least strongly? Do you disagree with our interpretation of any of the cases? In what way?

7. What are some other possible motivations to teach which we haven't mentioned?

FOR FURTHER READING

Allen, George N. *Undercover Teacher*. New York: Doubleday, 1960. "Inside story" by a reporter who disguised himself as a teacher in a Brooklyn junior high school. Somewhat sensational, but an interesting glimpse of the teaching profession.

Braithwaite, Edward R. *To Sir, With Love*. Englewood Cliffs, N.J.: Prentice-Hall, 1960. A British Guianan living in London becomes a teacher in a British secondary school. The book describes his trials and eventual success teaching lower-class London teenagers.

Brembeck, Cole F. *The Discovery of Teaching*. Englewood Cliffs, N.J.: Prentice-Hall, 1962. The book is composed of actual case situations centering on students and teachers.

Burrup, Percy E. *The Teacher and the Public School System*. New York: Harper and Row, 1967. An analysis of the structure, functioning and offerings of educational institutions, the nature of teaching and teachers and weaknesses needing correction in teaching and teacher education.

Chase, Virginia. *The End of the Week*. New York: Macmillan, 1953. An account of the lives of thirteen elementary school students both in and out of school. A touching and insightful view.

Hentoff, Nat. *Our Children Are Dying*. New York: Viking Press, 1966. An account of a New York City principal, Elliot Shapiro, as he deals with the massive problems of educating children in New York City slums. The author, a skilled journalist and commentator, depicts the frustrations and hopes of a dedicated educator making his daily rounds.

Hersey, John. *The Child Buyer*. New York: Alfred A. Knopf, 1960. A biting satire of American values and of the school as an extension of those values. The author is a major American novelist.

Hilton, James. *Goodbye, Mr. Chips*. Boston: Little, Brown, 1934. A short and sentimental novel depicting the life of a British schoolmaster from youth to old age.

Hunter, Evan. *Blackboard Jungle*. New York: Dell, 1966. A very popular novel about a new teacher's uphill struggle in an urban high school. Although quite absorbing, somewhat stereotypic and excessively violent.

Kaufman, Bel. *Up the Down Staircase*. Englewood Cliffs, N.J.: Prentice-Hall, 1964. An easy-to-read, humorous and poignant semi-fictionalized account of a beginning teacher's experience in a New York City high school. A thoroughly enjoyable book.

Kozol, Jonathan. *Death at an Early Age*. Boston: Houghton Mifflin, 1967. A first-year teacher's account of life in a Boston ghetto school. Tyrannization of the children, cynicism, condescension, racism and anti-intellectualism are dominant themes in Kozol's account. The book has become a rallying-point for critics and educational reformers.

Ladd, Edward T., and Sayres, William C., eds. *Social Aspects of Education: A Casebook*. Englewood Cliffs, N.J.: Prentice-Hall, 1962. Approximately twenty detailed cases of actual school experiences involving racial segregation, discipline, school organization and curriculum reform. Each case is followed by an insightful analysis.

Morris, Van Cleve, *et al. Becoming an Educator*. Boston: Houghton Mifflin 1963. Several major figures in American education discuss a key area, a grey level, or a foundation field of education. A valuable book for those contemplating teaching.

Moustakas, Clark E. *The Alive and Growing Teacher*. New York: Philosophical Library, 1959. A group of teachers and principals discuss an array of personal and professional problems and activities. The author concludes with an analysis of the teacher.

Rasey, Marie Y. *It Takes Time*. New York: Harper and Row, 1953. A novel which focuses on a young woman's choice to become an elementary school teacher. Much valuable description of various teaching methods.

Redefer, Frederick L., and Reeves, Dorothy. *Careers in Education*. New York: Harper and Row, 1960. An aid to prospective teachers deciding whether to teach and at which level. Essentially a source book dealing with opportunities in education.

Stuart, Jesse. *The Thread That Runs So True*. New York: Charles Scribner's Sons, 1958. An autobiographical account of the famous writer's experience as a teacher in a one-room school. Interesting description of the problems and successes of a beginning teacher, and of life in rural America.

Updike, John. *The Centaur*. New York: Fawcett World Library, 1964. A novel about a high-school teacher and his son, with parallels from Greek mythology, by a major American novelist.

Williams, Emlyn. *The Corn is Green*. New York: Random House, 1941. A moving play dealing with the life of a Welsh schoolmistress.

Abraham Kaplan (Indiana University Audio-Visual Center, 16mm, b&w, 59 min., NET) One of a series of five films about "Men Who Teach." Abraham Kaplan, professor of philosophy at the University of Michigan, explains his beliefs and attitudes toward teaching, as well as the differences he sees between instruction and education.

Blackboard Jungle (Films, Inc., 16mm, b&w, 101 min., 1955) Although made quite a few years ago, this film's depiction of a large-city vocational training school is still quite interesting. The problems encountered by teachers are not very different from those presented in *To Sir, With Love*.

Cloud 9 (EDC Film Library, 16mm, b&w, 25 min.) Documents the reactions of fifth-graders in the Cardozo Model School District in Washington, D.C., to the death of Martin Luther King.

Incident on Wilson Street (Contemporary/McGraw-Hill, 16mm, b&w, 51 min., 1964) A documentary on one school's special program to deal with the learning problems of emotionally-disturbed children from a poor neighborhood. The film focuses on Angela, a fifth-grader, and the school's attempt to get her back into "regular" classes.

Norman Jacobson (Indiana University Audio-Visual Center, 16mm, b&w, 59 min., NET) One of the films from the "Men Who Teach" series, *Norman Jacobson* is an intimate portrait of a professor of political science at the University of California, Berkeley, made up of scenes of him with students at seminars, scenes of student involvement and filmed interviews.

To Sir, With Love (Columbia Cinemathèque, 16mm, color, 105 min.) Based on E. R. Braithwaite's award-winning autobiographical novel, this film stars Sidney Poitier as a teacher in a "rough" school in London's East End. The film catalogue claims that he "treats them as adults and imbues them with standards of decency."

Warrendale (Grove Press Film Division, 16mm, b&w, 105 min., 1968) A powerful film study of emotionally-disturbed children made at a residential treatment center in Toronto. Many issues are raised and explored during the film, including the essential dynamics of the learning experience.

The Way It Is (Indiana University Audio-Visual Center, 16mm, b&w, 60 min., 1967, NET) Depicts the chaos of the New York City schools, focusing on what is being done in one school in the Bedford-Stuyvesant section of Brooklyn to improve the situation. Participants in a New York University special learning project are shown visiting with parents, teachers and students.

What Makes Man Human? (University-at-Large, 16mm, color, 15 min.) One of a series on Jerome Bruner's fifth-grade curriculum, *Man: A Course of Study,* this film reveals one teacher's feelings about the curriculum: how it affects her students, as well as her own teaching methods and theories. Bruner himself appears occasionally to interject theoretical descriptions and hopes for the curriculum.

SLIDE-TAPES

Project Inc. (Project Inc., 280 35mm color slides, audiotape, 22:22. min.)
A "portrait" of a storefront community art center through the voices and
images of teachers and students. This slide-tape presents a variety of
different "teaching situations."

AUDIOTAPES

George Leonard: Ecstasy in Education (Big Sur Recordings, reel or cassette,
mono or stereo, 60 min.) George Leonard, author of *Education and Ecstasy,* explains why education until the present has had to be repressive,
and why it can now involve joy, ecstasy and positive motivational conditioning forces.

Refer to Appendix for distributors' addresses.

Photo by Patricia Hollander Gross
through Stock, Boston.

175

Who Are Teachers?

What do *they* do all day? How much do they actually get to teach? Where do they draw the line at getting involved with their kids and with school activities? How can they keep themselves enthusiastic? calm? sensitive? empathetic? informative? not exhausted?

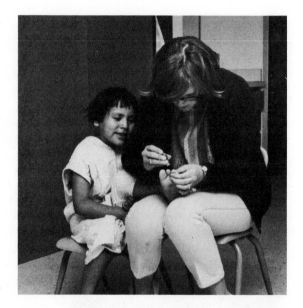

5 What Makes a Teacher a Teacher?

KEY POINTS

CLASSIFICATIONS
Theoretical and practical knowledge

STUDIES
Ryans' study of teachers' characteristics
Jersild's survey of teachers' attitudes to self-understanding
Haberman's study of successful and unsuccessful interns

CONCEPTS
Reinforcement
Range of challenge
Translation of theory into practice
"Single-solution" behavior
Externalization, internalization
Self-concept
Training vs. education
Need configurations
Teacher expectancy
Self-fulfilling prophecy

FACTS
Feeling and cognition as components of attitudes

THEORIES
Flexibility as outstanding characteristic of good teacher
Empathic personal relationship as crucial to learning (Rogers)

RELATIONSHIPS

Attitudes to teaching effectiveness

Self-understanding to understanding of students

CHAPTER CONTENTS

WHAT THEORETICAL KNOWLEDGE DOES THE TEACHER NEED?

What is theoretical knowledge?

How does one acquire theoretical knowledge?

How can theoretical knowledge be used?

WHAT TEACHING SKILLS ARE REQUIRED OF AN EFFECTIVE TEACHER?

Knowing vs. doing

A repertoire of teaching skills

WHAT ATTITUDES DOES THE EFFECTIVE TEACHER POSSESS?

What research reveals

The teacher's attitude toward himself: self-understanding

The teacher's attitude toward children

The teacher's attitude toward peers and parents

The teacher's attitude toward the subject matter

WHAT SUBJECT-MATTER KNOWLEDGE DOES THE TEACHER NEED?

"Teaching! What a deal!"

"That's the life—two weeks off at Christmas and three months' vacation every summer."

"What're you getting paid for, anyway? Just talking to kids!"

"*Anybody* can do that. . . ."

But *can* just anybody teach? Is "just talking to kids" the essence of teaching? What should a teacher know and be able to do which will make him more capable and effective than a nonteacher? This question is the central focus of this chapter. It is our goal that while reading you continually ask yourself what kind of teacher you would like to be, and what you can do to make your ideal self-image as a teacher a reality.

The teacher's role is much more complex than it appears to the casual observer. Colleges and universities, however, generally operate on the assumption that knowledge of the subject matter is all that's necessary to become a teacher. This is undoubtedly why so many college professors—despite their Ph.D.s and expertise in their fields—can't communicate their knowledge.

Until recently, almost nothing has been known about what constitutes good teaching or about how one could be trained as a good teacher. Thus, historically, colleges did not neglect pedagogy out of contempt for the subject, but because so little reliable data existed about teaching that it was not considered a subject at all. Although we are still far from having all the answers, educational research during the last decade has brought us much closer to understanding teaching and learning. Some people, such as management consultant Peter Drucker, believe that most teachers differ not at all from any other comparably educated adults. Consider the following statement:

It will be argued that we have teacher-training institutes with all kinds of courses in all areas of education. But this is self-delusion. What our teachers colleges do is something badly needed and useful; but it is not to teach anyone how to teach. They are recruiting agencies. They procure potential teachers and give them a seal of approval that guarantees their employment and entitles them to tenure. It also gives them self-confidence, and this is no small thing. But beyond that it is hard to see what the graduate of one of these institutions knows or can do that the seventeen-year-old high school girl of yesterday did not know or do when she started to teach elementary school in the rural midwest.[1]

The opposite extreme is represented by statements like this:

A revolution is underway in the education of teachers. The path to the teaching profession is changing as dramatically as the path to the medical profession changed following the historic Flexner Report on medical education in 1910.[2]

Most observers would agree that elementary and secondary teachers require knowledge and skills unique to the teaching profession. A teacher must ask himself not only "What am I going to teach?" but also "What should my students be learning?" "How can I help them learn it?" and "Why is it important?" To answer these questions the teacher must be familiar with children and their developmental stages. He must know something

---

[1] Peter F. Drucker, *The Age of Discontinuity: Guidelines to our Changing Society* (New York: Harper & Row, 1968), p. 338.

[2] *The New Teacher: A Report on Ford Foundation Assistance for New Patterns with the Education of Teachers* (New York: Ford Foundation, 1962).

TEACHERS

about events occurring outside the classroom and about what society needs and requires from the young. He must have enough command of the subjects he is going to teach to be able to distinguish what is peripheral from what is central. He must have a philosophy of education to guide him in his role as a teacher. And he must know something about how human beings learn and how to create environments which facilitate learning.

What are the specialized skills and attributes of the effective teacher? The four areas of competence which we consider essential for a teacher are:

1. Command of theoretical knowledge about learning and human behavior
2. Control of technical skills of teaching which facilitate student learning
3. Display of attitudes which foster learning and genuine human relationships
4. Sureness and adequacy of knowledge in the subject matter to be taught

The rest of this chapter will examine these four areas of competence in depth.

WHAT THEORETICAL KNOWLEDGE DOES THE TEACHER NEED?

Teacher education programs are frequently criticized by prospective teachers on the grounds that they overemphasize theory at the expense of practice. Experienced teachers commonly tell beginners, "Forget all that theory they're giving you at the university. Here's what works in the real world . . . ." The problem, though, is not that theory is wrong or unworkable, but that many teacher education programs offer students no opportunities to apply theory to practical situations; it is usually up to the neophyte teacher to translate theory into practice on the job. But theory is no less important for the failure to apply it effectively.

Theoretical knowledge about learning and human behavior equips the teacher to draw on concepts from psychology, anthropology, sociology and related disciplines to interpret the complex reality of the classroom. The

teacher who lacks theoretical background will be obliged to interpret class-room events according to commonly-held beliefs or common sense, much of which is, unfortunately, based on outmoded notions of human behavior. As Josh Billings said almost a century ago, "The trouble ain't that people are ignorant; it's that they 'know' so much that ain't so." Consider the following statements:

The more content a person knows, the better a teacher he is.

Content is best kept pure by departmentalizing instruction.

Content or subject matter has a logical structure or logical sequence which dictates how it should be taught.

Bigger schools are better than smaller schools.

Smaller classes are better than bigger classes.

Homogeneous grouping makes learning more efficient.

Classes must last for about an hour for optimal learning to take place.[3]

All of these contentions are commonly believed among educated people, including educators, yet there is no evidence to verify any of them and considerable evidence to refute them.

Every teacher should be familiar with currently-respected theoretical knowledge about human behavior and social systems. In addition to such general knowledge there exists specialized theoretical knowledge which is the unique province of the effective teacher. Teaching is neither static nor a matter of intuition; it has given rise to a body of theoretical knowledge which is constantly growing.

WHAT IS THEORETICAL KNOWLEDGE?

Theoretical knowledge which relates to teaching has been described by B. O. Smith as data which makes up a large part of the content of the disciplines and refers to the manipulatory level of human experience.[4] An example of relevant theory derived from psychology is the concept of *reinforcement,* defined as any event which increases the strength of a given response. A student who is praised for a certain behavior is likely to repeat it; the praise functions as reinforcement. Psychology is also the source of evidence that frequent reviews immediately after initial learning, followed by relatively widely-spaced reviews over a period of time, are likely to increase retention of knowledge. Thus, a teacher who consciously refers to a concept discussed

---

[3] Adapted from Neil Postman and Charles Weingarter, *Teaching as a Subversive Activity* (New York: Dell, 1969), p. 144.

[4] B. O. Smith, *Teachers for the Real World* (Washington, D.C.: American Association of Colleges for Teacher Education, 1969), p. 42.

WHAT DO WE KNOW ABOUT LEARNING?

1. *Behaviors which are rewarded (reinforced) are more likely to recur.*
2. *Sheer repetition without indications of improvement or any kind of reinforcement is a poor way to attempt to learn.*
3. *Threat and punishment have variable and uncertain effects upon learning; they may make the punished response more likely or less likely to recur; they may set up avoidance tendencies which prevent further learning.*
4. *Reward (reinforcement), to be most effective in learning, must follow almost immediately after the desired behavior and be clearly connected with that behavior in the mind of the learner.*
5. *The type of reward (reinforcement) which has the greatest transfer value to other life-situations is the kind one gives oneself—the sense of satisfaction in achieving purposes.*
6. *Opportunity for fresh, novel, stimulating experience is a kind of reward which is quite effective in conditioning and learning.*
7. *Forgetting proceeds rapidly at first—then more and more slowly; recall shortly after learning reduces the amount forgotten.*
8. *The most rapid mental growth occurs during infancy and early childhood; the average child achieves about half of his total mental growth by the age of five.*
9. *Not until eleven years of age do most children develop the sense of time which is required for historical perspective.*
10. *The most effective effort is put forth by children when they attempt tasks which fall in the "range of challenge"—not too easy and not too hard—where success seems quite possible but not certain.*
11. *Children are more apt to throw themselves wholeheartedly into any project if they themselves have participated in the selection and planning of the enterprise.*
12. *Reaction to excessive direction by the teacher may be: (a) apathetic conformity, (b) defiance, (c) scapegoating, (d) escape from the whole affair.*
13. *Over-strict discipline is associated with more conformity, anxiety, shyness and acquiescence in children; greater permissiveness is associated with more initiative and creativity in children.*
14. *What is learned is most likely to be available for use if it is learned in a situation much like that in which it is to be used and immediately preceding the time when it is needed. Learning in childhood-forgetting-and relearning when needed is not an efficient procedure.*
15. *If there is a discrepancy between the real objectives and the tests used to measure achievement, the latter become the main influence upon choice of subject matter and method.*

Goodwin Watson, "What Psychology Can We Feel Sure About?" *Teachers College Record* (1960), pp. 253–257. Reprinted as a separate pamphlet under the title, "What Psychology Can We Trust?" (New York: Bureau of Publications, Teachers College, Columbia University, 1961).

earlier in the week and continues to draw parallels to it throughout a unit is likely to help the students grasp and remember the concept.

HOW DOES ONE ACQUIRE THEORETICAL KNOWLEDGE?

Theoretical knowledge relevant to teaching is derived from courses or disciplines such as educational psychology, educational sociology, educational anthropology, linguistics, foundations of education, texts and measurement and classroom management. But because the relationship of theoretical knowledge to a given occupation is typically indirect, as Smith emphasizes, it is not enough for you simply to take the appropriate courses. Theory develops within a discipline and is formulated in terms suitable to that discipline but usually unsuitable or inadequate for a learning situation. For teachers this means that principles derived from psychology must be adapted to a classroom before they become useful. A classroom is always subject to a number of variables absent in the experimental situation. In the late afternoon of a school day, for instance, both teacher and student are likely to be tired, and their behavior then is likely to differ from what it would have been in the morning. In contrast, the laboratory experiments from which theory is derived are controlled to eliminate such variables. Thus, a teacher must have a command not only of the theoretical knowledge but also of the learning situation, in order to make the necessary adaptations.

Perhaps an example will clarify the need for adaptation. A student teacher "knows" from her educational psychology course that any behavior which is reinforced will be strengthened. Yet she deals with a noisy student by calling his outbursts to the attention of the rest of the class. What she doesn't realize is that by publicly acknowledging his behavior and attracting other students' attention to him, she may be reinforcing his noisemaking. The student teacher, of course, is at a loss to explain why the boy persists in his behavior despite her reprimands. Her theoretical knowledge has not been internalized to the point that she draws on it instinctively in the classroom. Many apparently inexplicable events of the classroom will make sense only when they are related to theories of human behavior. Make no mistake about it—this is a difficult task and does not come easily. It requires practice, insight and the advice and assistance of colleagues. You should view real or simulated classroom situations in conjunction with your courses in theory, and practice applying the appropriate concepts to your observations. It is also valuable to exchange ideas, interpretations and solutions with other teachers, both to verify your own views and to gain insight into other valid interpretations of the same events.

HOW CAN THEORETICAL KNOWLEDGE BE USED?

A teacher's theoretical knowledge can be used in two ways: to interpret situations and to solve problems. (Practical knowledge, on the other hand, is more limited in applicability and is used primarily to respond to familiar situations.)[5] For example, a teacher may see a child acting like a bully and interpret the child's aggression as a reaction to some frustration the child had experienced. In doing so the teacher would be drawing on theoretical knowledge about frustration and its possible consequences to interpret the child's behavior. To solve the problem, the teacher would avoid shaming the child but would seek the causes of his frustration and try to channel the child's energy in a more constructive direction. Adults lacking theoretical knowledge would be likely to attribute the child's aggression to "bad character" and to be unable to deal further with the situation.

Problem-solving is a primary aspect of the role of the teacher. He is constantly required to make diagnoses and decisions about problems related to learning and to human relations. In order to do this effectively the teacher must possess a high degree of theoretical understanding. He applies this understanding by formulating hypotheses both about the interpretation of problems and about the actions he should undertake in response to them. But there should be no air of finality about his proposed solutions. If the actions the teacher has chosen do not solve the problem, the situation should be reinterpreted and alternative responses sought and tested.

Classroom problems are rarely entirely original, except in the case of the new teacher, to whom nearly all are unprecedented. As a result, once a teacher has developed and incorporated a solution to a given problem, he will tend to use the same solution, with appropriate modifications, when confronted by similar situations; a solution that worked once in a particular situation is habitually relied upon as the "correct" way to handle all related problems. One teacher's means of handling disruptive outbursts might be to separate the offending child from the others by putting him in the corner. This solution deals only with the symptom, rather than the problem itself, which might vary from insecurity due to parental neglect to dislike of the school environment. Single-solution behavior is dangerous because it fails to take into account all the variables of individual situations. Also, a solution which is overused tends to become ineffective. Teachers must guard against the "single-solution rut."

Because of their insecurity and lack of theoretical knowledge, beginning teachers often seek "recipes" to solve certain categories of problems. "What do I do when one child hits another?" Questions of this type are requests for pat answers which can be automatically "plugged in" when needed. Unfortunately, this approach rarely works because the reasons why one child hits another are as numerous as are the possible and appropriate teacher responses. As a teacher you should not only refrain from using "single solutions" but also avoid seeking them; instead, you should concentrate on acquiring knowledge about learning, patterns of behavior, how children from different cultural backgrounds behave and what values they possess,

---

[5] *Ibid.,* p. 44.

and familiarity with such concepts as motivation, self-concept, feedback, reinforcement, attitude formation, perception and peer approval.

Arthur Jersild makes an interesting point about seeking solutions to problems. He suggests that when teachers insist on a practical application—a method, a gimmick, a prescription or a rule of thumb—they are often trying not to grasp but to avoid the implications of the theory under discussion.[6] Thus theory and practice are often out of phase because teachers, like all human beings, tend to externalize rather than internalize a theory. We see a theory's applicability to others more easily than we see its relevance to ourselves. As a result, we tend to react manipulatively, wishing to do something to someone else, rather than looking inward and becoming personally involved.

Let's consider an example of how theoretical knowledge can help a teacher interpret classroom events and solve the problems arising from them. In psychology, *self-concept* is defined as the sum of a person's beliefs about and evaluations of himself as a person. Every individual has an image of the kind of person he is, derived from previous experiences, and he tends to behave in ways that are consistent with that image. A child's self-concept is an important factor in both his ability to learn and his interaction with other children and his environment. For instance, if a child views himself as likeable and outgoing, he is apt to respond in a friendly manner when meeting new children. If a child is insecure because he views himself as weak, ugly or unwanted, he will not respond easily to a group of new children.

Suppose a teacher observes that a particular child is doing poorly in science. The problem at issue is how to help this child improve his performance in that subject. A number of factors may be influencing his performance— he may possess inadequate scientific concepts; he may not be interested in science; he may not be very intelligent; or he may view himself as poor in science and as a result not try as hard as he might. Several of these factors may be interrelated in complex ways.[7]

A teacher who functions as a problem-solver would hypothesize that the child's poor performance could result from any of these factors and proceed to investigate further by collecting information about the child's previous performance in science, his intelligence level and his self-concept. In this way the teacher can determine whether the child's self-concept is an important determinant in his poor science performance.

If the child's intelligence level is high and his previous experience indicates that he should be doing reasonably well in science, it might be hypothesized that the principal reason for the child's poor performance is his conception of his own abilities. What can the teacher do? Can a teacher help change a

---

[6] Arthur Jersild, *When Teachers Face Themselves* (New York City: Teachers College Press, 1955), pp. 86–87.

[7] The authors are indebted for this example to Frederick J. McDonald, *Educational Psychology* (Belmont, California: Wadsworth, 1965), pp. 439–441.

child's self-concept? The answer is an unequivocal maybe. If the teacher is one of the child's major sources of self-information, he may be able to encourage a revised self-concept through a guidance program designed to help the child gather reliable information about himself. Sometimes children lack self-understanding to such an extent that they must be referred to specialized professional help before progress can be made. Again, the teacher may have to make that decision on the basis of his own observations and knowledge.

If the child's problem does not seem serious enough to require referral to a specialist, the teacher himself might try any of several approaches to improve the child's self-concept in science. Discussing his abilities with him, helping him view his abilities more realistically and arranging for a successful experience are among the potential ways to change the child's self-perception. The teacher proceeds throughout as an hypothesis-maker, forming tentative ideas about experiences which might improve the child's self-concept, and testing those ideas. The teacher's hypotheses will become more perceptive and accurate as his understanding of the variables which influence the child's self-concept increases.

A teacher needs much more than common-sense understanding of human behavior. The capable and effective teacher uses theoretical knowledge drawn from various education-related disciplines to formulate and test hypotheses about human behavior in the classroom. In our opinion, the translation of theory into practice cannot be left to chance; you must constantly seek experiences which allow you to apply theoretical concepts to classroom situations and to receive guidance and feedback about their application.

WHAT TEACHING SKILLS ARE REQUIRED OF AN EFFECTIVE TEACHER?

KNOWING VS. DOING

Simply knowing something does not guarantee the ability to act upon that knowledge; there is a profound difference between *knowing* and *doing*. A teacher may know, for example, that he should ask his students questions which require more than mere factual answers, but he is not always able to act upon that knowledge. No teacher education program can afford to focus exclusively on theoretical knowledge at the expense of the practice, or "doing," dimension of teaching, just as no individual teacher can rely solely on knowledge of subject matter. Every prospective teacher needs to develop a repertoire of teaching skills to use as he sees fit in varying classroom situations. In contrast to the theoretical knowledge component of a teacher's preparation, which focuses on the situation in which the teacher finds herself, the teaching skills component focuses on the trainee herself—the observation, analysis and modification of her teaching behavior.

Research has not yet conclusively identified the teaching skills which have the most beneficial impact on student learning (the results of some very revealing studies, however, were reported in Chapter Two), but many educators have independently defined the skills they believe essential to good teaching, among them the following:

The ability to ask different kinds of questions, each of which requires different types of thought processes from the student

The ability to effectively reinforce certain kinds of student behavior

The ability to diagnose student needs and learning difficulties

The ability to continually vary the learning situation in order to keep the students involved

The ability to recognize when students are paying attention and be able to use this information to vary behavior and, possibly, the direction of the lesson

The ability to utilize technological equipment, such as motion picture projectors

The ability to judge the appropriateness of instructional materials

The ability to define the objectives of particular lessons and units in terms of student behaviors

The ability to relate learning to the student's experience[8]

A REPERTOIRE OF TEACHING SKILLS

This list is far from complete. It does make clear, however, that teachers need a large repertoire of skills to work effectively with students with varying backgrounds and different educational goals. There is some evidence that the outstanding characteristic of a good teacher is flexibility,[9] since varied approaches are necessary to meet the multiple needs of students.

We believe strongly that a teacher education program should train candidates in the performance of selected teaching skills. Many teachers and teacher educators, however, blanch at the term "teacher training." They regard training as something one does with animals, not human beings; human beings, they say, should be educated, not trained. We don't agree. We believe that a teacher's preparation must consist of both education and training. The objection that training a teacher makes him a robot and prevents the release of his creative energies is contradicted by what we know of training in other occupations. Surgeons and pilots, for example, are

---

[8] Partially adapted from Smith, *Teachers for the Real World,* p. 71.

[9] Donald Hamachek, "Characteristics of Good Teachers and Implications for Teacher Education," *Phi Delta Kappan* 50 (February 1969): 341–344.

WHAT WOULD YOU DO?

Case Number One

You are a first-year female teacher, in a ninth-grade English course. As the first semester proceeds you notice that Fred has a crush on you. He is constantly volunteering to help you pass out papers, and lingers after class each day to talk to you. He found out your home address and came to visit you one Saturday morning. His actions are becoming obvious to the other students, who are starting to kid him about his infatuation.
   What would you do?

Case Number Two

You are generally recognized as one of the most popular teachers on campus. The students look upon you as a friend who can be trusted, and you have told them that if they ever have problems, school-related or personal, they should feel free to come to you. One day Maryanne, a junior in one of your classes, seeks you out. She is close to hysteria, and tells you that she is ten weeks pregnant. You are the first person she has told. She begs you for advice, but insists you do not tell her parents.
   What would you do?

Case Number Three

The school in which you are teaching has recently been integrated. There are seven black students in one of your classes. Because you fear alienating the blacks and being accused of prejudice, you make special efforts to treat them fairly. One day three of your white students come to see you and accuse you of coddling the blacks and discriminating against whites.
   What would you do?

trained to perform certain operations proficiently and even automatically. This level of mastery enables them to turn their attention and energy to tasks more worthy of their creativity. As B. O. Smith says, "A trained individual has relaxed control which frees him from preoccupation with immediate acts so he can scan the new situation and respond to it constructively. Training and resourcefulness are complementary, not antithetical, elements of behavior."[10]

   The skills in which a teacher is trained should depend upon the age level and cultural background of the children he will teach, the subjects to be

---

[10] Smith, *Teachers for the Real World*, p. 80. Reprinted by permission of the publisher.

taught, research evidence on the effectiveness of certain skills and other factors. Once the necessary skills have been selected, a training procedure is developed. Smith argues that the training process must have the following components:

establishment of the practice situation

specification of the behavior

performance of the specified behavior

feedback of information about the performance

modification of the performance in the light of the feedback

performance-feedback-correction-practice schedule continued until desirable skillfulness is achieved[11]

Probing Questions—A Representative Teaching Skill. Before teaching skills can be acquired they must be specified. The specific behaviors, or components, which must be learned to master the skill must be described explicitly—vague or general descriptions will not provide adequate guidelines for the trainee. Consider the following material designed to teach the skill of asking probing questions. This skill description was developed as part of a training experiment with beginning teachers at Stanford University.[12]

Today you will have an opportunity to develop skills in basic classroom questioning techniques. The session is designed to help you extend the range and quality of your questioning techniques in such a way that the pupils you teach are led to think more deeply about problems raised in class.

The techniques outlined below are designed to be used in discussion, review, and inductively organized lessons where active pupil participation is prerequisite to the realization of the goals of instruction. Any given technique may be appropriate in one situation but not in another. The selection of a particular technique depends upon the extent to which, in your judgment, it requires the pupil to analyze critically a problem or to justify rationally his answer. Do not use a given technique unless you feel it contributes to the educational relevance of the lesson.

Your goal is to ask penetrating and probing questions that require pupils to go beyond superficial, "first answer" responses.

BASIC QUESTIONING TECHNIQUES: There are two ways of achieving the above goal: 1) The teacher asks penetrating questions that require pupils to get at the heart of the problem. This forestalls superficial answers. Whether you are able to do this largely depends upon your knowledge of relevant content; 2) The second approach is based on specific techniques that may be used *after* the pupil has responded in some way (i.e., a question, a comment, an answer to a teacher's question). The goal here is to get the pupil to go beyond his first response. You are attempting to produce greater

---

[11] *Ibid.*, p. 71.

[12] Frederick J. McDonald and Dwight W. Allen, *Training Effects of Feedback and Modeling Procedures on Teaching Performance* (Palo Alto, California: Stanford University, 1967), pp. 188–191.

critical awareness and depth by *probing*. Your cue is the pupil's response—once it has occurred, don't immediately go on with the discussion yourself. *Probe* his answer by means of one of the techniques outlined below.

I. *Teacher Seeks Further Clarification by the Pupil:* You may ask the pupil for more information and/or more meaning. You may respond to the pupil's responses by saying such things as:
   a. "What do you mean?"
   b. "Could you put that in other words to make clearer what you mean?"
   c. "Can you explain that further?"
   d. "What do you mean by the term . . . ?"

II. *Teacher Seeks Increased Pupil Critical Awareness:* Here you are requiring the pupil to justify his response rationally. You may say:
   a. "What are you/we assuming here?"
   b. "Why do you think that is so?"
   c. "Have we/you oversimplified the issue—is there more to it?"
   d. "Is this one or several questions?"
   e. "How would someone who took the opposite point of view respond to this?"

III. *Teacher Seeks to Refocus the Pupil's Response:* If a pupil has given a high quality answer, it may seem unnecessary to *probe* it. However, you can refocus his or the class's attention on a related issue.
   a. "Good! What are the implications of this for . . . ?"
   b. "How does this relate to . . . ?"
   c. "Can you take it from there and tie it into . . . ?"

IV. *Teacher Prompts Pupil:* In *prompting* you are giving the pupil a hint to help him go on and answer a question. Suppose a pupil has given an I-don't-know or I'm-not-sure type of response. Rather than giving him the answer or redirecting the question to another pupil, you may give the puzzled student a hint.
   Teacher: "John, define the term 'polygenesis.'"
   John: "I can't do it."
   Teacher: (*Prompting*) "What does poly mean?" or, "Well, genesis means origin or birth, and poly means . . . ?"
   This technique allows you to *probe* even though at first it appears that the pupil can't answer the question.

V. *Redirect:* This is not the *probing* technique per se. It helps you bring other students into the discussion quickly while still using *probing* techniques. In *redirecting*, you merely change the direction of interaction from yourself and the first pupil to yourself and the second pupil.
   Teacher: "What is the relationship between pressure and volume?"
   First Pupil: "As the pressure goes up, the gas is condensed."
   Teacher: (to Second Pupil) "Can you tell us what is meant by condensed?" Or, "Can you restate that in terms of volume?"

To sum up, the techniques outlined above have two things in common:
1. They are initiated by the teacher immediately after the pupil has responded.
2. They require the pupil to go beyond the information he has already given.

Concluding Remarks: Try to use the techniques as frequently as you can. Do not stay with one given technique for too long at one time. In addition, don't forget to reinforce when you *probe*—if you are not at ease you may otherwise behave like a "Philadelphia lawyer."

If you prefer to run through the first five-minute lesson as a warm-up, this would be fine. You may teach the same lesson over two or three times. We will focus more on *probing* than on transmitting new or complex material. The maximum amount of time for the session will be two hours.

Many skills can be acquired in a simulated teaching situation in which the trainee is presented specific information and asked to take appropriate steps to solve the problem. Similarly, many teaching skills, such as the ability to ask probing questions, can be acquired through a relatively new training procedure called microteaching. Both simulation and microteaching will be discussed in more detail in Chapter Six.

WHAT ATTITUDES DOES THE EFFECTIVE TEACHER POSSESS?

WHAT RESEARCH REVEALS

Many people believe that the teacher's personality is the most critical factor in successful teaching. If the teacher possesses warmth, empathy, sensitivity, enthusiasm and humor, he is much more likely to be successful than if he lacks these characteristics. In fact, many people argue that without these attributes an individual is unlikely to be a good teacher.

For years educational researchers have sought to isolate the characteristics essential to good teachers. In a massive study, David Ryans concluded that effective teachers are fair, democratic, responsive, understanding, kindly, stimulating, original, alert, attractive, responsible, steady, poised and confident. Ineffective teachers were described as partial, autocratic, aloof, restricted, harsh, dull, stereotyped, apathetic, unimpressive, evasive, erratic, excitable and uncertain.[13]

But this information is not very useful. After all, what human interaction wouldn't be improved if the participants possessed only positive traits? Getzels and Jackson, summarizing fifty years of research on teachers' personalities and characteristics, conclude: "Despite the critical importance of the problem and a half-century of prodigious research effort, very little is known for certain about the nature and measurement of teacher personality, or about the relation between teacher personality and teaching effectiveness."[14]

---

[13] David Ryans, *Characteristics of Teachers* (Washington, D.C.: American Council on Education, 1960).

[14] J. W. Getzels and P. W. Jackson, "The Teacher's Personality and Characteristics," in *Handbook of Research on Teaching,* ed. N. L. Gage (Chicago: Rand McNally, 1963), p. 574.

DIALOGUE

Kevin: *Jim, as a teacher trainee what concerned you most about teaching?*

Jim: *I can remember telling my advisor one day that if my students didn't like me I would probably quit teaching. I guess I had a very high need to be liked.*

Kevin: *Did they like you?*

Jim: *Well, for the most part. I remember I could hardly wait to read my students' evaluations of me after my supervisor had collected them. I must have spent a couple of hours reading and rereading them. It's interesting, though, that because of an old skill of mine I was quickly able to become a center of attention.*

Kevin: *What was that?*

Jim: *Well, you have to understand that I taught seventh grade at a junior high school, and had playground duty every noon hour. I was an expert Yo-Yo performer, and Yo-Yoing was very big with seventh-graders. So at noon I would give exhibitions of around-the-world, rock-the-baby, man-on-a-flying-trapeze, reaching-for-the-moon and a lot of my other specialties.*

Kevin: *Wow! It must be nice to know you can always fall back on a show biz career!*

A person's *attitudes,* or predispositions to act in a positive or negative way, toward persons, ideas and events, are a fundamental dimension of his personality. Although little empirical evidence exists relating specific attitudes to teaching effectiveness, almost all educators are convinced of the importance of teacher attitudes in the teaching process. Attitudes have a direct—though frequently unrecognized—effect on our behavior in that they determine the ways we view ourselves and interact with others.

We believe that there are four major categories of attitude which affect teaching behavior: 1) the teacher's attitude toward himself; 2) the teacher's attitudes toward children and his relationship with them; 3) the teacher's attitudes toward peers and parents, and 4) the teacher's attitude toward the subject matter.

THE TEACHER'S ATTITUDE TOWARD HIMSELF: SELF-UNDERSTANDING

If the teacher is to help a student have meaningful experiences, discover his aptitudes and abilities, face his inner difficulties and accept himself as a person, he needs to know and understand that student. But before a teacher can do that, he must work at knowing and understanding himself. Empirical evidence from psychology indicates that a person who denies or is unable to cope with his own emotions is unlikely to be capable of respecting and dealing with others' feelings. A person who never admits to feelings of anger and hostility, for example, may overreact to, ignore or deny the legitimacy of another person's anger. He may consider it "bad" to feel anger. The same is true of fear, feelings of inadequacy and most other natural human emotions.

Thus if a teacher is to understand and sympathize with a student who is hostile, he must face hostile tendencies in himself, and recognize their implications for his students and others with whom he has dealings. Unless the teacher recognizes his own anxiety, he will be unlikely to understand and empathize with his students' expressions of anxiety. He may not recognize that a student's inability to learn, inattentiveness, impudence or irritability may be the result of anxiety. The teacher also needs to recognize that his own anxiety may make him irritable, causing the students in turn to feel anxious and display similar symptoms. As Arthur Jersild has said, "A teacher's understanding of others can be only as deep as the wisdom he possesses when he looks inward upon himself. The more genuinely he seeks to face the problems of his own life, the more he will be able to realize his kinship with others."[15]

The question remains, "How can one achieve understanding of self and, after achieving it, accept it?" Jersild suggests that "to gain knowledge of self, one must have the courage to seek it and the humility to accept what one may find."[16]

There are a number of potential sources of increased self-understanding. Jersild suggests that books by sensitive and compassionate people who have made progress in their own struggles to know themselves can be a valuable aid in self-examination. For prospective teachers, such books might include Sylvia Ashton-Warner's *Teacher,* an account of her teaching experience in a Maori Infant School in New Zealand, and Herbert Kohl's *36 Children.* Another method he suggests is "participant observation," the process of observing a class and recording what you hear, see and feel as you observe. Your record is then compared with the records of other observers. This experience may demonstrate to you that what you notice in any given situation is determined in large part by habits of thought which you take for granted. It may also illustrate that your "objective" perceptions are often projections of your own subjective state, and thus may tell you more about yourself than about the people you have observed.

In recent years a number of techniques have been developed to help individuals better understand themselves and their relationships, feelings and attitudes toward other people. These processes, which include sensitivity training, T-grouping, awareness experiences and encounter sessions, share no standard format or common set of experiences, but all emphasize intro-

---

[15] Jersild, *When Teachers Face Themselves,* p. 83.

[16] *Loc. cit.*

spection, self-evaluation, small-group activities and a "here and now" existential orientation. They are usually characterized by strong emotional interaction. A more detailed discussion of sensitivity training appears in Chapter Six.

While at one time group sessions were considered "freaky" or of dubious value, more and·more people are recognizing their validity and effectiveness in helping people gain self-understanding. Jersild's survey of 1,032 teachers revealed that over 40 percent thought they would need personal help, such as group therapy, if they were to put the widely-endorsed concept of self-understanding into practice in their teaching.[17] In group therapy sessions, a person may be helped to see his anger, fear and self-protective maneuvers as others see them. The way others respond to him may help him perceive facets of his personality or behavior of which he was previously unaware. A structured exercise in which someone mimics his conduct, for example, might illuminate for him certain aspects of his behavior.

Self-examination can also grow out of day-to-day relationships with others. The procedures by which one gains self-understanding are less important than the courage and desire to do so. We constantly find ourselves in new situations with new people who challenge us in new ways, and as a result understanding oneself is a continuous process. Because teachers interact with and influence so many young children, they must work particularly hard to understand themselves and their actions in order to understand the children in their charge.

Your college years are likely to be a time of protracted self-examination. As you gain new independence from your family, examine values you may have taken for granted, test yourself against rigorous academic standards, encounter new ideas and live in close quarters with others your own age, you probably find yourself experiencing new feelings and recognizing unfamiliar things about yourself. College is also likely to offer you more leisure than any future period of your life (believe it or not!) to explore and learn about yourself. Most colleges offer sensitivity sessions run by trained leaders, as well as personal counseling sessions, to help you face and cope with feelings of limitation, insecurity, inferiority or confusion, the need to be liked and approved of, lack of direction and other problems. We urge you to regard self-examination as a serious commitment, and to undertake it *as a prospective teacher,* in an effort to make a good decision about whether to teach and to become the best teacher you are capable of becoming.

Consider for a moment a need basic to most people—the need to be liked. Teachers, too, especially beginners, need to be liked by their pupils and their peers. Many teachers do not realize how strong their need for approval is; a teacher may approve particular student actions not because they are in the student's best interests but for fear that if he disapproved he might lose

---

[17] *Ibid.,* p. 84.

It is not of supreme importance that a human being should be a good scientist, a good scholar, a good administrator, a good expert; it is not of supreme importance that he should be right, rational, knowledgeable, or even creatively productive of brilliantly finished objects as often as possible. Life is not what we are in our various professional capacities or in the practice of some special skill. What is of supreme importance is that each of us should become a person, a whole and integrated person in whom there is manifested a sense of the human variety genuinely experienced, a sense of having come to terms with a reality that is awesomely vast. The-odore Roszak, The Making of a Counter-Culture, *as quoted in the* Phi Delta Kappan *52 (October 1970): 74.*

their affection. Unfortunately, the teacher rarely recognizes his own motivations when such incidents occur. Unless the teacher is aware of the strength of his own need, he will be in no position to examine and judge his actions correctly.

Another configuration of needs which can influence classroom behavior is represented by the teacher who needs to have students depend on him. This teacher feels pleasure when the students demonstrate that they need him. Thus the teacher habitually engineers situations in which the students have to depend on him in order to accomplish the assigned tasks. This teacher usually behaves like a benevolent dictator in the classroom, kindly but relentlessly building a "cult of the individual." The novel, play and movie of *The Prime of Miss Jean Brodie* depict this type of teacher very well. In order to be considered one of "Miss Brodie's girls," a student must adhere to a code of Miss Brodie's invention. This type of teacher is potentially very damaging to her students. Instead of producing students who are self-directed and who can make choices for themselves, such a teacher inhibits growth. She may not behave consciously in this fashion; she is probably unaware of her own need for others to be dependent on her. This teacher needs counseling to make her aware of her need and of its negative effect on students. The situation may even be serious enough to warrant psychotherapy.

As we stated earlier, a person's attitude toward himself has a direct influence on his attitudes toward others. If, for example, a teacher sees himself as friendly but is not considered friendly by his students and does not, by every objective criterion, behave in a friendly manner, he is not likely to change his behavior until he acquires some insight into his inaccurate self-image. He will be perplexed when his students do not respond warmly to what he considers friendly behavior, and will probably form negative attitudes toward them. If, on the other hand, he is able to adopt a more realistic self-concept—to recognize that he is not naturally friendly and that he will

TEACHERS

Dec. 4, 1969   *c*   David
                                          Year 4

I am a Belly Button

    I am a belly button. X I belong to a fat man. My name is Jay. Now I don't like the fat man I belong to. I don't like all the tall tall hairs or when the fat man slapps me. So one night when everbody was asleep I rolled off of the fat man and rolled out of the door. I rolled into another house and found a pretty girl asleep. I rolled onto her and rolled beside her belly botton. When she ~~a~~ woke up she screamed. When the fat man woke up he was ~~scared~~. ~~Fnly~~ Finally the fat man found out what had happened he went over to the girl's house and got me back.

                                   A weird story, David, and I think in bad taste.

Mind-Murdering, Grade 4   *A parent sent this to a magazine, angry that David's fantasy should be put down so brutishly by his teacher.*

From *Media and Methods,* April 1970, p. 33.

have to change his behavior patterns—he will be on the road to changing his attitudes toward his students and improving his relationship with them.

We hope that these examples illustrate vividly how a teacher's personal needs and attitudes can influence his behavior, and how self-knowledge can deepen insight and even change behavior.

THE TEACHER'S ATTITUDES TOWARD CHILDREN

Children are sensitive observers of adult behavior, and they frequently recognize, and become preoccupied with, aspects of the teacher's attitude toward them of which the teacher may be unaware. There is a variety of attitudes or feelings toward students which can decisively reduce the teacher's effectiveness; the teacher may have:

strong dislikes for particular pupils and obvious fondness for others

biases toward or against particular ethnic groups

low learning expectations from poverty-level children or those with certain ethnic backgrounds

a bias toward certain kinds of student behavior, such as docility or aggressiveness

Few teachers are entirely free of such attitudes at the outset, and self-awareness can be the crucial factor distinguishing a biased teacher from a fair one. Thus, it is important that the prospective teacher confront his own attitudes early, perhaps through group discussions, role-playing, or simulated and real experiences. It is quite likely that your own teacher education program will provide you with such experiences. It is necessary to acknowledge one's attitudes in order to change them, but even then change is neither easy nor automatic. Any attempt to change attitudes must take into account both of their components, feelings and cognition. Attitudes may be based almost entirely on feelings, as when a teacher's dislike for a particular student causes her to refuse to let the student participate in a particular activity. Or, if a teacher feels strong rapport with a certain child, he may have a ten-

dency to let the child "get away with" more than other students are allowed. An example of cognition as the primary component of an attitude is the assessment of a student's needs causing a teacher to require the student to participate in particular activities, even those the child might dislike.

If an attitude is based on a negative feeling, it is usually amenable to change through counseling or role-playing techniques. In a role-playing situation each of the participants is asked to portray as realistically as possible the behavior and feelings of another person, perhaps a member of a minority group. Rather than intellectualizing his feelings, the role-player attempts to suspend his own feelings and to draw on his capacity to feel what the other person is experiencing. The result is that the individual playing the role begins to project himself imaginatively into the identity of the other person. Role-playing as a technique is based on the belief that one of the most effective ways to change attitudes is to participate in experiences in which one can observe the effect on others of attitudinal behavior; the process creates the content.

If, on the other hand, an attitude is primarily based on cognition, new information may be effective in producing attitude changes. An excellent illustration of this effect involves the notion of *teacher expectancy.* If a teacher expects a student or group of students to behave in a certain way, the teacher's attitude may serve as a *self-fulfilling prophecy*—that is, the students may behave in the predicted manner in response to the teacher's attitude and not as a result of the other factors on which the teacher's expectations are based. A teacher who is told that his students are "slow" will have different expectations for their performance than he would if he was told the students were "fast."[18] Regardless of their innate ability, students deemed "slow" may respond poorly precisely because of the teacher's low expectations. Many teachers have low expectations of poor children. This phenomenon is cited by many educators as a major cause of low student performances in urban schools attended by poor children. The teach-

---

[18] For further discussion of teacher expectations, see Robert Rosenthal and Lenore Jacobson, *Pygmalion in the Classroom* (New York: Holt, Rinehart & Winston, 1968). Although the book has received methodological criticism, the phenomenon they report is probably accurately described.

EXCERPTS FROM A DIARY OF A BEGINNING TEACHER

September 7. *I'm exhausted today. I gave them all back their papers which, thank goodness, took up part of the class time. I also assigned them four questions to do for homework. I didn't write the questions on the board, which was a mistake; I ended up repeating everything five or six times.*

I feel so pushed, preparing and correcting papers; hope things calm down soon.

September 9. *I tried playing a game with them in class today. It didn't go very well. One of the biggest problems was that I didn't have a firm enough control over the class to do it. I had them asking each other questions. They were divided into two teams and all that. I even set up a panel of judges who decided whether the answer to a question was right.*

I also gave them a pop quiz at the beginning of the period. I tried it in one class at the end, but that didn't work as well; they were too excited from the game to settle down.

One real catastrophe today. The map fell on my head during fourth period. The class went wild, luckily the assistant principal was right outside the room, and came in and rescued me.

September 13. *I gave the quiz today and they did pretty well and then I finished up discussing geography—I hope. I only gave them twenty of the spelling words and left off the longest and most difficult. They were very upset because they said they had all learned that one.*

The day has finally come. Despite all of the work and how tired I am, I think I am really going to like teaching.

September 26. *I'm having a problem getting the classes to keep quiet now. For a while they were pretty good, but now they're beginning to get to me. Even the good students are starting to talk during class. I don't think its because they're not interested because the talk is almost always about what I'm discussing, but still they're talking without permission. If it was only a little I wouldn't mind, but it's beginning to get to the point where I can't go on because of the talking.*

September 27. *The assistant principal came and visited one of my classes today. Before class I was talking at my desk with one student and all of a sudden I heard this deathly silence hit the class. (I guess that's not the right way to say it, but anyway.) I looked up and there he was. I started the class. I'd ask a question and there was absolute silence. Nothing. It was terrible! It's bad when they're all talking at once, but it's horrible when they're afraid to move.*

September 29. *I've been getting bored, teaching the same thing over and over and so today I did different things in different classes. I discussed* *with some, gave some a quiz and had others writing. I tried discussing with my sixth-period class but they're just impossible after about ten minutes. I got really mad at them and told them to take out their books and study quietly for ten minutes and then I would give them a quiz. While they studied, I made up the quiz and it was a dilly—only four people passed. I suppose it isn't good educational psychology to do that but it made me feel much better, and at that point it was either them or me.*

October 14. *I have now firmly and purposely gotten my classes separated. That is, I am no longer doing the same thing five times a day. At first it was a big help being able to prepare only one lesson each night. But I realized that it was terribly boring for me, and my boredom would be reflected in the kids. Once I felt that I had my bearings, I decided to change all that. Well, it's taken me this long to carry out my plan. Although I use much of the same material in all of my classes, I do not use it all at the same time or in the same manner. I can really see the difference in the classes.*

October 19. *Tonight was the PTA open house. I was pleased at how well it went. I guess that parents are not really ogres after all. But it was an awfully long day. I really do love teaching and I look forward to all of my classes, but I often feel that I am not doing my best for these kids. Teach and learn—and have I learned a lot in these seven weeks!*

November 4. *Teacher's Convention—WHAT A FARCE!*

November 9. *Every day I learn so much. I hope that the children are learning some too, but they couldn't possibly learn more than a fraction of what I have. I think there is hope for me yet. I already know so much more than I did in September. Sometimes I feel the huge mountain of things yet to learn pressing down on me but I think I've made a significant dent in the mountain. I may live through the year. But then again, it seems overwhelming.*

November 30. *Beautiful day! Introducing a new unit and the kids were great—love it. Everything went well.*

December 8. *Ugliness! Nothing went well at all. Jabber, jabber, jabber—I don't know. Sometimes I get so upset and depressed it's horrible. They don't listen or follow instructions, or learn anything. I guess it's a normal feeling for new teachers.*

December 12. *Almost the end of the period before vacation. I guess not really but it seems like it must be. Happiness!! They announced that all evaluation meetings are cancelled until after Christmas. Hurray! Except for the faculty meeting Thursday.*

From Jean Morris, "Diary of a Beginning Teacher," *National Association of Secondary School Principals Bulletin* 52 (October 1968): 6–15.

ers' expectations can be changed by providing proof that their ability is not inherently inferior to that of other children. The teachers' attitudes toward these youngsters are likely to change somewhat as a result of their raised expectations.

At this point let us consider the position, most eloquently expressed by Carl Rogers, a noted counselor, psychologist and therapist, that significant learning depends on certain attitudinal qualities which exist in the personal relationship between the facilitator and the learner. Note that Rogers uses the term "facilitator," rather than "teacher," because he believes it puts emphasis on what happens to the learner rather than on the performance of the teacher. The term "facilitator" also implies significantly different functions than does the term "teacher."

The attitude most basic to the learning relationship, according to Rogers, is realness or genuineness. Instead of playing a role or presenting a front, the facilitator must enter into a relationship with the learner. He must be a real person, one who "... is *being* himself." He is free to be enthusiastic, bored, interested, angry, sensitive and sympathetic. As Rogers says,

> Because he accepts these feelings as his own he has no need to impose them on his students. He can like or dislike a student product without implying that it is objectively good or bad or that the student is good or bad. He is simply expressing a feeling for the product, a feeling which exists within himself. Thus, he is a person to his students, not a faceless embodiment of a curricular requirement nor a sterile tube through which knowledge is passed from one generation to the next.[19]

Another essential attitude Rogers describes as valuing the learner—his feelings, his opinions and his person—as he is and as worthy in his own right, and accepting both his imperfections and his potentialities. The facilitator who possesses this attitude can accept a student's occasional apathy, fear of failure or hatred of authority, as well as his more positive characteristics. In short, this attitude is an expression of the facilitator's confidence and trust in the capacity of the human being.

A third attitude which Rogers considers essential to the establishment of a climate for self-initiated, experiential learning is empathic understanding. "When the teacher has the ability to understand the student's reactions from the inside, has a sensitive awareness of the way the process of education and learning seems *to the student,* then again the likelihood of significant learning is increased."[20] Empathic understanding implies that the facilitator understands the learner, but does not judge or evaluate him. Rogers urges that a teacher initially set himself the goal of making one nonevaluative, accepting, empathic response per day to a student's demonstrated or verbalized feelings. By doing so, he believes, the teacher will discover the potency of this approach.

---

[19] Carl Rogers, *Freedom to Learn* (Columbus: Charles E. Merrill, 1969), p. 106.

[20] *Ibid.,* p. 10.

Jim: *We may be giving readers the impression that a person has to be "Superteacher" to step into a classroom.*

Kevin: *I think I know what you mean. Very few, if any of our readers will have mastered by the time they graduate all the characteristics, skills and knowledge that we say makes a teacher effective. It'll take years of study and self-study to become "master" teachers.*

Jim: *That's part of it, but I was thinking of something else too. We've been describing a teacher who is like the ideal Renaissance man, able to do all things well. I think that part of our problem in education has been that we require too much of individuals. I foresee much more specialization on the part of teachers in the future—all teachers won't try to be all things for all children.*

Kevin: *There's no doubt about that in my mind. It means, though, that the school will have to organize its personnel into teaching teams in order to take advantage of the unique contributions each person is able to make. I can visualize teams comprised of specialists in media, aesthetics, human relations and specific subject matter as well as generalists. The composition of these teams will vary tremendously.*

Jim: *This means, of course, that teacher education programs will have to become more diversified in order to prepare teachers with all these different competencies.*

Kevin: *And the problem is that the universities don't want to prepare these kinds of teachers until they think there are going to be jobs available for them.*

Jim: *And the schools don't want to commit themselves to this approach until the universities can provide them with people trained to do these kinds of jobs.*

Kevin: *It looks like a rerun of the old chicken-and-egg routine.*

Rogers' approach is intended to create classroom environments conducive to self-initiated learning. He maintains that the teacher's skills, his knowledge of his field, his curricular planning, his lectures and his selection of books and other learning aids are all peripheral; the crux of the learning situation is the relationship between the facilitator and the learner, which should be characterized by the three attitudinal predispositions described above. Unless the learning environment is characterized by *realness, valuing* and *empathy,* according to Rogers, it is sterile and cannot produce significant learning.

It is interesting to compare Rogers' ideas with the findings of Martin

Haberman, who studied the teaching behavior of students in the Intern Teaching Program at the University of Wisconsin.[21] The interns, under the dual supervision of the university and the school, had been given a minimum of theoretical knowledge prior to instructing fulltime in the classroom. The teaching behavior of the more successful interns was compared with that of the less successful interns. Haberman's studies indicated that academic achievement at the graduate level, communication skills and positive attitudes toward children, as measured both verbally and on written instruments, were all irrelevant to success as an intern. There were, however, five factors which significantly distinguished the successful and unsuccessful interns: belief in the youngsters' potential, ability to organize the classroom situation, genuine enthusiasm for the subject matter, ability to set appropriate standards and willingness to listen to the youngsters and utilize their comments in teaching. The results of this study seem generally to support Rogers' theories, except that Haberman found a positive attitude toward children to be insufficient for success in teaching; belief in their abilities must be demonstrated by continual use of student input in the classroom.

In any case, there is little question that if you have empathy for your students, value them as unique individuals and are secure enough to be yourself without playing a role, you will be a more successful teacher and the atmosphere in your classroom will make possible for you and your students a joy, excitement, and closeness absent from many classrooms.

THE TEACHER'S ATTITUDE TOWARD PEERS AND PARENTS

The teacher is not isolated in his classroom. He interacts daily with fellow teachers, administrators and other school personnel, and he must often have very sensitive dealings with parents. It can happen that a teacher who is very gifted in his work with children has a disastrous professional life because of his uncontrolled attitudes toward the adults he encounters. However, most teachers do not have significantly different attitudes toward adults than they would toward children possessing the same characteristics. Therefore, much of what we have already said about the teacher's attitudes toward himself and toward children also applies to his attitudes toward peers and parents.

Authority. The teacher's attitude toward those who represent authority (ordinarily administrators, but for prospective teachers the university supervisor or the cooperating teacher) is often a source of conflict. A teacher may find it hard to be himself while dealing with people who outrank him in position or prestige, though he may feel perfectly comfortable with people who are his equals or in a lesser position. Sometimes a teacher finds that he

---

[21] Martin Haberman, "The Teaching Behavior of Successful Interns," *Journal of Teacher Education* 16 (June 1965): 215–220.

yields too readily to demands from others, especially those in positions of authority, and as a result feels guilty about complying rather than standing on his own convictions. When this occurs, the result is often a continuing undercurrent of resentment toward the person making a request.

These responses to authority are dysfunctional in that they impede communication and understanding. A teacher must examine his reactions to persons in authority positions and strive to overcome predispositions to hostility or anxiety unwarranted by reality.

Competition. Some teachers develop a strong drive to compete with other teachers for recognition from both authority figures and students. They strive to have the best lesson plans, to be the "most popular teacher" or to maintain the friendliest relationship with the administration. Such persons are striving to be recognized and rewarded. As a result of this attitude, they sometimes cut themselves off from much-needed help and severely limit their ability to be of help to others. They are unable to recognize the need for cooperation and sharing of ideas for the benefit of both staff and students.

Superiority and Prejudice. One attitude which never fails to cause trouble for the teacher is a feeling of superiority to his fellow teachers and the parents of his students. He may feel intellectually superior to his colleagues or socially superior to his students' parents, or both. Some teachers simply have little tolerance for people who differ from them in values, cultural background or economic status and, as a result, treat others with disdain and contempt, rather than patience and respect. Consider the following description of a teacher's meeting with lower-class Negro parents who have come to the school to lodge a complaint about their child being teased:

... the point was made by the Reading Teacher that this little girl actually was not so much teased by other kids as she was something of a troublemaker herself. It happened that this was not the truth . . . . The Reading Teacher then delivered an excellent and persuasive assessment of the little girl's incorrect behavior and she was so persuasive that the child ended up by apologizing to the Reading Teacher for all of the things that she had done wrong.
    . . . The parents come up with a just and proper reason to place blame, and they *get* it instead. Up they come angry and with proper outrage. Off they go, humbled, sad and weakly, having as it were apologized for the stupid thing they've tried to obtain. The look of embarrassed humility.[22]

Had the father been a lawyer or doctor, the scenario described above would undeniably not have taken place. Feelings of personal superiority can cause teachers to treat people in an offensive and humiliating manner.

---

[22] Jonathan Kozol, *Death at an Early Age* (Boston: Houghton Mifflin, 1967), p. 92. Reprinted by permission of the publisher.

This section is short because our message is simple—it is most important, whatever subject matter you teach, that you feel *enthusiasm* for it. Just as students can usually discern the teacher's attitude toward them, they are also very sensitive to the teacher's attitude toward the subject matter. One of the most striking characteristics of the excellent teacher is her enthusiasm for what she is teaching or "facilitating." The bored teacher conveys her feeling to the students—and who can blame them for failing to get excited if the teacher, who knows more about the subject than they do, doesn't find it engaging?

Some teachers find it difficult to feel enthusiasm for a curriculum they haven't constructed themselves, or don't identify with or don't want to teach. The surest way to guarantee that the teacher is enthusiastic about what he is teaching is to allow him to teach what he is enthusiastic about. And we do not mean this as a mere play on words. We would much rather see an enthusiastic teacher teaching Turkish military history or macramé than an uninspired teacher teaching Shakespeare.

One of the reasons we advocate the development of new curricula which concentrate on the problems of mankind, rather than the traditional disciplines, is that we believe most teachers can generate more interest and enthusiasm for problems dealing with mankind's survival than for mathematics or history *per se.* We also believe that students will feel more enthusiasm for this kind of curriculum. The teaching profession is filled with individuals who don't care about what they are teaching and don't care much more about the students. As one student put it, "Teachers should be more enthusiastic about their subject. There is nothing worse than sitting in a lesson knowing full well that the teacher is dying to get rid of you and rush back to the staff-room to have her cup of tea."[23] A thirteen-year-old boy expressed himself similarly: "I feel there is nothing like a teacher's enthusiasm for his subject to make learning a pleasure, and I am sure that a computer cannot show enthusiasm."[24]

Or, in the words of a teacher, ". . . the main hazard a teacher runs is to get bored and complaisant. He teaches the same things the same way and pretty soon all of the kids begin to look alike, too."[25]

Don't allow yourself to be pressured into teaching something you care little about. Make sure you have a positive attitude toward the subject you teach. Enthusiasm—if the teacher has it, life in the classroom can be exciting. If it is missing, there is little hope the students will learn much of significance.

---

[23] Edward Blishen, ed., *The School That I'd Like* (Harmondsworth, England: Penguin Books, 1969), p. 141.

[24] *Ibid.,* p. 143.

[25] Myron Brenton, *What's Happened to Teacher?* (New York: Coward-McCann, 1970), p. 147.

WHAT SUBJECT-MATTER KNOWLEDGE DOES THE TEACHER NEED?

The prospective teacher's subject-matter preparation can be seen as having two facets: study of the content of the discipline itself, and familiarity with the knowledge derived from it to be taught to the pupil.[26] In some fields, such as biology, the discipline is coterminous with the subject to be taught; other teaching fields, such as social studies, draw on many disciplines. In all fields, though, the knowledge to be taught is less extensive and advanced than the content of college disciplinary courses; the content of the school curriculum is selected from the available knowledge on the basis of the students' prior learning and the limitations of time. This is one reason why expertise in a discipline is not a guarantee of success at teaching the same subject at the elementary or high-school level. Another is that, in addition to the two kinds of subject-matter preparation described above, the teacher must possess *knowledge about knowledge.* By this we mean sufficient perspective on a subject to be able to analyze and convey its elements, logic, possible uses, social biases and relevance to the needs of the students.

We have assumed that the educated man is one who *knows;* yet *knowing* about literature may give one little sense of human tragedy or of belonging to humanity, little compassion. Knowing some science—let us say physics—may do little to help one sense the spirit of science. If we really believe in a liberal education, we must be more concerned with what students are and are becoming than with what they know and are learning in fact and skill. This does not mean that knowledge is unimportant but rather that the true teacher sees knowledge as a means, not as an end.[27]

It is precisely this concern for the uses of knowledge which most teachers lack.

Let's turn to the teacher's preparation in the disciplines which will comprise his teaching field. Most teacher education programs draw heavily on the disciplines. We consider training in specific disciplines as essential to a teacher's general education as it is to that of a doctor or a lawyer; and we are not advocating the total dissolution of disciplinary study. However, we feel that one of the major faults of existing teacher education programs is that the disciplinary approach fails to prepare teachers for the second facet of subject-matter preparation—the knowledge to be taught to the pupil. For instance, a teacher who majored in mathematics might find that his college courses, however rigorous, simply didn't prepare him to teach arithmetic or algebra. The mathematics courses required of a prospective teacher probably differ little from those prescribed for a mathematics major planning on a

---

[26] The authors are indebted to B. O. Smith, author of *Teachers for the Real World,* for many of the ideas expressed in this section.

[27] Ernest O. Melby, "The Contagion of Liberal Education, *Journal of Teacher Education* 18 (Summer 1967): 135.

Henry David Thoreau (1817–1862)

Henry David Thoreau, the American writer, naturalist and dissenter, spent a relatively short period of his life as a teacher. In the opening chapter of *Walden,* he writes, "I have thoroughly tried schoolkeeping. As I did not teach for the good of my fellow-man, but simply for a livelihood, this was a failure." Although Thoreau was passionately interested in education, he quickly recognized that he was not personally suited to teach in conventional schools.

Nevertheless, education remained one of his absorbing preoccupations. Thoreau thought of his entire life, and particularly the twenty-six months he spent at Walden Pond, as an educating act, undertaken not only to teach himself how to live but also as an example to his fellow men who had lost the art of living.

After graduating from Harvard, Thoreau applied for and was appointed to a position as teacher in the Concord village school. He had not yet been teaching for two weeks when a church deacon came to complain about his class and to warn that if he did not apply the rod, he would spoil the school. The story is that the same afternoon Thoreau selected six male students at random, beat them and walked abruptly out of the school and to his lodgings to write a resignation.

The following year Thoreau and his brother John founded a school in Concord in which they could teach on their own terms. They began the year with four pupils, but the school was an instant success and they soon had as many students as they could handle.

Contrary to the common practice of the day, there was no corporal punishment in Thoreau's school; nevertheless, discipline was strict. One afternoon a week, the school went on a nature-study walk as a regular part of the curriculum. Here "the Captain of the Huckleberry party," as his friend Ralph Waldo Emerson called him, was in his element. A student later wrote that Thoreau could tame the fishes in the pond, feed the mice from his fingers and keep up a fire of conversation while birds lighted on his head and shoulders. Pupils were amazed to discover that he knew every spot where wildflowers grew and every sheltered nook where climbing ferns hid. They found Thoreau a winning combination of the Pied Piper, St. Francis of Assisi and Daniel Boone.

But this wonderful school was short-lived. After two years, John became ill and died. Henry was so deeply shaken by his brother's death that he made no effort to carry on the school.

Throughout his lifetime, Thoreau chided the schools, colleges and general populace for their failures to improve education. His favorite target was Harvard, because of the remote-from-life quality of its curriculum. He claimed astonishment when he was informed upon leaving college that he had studied navigation. "One turn about the harbor would have given me more knowledge than four years as a student," he wrote.

Thoreau set great store by the educative powers of physical labor. He argued that students should not play at life, or merely study it while the community supported them, but should work at and live through a profession from beginning to end. He proposed that colleges be built by students and teachers, not by contractors and laborers.

Thoreau was also concerned with the lack of educational opportunities for adults. He pioneered the cause of adult education, becoming enraged when the town of Concord spent sixteen thousand dollars on a town hall and nothing to educate adults. He saw no reason why the townspeople could not spend less for big barns and set aside something for works of art, journals, books and scientific instruments. Every village, he said, should have a fine museum.

Thoreau was an ardent ecologist, convinced that nature should be the source of education. He begged townspeople to preserve the rivers, waterfalls and meadows, both for their beauty and because he believed them more capable of educating than hired teachers and school systems. He admired American Indians for conceiving of education as learning to live within nature. The Indian's life, he suggested, was in harmony with the nature of man and the universe.

For all his praise of Indians, however, Thoreau never proposed that man give up booklearning. He imagined education as the process of achieving the best of both worlds: intimacy with nature and with the finest creations of civilization, the classics.

career in industry. As a rule—despite the involvement of many scholars in the curriculum reform movement—university professors are not concerned about preparing teachers to teach the subject matter that elementary- and secondary-school students are expected to learn. Most college courses are designed to prepare students for more advanced study within the discipline. The methods courses offered in schools of education represent an attempt—not always successful—to remedy this situation. In short, much of what the prospective teacher learns from his study of the disciplines is not taught to children, and thus it is not directly applicable to teaching. This is particularly true for the elementary school teacher, who is called upon to teach content virtually ignored by the academic departments of the universities.

In Chapter Three, we expressed our belief that the discipline-oriented approach to the public school curriculum must be replaced by a curriculum organized around societal problems and the concerns and interests of the students. If a teacher's college education should include the study of various disciplines, and if the disciplines in themselves are inadequate preparation for teaching youngsters, what then do we propose? The teacher education program should offer opportunities for prospective teachers to develop curriculum units apt to be of interest to students, drawing on concepts and approaches from several disciplines. In addition, the courses taken by the prospective teacher should serve as models of the issue-oriented inquiry approach, thus requiring the prospective teacher to experience the same mode of learning he wishes his students to experience.

The mode of study should focus on problem-solving, with the prospective teachers themselves assuming a major share of the responsibility for analyzing the problems, selecting and organizing the materials and carrying on discussion. Through this process they would learn to think through problems on their own and would acquire the skills necessary to identify and locate relevant materials. By experiencing the same kinds of difficulties that their own students will be likely to encounter, prospective teachers would be better prepared to deal effectively with them. "To be prepared in the subject matter of instruction is to know the content to be taught and how the content can be related to the interest and experience of children and youths. To prepare the teacher in this subject matter will require courses oriented to the teacher's need for knowledge that can be tied in with the life of children and youths rather than discipline-oriented courses."[28]

Translating the content of discipline-oriented courses into a more appropriate mode of instruction will be a difficult undertaking. But we are convinced that allowing the prospective teacher to organize materials to focus on meeting the students "where they're at" will make the job of translation easier.

We thus urge that the prospective teacher know intimately the content he is to teach, and that this content be centered around man's physical and

---

[28] Smith, *Teachers for the Real World,* pp. 121–122.

social problems and issues relevant to the students' lives. It is equally important for the teacher to be well-versed in the disciplines from which the instructional subject matter is derived. In Smith's words, "The first is necessary for teaching anything at all. The second supplies a depth of knowledge essential to the teacher's feeling of intellectual security and his ability to handle instructional content with greater understanding."[29] Finally, a teacher must have knowledge about knowledge as a whole, so that he can bring perspective and a command of the logical operations used in manipulating information to any subject-matter content. These three types of knowledge, we believe, are essential for the effective teacher.

DISCUSSION QUESTIONS

1. Do you agree with Peter Drucker's statement that "the graduate of one of these institutions knows or can do [nothing] that the seventeen-year-old high school girl of yesterday did not know or do when she started to teach elementary school in the rural midwest"? Try to construct an effective argument for or against it, using evidence from Chapters Two and Five.
2. Which of the theoretical principles listed on p. 187 strike you as simple common sense? Which are new to you? If any surprise you, to what do you attribute the surprise? Which seem most important to you as a prospective teacher? For what kind of theoretical knowledge do you feel the greatest need?
3. Which of the skills listed on p. 192 seem most important to you? What skills would you add to the list? subtract?
4. We say on p. 206 that teachers' low expectations of poor children can be changed by providing proof that their ability is not inherently inferior to that of other children. What might constitute such proof?
5. Is there any group or type of people toward whom you have negative feelings? Can you identify the basis of those feelings? Do you want to change them? How might you try?
6. Carl Rogers argues for a teacher who "is *being* himself" and shows his feelings. Do you agree? Have you known any teachers who did so? Do you think children can cope with any reaction from the teacher as long as it is honestly expressed? Do you think this kind of teaching requires any particular prior training?
7. Analyze the five factors which Haberman found to characterize successful interns (p. 208). Which seem to you the result of training? which of individual attitudes? which a combination of the two?
8. Do you agree that it is preferable for an enthusiastic teacher to teach an irrelevant subject than for an uninspired teacher to teach a crucial sub-

---

[29] *Ibid.,* p. 122.

ject? What implications do you see in this remark? On what assumptions about teachers, students and subject matter is it based?

FOR FURTHER READING

Borton, Terry. *Reach, Touch, and Teach.* New York: McGraw-Hill, 1970. Focuses on the affective concerns of teachers and students. Borton believes that what a student learns in school and what he eventually becomes are significantly influenced by how he feels about himself and the world outside. Thus, the teacher's goal should be to help each student increase his understanding of his feelings, and expand that self-awareness by utilizing his intellectual resources.

Fuchs, Estelle. *Teachers Talk.* New York: Doubleday, 1969. A collection of teachers' statements about themselves, schools and learning. The author analyzes these teacher statements from the perspective of an anthropologist.

Holt, John. *How Children Fail.* New York: Pitman, 1964. Holt insists that schools often teach children to think badly, to give up a more natural way of thinking in favor of one that does not work for them and that we rarely use ourselves. As a result, he maintains, most of them get humiliated, frightened and discouraged. Very readable and enjoyable.

Holt, John. *How Children Learn.* New York: Pitman, 1967. In the sequel to *How Children Fail,* Holt tries to describe situations in which effective learning occurs. The reader will take away new perceptions, techniques and, possibly, even a new philosophy.

Jersild, Arthur. *When Teachers Face Themselves.* New York: Teachers College Press, 1955. Jersild's major thesis is that before teachers can understand their students, they must understand themselves. He develops a case for this premise, followed by suggestions as to how teachers can go about better understanding themselves.

Neill, A. S. *Summerhill.* New York: Hart, 1961. A personal account of one man's philosophy of education, based on freedom for the learner, and of the school he established in England to implement his philosophy. For those concerned with expanding the student's freedom and allowing him choice in the direction of his education, this book is a must.

Passow, A. Harry, ed. *Education in Depressed Areas.* New York: Teachers College Press, 1963. A collection of research-based articles that focus on culturally disadvantaged learners and their special educational difficulties. Written by leading sociologists, educators, psychologists and teachers, the selections cover such topics as teaching techniques, strategies and devices which appear effective in this area of education.

Raths, Louis E.; Harmin, Merril; and Simon, Sidney B. *Values and Teaching.* Columbus, Ohio: Charles E. Merrill, 1966. This very useful book presents techniques to help the teacher assist students in clarifying their own values. Focuses not on instilling values, but on helping students recognize how the values they hold influence their decision-making.

Rogers, Carl. *Freedom to Learn.* Columbus, Ohio: Charles E. Merrill, 1969. The major theme is that students can be trusted to learn and to enjoy learning when a facilitative person creates a responsive environment and encourages responsible participation in the selection of goals and ways of reaching them. Includes case studies of three facilitators at three levels of education, all of whom have, in quite different ways, provided their students with freedom to learn.

Sanders, Norris. *Classroom Questions: What Kinds?* New York: Harper and Row, 1966. Designed to help teachers develop the ability to ask questions that are not limited to factual recall. Through the use of discussion and examples, the author helps the reader recognize how different types of questions can stimulate various levels of thought processes on the part of students.

Schutz, William C. *Joy.* New York: Grove Press, 1967. Focuses on helping people expand their awareness through a number of theories and exercises. The book emphasizes openness and honesty and assumes that joy will result when our feelings are expressed and explored.

Smith, B. O. *Teachers for the Real World.* Washington, D.C.: American Association of Colleges for Teacher Education, 1969. Focuses on the knowledge, skills and attitudes teachers need to possess.

FILMS

The Best of the Real: Teaching in the Inner City Elementary School (Center for Urban Education, 1st film 28 min., 2nd film 22 min., 3rd film 40 min., all 16mm) A series of three films documenting the classroom work and techniques of a New York City fifth-grade teacher who was identified as "effective" by students, teachers, supervisors and parents. The first film shows him teaching an elementary algebra class; the second, a humorous short poem, and the third records an analysis of his teaching techniques.

Children Without (Mass Media Ministries, 16mm, b&w, 30 min., 1964) This film documents the efforts of teachers in a school in an economically substandard area of Detroit. Through a dramatization of the experiences of one little girl who attends the school, the viewer is shown how these teachers are concerned not only with the mental development of their students but also with their emotional, psychological, social and physical needs.

Education for Psychological Maturity (Indiana University Audio-Visual Center, 16mm, b&w, 29 min.) Featured personality in this film from the "Philosophies of Education Series" is Arthur Jersild, Professor in the Department of Psychological Foundations and Services at Teachers College,

Columbia University. The film explores theories presented in Dr. Jersild's book, *When Teachers Face Themselves.*

Four Teachers (National Film Board of Canada, 16mm, b&w, 59 min., 1961) Although a little dated, this film presents an interesting comparison of classrooms, student-teacher relationships and of the importance placed on education in four parts of the world—Japan, Poland, Puerto Rico and Canada, with intermittent comments by a university professor and a grade-school teacher.

I Have an Egg (Contemporary/McGraw-Hill, 16 mm, b&w, 15 min., 1966, Poland) An awardwinning documentary film about an extraordinarily patient teacher and group of blind children. The students are being taught how to answer a very difficult question using only the tactile sense: define an egg.

Lloyd Reynold/William Geer (Indiana University Audio-Visual Center, 16mm, b&w, 59 min., NET) This film from the "Men Who Teach" series presents an interesting comparison between two people with very individual teaching styles. Portraits of William Geer, lecturer in modern civilization and history at the University of North Carolina, and Lloyd Reynold, art historian at Reed College, are built from scenes of their lectures, their methods of counseling students, their philosophies and interviews with present and former students.

My Name Is Children (Indiana University Audio-Visual Center, 16mm, b&w, 1967, 60 min., NET) This film presents scenes of children and teachers at Nova Elementary School in Fort Lauderdale, Florida, to show how one school uses an "inquiry approach" to motivate students. A montage of activities is accompanied by natural, spontaneous dialogue by students and teachers.

The Prime of Miss Jean Brodie (Films, Inc., 16mm, color, 116 min.) Although it takes place in Scotland in the Thirties, this film deals with relevant and provocative issues in contemporary society: the relationship between teachers and students, and the responsibility of a teacher toward her students.

Sir! Sir! (Contemporary/McGraw-Hill, 16mm, b&w, 20:23 min.) Documents an interesting role-reversal between students and teachers in a Toronto classroom. This film, which grew out of a creative drama class, portrays what happened when teachers occupied students' desks and students became teachers.

Who Teaches Them (Indiana University Audio-Visual Center, 16mm, b&w, 30 min., NET) Part of the NET "Radical American Series," this film examines through on-location reports and interviews the differences between schools with a radically left-wing or right-wing orientation. Among the people interviewed are the director and faculty of the Free University of New York; the President of Harding College, Searcy, Arkansas; and the Dean of Rampart College, Larkspur, Colorado.

Abraham Maslow: Self-Actualization (Big Sur Recordings, 3.75 ips, ½ track, mono, 60 min.) A one-hour tape made at the Esalen Institute in which Maslow defines "self-actualization," discusses his own extensive research on the motivations of self-actualized people and makes observations on the "business organization."

R. D. Laing: Politics as Experience (Big Sur Recordings, 3.75 ips, ½ track, mono, 60 min., 1970) This tape, excerpted from a longer discussion, presents Laing's views on the "binds" and "double binds" which can prevent a person from knowing who he really is.

Scott Buchanan, Teacher (Center for the Study of Democratic Institutions, #473, 3.75 ips, ½ track, 31:24 min., 1969) A group discussion with Scott Buchanan, New Program Director at St. John's College in Annapolis, Maryland. Through reminiscences on his life's work as a Socratic teacher, Buchanan explains his view of teaching and of the teacher's role in the learning process.

A Sixth Grade Teacher Reports: Two Approaches (National Education Association, 3.75 ips, reel or cassette format, 14 min.) One section of an hour-long tape on *The Teacher,* this report tells how a sixth-grade teacher uses both "hard" and "soft" approaches with her students in order to help them understand themselves and each other in relation to society.

Refer to Appendix for distributors' addresses.

6　How Do People Become Teachers?

Becoming a teacher can be compared to sculpting a work of art from a piece of stone. The difference is that the prospective teacher is both the sculptor and the stone. He begins with a vision of what he wants to be and then sets to work transforming the vision into a reality. The process takes an understanding of the material with which one is working—the self—and the tools at one's disposal. It takes long hours of chipping away at and smoothing surfaces. It takes commitment. Perhaps this comparison is unduly poetic. We are using it, however, to highlight two points fundamental to this chapter: that becoming a teacher is an active, dynamic process, and that you bear the responsibility for the kind of teacher you become.

The task of the teacher is to show that time is limited, that in perspective human existence can be condensed into a few climactic moments. Man is a product of limitation and yet always yearns for transcendence. To know our limitations is the foundation of education; to transcend them is the vocation of the teacher *(emphasis added).* Frederick Mayer, The Great Teachers *(New York: Citadel Press, 1967), p. 18.*

In Chapter Five we discussed our ideas about the special skills, competencies, knowledge and attitudes the effective teacher should possess. The competencies we prescribed can be considered a blueprint or, to continue the teacher-sculptor analogy, a rough outline of the shape of the potential work of art. This chapter will focus on *the process of becoming,* the process of making yourself a teacher. To make yourself the kind of teacher you want to be, you need to know yourself and to know what tools are available to help you and how they can be used most effectively.

LEARNING TO BE A TEACHER

When a college student enters a teacher training program, or begins taking courses for certification as a teacher, he is much further along in his training to be a teacher than he ordinarily realizes. He has been in training since he was in diapers, and already knows an immense amount about the field he has chosen to enter. Because most of this training is unstructured or informal, however, we mistakenly tend not to take it seriously. Some aspects of this informal curriculum, as well as the formal curriculum, will be examined below. The major emphasis of this chapter, however, will be on teacher attitudes and behaviors, rather than on the content or subject matter one teaches. As you read about the portion of the informal curriculum that is already behind you, ask yourself, "What effect has it had on me?" and "How have these experiences shaped me and my vision of what a good teacher is?"

INGRAINED HUMAN TENDENCIES

It seems to be a natural human tendency to teach one another. Humanity has survived because we have this special capacity to pass on what we know, and no one is required to discover everything for himself. Man taught man not to fool around with huge furry cats with sharp teeth and blood-stained claws—unless he carried a heavy club or a sharp stick. Man taught man how to rub sticks together and make a life-preserving fire. Man taught man that he could make marks on stones to represent words and ideas. And so on and on.

From the time we can crawl we are constantly being taught by other humans. "That's a no-no!" "You can hurt yourself putting the steel nail file in the electric socket." "You'll never grow up to be a pro football player if you don't eat your turnips." "Say 'thank you.'" "Nice girls simply don't use language like that!" (The rationality or usefulness of what we are taught is sometimes, in retrospect, open to question.) In this way, children learn to respect electricity, eat their vegetables and curb their language (at least in the presence of adults), and they also learn to be teachers. Have you ever observed three- or four-year-old children playing together? Much of their play is imitative of their parents. One child tells another how to do something, or scolds him for leaving his toys around, mimicking the tone and words his own parents use to instruct him. The child-teacher has learned both his parents' message and the teaching medium.

Thus, human beings have survived as a result of their deeply-ingrained habit of correcting one another, reporting what they know, moralizing and responding to the behavior of others.[1] These behaviors precisely duplicate much of what teachers do in classrooms. Teaching skills, then, are acquired by the vast majority of people in the normal flux and flow of life. They are lodged in the very marrow of the human race.

TEACHER-WATCHING

Teacher-watching is a major pastime in American schools. By the time we graduate from college we have spent sixteen or seventeen years observing sixty or seventy teachers. Since most of us have experienced traditional teacher-centered schooling, with the teacher invariably facing the students and all the students facing the teacher, it is difficult to avoid being a teacher-watcher. Teacher-watching is a variety of people-watching, one of mankind's most enduring pleasures—but it is often undertaken with more intensity since it frequently contributes to a student's very survival in school. Trying to understand or "psych out" the teacher can be more crucial (and occasionally more interesting) than mastery of the subject matter. "I just can't figure out my history teacher. What does that man want?"

The result of this none-too-casual teacher-watching is difficult to determine precisely. But when we consider the amounts of time students devote to analysis of their teachers' personalities, motivations, instructional methodologies and general effectiveness, the suspicion grows that its impact is massive. One obvious effect of watching so many teachers for so long is that the prospective teacher compiles a highly detailed mental catalogue of the

---

[1] J. M. Stephens, "Research in the Preparation of Teachers: Background Factors that Must be Considered," in *Psychology in Teacher Preparation,* ed. John Herbert and David P. Ausubel (Toronto, Ont.: The Ontario Institute for Studies in Education Monograph Series, no. 5, 1969), pp. 55–61.

Photo courtesy of Harvard Graduate School of Education.

teacher behaviors he finds acceptable and unacceptable. He has stored up observations of methods and motivational approaches. He has collected techniques of handling children which he considers workable and with which he feels comfortable. Although it is unusual, we are sure there are other cases like that of the young third grade teacher who had decided when she was in the third grade that she wanted to be a teacher, and had never wavered from that desire. Having made her career choice at eight years, she consciously spent the next thirteen years preparing to teach her own third grade class. And, as she reported, she had plenty of good and bad teaching models on which to draw. But even those who decide on a career in teaching during their last year of college have been seriously engaged in teacher-watching and have stored away countless observations of life in classrooms and student and teacher behavior.

MEDIA MODELS

"Who's your favorite teacher?"
"Mr. Dixon—of *Room 222.*"

The American people's growing interest in the public schools is manifested, among other ways, in the emergence of the teacher as a stock character in the mass media. The movies have given us *To Sir, With Love, Up the Down Staircase, The Prime of Miss Jean Brodie, Kes* and *Getting Straight.* On TV we had *Mr. Novak* a few years ago, and more recently the *Bill Cosby Show, Room 222* and the popular preschool program *Sesame Street.* Nightowls can still see *Good Morning, Miss Dove* and *The Black-*

board Jungle on the late show. These media teachers are providing us a new set of role models, whom we experience with a different kind of intensity from that we invest in "live" teacher-watching. For one thing, media teachers are almost uniformly immensely attractive young people, and the viewer gains a much more intimate knowledge of their private lives than he does of the lives of his "real" teachers. Second, they are usually models of what is traditionally considered good teaching. Third, dramatized classroom situations are more intense than reality, and thus often tend to make a deep impression. And finally, the media teacher can be observed dispassionately because there is no need to psych him out for survival purposes. One can relate to and learn from the media teacher without complications.

The impact of media teachers on the student of teaching has not been studied but, unfettered by facts, we will make some tentative observations: first, the fact that some media teachers have become culture heroes may help to raise the status of teaching and underline its importance. Second, media teachers rarely perform the traditional information-dispenser function of the teacher. Third, media teachers are often shown responding to the emotional and social needs of children. Fourth, media teachers are portrayed as warm human beings who fall in love, enjoy life and, especially, gain deep satisfaction from their work—a view of teachers rarely available in the classroom.

ED COURSES

During the Colonial period, and well into the late nineteenth century, a person who wanted to teach simply declared himself a teacher. A high school or college diploma was considered nice to have but in no way necessary. If you could do readin', writin' and cipherin', there was sure to be a school waiting to hire you. The self-declared teacher competed for a job and, if he got it, continued teaching as long as his clients were willing to pay. Today, however, the nation's institutions of higher education have taken on responsibility for initially training teachers. While this is a well-entrenched practice, it is essentially an arbitrary one. As a society, we could conceivably turn over the job of teacher education to the public schools, private industry or even to public corporations.

By and large, higher education institutions discharge their responsibility for the professional training of teachers through two channels: education courses, which will be discussed here, and practice teaching. At their best, education courses prepare teachers to translate into practice knowledge and principles derived from such disciplines as psychology, philosophy, sociology and anthropology. At their worst, education courses offer useless and outdated theories or a potpourri of unrelated anecdotes about schools and children.

Each college or university with a department or school of education offers an array of education courses, some required and some elective, reflecting its own judgments and those of the state legislature on how a teacher should be trained. As a minimum, though, the teaching candidate must take the sequence of courses which leads to licensing or certification. After successfully passing the required education courses, including practice teaching, and graduating from college, the student is eligible for state certification.[2]

Education courses are normally embedded in what is called the professional sequence, which means, very simply, that they are designed to prepare one for work as a professional teacher. Like courses in medicine, architecture, baking or computer programming, they are vocational. Not all of the material presented, however, is immediately usable or relevant to "nitty-gritty" situations. Courses in the history of education are a case in point. Such courses rarely help the teacher who is struggling to find material that will interest her students or who is trying to find ways to get the sullen kid in the back of the room to put aside the chip on his shoulder. It does, however, let the prospective teacher know where her profession has been and what its accomplishments and failures have been. And it may, too, save the teacher from, in effect, reinventing the wheel.

Most of the content of a teacher education program, however, should have obvious transfer value to one's future teaching situation. When students fail to use their courses for that purpose, it is usually for two reasons. First, they are so familiar with teachers and schools that they underestimate the difficulty of teaching well. This is like the boy who sat at the end of a pier all summer watching other boys swim. Finally, convinced he "had it," he jumped in—and, of course, drowned. Education courses are like the swimming lessons the boy should have taken.

A second and related problem is inherent in the nature of courses themselves. We frequently take courses because they sound interesting, or we have heard the instructor is great, or we are required to take them or we don't know what else to do with our tuition money. We "take the course" as if we were taking a pill. While this is always unfortunate, it can have serious consequences for the future professional. Just as no one wants to be treated by a doctor who sat passively through a course in the malady afflicting him, no one wants to send his child to the class of a teacher who inertly and obediently took the course in reading instruction. What we are somewhat laboriously trying to point out is that there can be minimal transfer value from just "taking a course." A much more active approach is needed. The best way for this to happen is for you to go into a course with your own questions about teaching and learning. Incidentally, some teacher education programs are introducing their students into the schools as aides and observers at the beginning of their teacher training experience. One purpose of this approach

---

[2] A word of warning: We live in a very mobile society, and many teachers prepare in one state to teach in another. Efforts are being made to establish national certification standards, but at present what fulfills requirements in one state may not be satisfactory in another. Therefore, it is good to know where you hope to teach.

To erect fine buildings and to seek to meet the needs and abilities of all individuals who desire to avail themselves of the opportunities so generously offered without providing teachers with qualifications commensurate with the ideal is a sham. I. L. Kandell, quoted in Alma S. Wittlin, "The Teacher," in The Professions in America, ed. Kenneth S. Lynn (Boston: Houghton Mifflin, 1965), p. 94.

is to give the students an opportunity to generate their own questions and to recognize their own "felt needs." A course is much more likely to be valuable to a student if he is using it to solve his own questions and problems. Regrettably, too few people approach education courses (and others) with this active posture.

REAL TEACHING

When we leave education courses behind and enter the classroom, we move from words and personal fantasies to real children and hard realities. The major difference between the traditional ways people learn to be teachers and teaching itself is the difference between passive and active learning. First you observe and think and read about teaching; then you find yourself actively engaged in the process, struggling to respond to your unique situation in a constructive way and working to master many aspects of your role all at once.

Universities ordinarily treat student teaching as a course for which there is credit and some evaluation procedure. The student teacher is supervised by the university staff and a master teacher from the school. For students it represents an opportunity to test out their ideas and previously untried skills in the real world. For the supervising teachers it is an opportunity to monitor their own profession, screening out those who might be harmful to children —the whackos—and those who don't measure up to minimum standards— the incompetents.

The first few years in the classroom are also periods of intense learning. This is especially true of the first year of teaching, which differs from student teaching in that the beginning teacher has full responsibility for her class. Although she is typically supervised by an administrator or department chairman, she is normally on her own. She has to start from scratch, setting the goals, procedures and tone for the year. Most first-year teachers learn as much about themselves as they do about children. Many struggle with the role of authority figure. Some find the search for appropriate and teachable material all-consuming. Others devote the majority of their time and energy to questions of methodology. And still others stride through the first year with few serious problems. The problems commonly encountered by beginning teachers are the subject of Chapter Seven.

Photo by Donald Patterson
through Stock, Boston.

TEACHERS

The first real teaching encounters are periods of testing. Primarily, the teaching candidate is testing whether or not he is going to gain satisfaction as a teacher. Then there is a whole range of testing, from alternative ways of handling content to different styles of leadership with one's students. As at no other time in his teaching career, the beginner is continually testing approaches, evaluating what he is doing and refining or discarding on the basis of this feedback. It is a long process, becoming a teacher. And, as we shall see next, it is not without flaws.

LEARNING HOW *NOT* TO BE A TEACHER

We have spent the preceding several pages pointing out how much teacher training you have already had. Teaching tendencies are ingrained in you simply as a consequence of growing up in our culture. You have watched dozens of teachers and stored up countless techniques and biases. You have been exposed to media teachers who may have prompted you to look at teaching and schools in a new light. Education courses and real teaching encounters still lie ahead of most of you. It would be wonderful if each of these experiences contributed beneficially to your professional development and each built on each until you achieved a state of flawless excellence. Or if, to put it another way, as a result of these learnings "every day in every way we become better and better." As most of you are profoundly aware, things don't very often work that way.

INGRAINED HUMAN TENDENCIES

The same experiences from which people learn to be teachers teach them how NOT to be teachers. Or, more precisely, how to be nonteachers. In other words, each of the sources of knowledge about teaching has drawbacks or counterproductive aspects. We need to be aware of these limitations if we are to correct for them, and thus gain more than we lose from each experience. For instance, our ingrained tendency to teach others—that is, to moralize, tell what we know, criticize, correct and volunteer right answers—gives rise to behavior which may have been very appropriate to a relatively static society. At a time when there was less to learn, and when knowledge expanded less rapidly, these teaching tendencies were more in tune with student needs. Now, however, the task of school is to help children live in the twenty-first century. And since there is no guarantee that the knowledge the teacher possesses will be accurate or useful in thirty years, students can no longer be regarded as empty vessels to be filled by the teacher's words and moralizing. Students need to learn to think independently, to work both independently and cooperatively and to adopt a fluid approach to learning. They must be helped by the teacher to become liberated human beings who possess the ability to evaluate new information and new situations and come up with independent solutions. Students need to be much more involved in their own learning and they should be learning skills which transfer from one situation to another, rather than time-bound facts. What we have, then, is a severe conflict between students' needs and our own ingrained tendencies to impose our knowledge, biases, morals and answers. Normally this is done without giving children the opportunity and, especially, the skills to properly evaluate what they are learning from us . . . and from the rest of the people in society. If the schools do not develop individuals with the skills and habits of independent judgment and action, they will not be able to cope with life. If they don't cope, they are not free. If they are not free, they (we) are slaves. This is a fundamental issue. Our job as teachers is to free people from ignorance. But ignorance can no longer be defined as simple lack of information or awareness. Access to television, magazines, newspapers and books is making that kind of ignorance obsolete. Ignorance in a fluctuating world is the inability to process information. (For instance, you have or will soon have more than enough information on teaching as a career. The crucial question is, "Do I have the ability to process this information and come up with a good decision?") What this means is that in order to be effective teachers we must in a sense suppress our ingrained tendencies to teach—in the most primitive sense of that word.

A fundamental problem of modern man is that he is trapped in outmoded forms and concepts. Politicians spend huge amounts of public funds on roads for individual cars, when it has been self-evident for a decade that such action is disastrous and that we need better mass transportation. At a time when our energies should be spent on finding ways for nations to live together in harmony, no government in the world has a Department or Ministry of Peace, and many spend massive sums on weapons of war. We have become prisoners of the way things used to be. The same thing happens to prospective teachers. Having sat in classrooms for sixteen or more years, we limit our definitions of what a school is, what a teacher is and what constitutes being educated to what we are familiar with. Perhaps what all of us who aspire to be teachers (and that very definitely includes the authors) need is new models of what it is to be a teacher.

TEACHER-WATCHING

Teacher-watching has its pitfalls too. It is not uncommon for a prospective secondary school teacher to model himself on a favorite college lecturer who can captivate three hundred people for ninety minutes at a time. He goes off to teach in secondary school hoping to duplicate the performances of his idol, and fails utterly because, first, he just isn't as fascinating or effective as his idol and, second, high school students have different tolerances and motivations than college students. Then there is the problem of the prospective teacher who admires all her mild and gentle former teachers, but who herself naturally exudes energy and enthusiasm. She may try to

August examples show that no limit can be set to the power of a teacher, but this is equally true in the other direction: no career can so nearly approach zero in its effect. Jacques Barzun.

deny her strengths in a misguided attempt to be something she is not. We may, too, have admired the wrong models. For instance, we may hope to emulate the very clever teacher who was so bright and humorous, but who wasted a tremendous amount of time drawing attention to himself and who controlled students with a sharp tongue.

It is worthwhile to acknowledge explicitly who our favorite teachers are and why we find them attractive. If we consciously choose to emulate a certain teacher, we need to think seriously about how such a choice is likely to affect our teaching. Will modeling myself after Mrs. Y or Mr. X enhance or undercut my strengths? Are our personalities similar? Where should I draw the line between myself and my model?

MEDIA MODELS

Media models don't pose as serious a problem as real teachers can, but they may teach us things about teachers and schools which should be quickly forgotten. The trouble with media models is that they are usually variations on Superman, disguised as a mild-mannered public school teacher. No matter what the problem, he plunges right in and saves the day for Western civilization. He throws himself into the lives of children with very little understanding of the situation. He knows no failure. He is a stranger to depression and insecurities. He easily strikes a balance between his family life and his professional life. He never makes a serious mistake that he simply has to live with. As a teacher, he is always up front running the show and dispensing wisdom. Great entertainment—maybe—but not the best model for us poor mortals who can't quite keep up with a speeding bullet.

Another shortcoming of media models is the conventional schools in which they perform. It seems to be a basic tenet of the mass entertainment industry that the characters can be idealized but the settings must be commonplace. If media schools have to be instantly recognizable to a mass audience, the result is that the media cannot use their programs to champion or even illustrate educational reform.

ED COURSES

Discussing education courses earlier in this chapter we wrote about *how not to learn* how to teach from education courses, that is, to be a passive recipient. Here we want to talk about the issue of how to learn *how not to teach* from education courses. Many students expect to learn how to teach from observing their education professors, whom they assume to be paragons of pedagogical finesse. Evidently they haven't heard about education professors who deliver impassioned lectures on the evils of the lecture, or about the professor who teaches Principles of Teaching and breaks every rule in the book.[3] Unfortunately, professors of education are just as frail and fallible in this regard as are other teachers.

Loss of perspective is another pitfall. Occasionally prospective teachers embrace a particular principle of teaching so fervently they lose their grip on common sense. For instance, a teacher who adopts the practice of verbally reinforcing or praising student participation in class ("That's an interesting answer, Sara. That's the kind of thinking we should have more of around here.") may overdo it. In excess, supposedly reinforcing statements become meaningless and even embarrassing to students ("You don't say much in this class, Ralph, but when you do, it's really a top-drawer contribution! Keep up the keen thinking!") A similar case is the elementary school teacher who, as a result of her education courses, is converted to teaching for problem-solving and commits herself to using that approach in her classroom. Things go relatively well until a girl asks to go to the washroom and the teacher tries to make a problem-solving session out of it. Remember . . . perspective.

A related issue is extravagant expectations for education courses. It is our view that teaching and learning are very complex phenomena, and that the training of teachers is a more massive task than is typically acknowledged. We find excessive the expectation that nonteachers will be transformed into superior teachers by six or eight courses. Think back for a moment to Chapter Five. To become the kind of teacher we described there requires the acquisition of considerable knowledge and a wide repertoire of skills and strategies. It calls for a good deal of behavior change in the prospective teacher. What many critics of education courses are really saying is that the magnitude of the task is such that it cannot be accomplished within the traditional course format. More on this later.

REAL TEACHING

"Experience is the best teacher." Maybe, but experience can also be a poor teacher, and teaching is no exception. Real teaching encounters, whether tutoring experiences or student teaching or the first years of full-time teaching, can have a negative effect on proficiency. The fact that poor teaching is not the exclusive province of the beginning teacher is proof enough of this point. The explanation is not that teachers get too little practice. If anything, teachers get too much practice. What is missing is knowledge-of-results, or *feedback*. Years ago the great learning theorist E. L. Thorndike,

---

[3] If you ever come across this elusive book, please send a copy to the authors.

in the process of formulating his "law of exercise," discovered that if the target was hidden from view people could throw darts over and over without improving their performance. The lack of feedback about where their darts were landing made self-correction impossible.

In this sense, dart-throwing seems to be analogous to teaching. Teachers receive relatively little feedback on their performance. Although colleges and universities employ supervisors for student teachers and school districts do so for beginning teachers, the cost prevents both institutions from providing as much supervision as they would like. Also, supervision is a difficult process which depends for its success on many variables.

The beginning teacher often has trouble making sense of the feedback he does get from his students, such as looks of attention or inattention, questions, responses to questions, and signs of confusion. For instance, it is common for neophyte teachers to be shocked and upset after giving their first test. They had been convinced by the looks on their students' faces and by the silence when they asked, "Do you understand? Are there any questions?" that their students really understood. What little feedback we receive may not be very good—in fact, it may seriously mislead us.

If the teacher does receive accurate feedback, and knows, for example, that the majority of her students are not learning subtraction or that three of her driver education students have racked up cars this week, what does she

Photo by Norman Hurst through Stock, Boston.

Raymond Fleming *(1919–1969)*

When Ray Fleming died, three days before Christmas in 1969, Palo Alto felt the loss. Ray taught American history at the local high school. He also taught his students, his colleagues and the community something about what it is to be black in a predominantly white society, and about what it means to be a man.

When he was still a young boy in South Carolina, both of Ray's parents died. A family friend in White Plains, New York sent for Ray and raised him. Ray wanted to become a labor arbitrator, but couldn't afford to go to college. Instead, he went to work, hoping to save enough to continue his education. However, World War II changed the course of Ray's life. He joined the Army and became a highly-decorated combat paratrooper.

Because many opportunities denied Ray as a black civilian were available to him as a soldier, he decided to stay in the military after the war. During his military career he married, rose to the rank of major, spent tours of duty in Japan, Korea, Germany and the Philippines and fathered four sons and a daughter. During the service Ray's desire for education became insatiable. He read constantly and took courses at nearby colleges whenever he was stationed in the United States. Finally, Ray earned his B.A. from the Munich branch of the University of Maryland. He was 42. Shortly afterward he retired from the military. His own struggle for education had given him a new vocation. He wanted to be a teacher.

Ray took his wife and family to California. He had been accepted in a graduate teacher education program at Stanford University, where he took courses in education and history and became a teaching intern at Palo Alto's Cubberley High School, one of California's fine secondary schools. At the end of a year he was certified as a teacher, earned a master's degree and was voted the school's most outstanding teacher. Ray was invited to stay on at Cubberley and since his frequently-uprooted family seemed settled, he decided to stay.

Ray Fleming was a passionate man dedicated to rational investigation. He used history as a vehicle to teach his students how to think about the world and about themselves. Ray was always putting books in students' hands and urging them to dig beneath the surface. From his study of history and his own experience as a black man, he knew how standardized textbooks can distort reality, and stressed the value of original sources and the danger of unquestioningly accepting someone else's synthesized view. He worked to develop a spirit of inquiry and a capacity for independent investigation in his students. He presented students with evidence, frequently inconsistent or conflicting, and forced them to come up with their own rational evaluations.

Ray was soon made department chairman and, although he had many obligations at home and at school, he felt a duty to the larger community. He was active on the Human Relations Council. He served on an advisory board for the Office of Economic Opportunity. He spoke frequently to groups throughout California about the inequality of educational opportunities for blacks, Mexican-Americans, Indians and other minorities. In 1967 the racial tensions that inflamed the rest of the country began to be felt in white, affluent Palo Alto. Blacks from East Palo Alto began attending Cubberley in search of a better high school education. When these black students demanded fairer treatment from the faculty and more attention to the black experience in the curriculum, tempers flared and communication broke down. The role of arbitrator he had once hoped for was thrust upon Ray. Ray helped the dissident black students shape their anger and disappointment into an instrument for change. He showed the predominantly liberal faculty that their sympathy and leniency were patronizing and insulting to the students. He made others see the cruelty of their indifference. The combined efforts of teaching and endlessly arbitrating in the troubled school sapped his energy. It was at just about this time that Martin Luther King was assassinated. Ray was deeply discouraged but, realizing the importance of that moment in history, he rallied himself. He had always lectured to church and civic groups on black history and black problems. Now he redoubled his efforts. He established the Martin Luther King Memorial Scholarship Fund to enable Cubberley students to go to college, and contributed his lecture fees to it.

Ray never compromised his academic standards. In the fall after the black students had voiced their demands, Ray offered a black history course. Some students apparently expected an extended rap session. They found, instead, that their teacher expected them to study, learn and question rigorously. Some dropped the course, but most remained to meet Ray's challenges.

That same fall, Ray's students and friends noticed that the ordinarily strong, energetic man was walking more slowly and often seemed to be in pain. In November Ray entered the hospital, and in less than two months he was dead of cancer. Young and old stopped to mourn; in his death they rediscovered their teacher.

One of Ray Fleming's students wrote, "If ever there comes a time in one's life where a genuine grasp on living renews itself, let it come now. Just as life comes only at death in the phoenix legend, so must the humanitarian in all of us renew his efforts with the death of Mr. Raymond Fleming. For this hope and toil to benefit mankind were his life work."

do about it? How does she remedy the problem? It is not only a matter of knowing the results, but also of knowing the available and constructive alternatives. It is at this point that people learn how *not to teach.* Take as an example the case of a beginning teacher interested in having her students do group projects. After she divides the students into groups, outlines the tasks and gets them started, things begin to fall apart. She envisions another fall of Rome taking place in her class. Tension begins to build up. She does not know her alternatives and does not know how to proceed. As a result, she does what many teachers do—retreats to what she knows well from her own elementary and secondary school experience. She abandons the group work, rearranges the students' chairs in rows and conducts a highly teacher-directed class. Retreating to the safe and traditional is a common reaction in a teacher who is frustrated and does not know the available alternatives. This attitude of "when in doubt, retreat," coupled with the strong influence of our ingrained tendencies and our own experience with teachers, may account for the very conservative quality of most instruction.

This is not to say that teachers cannot grow and improve "on the job," or that they cannot use the feedback available to them to help analyze, and gradually eliminate, their weaknesses. We simply want you to put the old cliché about "learning from experience" in balanced perspective.

SOME APPROACHES TO YOUR EDUCATION AS A TEACHER

Refreshing winds of change are blowing in higher education. College students have more curricular variety and choice available to them now, and more voice in campus affairs. The foregoing analysis of how people learn to be teachers (or nonteachers) may seem somewhat discouraging, but it is presented in a spirit of hope. By understanding what has already happened to you and what may be in store for you, you are much more likely to be able to transcend the limitations of those experiences. This is particularly true today, because higher education is increasingly responsive to student needs and desires.

In *The World and the American Teacher,* Harold Taylor suggests that deciding to become a teacher is like choosing to become a poet. "The preparation begins in a decision to become something, a commitment made about one's life and the purpose of it."[4] This statement is reminiscent of the analogy to sculpture with which we began this chapter. Both suggest that the process of becoming a teacher requires you to expend energy and imagination, rather than simply sitting back and letting it happen.

Adopting an active, aggressive approach to your education can have some intriguing implications. For instance, you may find it useful and revealing to

---

[4] Harold Taylor, *The World and the American Teacher* (Washington, D.C.: American Association of Colleges for Teacher Education, 1968).

The teacher must keep alive the spark of wonder, to prevent it from becoming blasé from over-excitement, wooden from routine, fossilized through dogmatic instruction, or dissipated through random exercise upon trivial things. John Dewey, How Teachers are Prepared.

behave like a critical "consumer" of the education that is offered to you. Analyze the instructional strategies, motivational techniques, human relations skills and evaluation methods of your professors. If you think it would be helpful, ask them to discuss their teaching methods with you. Look for opportunities to teach someone else what you have learned or are learning. It has been said—and our own experience confirms this—that the most effective way of finding out what you know and discovering how to apply it is to teach it to someone else. You might also look for opportunities to relate your other courses to some aspect of teaching that interests you. For instance, do your sociology term paper on an educationally-related topic, such as the correlation between social class and tracking assignments in a nearby school. Or study local Boards of Education for a political science class to determine which political and social groups are represented (and unrepresented) by their members. You might try to arrange an independent study project to visit, and perhaps teach in, experimental schools. If certain experiences which you feel you need for your education are not available on your campus, see if arrangements can be made to acquire them someplace else. You might be able to cross-register at another school or receive credit for an independent study project.

We are not suggesting that you try to make everything you do immediately relevant to your career choice. Rather, we are advocating a more active and creative response to the curriculum and to your decision to teach.

The informal education of a teacher involves many of the factors we discussed earlier—ingrained tendencies to teach, teacher-watching and the like. We should not ignore, however, the importance of the individual teacher's growth and development as a person. The informal education a person gains as he learns to work with other people, to develop his own standards and value system and to become independent and self-reliant is of central importance to his effectiveness as a teacher. Looked at in this perspective, the discipline one gains from learning to play a musical instrument, the give-and-take skills one acquires from living in a dormitory, the deepened maturity gained from doing service work—all contribute to one's development as a person and as a teacher. The same thing could, of course, be said about the personal development of an engineer. But it is especially important in the case of the teacher because her "person" is continually on view to her students, and may in the long run be her most important contribution to their search for maturity and personal growth.

There is an old tale about a student who wanted to learn how to live the good life. The student heard that in a distant land there lived a teacher of abundant wisdom, and he decided to travel there to study under the wise teacher. When he arrived in the city where the great teacher lived, he was directed to an opulent mansion. The teacher's servants cringed at the mention of the teacher's name. After a very long wait while the teacher meditated, the student was ushered into his presence. He bowed, sat before the richly-dressed teacher and said, "Teacher, I have come a long way to inquire of you how to live a good life." The teacher smiled, saying, "You have come to the right person," and began to hold forth on the "good life." After five or six minutes, the student rose and explained that he had to leave because he could not hear the teacher. "What is this? Why can't you hear me, simpleton, you're right in front of me!" "I cannot hear what you say because *what you are* speaks so loud. I must seek elsewhere."[5] Our students, confirmed teacher-watchers all, are seekers just like the student in the fable.

If you are interested in a further discussion of teacher education, particularly its problems and new developments, keep reading. If not, turn to page 249, the closing section of the continuing education of teachers. (If you do this, we would be a little hurt. But then again we'll never know.)

SOME PROBLEMS IN TEACHER EDUCATION

A young sage once said, "Everyone cares about teacher education . . . but not very much."[6] The United States of the Sixties and Seventies has so many more attention-getting problems to grapple with that little public energy is left to expend in sustained attention to teacher education. Compared with war, pollution and unrest among the young, teacher education is, admittedly, not much of a drawing card. However, it has for some time been a matter of sustained national concern. In the fifty-year period between 1920 and 1970, there have been ten major national studies of teacher education, each accompanied by recommendations for action. By and large, these reports have been negative in tone. And the public has by and large responded with apathy. This response has been deeply disappointing to many teacher edu-

---

[5] This fable was told to one of the authors on a bitter cold night in Mobile, Alabama. As reported by said author (whose name will be withheld because he was supposed to be visiting a sick friend in Perth, Maine), "On a dingy back street this old man with a heavy foreign accent shuffled up and asked if I would buy him a drink in exchange for a story. Being a seeker of truth and having seen all the movies in Mobile anyway, I agreed. What followed is reported above. When the story was ended, I had a deep intuition that the old man had been more involved in the story than he let on. As he got up to go I looked deep into his watery eyes and said, 'Sir, I have a deep intuition that you are involved in the story more than you let on.' He winced and then replied, 'Look, fella. Three shots of bar whiskey don't give you the right to pry.' With that he shuffled off into the wintry night, in the general direction of Winnipeg, Manitoba."

[6] Modesty keeps us from identifying the young sage.

cators who realize that major change will not occur until the public takes the issue of how teachers are educated much more seriously. If the public were told that its doctors were being badly trained or that bridge-builders were plying their trade in a dubious manner, action would be taken swiftly. The health and safety of the body apparently takes a higher priority than that of the mind and spirit.

THE VICIOUS CYCLE

What, exactly, is the problem? Few teachers are fully prepared before they begin teaching and, once on the job, they are forced to learn by trial-and-error. In other words, our formal system for preparing teachers is not the major influence on their classroom performance. Teacher education is caught in a vicious cycle which makes significant improvement especially difficult. Its components are so deeply interrelated that the cycle can be entered at any point.

There is a lot of competition for resources—that is, money and personnel —within a university. The university can give only so much of its resources to teacher education without getting itself into political trouble both on and off the campus. As a result, the teacher training program is rarely what the people involved would like it to be, but is "the best we can do *under the circumstances.*" And frequently it is. Field work, clinical exercises and technological aids like videotape recorders are often too expensive. Therefore the primary modes of professional education become those that are least costly—lectures and student teaching. Because of its limited resources, the professional education program is designed to consume very little time. This is particularly striking when teacher education is compared with the training of such other professionals as veterinarians and civil engineers. In sum, the education student does not have to put out a great deal. Nor does he risk much, since normally one can acquire a college degree and professional training as a teacher at the same time.

Approximately 50 percent of all certified teachers either never teach or leave teaching by the end of their second year. Although there are many reasons for this high turnover rate, it is apparent that insufficient training accounts for much of it. The undertrained teacher makes frequent mistakes, knows enough to realize it and thus feels more frustration than satisfaction at her performance. Familiar with the high turnover rate among beginning teachers, administrators and experienced teachers are unwilling to offer much in the way of in-service training to make up for insufficient pre-service training. The high turnover rate thus makes it difficult to build a strong professional staff in a school. Furthermore, the local community is understandably reluctant to support expensive in-service training courses if the participating teachers keep leaving, because local children too often do not reap the benefits. And the nation as a whole cannot understand why more money should be spent on long and expensive teacher training programs if teaching is a revolving-door profession. To complete the cycle, lack of strong public support for more rigorous, longer and more expensive training reinforces the *status quo* in the education of teachers. This brief summary is, admittedly, a simplified version of the situation, and it does not take into account changes which have taken place recently. It may be unduly pessimistic. But these qualifications aside, teacher education appears to be trapped in a vicious cycle of low expectations.

INSUFFICIENT COMMITMENT

In addition to this massive dilemma, there are a number of more specific difficulties which contribute to the poor state of teacher training. An issue we have already mentioned, but which needs amplification, is the low level of commitment. Thirty percent of the people who are trained as teachers in our nation's universities and colleges never teach a class. In analyzing this troubling phenomenon, B. O. Smith and his coauthors of *Teachers for the Real World* write:

Photo by Anna Kaufman Moon.

Perhaps the main reason that so many trained teachers never enter the classroom is a lack of commitment to the profession born of little investment in preparation for it. Not many people who are prepared to practice medicine or law fail to follow their profession: in all probability they would consider their failure to practice a waste of knowledge and training. Apparently those who are prepared to teach but never enter the classroom do not feel this sense of waste. Perhaps they feel that the amount of knowledge wasted is not that great or that valuable. If physicians were trained by giving them only basic liberal arts and science courses and four or five courses in medicine in the junior and senior years, perhaps, they would not feel committed to their vocations or competent to practice. Yet this is the way teachers are now trained.[7]

Smith goes on to state that because prospective teachers take a basic liberal arts program, glossed over with a thin veneer of pedagogy, they have lost next to nothing if they decide not to enter teaching. Their preparation has been essentially the same as that of a liberal arts graduate. Smith goes on to suggest that if the prospective teacher were required to make a heavy investment in his preparation, he would either not enter teaching at all or would feel committed to it as a career. Lack of commitment seeps into many aspects of teacher education. Even those who do teach often don't look upon it as a lifetime career. As we have said earlier, many people see teaching as a respectable way to bide time until marriage, "a good insurance policy" or a stepping-stone to administration. If people look upon teaching as a transient occupation, something they are traveling through, the intensity of their commitment is bound to be seriously diminished.

A related issue is lack of competition and the commonplace image of a career in teaching. The nation's higher education institutions train almost a quarter of a million teachers each year. Given such vast numbers, teacher education programs are bound not to be very competitive. If a person is not admitted to one program, there are around 1200 others to choose from. As a result, the individual who is accepted into a teacher training program does not feel that he has been admitted into a small group of elite and highly dedicated professionals and professionals-to-be. A major consequence of this is the commonplace image of teaching. Being accepted into a teacher training program carries about as much prestige as being eligible to join the armed services or to pay taxes. (We feel compelled to say that we consider this lack of commitment a reflection of a severely warped system of values. It is difficult to imagine a career whose potential for impact on people is as great or more important to society than the education of its young. We are somewhat cheered, however, by signs that many people are waking up to the importance and significance of a career in teaching. We will be even more optimistic when university professors in the liberal arts actively encourage their best students to enter elementary and secondary education.)

---

[7] B. O. Smith, *Teachers for the Real World* (Washington, D.C.: American Association of Colleges for Teacher Education, 1969), p. 24. Reprinted by permission of the publisher.

THE LEADER-FOLLOWER DILEMMA

There are numerous alternatives to the way we are presently conducting school. Various unorthodox approaches are being experimented with on a small scale, and some are being considered for wider adoption. New curricula and new ways of organizing the school day and the teaching staff are being suggested. Some critics are beginning to question the very idea of schools in such a society as ours. All of this controversy raises a very pressing issue for teacher education: whether to prepare (and again with very little time and few resources) teachers for the way schools are now or for the way they may be in the future. Both alternatives are fraught with problems. If a given program undertakes to train teachers for the future, it must confront the question of what future schools will be like. Dozens of loud voices begin to vie with each other to assert very different views of how the schools will change. The danger, of course, is that a program may train teachers who are ineffective in existing schools and perfectly suited to schools that never come into existence. For example, should teachers be trained for the traditional self-contained classroom, or for team teaching? Or should we assume that all schools will soon have highly differentiated staffs of paraprofessionals, master teachers and education specialists? Should teachers be trained to function in a school which uses individualized self-directed instruction and relies heavily on media for instruction? In sum, should teacher education lead or follow?

We are undergoing a revolution in our thinking about education and schools. Like most revolutions, it will undoubtedly occur sloppily and unpredictably. At the very least, future teachers need to be educated to what is going on in education so that they can play an active part in directing the revolution in our schools.

THE PRODUCER-CONSUMER RELATIONSHIP

The relationship between the schools and the teacher education institutions is troubled not only by the leader-follower problem, but also by the consumer-producer problem. At present, colleges and universities almost singlehandedly "produce" the teachers for American schools. The schools, on the other hand, act as passive consumers of teachers. The inefficiency of this situation is reminiscent of Russian industry twenty years ago, when huge factories blindly turned out suits and dresses, impervious to consumers' desires and needs. The consumers, having no say in the operation, were frequently stuck with outdated styles or shipments of dresses all uniformly extra-large.

Teacher-trainees and schools lose a great deal in the isolation of training from practice. For one thing, students of teaching are usually taught to teach in the absence of children. The public schools, too, miss the youthful spirit and energetic service of prospective teachers. This problem has been getting special attention recently. Universities and schools are beginning to develop collaborative teacher training programs which capitalize on the skilled teachers and the availability of children which the schools can offer. This in turn allows the university to focus its efforts on what it can do best.

WHAT'S NEW IN TEACHER EDUCATION

We have run the risk of depressing you by talking about what's wrong with teacher education, and a corrective is in order. There have been some very encouraging developments within teacher education in recent years. The knowledge base—what we know about teaching—is being expanded. New institutions, such as federally-funded research and development centers and regional laboratories, have been created for the purpose of expanding the knowledge frontier. Universities and industry have shown renewed interest in the education of teachers. While these new efforts have not yet brought about any major breakthroughs, the climate is encouraging. Interest is high, and individual contributions to a solution of our teacher education problem are emerging.

What follows, then, is a brief description of some new approaches to the training of teachers. Some are in an embryonic stage of development. Others have been tried, tested and found effective. They are very dissimilar. They are more like apples and plums and bananas than a bunch of grapes. All of them, though, represent new directions for teacher education.

EARLY TEACHING EXPERIENCES

For a number of decades the standard method of training teachers has been to rely almost exclusively on university course work and student teaching. The study of education tended to be overly academic, and student teaching was too short and too unpredictable to serve as a satisfactory antidote. A number of universities have attempted to improve their programs by providing their teaching candidates with early, clinical experiences in the schools. Early in their programs teaching candidates are attached to schools, often to perform tasks that contribute to the learning of children. A candidate may be assigned to a particular teacher or team of teachers as a teacher aide, or she may be rotated weekly among a number of positions, assisting behind the main desk in the office, helping the school librarian, working as a tutor in the remedial reading lab and so on.

Participation in community affairs is a feature of some of these programs. The future teacher is assigned to a community agency or service group and, ideally, has opportunities to meet parents and children in nonschool settings. Also, he is enabled to see from an unfamiliar vantage point how the school fits in the total life of the community.

The purposes of these early school experiences are many. First, by returning to school in an authoritative but nonteaching role, the future teacher can begin to encounter some of the problems of that role without having also to deal with the issues of teaching. Second, through real-life encounters he can deepen his understanding of children and their needs. These experiences provide a reality base on which to draw while studying educational theory in the university. The study of education thus loses its cold, abstract quality. Third, such arrangements allow public school teachers and administrators to take their rightful place in the preparation of teachers. Fourth, these early experiences can serve as testing grounds enabling students to make more realistic decisions about whether they wish to teach or not.

Teacher education programs vary tremendously in the use of early teaching experiences. Some programs have developed a core of highly structured clinical experiences. Some confine the early experience to a short period of time, linking it to a specific education course. Despite this diversity, all of the programs are motivated by a common belief that "experience in school may not be the best teacher, but it does vitalize the study of education."

SIMULATION

Since World War II the U.S. armed forces have used "war games" to prepare military men, from privates to generals, for the trials of warfare. War games are designed to reproduce the conditions of battle without its hazards, and are based on the principle of *simulation*. In a simulated situation, real conditions are artificially reproduced, and the participants enact the appropriate roles in problem situations. Simulation has been introduced into teacher education only recently, but it has aroused great interest and high expectations. The principle of simulation can be applied with equal success to the problem of running an entire high school or dealing with an angry parent. One commercially available set of materials simulates an elementary school classroom in an urban setting. It describes the socioeconomic background of the community and provides test scores, records and past teachers' reports for each of the teacher's students. A teacher education student plays the role of the teacher, and after being introduced to the rules of the game and all the information about the school and the class, the game begins. Sometimes a problem is introduced by means of a short film. Other times, the problem is presented verbally to the "teacher." Typical problem-solving situations deal with student misbehavior, the teacher's relationship with administrators and parents, curriculum planning and teaching methods. Although there may be an initial "let's pretend" quality to simulation activities, the participants almost invariably take them quite seriously once the problem-solving situation begins to evolve.

Simulation can have many different uses. Like early teaching experiences, it can be used to introduce the future teacher to some of the issues and problems that must be confronted in the schools. At a later point in training, simulated experiences can be used to see if teaching candidates are able to apply educational principles in teaching situations. Simulation can also serve to initiate discussion of specific issues. For instance, a class studying teaching by inquiry can begin with a simulated lesson, and an analysis of the lesson can be used to illustrate the underlying principles of inquiry.

One of the drawbacks of field experiences for teacher trainees is the reality of making a mistake with real children. Call it what you will, student teaching is real teaching, and the beginner is bound to make mistakes. Simulation allows him to deal with complex issues and to make mistakes in a safe environment. Another of its advantages is that mistakes can be immediately analyzed and constructive alternatives can be presented on the spot. Simulation shares many of the objectives of student teaching, but is more controlled, more open to analysis and more economical in terms of time and human resources.

MICROTEACHING

Microteaching is a training setting for teachers. The normal complexities of the classroom are reduced and the possibilities of providing immediate growth-producing feedback are increased. A teacher, either beginning or experienced, can use microteaching to practice a particular skill or strategy. The impact of microteaching lies in the fact that it provides actual classroom practice *and* instantaneous feedback on one's performance. First, the normal dimensions of classroom teaching are reduced. The length of the lesson is reduced, frequently to only five minutes, its scope is narrow and the teacher works with only a few students. At the same time, the feedback or knowledge-of-results mechanisms are maximized. The trainee reflects on his own performance immediately after the lesson. A supervisor who has watched his performance helps him think about what he did and how it might be improved. The students who have been taught (unless they are very young children) provide feedback on the teaching. Also, the lesson is videotaped and the trainee and supervisor later analyze the tape and, of course, search for ways to improve the performance. The cycle is repeated until the trainee and his supervisor are satisfied with his performance.

A typical microteaching session would proceed as follows: first, the trainee would receive some initial introduction to a specific approach or strategy or teaching skill. For example, if he is trying to master the skill of asking probing questions, he might watch a demonstration film, read about the uses of the skill, and then prepare a brief lesson. The lesson is, primarily, a vehicle for the teacher to practice a particular skill or approach, rather than a learning experience for the students. While it is important to have an interesting lesson, his major focus is on improving his skill in this one area. Arrangements having been made, the teacher teaches the lesson to a small group of students. After the lesson is over, feedback forms are handed out to the students. The teacher and the supervisor may also fill out these rating forms. The trainee and the supervisor then enter the critique phase. Normally, they both examine the written feedback forms and review the videotape. The critique sessions are not aimed at across-the-board improvement of the trainee's performance. Rather, the intention is to focus on the specific skill being practiced. Normally, a trainee would go through a full series of microteaching experiences to gain competence in an array of teaching styles, strategies and skills.

By design, microteaching is not "real world" teaching. Instead of learning by trial and error (or not at all) the trainee acquires new skills in an environment which is safe both for him and for the students. Like the other teacher training approaches described in this section, microteaching should not be interpreted as *the* approach, but as one of many approaches needed to train the highly competent professional teacher.

SENSITIVITY TRAINING

All of us have known teachers whose personalities or ways of interacting with people undercut their effectiveness as teachers. You may have had a teacher who reacted defensively to questions and, in turn, put students on the defensive. Or you may have known a teacher who was so shy that students either wanted to protect her or continually challenged her authority. Human relations problems not only limit a teacher's effectiveness, but also sap any satisfaction he might get from working with people. Such problems are the concern of a new movement in our culture, known by various labels such as T-grouping, encounters, the bod biz and therapy for normals. The most common and accurate label, however, is sensitivity training, since its aim is to make people more sensitive to themselves and to the ways they interact with others. This kind of awareness can lead to the discovery of more satisfying ways to interact.

Interest in sensitivity training is not confined to teachers. However, it can be argued that it is particularly pertinent to teaching, since effective leader-

Photo by Norman Hurst
through Stock, Boston.

ship and communication are essential components of the teacher's role. The aim of sensitivity training is to clear away communication difficulties and leadership problems. To accomplish these rather straightforward objectives, a variety of techniques, some quite unorthodox, are employed. Typically, individuals join a training group organized by a trained leader. Through a series of exercises and games whose purpose is to break through superficial communication, individuals gain a greater understanding of the way they are perceived by others. They also become involved in helping other group members see themselves accurately and adopt more fruitful methods of communicating. It is difficult to speak with any precision about the sensitivity training movement because it is new and highly diverse. Also, its effectiveness depends both on the skill and "sensitivity" of the trainer and on the mental health of the group member. It is no cure-all for someone who is emotionally unstable. It resembles microteaching in that it is an environment created to enable people to learn some things about themselves which they can later apply in real life.

Some educators regard sensitivity training as an antidote to what they consider the schools' excessive attention to cognitive matters. In their view, teachers have been overly concerned with the mind and minimally concerned with the body, and have largely ignored the emotional life of children. Sensitivity training, therefore, attempts to make the future teacher aware of the interdependence of his own mind, body and emotions and then of that of his students. When a particular sensitivity training encounter accomplishes these goals, it is undeniably enriching the training of a teacher.

NEW MEDIA

The primary mode of most formal education is the spoken word. While words have great power, they can have severe limitations as well. For instance, the word "radical" may be decoded by two different people in entirely dissimilar ways. Some words, such as "mother," carry so much emotional weight that a person cannot respond to them objectively. And, again, some uncommon words are devoid of meaning for many individuals. "Flagellation" is a meaningless sound to many people. These and other difficulties with words often make verbal communication, both written and spoken, imprecise and incomplete. This is always unfortunate, and it can be particularly so in teacher education when theories, concepts and principles are being discussed. Also, words can have limited value when a supervisor is attempting to talk to a student teacher about his teaching performance. The new communications media are a way of alleviating this problem by making the education process less exclusively dependent on words.

Film is hardly a new medium in teacher education, but promising new ways of using it are being devised, among them the development of protocol materials for teaching. Protocol materials are slices of life which have been captured on film or videotape and are used to analyze and gain understanding of people's raw behavior. Since all of a child's experience bears on his life in school, protocols are not restricted to classroom episodes.

Instead of talking or reading about the way children behave in certain classroom situations, a protocol may be shown in a teacher education class. The students might first watch it to identify the behavior occurring in the class. After a second and, possibly, third viewing, students make tentative hypotheses about the teaching-learning strategies exhibited. Finally, they may discuss and arrive at an evaluation of what is taking place in the class. One of the major benefits of protocol materials is that they capture life in the raw in a form which allows it to be analyzed over and over again. This, in turn, enables the student of teaching to look deeply into classroom events and to develop a precise vocabulary to talk about the complex phenomena of the classroom. Further, protocol materials allow abstract principles to be presented in the context of concrete situations, enhancing the potential for learning.

In teaching, understanding is not enough. Theory must become part of the teacher's practice. Making the transition from theory to practice is the job of training. The new media are making an important contribution to training in that they provide the means to present models and to provide feedback. In order to bridge the gap from theory to practice, it is helpful to have an explicit model of the behavior we want to acquire. This is especially true in the acquisition of complex teaching skills and strategies. Films and video-tapes can make models of teaching excellence readily available to beginning and experienced teachers. Understanding the principles behind a five-step problem-solving strategy, for instance, may not be enough to enable you to put it into practice. However, if you are able to observe repeatedly one or two models of this problem-solving technique, the chances of your being able to perform it would be greatly increased.

Feedback, the other important ingredient in the acquisition of new behaviors, has been enhanced in efficiency and effect by the wide distribution of videotape recorders. The videotape recorder, or VTR, can provide instant or delayed feedback in such varied training settings as tutoring, simulated and microteaching sessions and student teaching. The teacher-in-training can see his own behavior as it appears to others. He can observe it repeatedly, analyzing it for weaknesses and ways to improve. He can show it to others to gain their insights and observations. And, finally, he can use videotape recordings as a record of his progress over a period of time.

The new media have significantly extended the potential impact of teacher education, and have pointed teacher education in new directions. In addition, the new media have a second-level impact of some importance. For many years critics have complained that teachers do not use the media and audiovisual aids available to them in the classroom. Overhead projectors, films and records commonly sit in the corner gathering dust. Sometimes teachers don't even know how to operate the equipment. If there is any truth to the old saying that teachers teach as they were taught, the use of new media in teacher training could help break this dismal cycle. Marshall McLuhan claims that the medium is the message. If the medium of teacher education is a rich use of media, the message—that they can enhance instruction—will be taken seriously.

PERFORMANCE-BASED TEACHER EDUCATION PROGRAMS

Most teacher education programs have rather nebulous goals, i.e., educating the good teacher. The means of achieving the goal—courses and student teaching—are explicit enough, but exactly how they do so usually remains decidedly vague. Also, the customary way of testing whether a goal has been achieved is dubious. The usual criterion is satisfactory grades on paper-and-pencil tests at the ends of courses and the ability to survive student teaching. While the courses may be effective for most of their students and have strong individual components, this imprecise approach keeps teacher education in the dark about what it actually is accomplishing.

In the last few years a great deal of attention has been focused on the development of teacher education programs based on performance criteria. By this we mean that programs are designed to achieve very explicit objectives whose achievement can be measured. The objectives are identified as competencies which the teacher trainee can demonstrate that she has acquired. There are three kinds of outcomes of the training program which can be measured: first, specific knowledge which the teacher demonstrates he possesses; second, specific skills or behaviors which the teacher can exhibit and, third, specific changes in students' behavior which the teacher has brought about. The fundamental way performance-based programs differ from the traditional approach is that the number of courses one has taken no longer matters. The operative question is, "What can the teacher demonstrate he is able to do?" As a result of this change in focus, the structure of performance-based programs is very different. Many of the innovations mentioned earlier are utilized to achieve specific objectives. Courses, as such, shrink in importance, and the theoretical and the practical dimensions begin to merge.

These, then, are a few of the new directions in which teacher education is moving. No program we know of incorporates all these features. We discuss them here because we believe that teacher education will advance in direct proportion to the pressure applied from within the teaching profession. Some caution should be exercised because, first, these new directions are *new*. Although they appear quite promising we need more experience with them and more evidence of their effectiveness. Second, we need to acknowledge and respect the distance that teacher education has already traveled. Compared with training for the ministry or the law, its history is very brief. While complacency is unthinkable, we should recognize that we have come a long way from the one or two years of post-high-school normal school training in a very short time.

THE TEACHER'S CONTINUING EDUCATION

AFTER THE MORTARBOARD, WHAT?

To become a teacher is not only to commit yourself to your students; it is also a commitment to yourself to be a continuing learner. The idea that one's education ends with graduation from college is foolish for anyone. For the teacher, it is tragic. To be a teacher in the last quarter of the twentieth century is to try to make comprehensible to children a world which is constantly changing, and which many adults have difficulty making sense of. What is known is expanding moment by moment. New information and theories are replacing yesterday's ideas. Society's needs and those of the individual (which are frequently contradictory) are shifting and evolving. What is useful and relevant to life in a post-industrial society will not remain constant. In quieter times, just a few decades ago, the teacher did not need to know as much—and what he did know seemed to last much longer. To fulfill his commitments to society and self, today's teacher must be a continuous learner.

From one point of view there is nothing new in this. It has always been true that when someone stops learning himself, he cannot deal effectively with other learners. He loses the sense of what it's like to learn, and thus loses touch with what his students are experiencing. The nonlearning teacher becomes a mechanic. He may give out valuable information and aid people in acquiring needed skills, but he also exudes intellectual sterility. He is telling his students, "I really don't find learning exciting. I really don't enjoy the life of the mind."

TYPES OF CONTINUOUS LEARNING OPPORTUNITIES

One of the aims of education, according to school constitutions and college catalogues, is to develop the ability to engage in independent study. Independent study is jargon for being able to go it alone. Although it is much discussed by educators, students seem to get little actual practice in picking their own problems or areas of interest and systematically investigating them. Independent study, though, is one of the most important means available to the teacher for his continual self-renewal. The teacher is daily confronted with things he does not understand about children and knowledge and their interaction. "What are children really doing when they yell out answers to homework problems?" "What are the fundamental skills of composition that children should know?" "How can I help my students to use history for their own benefit?" Such questions are daily grist for the teacher's independent study mill. Of course, the teacher's study should not be confined to professional problems. His own interests may lead him into such areas as organic gardening, physical fitness, old movies, politics in colonial America or the humanizing of the corporate state. Not by professional problems alone doth the teacher live!

Group study is another common mode of continuing learning for the teacher. It frequently takes the form of committee work. Problems arise in the school for which there is no apparent solution, so a group of people take on themselves the task of exploring the problem with a view toward recommending an enlightened course of action. In recent years, teachers and administrators have begun inviting community residents to these study groups in order to have the input of opinions from outside the confines of the school. Typical issues these study groups might take on are "Alternatives to the present second grade reading program," "An analysis of the unused educational resources in a particular community" and "the potential benefits and cost of using paraprofessionals in our high schools."

A third way of continuing to learn is to take courses or work on an advanced degree. Most colleges and universities offer courses suitable and interesting to teachers. Special and regular courses are offered in the evening and during the summer vacation. These courses and degree programs not only allow teachers to gain a deeper understanding of their work, but also make it possible for some teachers to train for other jobs in education, such as guidance counseling, administration or college teaching.

Besides personal satisfaction, there are very real incentives for teachers to participate in continual schooling. In most school districts with a salary scale, the two major variables which affect a teacher's salary are his years of teaching experience and his formal education. A teacher with a master's degree frequently makes as much as a thousand dollars more than a fellow teacher with equal experience and no master's degree. While this is a rather crass reason to pursue graduate study, it does indicate the taxpayers' belief that teachers should be continually upgrading themselves. Many states require teachers to do advanced graduate work to keep their initial certification. Some require the master's degree for permanent certification.

In addition to the general categories of continuing education mentioned above, there is a considerable variety of activities which can enrich the professional life of a teacher, such as participating in a teacher education program, writing a new curriculum, joining an encounter group, working on a research project, taking summer employment in an entirely different field, taking a sabbatical year of travel and study or making a film. Not only can such activities be personally satisfying, but they can also make us more stimulating teachers.

Any human activity, even one as challenging and ever-changing as teaching, can lose its excitement. A commitment to continuing education is a way of dealing with this condition of life. Besides the activities suggested above, the habit of daily asking yourself, "What am I trying to do?" and "What is this about?" will help make you a continuous learner and an effective teacher.

DISCUSSION QUESTIONS

1. There is a proverb that "teachers are born, not made." What arguments can you marshal for or against it?

2. What are some of the outstandingly effective and ineffective teacher behaviors you have observed in your years of teacher-watching? What have you learned from the media models you have seen? What experiences have you had or do you expect to have in the teacher education program at your college or university?

3. What kind of educational experience would you like to design for yourself? Can you carry it out? Why or why not? How can you use your current courses to help you explore some aspect of education that interests you? What else can you do to make your education relevant? What will you do?

4. How does our statement that "we have become prisoners of the way things used to be" relate to teaching behavior, both personally and culturally? What's wrong with the traditional notion of a professional sequence of courses as the major vehicle of teacher education? What's right with it?

5. Can you think of any explanation other than those we proposed for the defection from teaching of many trained teachers?

6. Do you want to be trained for schools as they are or as they might be? What might be done to alleviate the isolation of teacher training institutions from the schools that will employ their graduates?

7. What are the advantages of practical experience early in teacher training? What are the disadvantages? Do you think that the principle behind simulation is valid? What are the advantages and disadvantages of simulation as a training method? of microteaching?

8. Which of the new approaches to teacher education we have discussed are available in your school's program? Would you like to experience some which are not currently available? What can you do about it?

9. What possible implications do you see in our suggestion that you become a critical consumer of your education? Try to imagine the attitudes, tactics and traditions of the marketplace, and of the consumer movement, applied to education. Suppose this idea were adopted in the schools?

FOR FURTHER READING

Sharp, Louise D., ed. *Why Teach?* New York: Holt, Rinehart & Winston, 1957. A dated but interesting series of short statements by prominent figures and famous teachers on the importance and value of teaching.

Silberman, Charles E. *Crisis in the Classroom.* New York: Random House, 1970. Sponsored by the Carnegie Foundation, Silberman's book argues that American schools are grim, joyless places—oppressive, intellectually sterile and aesthetically barren. This condition, Silberman argues, is due primarily to the mindlessness of American education. However, he finds hope in the implementation of concepts borrowed from British primary schools.

Smith, B. Othanel; Cohen, Sol B.; and Pearl, Arthur. *Teachers for the Real World*. Washington, D.C.: American Association of Colleges for Teacher Education, 1969. A major report by a high-level committee on teacher education. Building on what is already known about the preparation of teachers, it charts a sound and workable plan for the future. A milestone book.

Stephens, J. M. *The Process of Schooling*. New York: Holt, Rinehart & Winston, 1967. A distinguished educational psychologist presents a unique view of the effects of schooling and how children learn.

FILMS

Blackboard Jungle (Films, Inc., 16mm, b&w, 101 min., 1955) Although made quite a few years ago, this film's depiction of a large-city vocational training school is still quite interesting. The problems encountered by teachers are not very different from those presented in *To Sir, With Love*.

Education for Psychological Maturity (Indiana University Audio-Visual Center, 16mm, b&w, 29 min.) Featured personality in this film from the "Philosophies of Education Series" is Arthur Jersild, professor at Teachers College, Columbia University. The film explores theories presented in Dr. Jersild's book, *When Teachers Face Themselves*.

Good Morning, Miss Dove (Twyman Films, 16mm, color, 106 min.) Based on the novel by Frances Patton, this film tells the story of a small-town geography teacher. As Miss Dove reminisces about her life, the viewer is presented with many amusing examples of "how people become teachers."

A Lot of Undoing To Do (Philadelphia Board of Education, 16mm, b&w, 15 min., 1967) Another film from the series in the 1967 Philadelphia Cooperative Schools Program. Rather than describing the development of a particular curriculum, this film documents an attempt to train teachers in the general philosophy of a "process curriculum" by having them participate in sensitivity groups, improvisational drama and the like during a summer training program. The film effectively juxtaposes the reality of the school situation with the ideas explored during the summer program.

Making Things to Learn (EDC Film Library, 16mm, b&w, 11:27 min.) A film on the workshop process. Filmed in public, private and Head Start classrooms in the Boston area, *Making Things to Learn* shows adults building various kinds of educational materials and children using the materials in their classrooms.

This is Marshall McLuhan: The Medium is the Message (Contemporary/McGraw-Hill, 16mm, color, 53 min., 1968, NBC News) This discussion by Marshall McLuhan dramatizes his belief that electronic media are orienting society toward an "all-at-once" mode of perception. McLuhan's views on the effects of mass media have strongly influenced the "media movement" in education.

To Sir, With Love (Columbia Cinemathèque, 16mm, color, 105 min.) Based on E. R. Braithwaite's award-winning autobiographical novel, this film stars Sidney Poitier as a teacher in a "rough" school in London's East End. The film catalogue description claims that he "treats them as adults and imbues them with standards of decency."

Up the Down Staircase (Warner Bros., 16mm, color, 123 min.) Adapted from the book by Bel Kaufman, this film portrays a large-city school from the viewpoint of a young, idealistic teacher on her first assignment.

The Workshop Process (The University of California, 16mm, 12 min.) Documents the organization, operation and evaluation of a teacher's workshop in the Montebello School District in California.

AUDIOTAPES

Intensive Group Experience (Big Sur Recordings, 3.75 ips, reel or cassette, mono or stereo) The history and development of the encounter group method is explained by Carl Rogers.

On Staying Awake: Talks With Teachers (National Education Association, 3.75 ips, reel or cassette) These taped addresses to teachers are based on a written work by Ole Sand called *On Staying Awake,* which describes a multilevel approach to humanizing education.

The Person of Tomorrow (Big Sur Recordings, 3.75 ips, reel or cassette, mono, 90 min., 1970) Carl Rogers presents his views on rock music, violence on campus and the encounter group movement, and in so doing discusses some changes necessary in education.

Principles and Philosophy of Open Encounter (Big Sur Recordings, 3.75 ips, reel or cassette, mono or stereo, 1 hour) William Schutz informally discusses, with participants at the Esalen Institute, an overview of the encounter group movement, its philosophy and some underlying premises on which open encounter is based.

Psychology and Education for the New Age (Noumedia, 3.75 ips, $\frac{1}{4}$ track, mono or stereo, 5 hours) This long tape was made at the Menninger Foundation in Topeka, Kansas, in 1970, and covers a great deal of ground for teachers, therapists and others interested in psychology and education.

Rules of Thumb of Open Encounter (Big Sur Recordings, 3.75 ips, reel or cassette, mono or stereo, 1 hour) In this second tape, Dr. Schutz outlines his own guidelines for running encounter groups.

Seminar on Encounter and Education (Big Sur Recordings, 3.75 ips, reel or cassette, mono or stereo channeling, 4 hours) Carl Rogers lectures on the use of encounter methods in education and, in an informal seminar, develops the question, "How would we plan a college based upon encounter methods?"

Refer to Appendix for distributors' addresses.

7   What Problems Does the Beginning Teacher Face?

The first year of teaching has been described as an emotional roller coaster, filled with peaks of exhilaration, dips of depression and, *always,* intense involvement. It is a year of adult freedom, immense learning and great satisfaction. And much of the learning and satisfaction it offers is a direct result of working out or learning to live with problems. In this chapter we will examine some of the problems commonly reported by beginning teachers. However, before you read about what we consider to be the major problems encountered by new teachers—and we can't cover them all—we would like you to take a moment to write down seven or eight problems you would expect to be most common among beginning teachers. After you have done that, write down the two or three problems you feel you might be most concerned with as a beginning teacher.

Common problems encountered by beginning teachers:

1 _____

2 _____

3 _____

4 _____

5 _____

6 _____

7 _____

8 _____

Possible problems I might experience:

1 _____

2 _____

3 _____

A summary of a research study on the problems generally encountered by beginning teachers appears on page 257.

PROBLEMS! PROBLEMS! WHO NEEDS PROBLEMS!?

It might well be asked why we are devoting an entire chapter to the problems and difficulties experienced by beginning teachers. At face value, it seems a rather negative approach. Even sadistic. Aren't we running the risk of giving the reader a one-sided view of teaching? If we recount a series of demi-horror stories, are we liable to frighten away potential teachers? Perhaps we are. We believe, however, that there is a pervasive tendency in much writing about education and teaching to oversell. Joys and satisfactions abound. The teacher is portrayed in these writings as a modern-day Pied Piper leading a procession of happy, devoted students out of the Cave of Ignorance into the Light of Wisdom and Happiness. This kind of inspirational literature, in combination with our own tendency to kid ourselves, can be very misleading for the aspiring teacher. One of our aims in discussing the problems of the beginning teacher is to present a corrective to this rose-colored vision of teaching.

Another more positive reason for examining common problems is to give the reader time to develop solutions or responses before encountering them directly. The old chestnut about locking the barn door after the horse has been stolen has special applicability to many teachers. Only after they have made a mistake do they begin to seek a solution. On the other hand, a realization that he will have problems and an attempt to identify them and develop solutions in advance may save the prospective teacher and his students much grief.

As we have said before, the future teacher's encounter with problems can also enrich her study of educational theory. Future teachers frequently fail to utilize educational theory fully because they are simply unaware of the problems such knowledge can help them solve.

CATEGORIES OF TEACHING PROBLEMS

"Problem" is one of those all-purpose words which can be applied to situations as different as the threat of nuclear holocaust and chronic bed wetting. Even when limited to aspects of teaching, it can be assigned to widely varying phenomena. There is the problem of having a quiet voice and not being heard by all the children. And then there is the problem of an irreconcilable philosophical disagreement between you and the school authorities about how you teach. Problems are also quite subjective. A problem that might drive one teacher out of the profession and into the expensive hands of a therapist can be a stimulating challenge to another teacher.

To help us deal with this troublesome characteristic of problems, we have organized our discussion around six aspects of the teacher's experience: the school setting, administration, fellow teachers or peers, instruction, students and parents. We have drawn heavily on reports of actual experiences by beginning teachers to add flesh and some blood to our abstractions.[1]

---

[1] An uncomfortably large number of the reports in this chapter are drawn from a book one of the authors edited. However, these problem cases are the cases with which we are most familiar.

PROBLEMS OF BEGINNING TEACHERS

In 1964, Frank Broadbent and Donald Cruickshank of the State University College at Brockport, New York, conducted a study on the problems of the first-year teacher. They sent questionnaires to 282 graduates of their institution who had just completed their first year of teaching in elementary and secondary schools. Fifty-eight percent of the teachers responded to the 117-item questionnaire. The results were grouped into six problem area categories and scored for frequency and intensity. According to this study, first-year teachers are troubled by the following problems, listed in descending order:

1. *methods of teaching*
2. *evaluation of students*
3. *discipline*
4. *parent relations*
5. *classroom routines and materials*
6. *personal problems (primarily lack of self-confidence)*

These findings conflict with earlier studies which indicate that discipline is the most troublesome problem area for first-year teachers.

F. Broadbent and D. Cruickshank, *The Identity and Analysis of Problems of First Year Teachers,* 19 Oct. 65 ERIC Ed. 013–786 FP 001–282.

S. GROSS

Cartoon by Samuel H. Gross, copyright © 1969, Saturday Review, Inc.

One of the oddest phenomena related to becoming a teacher is the new teacher's sense of strangeness in what is, after all, a very familiar setting. A person who becomes an insurance salesman or a psychiatric social worker knows he is moving into a strange environment, and expects this new work world to present him with very different experiences than those he has had as a student. The new teacher, however, is reentering a familiar setting, even if it is not the same school in which he was taught. The school routine of classes, periods, bells, tests, homework and report cards is in his blood. The hierarchical system of principals, teachers and students is taken for granted. The rituals and pageants—assemblies, Thanksgiving class presentations, honor society induction, The Big Game—are all instantly recognizable. The existence of cliques, in-groups and out-groups among both students and faculty is no secret either. But despite all their experience and sophistication, beginning teachers are commonly overwhelmed by their initial exposures to school.

The beginning teacher's shock at the familiar is sometimes manifested in visible signs of mental and physical stress. In the early months of the school year it is not uncommon for the new teacher to experience depressions and self-doubt, outbursts of crying, physical exhaustion, insomnia, fits of vomiting before school, crankiness and inability to control his temper. The anthropologist Estelle Fuchs has studied the world of the beginning teacher. In her words,

> Most of us are aware of the tensions and strains accompanying unfamiliar routines or activities. However, the symptoms expressed by beginning teachers . . . go far beyond the ordinary fatigue associated with a new mode of employment. They are surprisingly similar to the phenomenon described by anthropologists as "culture shock."[2]

Culture shock is the feeling of dislocation people experience when they initially encounter a foreign culture. Peace Corps volunteers, foreign students, tourists and newly-arrived immigrants frequently report that when first thrust into the strange life patterns of a foreign culture they feel numbingly disoriented, forced to assimilate too much too soon and afraid they have made a drastic mistake to have come to a strange country. It is easy to explain culture shock among Peace Corps volunteers and immigrants, but why teachers? Haven't we just said that teachers, as ex-students, are accustomed to the culture of school? It appears, though, that the new teacher's very familiarity with life in schools is a problem in itself. "School" is a very

---

[2] From p. 21 of *Teachers Talk* by Estelle Fuchs. Copyright © 1967 by Hunter College of the City University of New York, Copyright © 1969 by Estelle Fuchs. Reprinted by permission of Doubleday & Company, Inc.

Cartoon by Bill O'Malley.

complicated series of structures, people and interactions, and knowing a part of it does not imply knowledge of the whole. Being one of twenty-five students sitting and listening to a teacher is very different from standing in front of twenty-five strange children and taking charge of their learning. People learn a great deal about teaching through teacher-watching, but there is a great deal they do not learn. Besides this, the new teacher has to learn not only a new set of school routines for her particular school, but also how to administer them. She has to learn her way around a new building and find out how to requisition the supplies she needs. She has to "learn" her administration, her fellow teachers and, especially, her students. And on top of all this, the first-year teacher has to develop lesson plans from scratch. She has to build complete units, design bulletin boards, devise an evaluation system and make up tests. The pressure of all this newness causes strain.

As attested to by the following account by a first-year teacher,[3] intellectual understanding of "culture shock" is not always an effective antidote.

Linda Corman/English:

Considering myself sophisticated enough to survive any experience the outside world was pleased to offer, I lent a deaf ear and bored spirit to academic discussions of the severe "cultural shocks" we, who then dwelt in University of Chicago ivory-towerdom, were likely to undergo on the job. I had attended the only public high school in my small midwestern hometown and had therefore been exposed, I thought, to the social, emotional, and intellectual lives of a socioeconomic cross-section of teenagers and to the academic dispositions of variously talented young students. I had also known urban youth, black and white, in college and before. I had known and liked very well the blacks with whom I became acquainted in college. Certainly, I asserted, I was altogether sympathetic with the plight of minority groups and totally without so-called prejudice. And I had traveled a lot on my own, and, after, had lived in Chicago's liberal melting pot, Hyde Park, for a year. On the whole, I concluded, I had met a varied lot of people and should no doubt find very little new—certainly nothing surprising—in anyone whom I should hereafter encounter.

Perhaps I had simply forgotten these people of my past. For it turned out that I was thoroughly shocked by a large portion of the high school community with which I sought to involve myself. Only now can I see that these people should have been familiar from the beginning. I had read about them in books—in novels and poems, in psychology texts and anthropological studies. And most of them I had indeed known very well before.

But I did not know myself, and I did not know the role I haphazardly tried to play. I had known tyrant-teachers and pushovers, bright ones and ignorant ones; but I had not known them as colleagues. I had known mischievous students and helpful ones, vicious ones and apple-polishers, but I had not known them as students in a class I was supposed to teach. I had known principals and assistant principals, and coun-

---

[3] All the cases in this chapter which are not accompanied by specific citations are slightly altered or fictionalized accounts of situations and problems experienced by the authors or by beginning teachers with whom the authors have worked. The names have been changed to save us all from embarrassment.

TEACHERS

selors and truant officers, but I had not known them as one who expected to be treated as the college graduate, the lady, and the professional I wanted desperately to be. In short, I saw strange faces because I looked out through the strangely new eyes of a teacher.[4]

Of course, not every kind of shock is equally overwhelming. Some teachers-in-training who are preoccupied with problems related to instruction forget how much clerical and administrative work is required of them.

John Canfield/History:
I couldn't believe all the paperwork that was required (in duplicate, if you please). Most of it was related to the home room. There were a thousand forms to be passed out, to be filed, to be passed to the student to be filled out, or simply to be read aloud. Late in the year one got the feeling that they all should be thrown out.

The first day of real school was a bookkeeper's nightmare. There were absence reports, homeroom size reports, class size records, tardy slips, and cut slips to be passed out; and there were three schedule cards per student to be passed out, filled out, returned, and filed. Then there were parents' voter registration cards to be collected to prove that the students lived within the school district. Half the students didn't have these, and even if they had, I wouldn't have known which addresses were in the district anyway. Add to this the physical and dental exam forms to be collected, the bus cards to be filled out, lockers to be assigned, and the locks to be sold.

Lockers! For thirty-eight students I was assigned sixteen lockers, twelve of which worked.[5]

Many new teachers have never come in contact with the rough-and-tumble, occasionally violent, aspect of school life. They may have attended schools where there was very little fighting and roughhousing, or they may have been smart enough, or timid enough, to stay out of the way. Whatever the explanation, their initial encounters with fists, screams and hairpulling can be, to say the least, unsettling.

Gail Richardson/Mathematics:
Near the end of the period, four of the girls who sat in the back were talking, and from the expressions on two of the faces, I knew that something was wrong. I walked over as the bell rang, but nobody would tell me anything, and all left the room for their next classes. I returned to my desk to gather my things when I heard shouting in the hall and saw a crowd of students outside the door. As I rushed out, Mary and Cathy's shouting match became a shoving match; so I grabbed one girl, and someone else restrained the other. I talked to Cathy for ten minutes until she was more calm, then sent her to the counseling office with a note explaining the incident. The counselor talked to both girls, and they were friends again the following day.

---

[4] Kevin Ryan, *Don't Smile Until Christmas* (Chicago: University of Chicago Press, 1970), pp. 104–105. Copyright © 1970 by the University of Chicago. Reprinted by permission of the publisher.

[5] *Ibid.*, p. 30.

My alarm clock rang at seven thirty, but I was up and dressed at seven. It was only a fifteen-minute bus ride from my apartment on 90th Street and Madison Avenue to the school on 119th Street and Madison.

There had been an orientation session the day before. I remembered the principal's words. "In times like these, this is the most exciting place to be, in the midst of ferment and creative activity. Never has teaching offered such opportunities ... we are together here in a difficult situation. They are not the easiest children, yet the rewards are so great—a smile, loving concern, what an inspiration, a felicitous experience."

I remembered my barren classroom, no books, a battered piano, broken windows and desks, falling plaster, and an oppressive darkness.

I was handed a roll book with thirty-six names and thirty-six cumulative record cards, years of judgments already passed upon the children, their official personalities. I read through the names, twenty girls and sixteen boys, the 6–1 class, though I was supposed to be teaching the fifth grade and had planned for it all summer. Then I locked the record cards away in the closet. The children would tell me who they were. Each child, each new school year, is potentially many things, only one of which the cumulative record card documents. It is amazing how "emotional" problems can disappear, how the dullest child can be transformed into the keenest and the brightest into the most ordinary when the prefabricated judgments of other teachers are forgotten.

The children entered at nine and filled up the seats. They were silent and stared at me. It was a shock to see thirty-six black faces before me. No preparation helped. It is one thing to be liberal and talk, another to face something and learn that you're afraid.

The children sat quietly, expectant. Everything must go well; we must like each other.

Hands went up as I called the roll. Anxious faces, hostile, indifferent, weary of the ritual, confident of its outcome.

WHAT WOULD YOU DO?

Case Number Four

You teach in a school that uses a letter grading system. You have assigned your students a term paper. You know that one of your students has spent hours and hours on his report, but its quality is quite poor. The student has already expressed his hope that you will take effort into account when grading the reports.

What would you do?

Case Number Five

You are the same teacher described in Case Number Four. When you assigned the term paper you distributed a sheet containing all the necessary information about the assignment, including the due date. All but two of the reports were handed in on time, and those were both a week late. Adequate time was allowed for the completion of the paper.

What would you do?

Case Number Six

Your seventh-grade students are all reading silently in their seats. Suddenly you notice that two of the boys are pushing and shoving each other. One of the boys, obviously very angry, shouts out a string of obscenities at the other. By this time all of the students are watching the incident. When the swearing occurs, all eyes turn toward you.

What would you do?

There were several reasons why this was one of the most upsetting incidents of my first year. In the first place, it was the first fight I had witnessed since I was a freshman in high school, and that had involved two boys; I do not remember ever having seen girls fight before. I was afraid that the trouble would continue after school and involve the friends of each; this was compounded by the fact that one girl was white and the other was black. Even though this had nothing to do with the cause of the dispute, it would certainly worsen the character of any continuation of the disturbance in a school where there were many racial tensions beneath the surface.

I went to my next class in a daze, trying desperately to stop my knees from shaking and to concentrate on the lesson. My nonviolent, pacifistic nature was greatly shaken by the sight of two girl students screaming at one another with such hatred, especially since both were from my class. By the end of the period I had regained my composure.

At the end of the year this incident looked as trivial as it really was, and I was amazed that I had been so deeply affected by it, even for a time.[6]

[6] *Ibid.*, pp. 70–71.

Then there is the straw that breaks the beginner's back. If the teacher had been sure of herself, and of the support from the principal, and if she had been rested and understood her students a little better, the following would not have happened.

Mrs. Bender/Grade 5

. . . Bobby, my "friend," has been taken from my class. He was transferred to a 5/4 class.

From the beginning of the term I have had discipline problems with him. I didn't call his mother because she was in the hospital having a baby. I don't know who the father is; I don't believe she does either. Anyway, I haven't been able to contact her. I did, however, speak to the guidance counselor, Mrs. Rogers, about him, and she's been watching him for a while. She's started a file on him but I haven't seen it yet.

Tuesday was an impossible day for me. I just didn't know what I was going to do with him. *I came home. I was hysterical. I cried all afternoon, all evening, and all night. I really felt that this was the end. I was not going back and what was the sense of knocking myself out? It wasn't worth it. Here I was trying to help people. They don't want to accept you and this is exactly what I felt, very useless* [author's emphasis]. I felt that I was not a teacher; I was a policeman. What did I need this aggravation for?

Wednesday, everything was fine. The class was marvelous. There was no problem.

Thursday, again, because of Bobby, everything went wrong. He had stolen . . . well, I didn't actually see him and couldn't accuse him . . . but paper clips were missing from my desk and while we were going up the stairs at lunchtime Bobby was throwing paper clips at the other children. I was afraid that one of these clips would end up in someone's eye. But, too, it was just one of those things. Everything that he did really got under my skin. I'd gotten to the point where I just wanted to take him and throw him down the flight of stairs we were on. He was just impossible!

On that same day, Mrs. Rogers, the guidance counselor, passed by my room to observe Bobby. He was in his seat so she just really couldn't understand what my fussing was all about. It just so happened that when she came in, he was in his seat taking a diagnostic test in math that I had prepared. She questioned me as to what was wrong and why I was so upset. I explained exactly what he was doing and told her that I just couldn't take it any more. "It's either him or me. I won't continue this way any more," I said, "because I'm becoming a manic-depressive. Monday, I go home; I'm fine. The next day I'm just very, very upset. I can't deal with my feelings any more." Well, she sent me out of the room and said that I should take a rest. She said she felt that I was very upset. She knew it! I'm sure she could see it!

I went down to the office to rexograph some stencils I had prepared and the principal walked in. All he had to do was say something nice to me! And that's exactly what he did. He said, "Well, Mrs. Bender, how is it going?"

I just started to cry. I could not control my feelings. I couldn't control anything. He asked what the problem was and all I had to say was, "Bobby."

"Is it just Bobby?" he said.

"Yes, it's just Bobby."

He said, "Well, if this is truly the problem, Bobby will be taken out of your class tomorrow. There is no need for you to feel so upset about it." Then he sort of scolded me, saying, "Why didn't you come to me before and tell me about this? Don't let things go so far. You are a human being; you have feelings. This isn't the way to react."

Now I was so upset that I just wanted to be left alone. I didn't want him to come near me. I didn't even want to go back to the classroom. I just wanted to go home.

I did go back to the classroom, however, and handed out the stencils I had run off and we did a music lesson. But my heart wasn't really in it because I felt that I was never going to come back. What's the sense?[7]

When problems and failures occur during the first year, the beginner has no backlog of successful teaching to reflect on and draw succor from. He feels swamped, as if he were sinking.

John Canfield/History:

It got so that I hated eighth period. I looked forward to it with apprehension and self-doubt. In the eyes of the school, I was not failing. None of my kids were in the hall, and there were no "undue disturbances." But I knew I was failing.

I brought in movies, had exercises with the newspaper, had the class write their own newspaper, did map exercises, and had them work on problems I brought in, but I felt that I was only occupying them—a sort of military holding action. I sensed no growth. I felt like Mr. Jonas, the teacher I had observed the year before on the West side. What a disappointing self-image! I began watching the clock, hoping the minutes would race by. They never did. It seemed like an eternity before the bell would ring. It would finally come, and I would drag myself to the first floor and prepare to get away from it all. Thank God it was my last class. I would be completely drained of emotional and psychic energy. Some days I would come home and fall asleep from four o'clock to ten o'clock. I am sure it was a symbolic return to the womb.

The next morning I would be reborn again and I would trudge off to school to face another day of trying to be a teacher.[8]

Many beginning teachers think of teaching as an intellectual and genteel profession which will make few physical demands on them. Before they develop the necessary stamina and learn how to pace themselves, many discover that sleep is the only healer.

Linda Corman/English:

Exhaustion—the exhaustion from endless improvisation, endless emotional torment, all too violent plunges and flights between rational and emotional extremes—this was my overwhelming reaction to this first year of teaching. Indeed there was shock— the shock of having a ninth-grade girl announce calmly to her homeroom teacher that she was tardy because she had slept with her boyfriend that night and, consequently, required an unexpected morning bath; and shock at the rage and disbelief I incited in an older student whom I had innocently befriended, when I tried to explain that the reason I wouldn't go out with him was that I was married, not that he was black. And I was often frustrated—when I used subject material too difficult or methods too boring, when class uproars prevented academic progress, when I had spent hours

---

[7] Fuchs, *Teachers Talk*, pp. 17–19.

[8] Ryan, *Don't Smile*, p. 43.

preparing a lesson the night before and nobody else in the class had read the assignment, when the audiovisual department refused to cooperate and confounded my plans for the day. Frustrations were endless, shocks enormously frequent! But beyond the shock and the frustration lay the final state: I was exhausted.[9]

Teachers who teach children from a different culture or subculture than their own experience an especially intense type of culture shock. This feel-

---

[9] *Ibid.*, p. 126.

"No, one thousand photocopies of 'I must not talk in class' is **not** acceptable!"

Cartoon by Hal Money for
Education Technology Magazine.

TEACHERS

ing is particularly common in this country among middle-class Americans who teach poor blacks or Indians. All of the turmoil of learning to teach is compounded by lack of understanding; all too frequently one loses appreciation of the style and values of the students one is teaching.

Miss Kooper/Grade 6:

I really can't explain why Jimmy is particularly more troublesome than the other children. It's just that he calls out all the time. He calls out in Spanish; he talks Spanish. He shows no respect for me. So far, two weeks in a row, I've given a spelling test and he doesn't take it. He just sits there with the paper. He creates a disturbance. He dances in the halls, he dances around, he sings, he calls out. He's always talking! He's always doing something wrong!

On Monday . . . well, Monday is always just a bad day. We have library on Mondays and somehow or other they're quiet while they're in the room. I don't have much of a discipline problem while they're in the room but the minute we go outside someplace it's just bedlam.

We went down to the library and Jimmy was his usual talkative self. He just talked and talked and talked the entire period. I yelled at him. The library teacher yelled at him; she threatened him that he was not going to be able to come to the library any more. It didn't make a bit of difference. He rambled on and on and on in Spanish. He didn't pay any attention to what anybody told him.

Then later, as we were coming up the stairs he was talking and talking and dancing around. He's the second person in line and the first boy was holding the door, so he was right under my nose. I was standing there waiting for quiet and he was dancing around and running up and down the stairs just making a general nuisance of himself.

I got so mad at him at that moment! I've never really gotten as mad as I did that time. I grabbed him by the tie to make him stand still and he said, "Man, let go! Man, don't do that!"

I just held his tie. I think I probably might have even choked him but he kept on saying, "Go ahead! Choke me, man! I don't care. I don't care."

Finally, I said, "When you stand still, I'll let you go."

He wouldn't, just in spite! He just kept pulling away and leaning back. Oh, I was so mad! Finally he just loosened his tie and took it off his head and I was left standing there with his tie in my hand.

This kept going on. As we walked through the halls Jimmy talked and talked. I said to him, "Jimmy, do you remember what Mr. Stark said about putting you back into the fifth grade? Don't think I wouldn't do it!"

He said, "Man, you wouldn't send me to the fifth grade. Nobody sends me to the fifth grade. I don't care."

"Well, we'll see," I said.

He was imitating me now and he said, "I don't care. I'd rather go to the fifth grade anyway. I'd rather have a man teacher; men teachers are more fun. I wish you could put me in the fifth grade."

This continued on and on in front of the whole class and I was really mad.

Finally, Mr. Stark came along. I just looked at him and said, "I don't want this boy in my class!"[10]

---

[10] Fuchs, *Teachers Talk,* pp. 27–28.

It is possible that if Miss Kooper had had some understanding of the Hispanic concept of *machismo*—a sense of pride associated with one's masculinity—she would have realized why Jimmy was acting as he was and certainly would not have offended his budding sense of manhood by laying hands on him in front of his friends.

Although the beginning teacher's culture shock is an intense and troubling experience, it is usually a one-time event confined to the first year of teaching. It can be painful, but it doesn't last forever. This is perhaps the reason why people who are contemplating teaching are told, "If you decide to become a teacher, promise yourself that you will teach for two years before making a definite decision about leaving or continuing in the profession."

THE ADMINISTRATION: THE FACE OF THE BUREAUCRACY

Most of us, as elementary and secondary school students, had rather simplistic notions of administrators. The superintendent was a vague presence we occasionally glimpsed in the hall talking to one of the staff or in front of a microphone on ceremonial occasions. The principal was much more a part of our school lives as someone beloved or feared, and occasionally both. Even though the principal was near at hand, our student's-eye view of him was rather one-dimensional. He represented AUTHORITY. In all but the rarest instances he stood directly beyond the teacher, supporting the teacher and the system. When as students we saw the principal in his office on official business, it usually meant we were in trouble.

The new teacher's relationship with the principal is not so simple, however. The school principal looms quite large in the life of a beginning teacher, and the teacher-principal relationship (and to a lesser degree the teacher's relationship with vice-principals, department chairmen and master teachers) is many-faceted. The principal is, first of all, a colleague, a fellow educator[11] joined with you in the common task of bringing civilization to the young. You are both professionals. You are part of a common tradition. You automatically share common goals (i.e., improving the educational opportunities of children) and attitudes (i.e., people engaged in the important work of educating the young need more support from the public than they get).

The principal is the official leader. He makes decisions, or acts as the funnel for the decisions of higher authorities. Decisions made by teachers or students are normally checked with him. He speaks for the school community to the superintendent, the press and the local citizens. While he is not necessarily the *de facto* leader, the most influential person in the

---

[11] One of the little curiosities of educationese, the official language of schools, is that administrators refer to themselves as educators—as in "leading educator" and "innovative educator"—and teachers are simply called teachers. Occasionally, when the principal attempts to rally the teacher-troops, he broadens it to "we educators. . . ." Some few, guilty, perhaps, for having left the classroom, insist that they are still "just teachers." One thing you can count on, though: "educators" invariably make more money than teachers.

school community, he frequently is. Nothing is ever quite "official" unless the principal has been involved.

He is a helper. He can dispense information and materials, and as an experienced teacher, he is a source of tips, shortcuts and helpful suggestions. The teacher can directly request his help. He also visits teachers' classrooms and, ordinarily, holds conferences with them. He is there to aid the beginning teacher encountering difficulties and confusion.

He is the initiator. A school system is a bureaucracy whose long arm extends from the State Commissioner of Education to the local district superintendent of schools to the individual school principal. The principal, in effect, acts in behalf of the bureaucracy by introducing you into the bureaucratic life of school and teaching you how to behave.

He is the crisis manager. When something happens which you cannot

Photo by Stefan Filipowaki for Harvard Graduate School of Education.

WHAT PROBLEMS DOES THE BEGINNING TEACHER FACE?

handle, the principal's office is where you naturally turn for help. Besides being a potential source of help, the principal needs to know about crises in the school in order to stay in touch with its problems.

He is the facilitator. Schools run on things—pencils, books, paper, heat, hot lunches, sanitary toilets, lights, construction paper, window poles, money and keys. It is the principal's job to keep you supplied so that you, in turn, can carry out the aims of the school.

He is the reward-dispenser. He is frequently the person who actually hires you. Later, he can give or withhold compliments on your performance and give or withhold extracurricular duty assignments. It is he who assigns classes to you, deciding what kind of children you will teach and whether or not they will be at the level or in the subject for which you are prepared.

He is the judge. His is the official view of "how you are doing." The first-year teacher is neither a permanent member of the faculty nor a permanently-certified member of the teaching profession. The principal makes decisions about your qualifications which can have a profound effect on your future in education. He can enhance or destroy your reputation as a teacher in his school. He can write recommendations for or against you. He can insure that you are not rehired. He can block certification. And, of course, he can judge you positively and be a very positive influence on your entire career. Obviously, the principal derives a great deal of power from his roles as reward-dispenser and judge.

He acts as a buffer between the teacher and angry parents (or, occasionally, angry students). Teachers can be quite vulnerable to public attack. Parents hear tales from their children or from other parents and, if they have a question or a complaint to make against a teacher, either go directly to the principal or to the teacher herself. If they do not get satisfaction from the teacher, they then go to the principal. The principal is thus the official "complaint department." This is a delicate position, requiring him to be open and responsive to complaints and at the same time to support the position of the teacher involved. Such situations call for the skills of high diplomacy.

He is the sacrificial lamb. If the community, the teachers or the school board become dissatisfied with what is going on in his school, the principal, who usually does not have tenure in that position, is vulnerable. The tenured staff cannot be dismissed. The community cannot be substituted for another. Thus the principal, who may or may not be responsible for the reported problem, is likely to be chosen to pay the penalty. The ease with which he can be dismissed is, incidentally, a position he shares with beginning teachers.

Having to perform all these roles makes for a complicated existence. The principal of a school today has a most difficult job, and to do the job well requires the strengths of a field general, a philosopher, a psychiatrist and a saint. In light of the general shortage of these strengths, it is not surprising that the new teacher often finds herself in conflict with her principal. He has to make large numbers of quick and difficult decisions, frequently with insufficient information or time, and he is sometimes wrong. A factor which contributes to conflict between the administrator and the beginning teacher is that the administrator is often playing several roles at once. When he appears in your room to observe your class, he is both helper and judge. He may say that he is there only as a source of aid, but some day in the future he must make recommendations about you to his superiors and he cannot help but be influenced by what he has seen during his "helping" observations.[12]

Therefore, it is to be expected that there will be confusion and the potential for conflict between the administration and the new teacher who is being initiated into the system. The following accounts may paint a picture that is unrealistically depressing. Remember, first, that you are hearing only one side of the conflicts. Second, harmonious relations between beginning teachers and administrators don't receive much attention, but they are by no means rare. You should bear in mind that the administrator wants an effective and happy faculty. He wants you to succeed, because his own success depends on your success and the success of the other teachers. Nevertheless, some beginning teachers and administrators encounter problems. What follow are reports from beginning teachers.

The beginning teacher sometimes does not know how to work in a bureaucracy (that is, make it work for her ends) and sometimes is anti-bureaucracy. This can lead her into direct conflict with her administrator, one of whose jobs, again, is to train the beginner in bureaucratic procedures.

Linda Corman/English:

The first unsettling relationship I experienced was between myself-as-bookkeeper and the assistant principal, who was chief disciplinarian for teachers as well as for students. . . .

Playing private secretary to thirty-five students was an exasperating but eye-opening experience. For who would have guessed that blanks requiring a guardian's name or a home address might constitute for some young people a legitimately difficult, perhaps impossible task? One boy had moved around from aunt to friend for the past two years, never quite sure where he would be wanted or want to stay. A girl didn't really know if the cousin with whom she had lived since her mother's disappearance a year ago was her guardian or not. And I had never known anyone who refused to reveal his phone number because his mother's welfare payments would be jeopardized if knowledge of her having a telephone fell into the wrong hands. But I did not have time to digest these strange new things, for unfilled blanks kept flowing in. The censure I received for my shortcomings in this role of private secretary was the final humiliation—and a useless one at that, for indeed, I was trying very hard.

This completely unexpected burden occupied more time than class preparations, or rather usurped the time allotted for class preparations during the first few weeks of school and frequently thereafter. And the assistant principal was the living symbol of

---

[12] Another potential source of difficulty is that the administrator must be like a ship's captain, concerned with keeping the ship afloat, running and moving in a particular direction, while the teacher, who is there to stimulate learning and creativity, has a different set of concerns. Bizarre or random activity, questioning and occasional chaos frequently play an important part in learning. And it is at this juncture that the administrator who puts too great a value on order most often collides with the teacher.

this burden to me, since it was usually he who stalked furiously in and out during class or homeroom periods to chastise me for my errors and delays in fulfilling my clerical duties. He also made a practice of sending for me while I was teaching, requesting that I come immediately to his office, where he would point out a mistake I had made in signing a readmission blank. By the time I returned to my class, the always tenuous state of readiness for learning had wholly dissolved into a chaos that I could not hope, at least that day, to subdue. Later I discovered that all teachers were treated precisely the same way—and all parents and students as well! I was not being singled out and I was not particularly inefficient. But in the beginning I did not know this and was not confident enough to oppose the assistant principal as, I learned later, everyone, to some extent, must do.[13]

Mrs. Bender/Grade 5:

Thursday was the day when I almost handed in my resignation. I just felt that there was no place for me to turn.

Dr. Frost had come into my room after Freddy and Thomas had had a fierce fight in the classroom, and he asked me about Freddy's record. Now, Freddy had just been transferred into my class; he was just admitted three weeks ago. I received his records only last week and I have not had the time to go through them. I told him, also, that I didn't like to make a practice of reading records before I knew the child. He told me that I was supposed to read them and I said that I disagreed. Then he said something to me which really made me feel very, very bad. He said, "When you have had twenty years' experience, then, perhaps, you can disagree with me."

This was the first time I had ever said I disagreed with him. I always went along with what he said because he was the principal and he had feelings and he had experience where I didn't. I felt that he was very wrong talking to me like this and I was very upset. New teachers sometimes see things that are hackneyed or that are in bad need of change and . . . oh, this wasn't a case that he had any right to . . . true . . . I should read the records but I feel that the opportunity will arise where I will read them. Until such time I feel that I really don't want to know, because every child is an individual and he's just justified on his own. I don't want to have in the back of my mind comments made by other teachers. Dr. Frost said to me, "Well, that's the purpose of the record card. You should know what the other teachers thought about him so that you will know how to handle him."

I really feel that by reading a record card you cannot understand how a child reacts.[14]

One of the principal's tasks is to combine teacher talents, student interests and aptitudes and school resources in such a way that important learnings take place. Sometimes it doesn't happen that way, though.

Ed McGrath, Jr./High School Science:

I really wanted to teach in an innovative school and one that would allow me a good deal of freedom. I don't mean freedom of speech so I can use my classroom as a political forum, but freedom to try out-of-the-ordinary things, like independent study projects for low-track kids, field trips, visiting speakers, students being given the chance and some responsibility to help other students. Since I'm a science teacher, it was all very safe, it seemed.

---

[13] Ryan, *Don't Smile,* pp. 105–107.

[14] Fuchs, *Teachers Talk,* p. 65.

CIRCULAR #61

Please keep all circulars on file, in their order.

TOPIC: HOMEWORK ADDENDUM

We have had an epidemic of unprepared students. A student unprepared with homework must submit to his teacher, in writing, his reason
or reasons for neglecting to do it. Please keep these homework excuses
on file in the right-hand drawer of your desk.

James J. McHabe
Adm. Asst.

Reasons Why the Homework Wasn't Done

I know homework is essential to our well being, and I did it but
I got into a fight with some kid on the way to school and he threw it
in the gutter.

_____

I fell asleep on the subway because I stayed up all night doing
my homework, so when it stopped at my station I ran through the door
not to be late and left it on the seat on the subway.

_____

The cat chewed it up and there was no time to do it over.

_____

As I was taking down the assigment my ballpoint stopped.

_____

My brother took "my" homework instead of "his."

_____

The page was missing from my book.

_____

There's no room in my house now my uncle moved in and I have to
sleep in the hall and couldn't use the kitchen table.

_____

What homework?

_____

My dog pead on it.

_____

From the book Up the Down Staircase by Bel Kaufman. © 1964 by Bel
Kaufman. Published by Prentice-Hall, Inc., Englewood Cliffs, New Jersey.
Pp. 198, 155-157.

When I went around interviewing I tried to make crystal clear what I wanted to do and what I thought I would need by way of support. A couple of principals told me directly that my aims were a little advanced for them. I respected their frankness. My future principal, however, got all excited about my ideas and said I was "just the kind of new blood the school needed." I was really turned on. He told me that he would set aside some money for some of my projects and that field trips would be no problem. The district had plenty of station wagons and busses. With that encouragement and more, I signed on the dotted line.

Come September, the tune changed. On a lovely fall day I took some of my classes outside and around the school grounds. I was trying to get them to describe the phenomenon of autumn. They discovered that a lot more was going on in nature than they were fully aware of. At the end of the day there was a rather sharp note in my box from the principal informing me that he hadn't granted permission to conduct classes outside. Also, such nature studies must be reflected in the weekly lesson plans. A few weeks later, I got my classes ready for a field trip to the big river basin about twelve miles away. It was originally the students' idea and it fit in beautifully with the unit on marine biology we were doing. I checked with the other teachers and they all agreed to release the kids. Then I wrote to the principal explaining the field trip, its purposes and the transportation needed. I wrote the note ten days before the date. Well, you guessed it. I was asking too late. Such requests have to be in three weeks ahead of the proposed trip, and there are special forms which I should have used (news to me!). Shot down again. After a while, I got my kids (oops! students) all fired up about independent study. They really came up with some great projects. Some needed special materials and equipment which when added all up came to thirty-eight bucks. I went in personally to see the principal and ask him how to go through channels and order things correctly. I didn't want to lose the money he had set aside for me. "What money? Oh, yes. I did set aside a little money for your classes, but when you failed to make application for it at the beginning of school, other priorities came into play." And so it went all year. We kept on good terms, and the principal gave me a great evaluation. My main complaint is that he guards the district's money and materials rather than letting them loose to do some good. Also, he does a lot of talking about innovation, but it stops at words.

A good quarterback is one who can get the best possible performance from his team. A corporate executive succeeds on his ability to make use of the talents of his subordinates. The principal, similarly, tries to encourage the abilities of his faculty. Sometimes, though, the faculty members feel more exploited than enhanced.

Miss Gould/Grade 5:
As far as the principal and the assistant principal sometimes taking advantage of the teachers and myself, I'd like to give three examples. First of all, there is one teacher who just came into the school this year, Miss Smith, and somehow or other the principal found out that Miss Smith was a professional dancer at one time. This was a big mistake on her part, to let him know this. I don't know if she did or not, but what happened was he told her he wanted her to start a dancing class for the children after school, of course without being paid, and that she would have to be responsible for a program in dancing for the assembly. This was an example of how the principal takes advantage of the teachers.

Photo by Frank Siteman.

Another example is Mrs. De Peuw, who is my buddy teacher and was my cooperating teacher last term. She also is given an awful lot of assignments. She has special course work in library, so she is given the job of ordering all the books for the library and taking care of the library when the librarian is not there. She also, being a very good teacher and being able to get the most out of her children, was given the added responsibility of the science fair. In other words, she is completely in charge of the science fair and has to make sure that everything is going according to what is expected.

Now, as far as I am concerned, I am in charge of the music assembly and the glee club. My principal went to a meeting with other principals at the superintendent's office and he heard other principals talking about a good glee club, so he figured he had to have one to show off too, and I am not kidding, this is just how he feels. Everything for him is show, so he came to me and he insisted in quite harsh words that I have a glee club. Now, I never worked with a glee club before. I didn't know what to do. And besides that, my class is not that bright that they can afford to lose me for an hour.

I was very annoyed over it, but there was nothing I could do, because he insisted and he said he would make it hard for me if I didn't do it. In this respect this is how the principal and the assistant principal as well try to take advantage of the teachers in the school, and this is why many of the teachers who can do other things do not. For example, the principal put up a notice saying that he would like someone who could teach Spanish. Now, I know Spanish, and I wanted to teach Spanish before I went into elementary school teaching, so that I could teach Spanish, but I would never let my principal know that I can even speak Spanish, because that's all I would have to do and I would get that position, which I cannot afford to do.[15]

The new teacher is ordinarily observed regularly by the principal during his probationary period. These observations, which bring into play the principal's antithetical roles as helper and judge, can be nerve-racking when handled badly.

Anonymous/Elementary:
One thing that happened this week was a trip we had taken on Friday to the museum. The trip worked out much better than I thought it possibly could. . . .

The least successful lesson during the last week, as was pointed out to me by my principal, turned out to be my trip to the museum. I had not had enough time to really motivate the children and tell them why we were going to the museum and what they were to see and really give them the background. I figured we had so many things to cover, and we would get to this after the trip was over. But as it turned out, the principal came up about ten minutes after I got back to the classroom and questioned the children on what they had seen, and where the museum was located and other things like that. The children knew where the museum was located, naturally, but he had asked what they had seen. One girl got up and said that she had seen armor and this was what he hit upon. He's a history bug, and he asked, "When did people wear this?" The child said, "Oh, when King Arthur . . . they worked for King Arthur." He asked, "What age in history is this associated with?" I knew this was way above their heads, and they just had no perception of what he was talking about. So it turned out he did

---

[15] *Ibid.*, pp. 115–117.

a time line with them, starting with the early Egyptians and the Romans and the Greeks, through the Middle Ages, which was what he was asking for—from 1200 to 1600, 1700 and through the modern ages.

Now this I would have gotten to if he had given me a free hand, but as it turned out he told me that I should definitely have a time line in the class. Yet I feel that these children have no conception of time, and what is the purpose of having it up in the room if the children don't understand? I sort of told him that we'd do it as soon as possible, but my heart is not really in it, and I feel that he's being very unfair. . . . Then he told me, also in front of the class, which upset me no end, that I should have this time line and a corner of my room devoted to our trip. He wanted to know if I had assigned homework, and I said that the children were doing a composition and art work on what they had seen. He walked out without any further comment, but left me quite upset.[16]

Very infrequently, a beginning teacher is foolishly or shabbily treated by an administrator.

Paul Klein/Grade 3:

During the special orientation meeting for new teachers, the principal told us all that whenever we have a problem to come and see him. He didn't expect us to be perfect and he felt his major job was to help new teachers. Later that week he stopped me in the hall and warmly repeated his offer of help. I really took him at his word. So in early October when I started having trouble planning and finding materials, I just went to see the principal. He was very cordial and, although he talked a lot about himself, he did give me some fairly helpful advice. I went to see him for three short visits. Just talking the problems out seemed to help. I started finding good materials and my classes really improved. I felt I was really doing well and I couldn't wait to get to school in the morning. Then in early December I started getting treated in an odd way by some of the senior teachers. They were always asking me whether or not they could help. Sort of like I had some incurable disease and could they get me a glass of water. It was weird. Finally, I asked two of them in the lunch room, "Why all the concern?" Well, it came out that the principal had told them that I was having big trouble and he had told a number of the senior teachers to do what they could for me. He had not been in to observe me once. Later in the year he came in for two brief observations (to conform to minimum standards in our district) and he never had time for a conference. He did, however, write up supervisor conference reports. They were lukewarmish and had no specifics. He did mention in both reports that I was improving and overcoming early problems. What improvement? What problems? All he had to go by was what I told him. I got so mad I wrote him a little note to the effect that my self-reported problems had cleared up some time ago and that I felt my teaching was better than that reflected in his report. I could see the handwriting on the wall, though. I started looking for another position, and got one without too much trouble. I liked the kids in my first school and many of the teachers. Somehow, though, I put myself in a box for the principal and he wasn't going to let me out.

---

[16] Reprinted with the permission of the publisher from Elizabeth M. Eddy's *Becoming a Teacher* (New York: Teachers College Press), © 1969. Pp. 53–54.

PEERS: A MIXED BLESSING

The new teacher is vulnerable to many outside forces and also to his own insecurities. In the same way that a supportive administrator can turn a potentially disastrous year into a year of growth, so too can one's professional peers. In learning how to teach and how to survive in the classroom, one's peers can be even more important. The following account attests to their importance.

Miss Samson/Grade 4:

I was quite depressed this week and down in the dumps. It was personal, and I also felt that the thought of the principal coming in to watch me this week sort of set me off, because he speaks very highly of me and every time I ask him a question he tells me how well I'm going to do and what great potential I have, how well everyone else thinks I'm going to do, and here he is coming into my classroom. He says all these things and, you know, he has never really seen me teach before. I'm afraid to really think of what he's expecting. So I developed this great feeling of insecurity.

I didn't know if I was teaching correctly. Nobody had come in to see me and I resented this now. I was just on the brink of tears on Monday and Tuesday.

I had a talk with Mr. Julian. I started to complain to him about how badly I felt and everything, and he started talking to me, helping me with suggestions of what I should be teaching, what they were covering and how he was doing it, and that I shouldn't feel like that, that all new teachers feel like that and that I really can do it. I haven't got such a bad class and I'll be able to manage with them. He gave me a few tricks and shortcuts. I told him what I was doing, and he was telling what I was doing wrong. I have two groups in spelling, and he said I should eliminate that because it's a great waste of time, and both groups could do the same work. He threw a suggestion at me for social studies on different people and the reasons that they come to New York. I don't even know if it's the suggestions or just the fact that he sat and talked to me that made me feel better. I was in such a blue mood and so afraid. The fact that he might just have sat down, that somebody was helping me and caring, I think, might have set it straight and helped me a lot.[17]

Although there are trends toward increasing cooperation among teachers, for the most part they work independently, in their own classroom and with their own students. When they are engaged in their professional work, teachers are isolated from one another. Still, though administrators are the official source of support and help for the beginner, his teaching peers are a much more accessible and much less threatening source of support. A teacher's peers can have a powerful influence on him, especially if he is at the beginning of his career. This influence can, of course, be positive or negative.

On the positive side, peers can be an ever-ready source of ideas and teaching tips. They can initiate the newcomer to the customs and folklore of the

---

[17] Fuchs, *Teachers Talk*, pp. 165–166.

DIALOGUE

Jim: *What do you mean by "learning how to survive"? Isn't that the same as learning to teach? If you learn to teach you survive.*

Kevin: *Usually, but not always. A lot of good teachers don't survive. We both knew and read about Ron Jones in Sylvia Williams'* Hassling *(Little, Brown, 1970). He was fired, essentially, because he was too good. He made students think in unorthodox ways.*

Jim: *Okay, but what is "learning to survive"?*

Kevin: *It's learning how to teach kids, how to ignite the human spirit, and not set the building and its administrators on fire in the process . . . or is that too heavy for you, Jim?*

Jim: *Ignite the human spirit? Well, I suppose that's what really good teaching is all about, isn't it?*

school. For instance, they can tell the beginner which administrative requests must be responded to promptly and which can be done late or ignored completely. Their friendship and reassurance can support one over rough days and weeks. They can suggest to the new teacher materials that "work" with his particular class. They can help with problems like making transitions from one part of a lesson to another without letting the lid blow off the class. They can share their planbooks, and suggest new approaches and insights on how to make up a planbook which will pass inspection. And, most important, they can be an inspiration to the new teacher seeking to gain mastery of his new role. By their example, they can demonstrate what the phrase "teacher as professional" means.

And, on the other hand, peers can have negative influence, undermining one's idealism, lowering one's standards and offering no help at all. Perhaps some capsule portraits will clarify this sad phenomenon. All organizations have people like these. They are a living witness to man's fall from the sublime.

Miss Pyrotechnics: She is a special effects expert. She and her students spend all their time decorating her classroom. The displays are beautiful and ever-changing. The desks and charts are always just right! Even while the class is decorating, the room is spotless. The principal loves to bring visitors to her classroom. She has four special lessons (or routines) she can perform for these occasions.

The Mouth: His hobby is gossip. His arena is the teachers' lounge. He thrives on the trade of secrets, and no morsel is too small to be shared with his colleagues. Nothing is too personal not to be passed on. He should have gone into advertising . . . or broadcasting.

Mrs. Coaster: She has had twelve years of teaching experience. Or, to be more precise, she has had one year of teaching experience which she has repeated twelve times. She still uses lesson plans from her first year of teaching. She knows not the words "outside preparations." She puts in time and nothing else. She has eighteen more years to go before retirement.

The Hoarder: His desk and cabinets are a veritable goldmine of goodies. He has chalk and paper enough to make it to the year 2000. He has materials that make the other teachers drool with envy. He is like a squirrel preparing for the long winter. Nothing is safe from his acquisitive hands. He is exceptionally nice to the office secretary and it pays off. He does not share.

The Big Planner: He is at his best in faculty meetings. He can create out of thin air the most exciting projects and eloquently invoke the need for unprecedentedly ambitious innovations. He disappears when volunteers are asked for.

The Sex Bomb: Appropriately, the Sex Bomb comes in two varieties. SHE: In the lunchroom with the girls she is rather quiet, even dull. But when he—any "he"—comes within range, she is transformed. Her clothes suddenly look too tight. Her conversation becomes animated, to say nothing of her flashing eyes. As the situation dictates, she is in desperate need of help or the font of all succor. It seems that he and she need to meet after school for some more private discussion. HE: He begins to stop by your classroom after school to check on "how things are goin'." He's helpful at first. He has a tendency to stand too close. His breath is hot, his hands moist. He knows a great deal about the proximity of intimate little cocktail bars where the two of you could talk about school in a more relaxing atmosphere. (Everyone on the faculty hopes that SHE and HE find each other soon.)

Mr. Up, Up and Away: He dresses nicely—carefully, that is. His shoes are shined. He volunteers for all committees. There is never any noise from his class. His students are always busy doing seatwork, but they seem a little glassy-eyed. It is difficult to tell whether he is bright or dull. He is beautiful to watch. He never makes a false move. He never makes a wave . . . unless the tide is running in his favor. He never tells jokes. Guess what he plans to be when he grows up?

The Ally Seeker: She courts new teachers. Shortly after you have met she tells you about The Great Injustice that was done her. She is telling you for your own good, she says. While it happened to her seven or was it eight years ago, it could be happening to you now. It seems it would be better for everyone if you approach the injustice-doer and slap him/her in the face before he/she does anything to you. Also, you would be proving that you are on the side of Justice. Avoid her. She bites.

The beginning teacher rarely has a dramatic clash with one of his peers. Peer influence is strong, but it is also subtle. Contact with peers only gradually shapes attitudes toward school, toward what constitutes good instruction, toward administrators and toward the children themselves. The following is from an account of a beginning teacher's first weeks of teaching.

The older teachers who have been there three or four years usually sit together. Yesterday I had yard duty, which meant I had to eat lunch a little earlier than the rest of the teachers, so I ate with two of the older teachers. . . . We discussed some of the idealism behind teaching. I was told they wouldn't advise someone to come into the school system. When I asked the reason, they told me that the children were getting too hard to handle. . . . They also told me how in a couple of weeks my idealism would have been worn off. It's easy to work with a slow class that is well behaved because you don't have to work too hard. I should not expect too much from these children whose I.Q.'s are in the high 60's and low 70's, and I should just try to teach them as much as I could. . . .

Mrs. Holtzman was a teacher last term, and now she's the library teacher. She usually takes my class if I have yard duty or a conference. . . . She told me, "I feel sorry for you having those kids for the whole term because they're a wild group." . . .

There's a teacher whose line is always behind me. . . . She's an experienced teacher. I don't know how long she's been teaching, but she's another one who reassures me that I'm doing well, and I have a bad class, and I have to make the best of it. . . .

Then an older teacher started in telling me that soon I would start getting letters with four-letter words. The kids start writing letters to the teachers using obscenities, and I shouldn't be surprised when I get these and think they are sending them just to me, because the older teachers get them.

And there's another teacher, Phoebe Epstein, who teaches the last fifth grade in the level. She's a lot of help to me because she encourages me. . . . We have yard duty together, and we talk. And I always say, "I just don't know what I'm going to do. I can't seem to cover anything during the day. I just do reading and arithmetic, and that's all I get to cover during the day." She encourages me. She's really terrific. She tells me, "Just do what you can; don't be disappointed. Everybody has the same thing. It's not only you." [18]

When new teachers join a faculty, the other teachers are understandably curious about how they are going to fit in. Since we all secretly want other people to be like us, it is not surprising that some people get anxious if an energetic newcomer tries to introduce new ideas.

John Canfield/History:
Students were not the only people that I confused during the course of the year. When one is a new teacher, he is looked upon as some kind of threatening animal which is ready to prey upon the older teachers, to turn the students against them, and to subvert the social order that they have carefully constructed over the many years that they have been there. Any innovation that one tries in the classroom or in operation of the school is looked upon as incompetence, negligence, or what is even worse, treason.

If one wished to take his students on a field trip, he was cross-examined at various levels as to the nature and purpose of the trip and was usually discouraged from its undertaking with stories of control problems, transportation difficulties and substitution difficulties. If one wished to eliminate a portion of the curriculum for something he felt was more relevant to the particular needs of the students at that time, he was reprimanded for not performing his task properly, or was questioned (even by members of other departments) as to what he was doing.

---

[18] Eddy, *Becoming a Teacher*, p. 111.

I remember once when I showed an award-winning movie on the concentration camps in Germany during World War II to illustrate a point about man's inhumanity to man during times of war, my students reacted to the movie with what I felt was the proper amount of repulsion and shock. The older teachers, on the other hand, were up in arms about the showing of this film and made it a point at one of our very infrequent teachers' meetings. With the exception of the few Jewish teachers on the faculty, who supported my showing of the film, the other teachers either supported the attack or stood by in quiet acquiescence.[19]

Teachers sometimes get in the way of one another. They can grate on one another's nerves. They sometimes find ways of avoiding one another. And occasionally they annoy one another professionally. One teacher may teach another's "specialty," thus spoiling the opportunity for his colleague. Or a teacher may assign so much homework that his students have no time to do the work assigned by a less punitive teacher. And sometimes a teacher may be so relaxed about rules that he makes another look like an ogre.

Linda Corman/English:

I declare at the outset that, though a teacher, I am altogether human: I want to be accepted, to be liked, to succeed, to feel strength or, perhaps, power. One way to do this—the quickest way, I found—is to appeal directly to the students. This doesn't necessarily mean turning one's classroom into a carnival, but it does mean seeking and taking seriously student feedback. A teacher who plays the role, consciously or otherwise, of an overgrown adolescent, a "with-it" hippie, or the like, often enjoys quite a headstart on the academic, theory-befuddled graduate. Once when I was playing a Donovan recording of Shakespeare's lyric "Under the Greenwood Tree," a student observed: "When we listened to this record in Mr. Krick's class, we turned the lights out and he let us smoke so we could really groove it; this is a drag." Thinking that I had been quite clever and appealing in bringing a popular folk ballad to my English literature class, my hopes fell painfully at this remark and I turned my disappointment into resentment against the other teacher, who had broken school regulations, I felt, at my expense, making my job even more difficult. Such feelings, I soon realized, were not unusual among teachers.[20]

While we strongly believe that the teaching profession has a larger percentage of dedicated, selfless people than any other profession (excepting, perhaps, the ministry), it nevertheless has its share of rogues and fools. The beginner should pick his way among this field of new colleagues with some care.

INSTRUCTION: SO MUCH TO LEARN

In an ultimate sense the teacher's only real problem is the failure of the children to learn and to develop. (All other conflicts, worries and defeats pale

---

[19] Ryan, *Don't Smile,* p. 45.

[20] *Ibid.,* pp. 117–118.

Jim: What exactly do we mean by "the closeness of the relationship between a teacher's instruction and his student's learning is frequently
overstated"?

Kevin: People often speak as if there were a one-to-one relationship between teaching and learning. This just isn't true. Teachers behave—
question, lecture, joke, drill—in front of their students, but how much
of this teacher activity results in student learning? I suspect not as
much as we'd like to think.

Jim: Are you saying that teachers are effective with some kids on some
days and some kids on another?

Kevin: Partly, but also that we have been overemphasizing the importance
of the teacher actively engaging in teaching students. Our schools
are organized on that teacher-dominant model and it just doesn't
work that well. It's sometimes valuable, but it is overdone.

Jim: Are you implying that emphasis on the closeness of the teaching-
learning relationship keeps teachers from letting kids learn from one
another or from other adults or independently, on their own?

Kevin: Yeah. I guess that's what I'm saying.
Jim: We agree, then.

in significance if the children are learning and developing their human potential.) The degree of the children's success as learners is the measure of
our success or failure. Although the closeness of the relationship between a
teacher's instruction and his students' learning is frequently overstated, it
is a crucial relationship. And teaching effectiveness, as we have said earlier,
is an area where there are few naturals. The new teacher normally has a
number of problems in the area of instruction.

A major difficulty is the sheer newness of the role. There is little in the way
of gradual immersion into the role of teacher. After a little student teaching,
you suddenly find yourself in charge of your own class and responsible for
taking it from the first day of school to the last.

Maxine Bell/Grade Two:
Now that it is over this whole first year seems unbelievable. So much has gone on.
I have changed so. So many of my cherished beliefs about myself and education have
gone down the drain or been drastically reshaped. I was so confident, but so ignorant
when I started. There were so many little things that I didn't know how to do . . . like
passing out papers or assigning them work. I had so many hot ideas and most of them
I didn't have the foggiest about putting them into actual operation. I was a bug on the
importance of individualized instruction. I wrote two or three papers on it during

teacher training. I knew all the right words to say about individualized instruction, but I *couldn't do it in my class.* I still believe in it . . . perhaps even more, but I'm just not able to make it operational, to make it go with my kids. Whenever I think back on this year, the image that keeps coming to mind is of a farmer plowing a new field and breaking fresh ground. I didn't have any old furrows to follow. I never knew when I was going to hit against a rock . . . and I did hit some rocks. Sometimes when I expected the plowing to be toughest, it was easiest. And the reverse was equally true. I have to be on my toes every minute of the year it seems. So much planning and adjusting and replanning. I'm glad it is over, and I'm tired. It's been a lot of trouble, this first year, but deep down I'm really proud of myself.

Funny thing about problems. They hurt, but they also make us strong.

During stable periods in the life of a society, there is little disagreement about what should be taught and how. These are not such gentle times. We appear to be in a transitional stage and, while it is not yet clear what kind of curriculum we need, it is increasingly apparent that the standard curricula of the Fifties and Sixties will not do. The search for effective curricular materials is engaged in by all conscientious teachers, but it is a special problem for the new teacher.

Marion Krug/Eighth Grade:

The overriding question of this year has been, "What works?" I'm in a constant search for materials. It is never-ending. My kids aren't that bright, but they devour material and look at me as if to say, "Well, what's next?" Our school has a curriculum guide that is only five years old, but it is terribly dated already. The students know a lot of the stuff already. They learned it in lower grades or just picked it up. They are bored by a good bit of the rest, too. I'm constantly squeezing ideas and tips from the other eighth-grade teachers. They are helpful, but they are in the same box I am. Then there is the problem of getting a big buildup on a particular workbook or special unit by a teacher who has had fabulous success with it. I try it and I fall on my face with it. Then there are the kids. They are so fickle. A couple of times I took their suggestion on things they wanted to study and work on. After much work and many late hours, I'd get these classes prepared and the very same kids who were so anxious to make the suggestions now couldn't care less.

My school district has curriculum specialists. Some of them are very good, too. Particularly the math specialist. He would give me too much material. I'd spend hours deciding about which approach to use to teach ten minutes worth of material. The language arts specialist was a sweet lady, but very rarely available and most of her ideas were really out to lunch. I was on my own there. When you get right down to it, you have to make the curriculum and the materials *yours* before they are any good to you. Someone else's brilliant materials are nothing until you have made them your own. This is hard to do the first year.

As the following illustrates, neither homemade nor prepackaged materials are completely satisfying.

Eleanor Fuke/Social Studies:

My advisor hit upon what sounded like the ideal solution. To relieve some of the pressure, he suggested I use only already-prepared materials. So far I had been creating my own course materials. These I would painfully extract from scholarly

TEACHERS

Men must be taught as if you taught them not,
And things unknown propos'd as things forgot.
  Alexander Pope, Essay on Criticism, *III, 15*

No man can reveal to you aught but that which already lies half asleep in
the dawning of your knowledge.
  Kahlil Gibran, The Prophet

books on the subject in question, and then edit down to the vocabulary level of a particular class. Such an attempt at creativity didn't always stem from a reformist zeal; often there simply were no materials available on the subjects I wanted to teach and my students wanted to study. The students suffered a double handicap in this respect. Not only were there no materials already prepared, but I am not an especially creative person, and what I came up with on my own wasn't the most stimulating work.

My advisor's plan, then, wasn't such a good one after all. To follow it, we would have to forget about drugs and other current topics, because there just are no materials available in cheap, easy-to-read, multiple copies. . . .[21]

It is not uncommon for the beginning teacher to find himself in conflict with administrators and other teachers over the appropriateness of certain materials or instructional procedures. Often excellent curriculum formulated in the universities or by publishing houses are unknown or not accepted in the real world of schools.

Miss Peters/Grade 4:
When I went downstairs for lunch the principal came over to me and he took up most of my lunch hour telling me about the observation. He criticized me on two things. Number one, the way that I teach the words—which is by teaching both groups' words to the whole class. This is what I've been told to do in the reading course and this was what the assistant principal told me to do and this is what I myself have found very effective. He criticized this, and the other thing he criticized is one of the drill games which I use and which I have also learned from this course. In short, the only things that he criticized me for were things that the assistant principal had told me to do and things which I had gotten from the reading course.[22]

Another order of problem develops when the teacher begins to doubt the importance of what he has to teach. The prescribed high-school curriculum in American literature is jocularly questioned by this young teacher.

Gary Cornog/English:
My first few weeks of futility with *Macbeth* in the junior classes and with Puritan thought in the senior class were not relieved when I contemplated the prospect which

---

[21] *Ibid.,* pp. 140–141.

[22] Fuchs, *Teachers Talk,* pp. 148–149.

Bruno Bettelheim (1903–   )

Bruno Bettelheim's life is a vivid illustration of the idea that any situation can be an occasion for learning: it was as a prisoner in Nazi concentration camps that he first observed the dramatic and reversible effects of environment on personality.

Bettelheim was born in Vienna to a family he describes as "assimilated Jewish bourgeoisie," and grew up during one of the most brilliant periods in Viennese artistic and intellectual life. He studied philosophy and art history, took a Ph.D. in esthetics, and then switched to psychoanalysis, largely as a result of his interest in mentally disturbed children.

In 1932, Bettelheim and his first wife took an autistic child into their home. Autism, a form of childhood schizophrenia characterized by total withdrawal from reality, abnormal subjectivity and extreme negativism, was believed at the time to be a congenital disturbance, but Bettelheim was convinced otherwise. For six years he and his wife created an environment in their home designed to undo the child's emotional isolation. This experiment ended abruptly in 1938 when the Nazis invaded Austria and Bettelheim was taken to the concentration camp at Dachau and, later, Buchenwald.

To fight despair during his stay in the camps, Bettelheim tried to make sense of the behavior of inmates living under extreme stress. As a Freudian, he had believed personality change to be a slow process, but in Buchenwald he observed men break in a few weeks. Later Bettelheim infuriated many people by criticizing European Jews for being insufficiently forceful in their opposition to the Nazis.

After his release in 1939, Bettelheim came to the U.S. and joined the faculty of the University of Chicago, first as a research associate in education and later as director of the Sonia Shankman Orthogenic School. What he had learned from psychoanalysis and in the internment camps led Bettelheim to ideas which he determined to put into practice in the school for disturbed children. If a negative environment could destroy human personality, he reasoned, an overwhelmingly positive environment might restore it. Under his direction, the school has become a bright and happy place, full of cheerful drawings, comfortable furnishings and good food. It is not unusual to see an 18-year-old's bed covered with stuffed animals—gifts from the school. "Dr. B.," as the children call him, believes that a patient can begin to realize that it is he who is sick—not the outside world—only as he becomes convinced that there is someone available to him who will help him get well. According to Bettelheim, only another person, not drugs or shock treatment, can lead the mentally ill back to reality.

When Bettelheim assumes the role of university professor of psychology, psychiatry and education, his style changes. He was recently introduced by one of his former students at a public lecture as the leading exemplar of "teaching by attack." He is intellectually stimulating, demanding and controversial as a teacher, and students often remark, "There's no one like him. You either love him or hate him."

Although a disciple of John Dewey, Bettelheim criticizes the schools' misapplication of Dewey's ideas. "The biggest nonsense in American education today," he told his graduate class in education, "is for the teacher to tell her pupils, 'Look, children, it's easy.' Make it attractive, not easy. The task must be made possible, and it must be meaningful. Ease has no place in it." This remark also sums up his attitude toward rebellious youth. Bettelheim believes the young need something to push against to find their identities, and became "something to push against" himself by telling student radicals that they are sick. The difference between the violent militant and the reformer, he maintains, is that the militant is motivated more by inner anger than by the wrongs of society. "We need a lot more people who work hard at reforming society," Bettelheim declares.

lay ahead of me. After Edwards, American literature seemed like a vast, hideous waste-land sparsely covered with stunted trees and unrelieved desolation—an intellectual Nevada—before an author of interest would provide us with an oasis. (Hawthorne, alas, seemed more like a mirage.) I would first have to slog through my colonial literati, then Irving and Poe, then Bryant (I decided to skip him), then Emerson (poor Waldo—so profound, so uptight on Nature, so uncool—I would have a hard time justi-fying the ways of Emerson to my seniors), then Thoreau ("He must be a communist!" they'll say, I know it; at any rate he's subversive), and finally to Melville. Oh, and of course the *Scarlet Letter;* I almost forgot that one. The menu of our literature would not be complete without that entrée: one has not had a high school education in Amer-ica unless one has had a pinch of Prynne and a dollop of Dimmesdale.[23]

The actual skills and strategies of instruction can be another problem area. Few teacher education programs have adequate staff to ensure that their graduates have mastered the teaching skills they will need in the field. Most programs are forced to rely on a rather academic study of the teaching pro-cess. As a result, the beginning teacher may know *what* to do, but not *how to do it.*

Rita Hodges/Grade 5:
I'm living proof that teaching is harder than it looks. I've always been a good student. I did very well in my education courses. In fact, I got an A in methods! However, I just about flunked once I had my own class. I really like working with the children inde-pendently and in small groups, but once I had to be up front, before the entire class, I'd have trouble. Little things that I had taken for granted became quite difficult to do well. I'd always admired teachers who can ask a lot of good questions and keep things really moving without having to step in and monopolize. Admiring is not doing, believe me! I discovered that asking questions is tricky business. First, it isn't that easy to come up with good ones. Then, calling on someone who you think can answer it or explore the question in an interesting way. Now, the tricky part. Listening carefully to what the student is saying and at the same time evaluating what he is saying and thinking of an appropriate response to his remarks *and* on top of that trying to figure out what the next move should be. Should I ask him another question? Should I call on Lois, who is falling asleep in the back? Should I try Sue who is so eager with that waving hand and always so painfully wrong with her answers? Where should I go? Should I correct what the first student said or get a student to . . . meanwhile losing the train of thought I was trying to develop. It's very complex, this teaching game.

Both the teacher and the student need to know if learning is taking place. This aspect of instruction is accomplished by means of evaluation. Having been on the receiving end of grades for years seems to be inadequate prep-aration for the job of evaluating the performances of one's students. The marking periods during the first year can be times of confusion and turmoil.

Wylie Crawford/Science:
At our school, however, the policy has been to give a non-weighted grade to all students. This meant that a B was a B was a B, no matter what brand of science was

---

[23] Ryan, *Don't Smile,* pp. 6–7.

being studied. After the first marking period it became clear that few of the new teachers understood this policy, for it was discovered that there were an excessive number of failures in the A and B [Advanced] tracks. The question that naturally arose was, how can a teacher be expected to compare a student's scientific savvy in, say, mechanics, with another's competence in general ecology? Even worse, since none of us had any contact with the student in the C-track, we were poorly qualified to judge the difference between a D and an F, since we had no idea how most of the students receiving these grades were doing. An experienced teacher, of course, has a better idea of the range of achievement of his students and is capable of grading any one student against a composite picture of all past classes. But I had no such scale to go by, and so had to rely on a somewhat mathematical approach. Since the science grades for all the juniors would theoretically yield the proverbial bell-shaped curve, and since by the junior year most students had presumably been placed in the right track, the vast majority of the C's should fall in the middle track. This group should also contain a moderate number of B's and D's and very few A's or F's. On any given test, then, the clump of students around the average score would receive a C. Medium-sized clusters above or below this C group would receive B's and D's. Then what about the stragglers? How far below the D range would still be a D, and how far below would be an F? Here, we were told, the teacher could be subjective (as he is in all grading, after all). Well, after much soul-searching, I was usually capable of justifying failing grades for students who really deserved them; but this was an unpleasant process, and the sort of thing that should only happen to a teacher once every few months, just in time for report cards.[24]

Becoming an "evaluator" is easier for some than for others. For a few the evaluation process is a source of great anguish and self-doubt.

Gary Cornog/English:
So absorbed was I in the day-to-day crisis that it came as a great shock to me to discover, close to the end of the first grading period, that I really did not have much data upon which to base a fair evaluation of my students. Having been some six years removed from the high-school environment myself, and having in the interim become accustomed to the mid-term exam, final exam, term paper routine of college course work, I had not given much thought to the matter of tests and papers when I began to teach. More because of a desire to vary routine class activities than to discover the effectiveness of my teaching, I had given quizzes to the juniors on *Macbeth* and one or two short theme assignments to the seniors. I recall noting with some embarrassment the sparseness of little red marks in my grade book in comparison with the handsome display of the same in the grade books of other teachers. The end of the first grading period, consequently, was a very trying experience for me.

It was puzzling to me how experienced teachers could grade as much student work as their grade books indicated. I found it extremely difficult at first to grade just one theme. Just as I feared making students mad at me by taking disciplinary action, so I also feared their ire as a result of the low grades I might give them on papers and tests. I think I rationalized this scruple (if that is what it was) by saying to myself, "Who am I to judge the excellence of a student's work?" Obviously the consequence of carrying

---

[24] *Ibid.*, pp. 90–91.

TEACHERS

Photo on preceeding page by T. C.
Abell through Stock, Boston.
Photos on this page by Mark Silber.

this sort of philosophy to various logical conclusions would be complete withdrawal from all evaluative activities—i.e., who am I to judge the worth of this presidential candidate; who am I to judge the sourness of this milk, etc. But at the time, that way of thinking had a definite appeal to my propensity for self-doubt.[25]

STUDENTS: FRIENDS AND FIENDS

What schools are all about is children. They are at the core of the teacher's sense of achievement or dissatisfaction. They are her victory and her defeat. So much of a teacher's work involves children that it is impossible that she *not* have problems with them. It is difficult, if not dangerous, to deal with such a complex and important topic in the space we have allotted. The subject involves so many variables: the personalities of different teachers; the ages of the children, all the way from nursery schoolers to high-school seniors; differences in the amount of contact a teacher has with her students, which can vary from all day every day to the once-a-week visits of a specialist teacher. In short, the complexity of the topic is outweighed only by its importance to the teacher's success and satisfaction.

The Minnesota Teacher Attitude Inventory, a test frequently given to college students planning to become teachers, is designed to measure attitudes which predict how well they will get along with students in interpersonal situations. Indirectly, it attempts to indicate how well-satisfied the test-taker will be with teaching as a vocation.[26] The test has been a very popular instrument for research on teaching, and has been used in over fifty research studies. One of these studies had curious results:

Large numbers of college students in teacher education programs, and a group of over one hundred beginning teachers, were given the test. The test asks many questions dealing with positive attitudes and feelings of warmth toward one's potential students. The test results show—and they show this very clearly—that the longer college students stay in teacher training programs the more positive and warm their attitudes toward students become. But among beginning teachers there is a sharp drop in positive attitudes toward students. In fact, beginning teachers' scores are significantly lower than those of students just entering teacher training. In other words, as people enter training, their attitudes toward students are positive and become increasingly so until they enter their own classrooms, when their attitudes become sharply less positive.

Why does this happen? How do you explain this phenomenon? As at a number of other points throughout this book, we would like you to stop reading for a moment and jot down some hypotheses about why beginning teachers' attitudes change this way.

---

[25] *Ibid.*, pp. 8–9.

[26] N. L. Gage, ed., *Handbook of Research on Teaching* (Chicago: Rand McNally, 1963), p. 509.

What happens between the time one is a college student preparing to teach and the time one actually becomes a teacher is undoubtedly a complicated series of events. We would like to offer our own hypothesis on the issue: College students alternate between being highly idealistic and highly realistic in their outlooks. However, when they enter teacher training, most become very idealistic (thank God!) about children and education. They believe deeply that teachers should have warm relations with students, making the classroom more relaxed and more responsive to the needs of students than it normally is. As the college student takes more education courses and observes in classrooms, his views of children become more idealistic and, as a result, more positive. By graduation, the rose-colored glasses are firmly affixed.[27] Also, he has usually managed to completely shut out some of the more realistic memories of his own childhood and adolescence. He forgets that he joined with the other seventh-graders to put four tacks on Miss Derriere's chair. He blots out all the juicy stories, most of which he knew were untrue, about the young home economics teacher. He forgets about how he enjoyed reading (writing?) obscenities about his math teacher on the lavatory wall. They all forget how cruel kids can be to kids.

---

[27] This analysis does not, we fear, account for the Lundquist Affect, named after our good friend, Ernie Lundquist. Ernie deviated (as is his habit) from the normal. As Ernie progressed through teacher training he began to dislike children more and more. By the time he graduated he had a well-developed distaste for, as he called them, "the little creeps." So Ernie decided not to become a teacher. He became an administrator. However, Ernie found sitting in his office quite lonely. The only people who came to see him were children. As Ernie talked to the children about what his school was really like, he gradually came to like, and eventually, to love children. But as for teachers . . .

"Alice, we've decided that from now on we're going to call you Fatso Alice. . . . Why are you crying, Fatso Alice?"

"We started this club, Roger, and it's called the Red Devils. But you can't be part of it because you smell real bad, Roger."

"PIMPLES! PIMPLES! EARL HAS LOTS OF PIMPLES. . . . Boy, look at old Earl run. And he's crying, too. What a sissy dope."

"My mother's a WHAT?!!"

"I can always spot a fruit. I can tell Paul's one just by the way he walks."

Need we say more? Just think back over your experiences with, and as, children, in and out of schools. Children are a mixed bag. So is the behavior of an individual child. One day he is eligible for canonization and the next day cannons should be aimed at him. Somehow, though, the dark side of human nature recedes from view during teacher education. Fear not. It reappears. The beginning teacher rediscovers human fallibility, in her children and in herself, and the result is that her affirmative attitudes toward children plummet. Normally positive attitudes make a comeback, although they rarely regain the euphoric heights they reached during the latter stages of teacher training.

A thorough discussion of the teacher-student relationship would take several volumes. Because of space limitations, we will restrict our attention to three areas: discipline, social distance and sex.

Discipline. Classroom control, classroom management or discipline (pick your euphemism) is one of those problems that shouldn't exist. After all, school is an opportunity for children. The teacher works hard to help them. It's simple: the teacher is there to teach and students are there to learn. Unfortunately, though, things do not work out this way.

The great majority of schools—whether kindergartens or high schools—are organized with the expectation that the teacher will be "in charge" of her class. You may not like this, and there are things you can do about it.[28] But it is still what is generally expected of a teacher by the children, the administration and peers. (We will return to this matter of expectations in the section on social distance.) Few (and lucky) are the teachers who do not have to come to grips with their role as disciplinarian.

A discipline problem occurs when the expected pattern of classroom behavior is violated. Normally, a breach of discipline is an overt act by one or more students which distracts attention from or interrupts the performance of the task at hand. Discipline problems are endemic to the first-year teacher. High-school students report that discipline is the most serious weakness of

[28] See Herbert Kohl, *The Open Classroom: A Practical Guide to a New Way of Teaching* (New York: New York Review/Vintage Books, 1969).

DIALOGUE

Jim: *I wish we could take care of this sticky topic of discipline with a few well-chosen clichés. For instance, "Well-planned and well-executed lessons are sure-fire insurance against discipline problems."*

Kevin: *How about "There is no such thing as a bad child. Only bad teachers."*

Jim: *Or "Be fair, firm and consistent."*

Kevin: *These sayings may be good advice, but this approach skirts the real problem. New teachers normally have discipline problems, and pretending they don't exist doesn't help.*

Jim: *The problem is that if we talk about discipline and control of students, we sound as if we're supporting the authoritarian-teacher model. On the other hand, we've probably made our bias clear earlier.*

Kevin: *I'm sure, too, that even teachers in open, more democratically-run schools have discipline problems.*

Jim: *I think you're right. Let's get to it.*

A BOY IS A BOY IS A BOY

The boy 1969 is still a boy not too unlike the Penrods of the past. He is neither alienated nor obsessed with sex or revolution, according to a four-year study of middle-class suburban high school boys conducted by Daniel Offer and a team of Chicago psychiatrists. The most systematic study of teenagers ever done, the Modal Adolescent Project is described in The Psychological World of the Teenager, by Daniel Offer.

The boys studied thought their single greatest problem was deciding on a career and completing the appropriate educational steps toward it. In spite of their preoccupation with careers, they couldn't wait to be finished with the means of attaining a career—school.

The typical suburban teenager really likes his parents—or at least one of them at a time. The boys could also be quite critical of their parents, but few had consistently bitter feelings towards them.

The teachers they liked best were athletic coaches, because they felt coaches treated them as individuals. Asked to describe the ideal teacher, their responses ranged from "How should I know? I never had one," to "He wants you to understand the subject, not just memorize a bunch of facts."

These boys largely shared their parents' middle-class values. About 90 percent planned to attend college, although as a group they were not particularly studious or intellectual. Despite parental emphasis on study, the *investigators found that the same percentage of both generations would choose a football game over a lecture by a famous scientist.*

The new generation is not idealistic. Asked what they would do with a million dollars, the vast majority said they would spend, save or invest it for themselves. They had opinions on the major issues of the day—the Viet Nam war and civil rights—but were not moved to work for causes.

The investigators felt that the boys' rebelliousness against parents and school was a normal step toward independence, not a new form of ideological dissent. Stubbornness over hair, dress and music are methods teenagers use to emancipate themselves from adult pressures. At the same time, they do not take issue with any of the fundamental values of their parents' generation. They do not drop out, use drugs or destroy property.

The study found that adults permit adolescents some latitude for experimenting before committing themselves to a role in life. For example, teachers quietly tolerate some infractions of school rules, like smoking. More overt acts like stealing or throwing bottles on highways were tried once or twice by a quarter of the boys. But most boys release their aggressive impulses in competitive sports.

Dr. Offer suggests that society has recently encouraged, rather than just tolerated, adolescent rebellion by romanticizing it. "We in the social sciences also glamorize the rebellions that offer us a possibility of change. Whether the young people of today, a sample of which we studied, will change the world and make it a better place is a sociological question. Social engineers like Paul Goodman feel that youth ought to change the world. It is our impression that the sample investigated by us is growing up to become very much a part of the culture into which they were born."

The myth of the increase of sexuality among high school students did not apply to these boys. Those who approved of premarital intercourse added "only after high school." The reason they gave was fear of the girl becoming pregnant. When means of preventing pregnancy were mentioned, they maintained they were "just not mature enough to handle it."

Psychologists are following up the 73 boys in the Modal Adolescent Project to find out how they adapt to the new demands of college, the Army, jobs and marriage. On the whole the boys were adjusting well.

Most of the boys had been good athletes in high school. When sports became less central in their lives, an important source of self-image disappeared. Most boys set about filling the vacuum left by their separation from parents and regaining self-confidence lost along with sports by involving themselves in new interests—studies, friends, girls, civil rights activities. About a quarter of the boys experimented with drugs and sex, but the majority seemed well on their way to conventional maturity.

Adapted from Rita Kramer, "The State of the Boy, 1969," *New York Times Magazine* (March 30, 1969): 97 ff.

first-year teachers.[29] Most supervisors and administrators (not to mention elementary students) would agree. The basic explanation for this phenomenon is simply that first-year teachers have had little practice in being "in charge." Few college students have had much opportunity to give orders, coordinate the activities of a group of people or tell others to do such things as "Quiet down," or "Stay in your seat!" Young women are often particularly unaccustomed to leadership roles. Students, on the other hand, are accustomed to being taught by experienced teachers who know how to control them, usually rather effortlessly. Further, students can sense inexperience and hesitancy in a new teacher. Finally, school is not all fun and games for children and they can get restless and bored. (Remember when you were in elementary and secondary school. Remember how long the schoolday was, how long you had to sit still at a stretch and how much you had to do that didn't interest you.) These conditions, plus the potential for friction in any group of so many people, make it almost inevitable that the first-year teacher have some trouble establishing the kind of productive relationship with students she seeks.

Anonymous/Elementary:

I had trouble with Roberto at the first of this week. He sits right in front of me . . . and he can talk to me. I'll be sitting at my desk, and he'll look over and take something from my desk. If I'm standing up and put something on my desk, he'll have to see what it is. He talks out constantly if I'm giving a lesson, without raising his hand, and he'll have the answers. He'll have wisecracks—like if I yell at someone to do something, he'll turn around and yell. I have my own little assistant teacher in there, and I keep saying, *"I'm* the teacher, not you. . . . Why are *you* telling them what to do?"[30]

Wylie Crawford/Science:

In the beginning, my fears about discipline and class control were abated. Instead of finding students who were organized for an all-out, massed offensive, I found students who wished for the most part to be left alone; instead of finding students who were outspoken and arrogant, I found students who were yielding and eager not to "make waves." For the first week or two, the vast majority of my students just sat, seemed to listen attentively, and asked questions when called for. . . .

. . . my ideal classroom was one in which everyone was happy, where everyone felt free to speak out when he had something important to say, without fear of harsh criticism or ridicule from me or from his fellows. To create such a situation, it was only natural to smile, and so I did. And eventually, the class did too, but in a slightly different way. As the first month passed, the routine and boredom of even this school began to set in. Many of the students did not understand why they were required to take four years of science (or English, or physical education, for that matter). The

---

[29] Roy C. Bryan, *Reactions to Teachers by Students, Parents and Administrators,* Report of Cooperative Research Project No. 668, U.S. Office of Education (Kalamazoo, Michigan: Western Michigan University, 1963).

[30] Eddy, *Becoming a Teacher,* p. 89.

happy, relaxed, loosely-disciplined class which I saw developing began to take strange and subtle turns in the wrong directions. The students were not just happy and relaxed, they were content and almost asleep. I started to get the message: their natural curiosity had not been aroused. I tried to spice up my presentations and asked more questions of individuals in the class, but this seemed to no avail. The symptoms persisted—one student would be looking out the window; another student would be sitting on a table when there were chairs still available; two girls would be gossiping just a little too loud, and would continue even when I approached and finally stood right next to them. While these were noticeable changes, no one of them was objectionable enough to make a big fuss about. After all, my own concept of the ideal classroom atmosphere was broad enough to allow for occasional disinterested students. There would be days when they, too, would become involved and some other students would lose interest. Besides, in the cosmic view of things, the state of the world today was not going to hinge on the fact that a few minor infractions were tolerated occasionally. Treating the students as adults, I felt that they knew they were pushing my patience a bit and that a gentle reminder would be sufficient to set things straight. And it did, for a while. But soon I found myself giving mild admonishments more and more often, and always to the same small group of offenders. Now, instead of just looking out the window, they were waving to passing cars while my back was turned. Instead of just sitting on the tables, a few were sprawled out on them. My resolve was still not shaken. They would soon tire of such shenanigans, and I could win them back through my artfully-designed presentations. After all, I had expected much worse, and we were still getting used to each other. When they saw the folly of it all, our little testing period would be over.

In reality, as far as the students were concerned, the testing period was already over, and they had won the game. I was going to be a pushover. And, since the other students had been watching the events of the first month, my list of offenders got longer as my blood pressure got higher. The situation got to the point where I had to brace myself before walking into certain particularly "liberated" classes.[31]

Social Distance. Establishing an appropriate social distance with students occupies a good deal of the attention and energy of a beginning teacher. Like discipline techniques, a correct social distance does not come with a teaching certificate or one's first job. Beginning teachers frequently take refuge in the two extremes of behavior. Many hide their insecurities by acting strict, businesslike and bordering on being hostile. Others attempt to be completely "natural." They reject the stiff "teacherish" image and seek to break down all barriers between themselves and their students. The first extreme, the overly strict teacher, can give rise to long-term difficulties, while the "natural" teacher usually has short-term problems.

The problem with playing the role of the overly strict, aloof teacher is that it might become a permanent habit. Acting like a Prussian officer might appeal to a hidden need for submission in others. Also, one might begin to believe that "a quiet class is a good class," education's version of "the only good Indian is a dead Indian."

---

[31] Ryan, *Don't Smile,* pp. 85–87.

Our actions are like pebbles dropped in a pool. After the initial splash, the ripples go on and on. The young teacher in this true account acted to solve a problem and the effects of her efforts are still reverberating.

EIGHTH GRADE REBEL

Eighth grade was my rebellious year, a year of testing authority to its break-ing point. For Miss B., a young and inexperienced teacher of English, the battle was lost before the fighting began. After several weeks, I was de-termined to humiliate her, to destroy what little domination she had over the class and over me. I talked loudly to my neighbor during grammar lec-tures, handed in assignments only when the mood moved me, and popped chewing gum into my mouth every day before class, despite almost daily requests to throw it in the wastebasket.

My relationship with Miss B. grew more and more strained and finally reached a crisis in early May when each pupil was required to write an autobiography for the permanent school record. Since it was to be a major production, Miss B. gave us several weeks to plan, prepare, and write. At first I had great plans for my life story. It was to be full of drama and humor, eloquence and symbolism.

But it was spring and my mind always seemed to slip out the window with the first lazy flies. Besides, I kept telling myself, I didn't care. The day before the papers were due, Miss B. called me up to her desk.

"Well, how's your autobiography coming? I haven't seen you working on it much during class."

I shrugged my shoulders. "Oh, it's O.K."

"May I see what you have, please?"

I found a rough outline I had made two weeks before and defiantly pre-sented it to her.

"Is this all you have?"

I nodded. She gazed out the window for a long time, then sighed and turned to me, "I want to see you at 3:30. Be prepared to stay a while."

War was finally declared.

When I came in that afternoon, she was working at her desk. She mo-tioned me to a seat, sat up a little straighter, then put her pen down and looked straight into my eyes. "Do you have any idea what a disappoint-ment you have been to me? Or how you've cheated yourself this year?"

I stared back at her, unfazed, and waited for her to continue.

"I have tried hard to understand what's bothering you, why you have completely rejected all my efforts to teach you. Frankly, I'm at my wits' end."

I was silent, determined not to show a hint of emotion. She tried again.

"The tragedy is that you could be one of my best students. You know as

well as I that you have both the interest and aptitude for English—if you'd only use them. Why do you refuse to?"

She was hitting hard. I stared at my chipped fingernails. "I don't like English," I finally blurted out, angered at my own sheepishness.

Miss B. countered quickly, "How do you know when you've never given it a try?" More silence.

"Laurie," she said, "I desperately want to instill in you a desire to learn, but I can't force you to do what you won't. Don't you see that you're only fighting yourself? I realize some of what we do in class is boring and repetitious for you, but some of it is important—like the autobiography. It will be a record of the feelings, thoughts, and events of your life up until now. It will be a reflection of you, something that will tell you years from now exactly what you were like at this stage of your life. Don't you think you're worthy of such a record? If you do, I think you should take some time and effort to write one. If not, I'm not going to say any more. I realize now that the decision must be yours. What's your answer?"

I gave a hollow little "Yes" that came from deep inside me and barely escaped as a whisper. Suddenly, to my mortification, I found I was crying. I don't know whether they were tears of self-pity, relief, or anger; but I remember exactly how the white circle of Miss B.'s face began running at the edges into her hair and how I bumped into the corner of a desk on the way out.

I never really learned much in Miss B.'s English class. I did write my autobiography, and I stopped chewing gum. But this young teacher's words and our relationship left its mark on my self-centered world. I had seen what was for me a new side of education—that of giving, of honesty, and, most of all, of respect. I don't know exactly when I started regarding education as much more than a one-way funneling tube or when I realized that learning was, in the final analysis, a highly personal decision to give and work and care. I think it might have been in Miss B.'s English class. Laurie Hedgecock, student, Pembroke College, Providence, Rhode Island.

The problem confronting the overly "natural" teacher is that his view of "natural behavior" is frequently not the same as the children's. The students expect their teacher to interact with them in certain recognizable ways—that is, they expect a certain degree of social distance. They are confused or put off when the teacher acts like "one of the gang." The crux of the problem, then, is that the beginning teacher often wants to be a friend or a pal, while the students expect and want the teacher to be an adult. Students, because they are uncertain and striving to be adults themselves, seek strength and maturity from their teachers. Often they interpret the beginning teacher's efforts at naturalness and informality as weakness.

Joan Poster/Seventh Grade:

Most of my year was spent alternating between being Wanda the Witch and sweet little Miss Muffet. I started out determined to be different from all those cold teachers I had had. I was going to be everyone's sweet Big Sister. I really was surprised when this didn't work. The children didn't respond. If anything, they seemed to be confused. Some of them started treating me like their big sister and I found myself getting annoyed. They became very familiar and started asking me all sorts of embarrassing questions—both in and out of class. The final straw came when one of my boys—one of my favorites, too—came up to me in the hall while I was talking to a senior teacher.

"What's my new teacher like? Oh, she's a tall, willowy blonde, about twenty-five, with green eyes and a husky, sexy voice."

Smiling, he patted me on the back and said, "How's it goin', Miss Poster?" I was mortified.

After that little incident, I became tough. I was all business. If anyone got close to being familiar, I cut them off at the knees. I really said some nasty things. I was just so uptight that I overreacted. I guess I was hurt that my Big Sister routine didn't work. Later I realized that one reason behind my wanting to be Big Sister was simply that I wanted to be loved . . . at any cost. I guess my insecurities led me to seek love from my students. Anyway, I spent most of the year going back and forth on this issue. One week Wanda and the next Miss Muffet. It was really a strain . . . for me and the kids. Finally, toward the end of the year things began to straighten out and I stopped playing a role. It was much more fun that way. I think everyone was relieved.

Sex. Sex is one of the great unacknowledged issues in the American school. Sexual attraction and romance between students, and even, believe it or not, between teachers, is recognized. But the idea that there might be sexual attraction or romance between a teacher and a student is taboo. It simply is not talked about. This doesn't mean it doesn't exist. Beginning teachers are more likely than others to be faced with this problem. For one thing, they are nearer the students in age. Another factor that makes beginning teachers more vulnerable than experienced teachers is that they are often single, new to the community and lonely. The strain of the new job may increase their need for affection, and this need may find expression in their relationships with students. In the same way, students often become attracted to their teachers. They sometimes attach themselves to young teachers, greeting them in the morning and walking them to their cars after school. This, too, can be a very awkward situation, in that the student wants to be treated as special and to feel that his affection is reciprocated. If the teacher rejects or embarrasses the student, he can hurt the student deeply.

Besides the platonic attachments teachers can have to young children, it is quite conceivable that a 22-year-old teacher would find a 16-year-old student sexually attractive. As the following account indicates, high-school teachers are particularly vulnerable to sexual attraction or manipulation. Our only advice in this area is DON'T.

Gary Cornog/English:

In one class there dwelt a fair young creature who found me to be an easily flustered appreciator of her many charms. She was a coquette and, to my way of thinking, a dangerous one. She had me at a great disadvantage. While she could liltingly ask special favors of me (such as my continued toleration of her misbehavior in class), I could not cope with her in anything like a spontaneous way. Unless I was in a phenomenally commanding mood, I could expect to hear such daily entreaties as "Oh, Mr. Cornog! Mr. Cornog! Could you come here and help me?" "Mr. Cornog, I just don't understand!" (All this spoken in a voice of tender urgency.) She would have her left arm raised, her right arm aiding it, and would be leaning forward and upward from her desk so that (I thought) I would not fail to notice her finer endowments (I didn't).

"What is it, Julie?" I would reply, hoping the fear in my heart would not be evident in my voice. It nearly always was.

"Mr. Cornog, there's something here I don't understand. Could you come here and look at it?"

Don't, I tell myself. *Don't.*

"Read it to me and I'll explain it." (*From here,* I almost added, but that would be too obvious.) No. She's getting up.

"I'll bring it up there."

She approaches. She arrives at my left side. I note a scent of lemony perfume; an attempt at make-up about the eyes. She leans over to place the book in front of me, and some of her long dark hair grazes my shoulder. By this time I feel thoroughly unwilling to answer any question regarding syntax. *What about private tutoring?* I hear my lecherous innards suggesting. Heaven forbid! My frustration causes me to blurt a response to her query, hoping that she'll return to her seat. The class by this time has observed me melting into a limpid pool behind the desk. She must be smiling triumphantly above me, her glory reflected in my devastation. If only she had been as innocent of malice in her manipulations as I had been tender in my innocence, then all would have been well. Alas, she was not. She thought it great sport to exercise her arts for the benefit of her friends, and I could think of no way to break the spell. I could not ignore her, because then the class would notice my attempt and think that she had really gotten to me. I could not allow her to continue to dominate me, for then the respect I sought would never appear. Who could respect a hen-pecked English teacher? The befuddled teacher doing battle with the temptress every day—what a tableau! What a cliché. It pained me to see myself in such a humiliating posture. It was so absurd.[32]

Some first-year teachers become terribly discouraged by their relationships with students. Most of us teach because we like young people and want to work with them. When we are rejected or make fools of ourselves, it is painful. Most problems with students are a result of inexperience, and the majority of second-year teachers find that most of their previous problems disappear and they feel very much at ease with their students. Developing satisfying relations with students usually involves some initial uncertainty. However, previous experience with children as a camp counselor, settlement house worker or tutor can ease the transition. Contacts with children and adolescents before beginning teaching helps you learn about how you relate to children best.

PARENTS: THE SOON-TO-BE-DIFFERENTIATED MASS

The parent and the teacher are natural allies. Both are concerned about the child. They are both working to help the child develop his potential as a person, and both want the child to be happy, sensitive, intelligent and well-balanced. Frequently, though, the relationship between teacher and parent runs amuck and natural allies become enemies. Instead of devoting their energies toward understanding the child and aiding him, they waste them on conflict with one another.

For most prospective teachers, the parents of future students seem very

---

[32] *Ibid.,* pp. 18–19.

YOU KNOW YOU'RE IN TROUBLE WHEN

—the principal comes in to observe your teaching and you hear him snoring in the back of the room.

—the principal asks you what you plan to be doing next year.

—your students chip in at Christmas to buy you a book on careers in the foreign service.

—you have your students correct their own tests and the lowest mark in the class is 96 percent.

—it is 10:15 and the class has ripped through three-quarters of the work you have prepared for the day.

—you return after being sick for three days and the students chant, "We want the substitute!"

—it feels like February and it's only late September.

—you have threatened that if there is one more sound in the classroom you will personally call every parent to complain—and there is a sound.

—the teacher across the hall comes in and offers to show your kids who's boss.

—the parents of eleven of your students ask to see the principal and you are not invited.

—unsolicited, your principal offers to write a recommendation for your placement file.

—you are convinced you have finally come up with challenging and interesting work for your class and when you present it they chorus, "We did that last year."

—your favorite student comes up after class and asks you why you ever wanted to be a teacher—and you wonder, too.

—after sitting in your class for five minutes, your supervisor starts to shake his watch.

remote. They do not seem particularly important in the light of all the more obvious issues and sources of difficulty. If you try to picture them, what probably comes to mind is a huge, undifferentiated mass of faces. Once you begin to teach, however, certain personalities and types come quite vividly to life. In an effort to speed the process of differentiation, we offer the following capsule portraits of some of the more troublesome types.

Mrs. Mysonthegenius: She has a nice boy. He seems to have average intelligence and he's rather nervous. After meeting her, you know why. If he doesn't make it to Harvard, she will be shattered. When she is not busy telling him to work harder, she is trying to convince you how lucky you are to have a future Supreme Court Justice in your class.

Mrs. Putdown: The first thing she tells you is that she was once a teacher. She then finds innumerable opportunities to indicate how much she knows and how good she was . . . and still is. She questions you about your "rationale" for teaching this content or using that procedure. When you answer her, she informs you that she prefers the old ways, the tried and true ways. She has dozens of ways of reminding you that this is only your first year of teaching. You wish she would go back to teaching.

Mrs. Latecomer: Her daughter has really been a problem. The girl is obviously unhappy and seems to have made little progress all year. You have looked for the mother at PTA meetings and Open House nights, but she has never shown up. You have written notes home, but they haven't been answered. You have called to make appointments, but she has missed them, having forgotten that she had to go to her Garden Club those days. You send home a failing report card. She complains to the principal that you don't like her daughter.

Mr. Heavyhands: You are at your wits' end with one student and you need help from his parents. He's picked three fights this week and his work is dropping off badly. Other teachers have been complaining about him. You call his father, who roars that he will be right over to school. He arrives breathing fire. You explain your concern, and he keeps socking his fist into the palm of his hand and describing what will happen when he gets his hands on "that no-goodnik." He is embarrassed and hurt by his son's behavior and he has a very old and simple solution. You are sorry you called him.

Mrs. Youthinkyouvegotproblems: She attends all the school functions. However, she never wants to talk about her child. She wants to share her trials and tribulations with you. She heard you took a psychology course once and has chosen you as her therapist. She goes on and on and on. You get a tight feeling in the pit of your stomach.

Mrs. Specialhelp: Her son is doing very well in your class. She doesn't think so. He is always happy and carefree. She reports that he feels schoolwork is no challenge. She is convinced that he needs special attention. How about after-school tutoring? Maybe Saturday morning? All his other teachers gave him special attention. Aren't you "dedicated"?

The sources of teacher-parent problems are the same as those involved in any human relationship, but encounters are more highly charged than in most relationships. This is to be expected since a child and his future are at issue.

As we pointed out in Chapter Two, differences in perception frequently cause disagreement and conflict between people. A parent and a teacher are quite likely to perceive the same phenomenon in very different ways. The nerve-frazzled teacher perceives a child as a wild, undisciplined, raucous menace. The mother perceives her child as energetic, spontaneous and wonderfully social. Differences in perception are enhanced by the different circumstances under which they see the child. An apparently quiet, shy child is frequently a chatterbox in the security of his home.

Evaluation is another area of difficulty. It is part of the teacher's job to make judgments on a child's performance, a process which can touch on some deep insecurities. It can wound the hopes and aspirations of parents.

That this is the Age of Anxiety becomes very apparent to the teacher in her contacts with some parents who look to the school as the royal road to success for their children. In our competitive society, being average is taken by some as failure. If a child is average, something must be wrong with him. Or with you, his teacher. "How can he get over being 'average'?" The thought that their child could be *below* average is more than some parents can bear. For these reasons, the teacher needs to be especially sensitive when dealing with issues of evaluation, and would do well to stay away from what are, after all, meaningless terms like "above average" or "below average."

Social distance can be a source of difficulty in relations with parents as well as with students. Issues of social distance have been at the nub of much parent-teacher antagonism in recent years. Since most teachers are middle-class or aspiring to the middle class, they have little intrinsic trouble communicating with middle class people. But when they deal with parents from a lower or higher class or a different ethnic group, or both, the potential for communications difficulties is heightened. Upper-class parents can look down on public schools and treat teachers condescendingly. Poor parents often have had unfortunate and unpleasant experiences with schools and, as a result, regard them with suspicion. Often these parents speak a different language or dialect than the teacher. They are put off by educational jargon. What the teacher sees as his humble classroom is to them part of a huge impersonal bureaucracy. In many urban areas this impression of the school as a cold, unfriendly and impersonal institution is supported by the evidence: the school doors are locked, and parents have to pass by policemen and assorted hall guards before they are given a pass to see the head secretary in order to see the teacher. The fact that many lower-class parents have as children encountered prejudice in schools and found attendance at school more discouraging than helpful makes communication even more difficult. Since they have neither wealth nor connections, these same parents are forced to rely heavily on the schools to provide their children a way out of the deprivation and futility that characterizes so much of their own lives.

Going to school changes children. It exists to help children change in specified ways: to read, to speak a foreign language, to solve problems. And, students do change. They master things. They acquire confidence. And they become increasingly independent of their parents. Some parents rejoice at the child's growing freedom from them. For others, this process of independence is painful. Hearing her little girl talk about how much she loves her teacher may arouse jealousy in a mother, and cause her to act hostile when she meets the teacher. When a high-school student comes home from school with political or social or religious views which conflict with his parents', it can cause resentment and confusion. Thus it is not uncommon for a parent to approach a conference with the teacher with a sincere mixture of appreciation and hostility.

The great majority of parent-teacher conferences are cordial, constructive and characterized by mutual respect. While there may be initial problems of perception or communication, the parents' and teacher's shared interest in the child is enough to overcome these minor blocks. However, problems do develop—and they are not always the fault of the parent.

Miss Bender/Grade 5:

This week was Open School Week. Parents visited the school on Thursday morning. Four parents showed up in my class. They started coming in at ten in the morning. They observed the reading lesson and then we moved on to our regular seats and we started social studies oral reports.

One of the girls, Roberta, gave her oral report and then William gave his. I noticed that the reports started serious oral discussion. Children whose parents were not there wanted to be recognized to answer questions—to do extra things. They wanted recognition. That was the entire thing. It is obvious to me at this point that these children definitely lack love and affection and I only wish I were able to divide myself into so many people and to just work with each one individually and give him the attention that he needs. As far as the children whose parents were there were concerned, they, of course, were interested in showing their parents exactly what they do in school and of course those are the children who are actually my good children, the ones who very rarely give me any problems. . . .

It was just four parents and I was very, very upset after the parents left, realizing that all of these children are actually lacking love and attention and they put on a good show, so to speak, only because there were parents in the room and they resented the fact that it was not their parent who was there to see what was going on in the school.[33]

It is common teacher folklore that the teacher always sees the parents of the good students, while the parents of underachieving or troublesome children never show up. The implication is that these unseen parents lack real concern for their children (which is rarely the case) and are major contributors to their child's difficulties (which may or may not be true). The young teacher quoted above is guilty of making some harsh judgments and unwarranted assumptions about parents who probably have to work and would find taking a day off to visit the school very awkward.

John Luke/History:

In the late winter we had our Annual Parents Night. It was a big public relations show, timed about three weeks before the bond issue was to be voted on. All the teachers were to work with students on displays and projects. And, of course, we had to get lots of student work up on the board. The drab old school building looked like the Rose Bowl Parade by the big night. We met the parents in our rooms and gave them an overview of what we were doing for the year. I thought I would be nervous, but somehow I wasn't. I was so distracted and fascinated by their faces. I never suspected that they would look so much like their kids! Or vice versa. And the way some features from one parent and some from the other found their way into their child's face was so absorbing! In the midst of my opening soliloquy in bounced the principal with his flash camera to take a picture of all the gay decorating I had done. Well, he just looked

---

[33] Fuchs, *Teachers Talk*, pp. 132–133.

around the room, decided to save a flash bulb and headed for the door. My classroom had all the gay carnival atmosphere of a men's locker room. We "chatted" about this a few days later.

When I finished my talk, I handed out folders of their children's work and told the parents I would be happy to talk with them individually. Most of my students had been doing fairly well, so most of the evening went well. The parents of my two prize ding-a-lings didn't show, an event I greeted with mixed emotions. Although I had been quite apprehensive about talking to these strangers, things were going well. I had been trying to be as direct and honest as possible. Looking back on it, I think I was especially intent on being honest because I felt the whole showboat atmosphere and intention of the Parents Night was dishonest. My overreaction got me in trouble, though. One set of parents hung back. I hadn't met them yet, but I knew immediately who they were. They were Dickie Krasno's parents. He, poor kid, had gotten the worst features of both parents. Dickie is a great big happy kid. He is not bright and he is quite lazy. All he likes to do is play his guitar, which he is pretty good with. The only time I have gotten any work from him was during a unit on the Civil War. I got him to look up the folk songs and marching chants of the Civil War. He gave a "singing and strumming" report to the class. But, after that . . . nothing! I'm an easy grader and he was carrying about a C– at that time. Well, the Krasnos asked a lot of questions and I stayed with my straight-facts approach and avoided generalizations. Then Mr. Krasno glanced anxiously at his wife, looked over his shoulder to see that none of the other parents was within earshot and said, "Tell me, Mr. Luke. We're both college men. My son, Dickie. Is he . . . you know . . . college material?"

I didn't know what to say, so I said, "What do you mean?"

"We just want to know if we should be saving to send him to college. Does he have it for college?"

All I thought of was that here was a guy who really wanted a straight answer, so I said, "No." Then I looked at Mrs. Krasno. I should have looked at her before answering. Her calm face just seemed to break up, to dissolve before my eyes. After the tears came the hostility. "How dare you prejudge my boy! Admit it, you don't like Dickie. You are trying to ruin his chances. We work hard to raise our only son and then some young know-it-all teacher ruins everything!" Underneath the hysteria, which subsided in about five long minutes, she was right. I had no right to make that judgment. Also, I didn't have enough data. Well, I made another appointment with them. During this I saw that frightening intensity behind their desire to get my class's number one guitar player into college. Some good things came out of this conference, though. Dickie's work picked up. I learned a good lesson, too. Somewhere T. S. Eliot says that human nature can stand just so much reality. I believe him.

Occasionally, the teacher is involved in bizarre misunderstandings. A parent hears something from her child or from another parent which troubles her. Instead of going to the teacher directly, she handles it "indirectly."

Linda Meehan/Grade 3:
I was having a great first year. Everything was going well. I was especially pleased by my rapport with parents. That is why I was so shocked when the principal, Mr. Carnes, called me into his office and told me he had just received a visit from two parents complaining about me. They were the parents of two of my boys. They claimed that I favored the girls. As evidence of this they charged that I systematically assigned

excessive homework on the nights the boys had Little League games. I was stunned. Homework! When I did give it, there was only about fifteen minutes' worth. I only gave it about twice a week, and there was no special day. Just when I thought it was needed. I was furious. Why hadn't they come to me! They had told him that they were afraid I would take it out on their children. That was even worse! I couldn't believe my ears. I left the office, stopped for a cigarette to calm myself and went back to my room. I certainly wasn't going to bring this up with my children, but I had to know one thing. I asked the boys what evening they played Little League baseball. Almost exactly half the class chimed out "Monday and Wednesday" and the other half said "Tuesday and Thursday." I went right to the principal's office and brought him back with me. I asked the question again. The boys chimed out like last time, but all—boys and girls—were very confused. The principal burst out laughing and after a few seconds so did I.

Contact with parents can lead to insight and growth or it can lead to sorrow and disappointment.

John Canfield/Social Studies:

It is very easy to forget how concerned these parents are about this matter: however, there are times when it is brought home very painfully. One such incident occurred after several social studies teachers had taken a group of students to the state capital at Springfield. The trip had cost each of the students eleven dollars. This paid for the busses, the guided tour, and the food, and it left about three dollars to help defray the cost of books for the history department that were not provided for in the budget.

During the beginning of the year, I had thought that eleven dollars would have been too great a strain on the budgets of most of the kids. But after I had seen all of the souvenir buying that went on during that trip, I didn't feel so bad about the eleven dollar cost. However, as we arrived home that night, about eleven o'clock, one bus was late. As we were explaining to the waiting parents why the other bus had been delayed, one of them began to talk about the trip. "I hope these kids learned something today," he said. "I hope the sacrifices that we parents make have some effect on what these kids learn. Eleven dollars is a lot of money. I hope they learned something as a result of this trip." I wasn't really at all sure that they had learned something; in fact, I was sure that there were several who hadn't. I began to feel very bad at that moment. Suddenly all of the fun had been taken out of the trip. But here I was reassuring the man that they had learned quite a bit about the history of the state and about the important things that take place in the state government. For several days I was very depressed by this whole incident.

Unfortunately, not all parents are as concerned about the education of their children as the man was that night. On the contrary, many are so unconcerned that they make the education of their children virtually impossible. I remember one girl in my homeroom who was very brilliant according to the battery of tests that the students submit to during their twelve years of education. However, she had what teachers commonly refer to as "a home problem." Her parents were less than cordial to her and to each other. This was caused by a drinking father and a promiscuous mother. The child, who was a freshman, was just beginning to discover the great potential that she herself had for getting into trouble. And she was beginning to emulate the behavior of her mother in very specific terms. As her school attendance record became a problem, the parents were called in for the customary parent conference with the personnel of the attendance office. The parents did not appear at the designated time. After a second appointment was made and not kept, the child was declared truant. The parents were contacted by a truant officer who informed them of their legal responsibility. Then a new conference was scheduled—this time with the parents and the child's counselor. At this meeting it became quite apparent that the parents looked upon the child as a mere liability, something which was in the way rather than something to be loved and cared for.

The parents of the child offered her no guidance or direction. The mother wanted no part of the girl. The father was a little different. In his more sober moments he felt a great deal of guilt about his neglect of the child, and he promised to take her to live with him. This never materialized. Meanwhile, the girl was getting deeper into trouble. Her circle of friends was becoming worse all the time, her grades were terrible, and her attendance was falling off even more. The father was finally induced to enroll her in a private school where she would get more individualized attention and where her activities would be more carefully supervised.

Even after all of this, one cannot help but feel sorry for the girl and somehow resent the parents for their lack of care for the child. Although one can intellectually understand the forces in our society that cause these situations, it is very difficult for one to face objectively the consequences of them.[34]

PROBLEMS IN PERSPECTIVE

Now, after having had a preview of some of the problems of teaching, you are probably giving serious thought to a career as a social worker or business executive. If you are vaguely apprehensive about becoming a teacher, count yourself among the fortunate few. If you are downright scared of the problems you may encounter, you are in the great majority. All but a handful of people are plagued by fears and worries. One of the authors, in addition to the more common fear that the children just would not respond when he asked them to do something, was afraid to write on the blackboard because his handwriting was illegible.[35] Perhaps we fear teaching because we know school so well, and because it has been for us a place where we have known fear: fear of being wrong; fear that the teacher would punish us; fear of getting hurt or beaten up; fear that the other kids wouldn't like us. It is to be expected that some of our childhood school-related fears become associated with our thoughts about an adult career as a teacher.

What can we do with fears and uncertainties? The worst thing to do is to deny them and hope they will go away. To decide not to become a teacher because of them is unfair to yourself. You may be denying yourself a rich and satisfying career as a teacher. The best approach to these worries is to

---

[34] Ryan, *Don't Smile,* pp. 47–49.

[35] Then there is the case of a friend, Jack Shay, who as a teacher education student was petrified by the thought of being in front of a class and discovering that his pants were unzipped. Overcome by this worry Jack finally decided not to be a teacher. The last we heard from him he was in the road company of *Hair.*

use them creatively. Explore them. Bring them out into the light. Grow and gain strength from them. Talk about them with your friends. (If you do this you will be surprised at how many friends who seemed the very essence of self-confidence are insecure in certain ways.) As practice in staying responsive to problems and fears, make a list of what you feel, after reading this chapter, will be your major problems as a teacher and then compare it with what you wrote at the beginning of the chapter. Like the other things you've written in response to questions, you may wish to save this and keep reexamining it. You may find as you work with children in student teaching and other capacities that the list changes and begins to shrink.

THE OTHER SIDE OF THE COIN

It would be misleading to leave the reader with the impression that problems dominate the life of the teacher—but it is much more difficult to write about joys and satisfactions than about problems. Problems, like an unresponsive class or a bullying supervisor, are concrete and identifiable. Joys, on the other hand, are personal, gossamer-like and seldom bear sustained scrutiny. The English novelist Joyce Cary has written that joy is not in the great events of our lives, but in the little everyday things, like a good cup of tea, which we easily overlook. So, too, with teaching. Its joys and satisfactions lie in everyday events and small surprises. As a teacher, you may find joy in

—those rare electric moments when you can *feel* the children thinking and *see* them making new connections.

—watching two lonely kids whom you brought together walking down the hall together, now friends.

—getting your planbook back from the supervisor with the comment, "These appear to be excellent lessons."

—a note in your box on a rainy Friday afternoon, written in a childish scrawl, "You are my most favorite teacher. Guess who?"

—correcting test papers and being surprised at how well your students know their work.

—shopping downtown and meeting one of your students, who proudly introduces you to his mother as "my teacher," and being able to tell by the way she responds that you are respected in their household.

—having a former student call to tell you that he has a problem and needs to talk with you.

—getting a note from the parents of the student you have been most worried about that makes you realize your concern is beginning to pay off.

—chaperoning a dance and having your most hostile student smilingly introduce his girl to you.

—hearing in the teacher's lunchroom that your supervisor called you "a real professional."

—dragging yourself back to school at the end of Christmas vacation and being enthusiastically greeted by your students as you enter your classroom.

—agonizing in advance over a conference with your most troublesome child's parents, only to have them back you up all the way.

—being observed by the principal and having your students make you look terrific.

—seeing the look of pride in a child's eyes as he brings up his artwork for you to see.

—surviving until June, being bone-tired, but proud of what you and your kids have been able to do.

—cleaning out your desk on the last day of school after the kids have been dismissed and finding a box of candy with a card signed by the whole class.

—knowing all the time that what you are doing with your life *really makes a difference*.

DISCUSSION QUESTIONS

1. Think of an occasion when you have experienced "culture shock"— abroad or in another part of this country, in an unfamiliar social milieu or, perhaps, on first entering college. Try to remember in as much detail as possible how it made you feel. Did you eventually overcome it? How? Can you trace the progression of your feelings and behavior from the first encounter to the final adjustment? What, if anything, does this suggest to you about ways to minimize the possible effects of culture shock when you begin teaching?

2. Learn to identify the psychological mechanisms people draw on to minimize feelings of anxiety: intellectualization, reaction formation, suppression or denial, rationalization, projection, regression or dependence. Try to characterize the outlook represented by each in one sentence, i.e., "Look what you made me do!"

3. Can you remember or imagine any common types of teachers, like Mrs. Coaster or The Big Planner, we have neglected to describe? Try writing a short description of one or two.

4. How do you explain the attitudinal differences between prospective and first-year teachers revealed by the Minnesota Teacher Attitude Inventory?

5. How do the findings of the Modal Adolescent Project differ from the stereotypes offered by the media? What do they suggest about societal and parental attitudes toward adolescents? Do the findings jibe with your own experience?

6. Where do you stand on the issues of discipline and social distance? Do you believe the school should be concerned with discipline? What is your concept of an effective degree and method of discipline? How much social distance do you feel is appropriate for you? Is there anything about these topics that frightens you? What can you do to prepare yourself?

7. If you agreed with Carl Rogers' statement, reported in Chapter Five, that the personal relationship between student and teacher is crucial, and that the teacher should "be himself," how do you reconcile this belief with the need for social distance?

8. If you were to begin teaching tomorrow, and were free to evaluate your students in any way you chose, or not to evaluate at all, what would you do? Be prepared to defend your position.

9. What do you expect to be the major problems you will encounter as a beginning teacher? What can you do now to begin solving them? What can you do after you begin teaching? What do you envision as the joys and satisfactions of a career in teaching?

FOR FURTHER READING

Braithwaite, Edward R. *To Sir, With Love*. Englewood Cliffs, N.J.: Prentice-Hall, 1960. A British Guianan living in London becomes a teacher in a British secondary school. The book describes his trials and eventual success teaching lower-class London teenagers.

Brembeck, Cole S. *The Discovery of Teaching*. Englewood Cliffs, N.J.: Prentice-Hall, 1962. The book is composed of actual case situations centering on students and teachers.

Cuban, Larry. *To Make a Difference*. New York: Free Press, 1970. A candid view of the problems faced by teachers in inner-city schools. The book's major thesis is that the individual teacher must match the methods and materials of instruction to the student. The author discusses different learning styles, the teacher as liaison with the community and as curriculum developer, and specific problems such as race, discipline and expectations.

Eddy, Elizabeth M. *Becoming a Teacher: The Passage to Professional Status*. New York: Teachers College Press, 1969. A recent study of twenty-one elementary school teachers in New York City. Using research methodologies from anthropology, the author analyzes the transformation from student to teacher.

Fuchs, Estelle. *Teachers Talk: Views from Inside City Schools*. Garden City, N.Y.: Doubleday, 1969. A collection of teachers' statements about themselves, schools and learning during their initial four months of teaching in an urban setting. The author analyzed these teacher statements, explicating the underlying assumptions of the teachers and suggesting alternative actions.

Hersey, John. *The Child Buyers*. New York: Alfred A. Knopf, 1960. A biting satire of American values and of the school as an extension of these values. The author is a major American novelist.

Hilton, James. *Goodbye, Mr. Chips*. Boston: Little, Brown, 1934. A short and sentimental novel depicting the life of a British schoolmaster from youth to old age.

Hunter, Evan. *Blackboard Jungle.* New York: Dell, 1966. A very popular novel about a new teacher's uphill struggle in an urban high school. Although quite absorbing, somewhat stereotypic and excessively violent.

Jersild, Arthur. *When Teachers Face Themselves.* New York: Teachers College Press, 1955. Jersild's major thesis is that before teachers can understand students they must understand themselves. He develops a case for this assumption, followed by suggestions as to how teachers can go about better understanding themselves.

Kaufman, Bel. *Up the Down Staircase.* Englewood Cliffs, N.J.: Prentice-Hall, 1964. An easy-to-read, humorous and poignant semi-fictionalized account of a beginning teacher's experience in a New York City high school. A thoroughly enjoyable book.

Kohl, Herbert. *36 Children.* New York: New American Library, 1968. A popular account of a Harvard-graduate teacher's first-year experience in a ghetto school in Harlem. The students' initial hostility to Kohl and the ways in which he overcomes their feelings are excellently described. The book also describes vividly the difficult conditions under which teaching is practiced in some sections of New York City.

Kozol, Jonathan. *Death at an Early Age.* Boston: Houghton Mifflin, 1968. A first-year teacher's account of life in a Boston ghetto school. Tyrannization of the children, cynicism, condescension, racism, and anti-intellectualism are dominant themes in Kozol's account. The book has become a rallying-point for critics and educational reformers.

Ladd, Edward T., and Sayres, William T., eds. *Social Aspects of Education: A Casebook.* Englewood Cliffs, N.J.: Prentice-Hall, 1962. Approximately twenty detailed cases of actual school experiences involving racial segregation, discipline, school organization and curriculum reform. Each case is followed by an insightful analysis.

Leonard, George. *Education and Ecstasy.* New York: Dell, 1968. Based upon the work of advanced innovative schools, brain-research laboratories and experimental communities, this book urges that education become an aesthetic unity of learning and living.

McGeoch, Dorothy M. *Learning to Teach in Urban Schools.* New York: Teachers College Press, 1965. Accounts by four beginning teachers of their experiences in urban elementary schools. Provides a realistic picture with hard-learned practical tips.

Patterson, William N. [G. F. Miller]. *Letters from a Hard-boiled Teacher to His Half-baked Son.* Washington, D.C.: Daylion, 1935. Over twenty letters from a veteran teacher to a son who is just beginning his professional life as a teacher. As the title implies, the advice is tough and practical.

Rasey, Marie Y. *It Takes Time.* New York: Harper and Row, 1953. A novel which focuses on a young woman's choice to become an elementary school teacher. Much valuable description of various teaching methods.

Ryan, Kevin, ed. *Don't Smile Until Christmas: Accounts of the First Year of Teaching.* Chicago: University of Chicago Press, 1970. A collection of six exceedingly honest autobiographical statements by six beginning high-school teachers. A concluding chapter on the first year of teaching by the editor.

Williams, Emlyn. *The Corn is Green.* New York: Random House, 1941. A moving play dealing with the life of a Welsh schoolmistress.

FILMS

Blackboard Jungle (Films, Inc., 16mm, b&w, 101 min., 1955) Although made quite a few years ago, this film's depiction of a large city vocational training school is still quite interesting.

The Fish Teacher (Audio/Brandon, 16mm, color, 1966, France) A delightful fantasy in which a class of French schoolgirls transform their teacher into a fish. A slight undercurrent of "revolution" is evident.

If (Films, Inc., 16mm, color, 111 min.) Described as "part humorous, part realistic, and part revolutionary," this film depicts problems which can be generalized to many different school situations.

Interaction in Learning (Indiana University Audio-Visual Center, 16mm, b&w, 29 min.) Different kinds of social interaction which occur during the school years are portrayed through scenes of students in informal group discussions, class presentations and interactions with their teachers.

A Little Younger/A Little Older (NBC Educational Enterprise Code# 0034C2, 16mm, b&w, 14 min.) An NBC special report on the youth revolution brought about by the first generation of "television children." The film asserts that the Sixties, characterized by affluence, mobility, political unrest and drugs, will be followed by years when the young will be even more influential.

No Reason to Stay (Contemporary/McGraw-Hill, 16mm, b&w, 27 min.) A look at the school dropout and what he drops out *from.* Through the eyes of a student we are shown both real incidents and fantasies about teachers who "bore to death thousands of innocent students." The film takes a deliberately biased look at the educational system and how it fails.

Semester of Discontent (Indiana University Audio-Visual Center, 16mm, b&w, 60 min., NET) Focuses on the thoughts of faculty, students and administrators at several major universities in order to investigate the issues behind the mounting unrest in the nation's universities.

Up the Down Staircase (Warner Bros., 16mm, color, 123 min.) Adapted from the book by Bel Kaufman, the film portrays a large-city school from the viewpoint of a young, idealistic teacher on her first assignment.

What They Want to Produce, Not What We Want to Become (EDC Film Library, 16mm, b&w, 1 hour) Presents the views of some Canadian high school teachers, students and principals on the problems of "school." The students explain why they are fed up with school, while the principal tries to explain his reasons for running the school the way he does.

The Teacher as Decision Maker (National Education Association, 3.75 ips, reel or cassette format, 6:40 min.) This brief discussion of the need for teachers to be allowed to take part in instructional decision-making is part of a longer tape called "The System." It can be used alone or in conjunction with the other sections.

Refer to Appendix for distributors' addresses

THE REAL WORLD

8 How Are Schools Governed and Controlled?

How do you explain the fact that:

—your favorite high school teacher was not given tenure?

—superintendents have a job expectancy of no more than two years?

—the black studies curricula which everyone was talking about a couple of years ago never got off the ground?

—in some schools teachers are expected to police bathrooms and lunch yards?

—two years after the new elementary school opened it needed major repairs?

—the last school bond issue in your town was decisively defeated?

—a textbook with a fresh approach to some aspects of "the system" was removed from circulation after a year, even though the teachers favored its use?

—your high school student newspaper was heavily censored?

—purchasing or construction contracts don't always go to the lowest bidder or the most qualified firm?

—in many school districts teachers have little or no voice in the selection of textbooks or supplementary materials?

How do you explain the school's image of conservatism and its slowness to change?

It is quite likely that at least one of these questions applies to your local school district; their answers all reflect the disparity between governance and real control of the public schools. The purpose of this chapter is to explore how schools are officially organized and governed and how they are actually controlled. While there is a legal authority for the schools and an organization established to exercise this authority, the school system is controlled in large part by informal forces which do not appear on any organizational chart. We will first examine the legal governing authority which exists in most school districts, and then discuss the influence of informal groups. Finally, we will explore the problems created by burgeoning bureaucratic structures which stifle creativity and discourage risk-taking, and some proposed alternatives to these structures will be discussed.

We have tried to draw from literature and experience to describe how things really are, not how they're supposed to be. The result will, we hope, give you insight into school control which will help you be a better teacher.

HOW GOVERNANCE DIFFERS FROM CONTROL

How is controlling different from governing? The right to govern is delegated legally, but domination or command which results in "control" of people or of a situation is not necessarily officially sanctioned. Often, however, the governing person or group also exercises control, as in the case of a strong president or a king whose powers are not constitutionally restricted. In other instances, those who govern exercise little real control, as in the case of a figurehead king who is manipulated by someone else behind the scenes. Such situations have occurred from time to time in monarchies when young boys have succeeded to the throne and the real power and control have been wielded by advisors and guardians. Between these two extremes is the situation in which those who legally govern share power with persons or groups possessing no legal authority. This state of affairs is prevalent in public education. Considerable control over the operation of our schools is exercised by persons without legal authority, largely through personal connections and the exertion of pressure on legal officeholders.

The experience of a group of women PTA leaders who decided to collect money for UNICEF illustrates the workings of the system.[1] The women prepared and submitted what they thought was a routine permit request to the city council. To their amazement, the council refused the permit. Outraged, the PTA group made plans to attend the next council meeting *en masse*. At this point some interesting developments began. In the words of one of the leaders:

I received a call from a lady down at the city offices and she said, "I hear you are getting up a group." I replied that we sure were, following which she asked, "Just what do you want, a permit or a public display?" I said, we want a permit, of course. Then she said for me to call three persons in town and tell them what we wanted. I called the three persons and we had a permit the next day.[2]

---

[1] This example is cited by Ralph B. Kimbrough, "An Informal Arrangement for Influence Over Basic Policy," in *Governing Education: A Reader on Politics, Power, and Public School Policy,* ed. Alan Rosenthal (New York: Doubleday, 1969), p. 111.

[2] *Loc. cit.*

The next time members of this PTA want something done at the city council, they will undoubtedly work through the same informal channels which secured their permit so effortlessly. They have learned that the legally elected city council is influenced and controlled by unofficial outside forces.

Another example of extralegal control might be the teacher who is a life-long community resident and has taught at least two generations of townspeople. If she disagrees with a position taken by the new principal, who has come from another state, she might command more influence outside the school than he could. Thus, even though he legally governs, she exercises more real control.

WHO LEGALLY GOVERNS PUBLIC EDUCATION?

In most countries, the public schools are a branch of the central government, federally financed and administered and highly uniform in curricula and procedures. In the United States, however, responsibility for the public schools has evolved as a state function. Each of the fifty states has legal responsibility for the operation and administration of public schools within its own boundaries. In most aspects of public education (we will discuss certain exceptions later) the authority of federal, county and city education agencies is subject to the will of the state authorities.

Although legal responsibility for school governance belongs to the state, policy decisions and administration are ordinarily delegated to local boards of education, which exist because Americans have come to insist on control of schools at the local level. However, the state does not relinquish all its responsibilities, and retains the power to revoke or countermand decisions made by the local units. One result of this delegation of authority to local units is that the efficiency and achievements of school systems vary widely across the nation, and even within individual states.

THE STATE BOARD OF EDUCATION

The state's legal responsibility for public education requires it to establish an organizational framework within which the local units can function. The result is the establishment of state boards of education to exercise general control and supervision of schools within the state. It is the state's policy-making body.

The Chief State School Officer.   The executive officer of the state board of education—whose title may be, depending on the state, "chief state school officer," "superintendent of education," "commissioner of education," "secretary of the state board of education," or others—generally has responsibility for teacher and administrator certification, organization of the program of studies, curriculum revision, application of the state finance law, approval of school sites and buildings, collection of statistical data and

Horace Mann (1796–1859)

Horace Mann was the radical educational reformer of his day. Though trained as a lawyer, he became eminently successful as an educator and politician. Asked why he had exchanged the practice of law for education, he answered that "the interests of a client are small compared with the interests of the next generation."

Born in Franklin, Massachusetts, not long after the Revolutionary War, Mann received only the most rudimentary schooling until he was fifteen. Most of his education was self-acquired, a circumstance which profoundly influenced his philosophy of education. He studied diligently in order to be admitted to Brown University, where he became a brilliant student. In 1827, Mann was elected to the Massachusetts House of Representatives, and a luminous political career lay ahead of him, but he became committed, instead, to education and to the use of political methods to bring about educational reform.

Mann made it his aim to abolish the cruel floggings that were then routine in the public schools. Schoolmasters believed it their duty to drive the devil out of their students, and many schools administered from ten to twenty floggings a day. Most school-keepers believed flogging to be an aid to learning. Not only were students treated cruelly; attendance at school was itself a punishment. Schools were often little better than hovels: the lighting was poor and many buildings were unsanitary and unsafe. Mann criticized corporal punishment and inadequate facilities in public speeches, lectures and letters, and lobbied for reform in the state legislature and in Congress. He was not always well-received. Once, when he and the Governor of Massachusetts were to address an audience, they arrived to find the hall dark and its floors unswept. Mann promptly took off his coat, lit the lamps and took to the hall with a broom.

Horace Mann saw education as a tool of liberation by which the poor could raise themselves, blacks could become emancipated and handicapped children could adjust to their disabilities. After all, Mann reasoned, education had brought him fame and position. It was over 100 years ago, then, that the idea of social mobility through education was born in America.

In order for education to be as powerful a force as he envisioned it, Mann thought it imperative to lengthen the school term and to raise teachers' salaries. To make learning more relevant and enjoyable, he helped introduce new textbooks designed to illustrate the relationship between knowledge and the practical problems of society. Mann organized libraries in many schools, to make books readily available to students. He believed less in the formal curriculum than in individual learning—undoubtedly because of his own self-education.

Mann was responsible for the establishment of the Massachusetts Board of Education, and for the founding in 1839 of the first normal school, in Lexington, Massachusetts. Although it opened with only three students, the concept spread and was widely imitated throughout the country. Mann was intensely interested in teacher training, and believed that teachers should be intellectual, moral and cultural models for their communities.

Many of Mann's ideas were controversial, but he was most violently denounced for his position on religion in the schools. Though a religious man, he believed that religious training belonged outside the schools, which should be run by the state. As a result of his views, Mann was attacked from many Boston pulpits.

Mann did not limit his reformist zeal to educational issues. When he was elected to Congress in 1849, he denounced slavery and attacked the industrial system, urging that workers be better paid, child labor be abolished, factories be made safer and slums eliminated. No educator, he said, could remain neutral about social injustice. Theories and ideals must be put into practice in society; otherwise, he argued, education is mere empty words.

Mann was regarded as a dreamer and a visionary by many of his colleagues. When he took over the presidency of Antioch College in 1852, opened its doors to all races and religious sects, and admitted women on an equal basis with men, some educators predicted that these measures would promote the collapse of higher education. Mann aroused further annoyance by remarking that many Antioch students were more brilliant than their professors.

Were he alive today, Mann might still be fighting for ideas he espoused more than a century ago. Many people have not accepted them yet.

direct supervision of elementary and secondary educational programs. He exercises little direct administrative authority over local educational officers, but his indirect influence is widely felt on the local level. In some states he is elected by the voters, while in others he is appointed by the state board of education.

THE LOCAL SCHOOL DISTRICT

To facilitate local control of education, the state creates local school districts for the purpose of carrying out the educational program in conformity with state educational policy. The school district is thus a unit of the state government and is usually distinct from the local municipal government.

The School Board.   The policy-making body of the school district is the local school board of education, which represents the citizens of the district in setting up a school program, hiring school personnel to operate the schools, determining organizational and administrative policy and evaluating the results of the program and the performance of personnel. Although school board members are elected by the citizens of the local district, they are state officers and not, as many people think, simply local representatives. Thus board members must operate the schools in conformity with the guidelines and policies established by the state board of education, and not on a strictly local perspective.

The Superintendent of Schools.   The superintendent, who is selected by the local school board to act as its executive officer and as the educational leader and administrator of the school district, is undeniably the most powerful officer in the local school organization. Theoretically, the superintendent's role is administrative and executive—he keeps the schools functioning—while the board of education retains legislative and policy-making responsibilities. In practice, however, the superintendent has become the major policy-maker in the public schools. Consider the following description of his powers:

. . . the administrator is in a position either to promote broad participation in decision-making and creativity on the part of individuals in the organization or to run a tight ship and discourage the efforts of any of the participants to rock the boat. The administrator does more than set the climate for the participants of the organization. He establishes certain goals; he allocates resources; he develops the criteria for the selection of personnel; he is the bridge between the organization and the broader society from which he derives the resources with which it has to operate. He controls the use of sanctions, both positive and negative, within the organization, and by his use of them, he establishes the determinants for the behavior of subordinates.[3]

The superintendent will be discussed in more detail in Chapter Nine.

WHO ACTUALLY CONTROLS AMERICAN PUBLIC EDUCATION?

There is no easy answer to this question. It is like asking who controls America. The President does—but so does Congress. The Supreme Court does—but so do the local police. The giant corporations do—but so does a small but influential group of political activists. Similarly, the formal, legally-constituted bodies control or influence certain aspects of public education as a consequence of the authority invested in them. The federal government exerts influence on public education through the passage and enforcement of legislation. Professional educators, including superintendents, principals, university professors and leaders of organizations, possess a major portion of the control and decision-making power over public education by virtue of the offices they hold and the organizations to which they belong. These professional organizations, though they lack legal authority, have considerable influence.

It is not the intention of this chapter to examine the authority and power possessed by each of these groups which enable them to control certain aspects of public education. However, a brief look at the roles of the professional educator, informal group power and the federal government yields some fascinating insights into how decisions about public education are actually made.

PROFESSIONAL EDUCATORS

One observer of American education, James D. Koerner, has charged that important decisions in education emerge from a "labyrinthine structure of forces and countervailing forces, but that the interests of professional educators tend to be dominant."[4] When Koerner refers to "professional educators," he does not, unfortunately, mean classroom teachers. He is speaking of several organizations he considers to have disproportionate influence on the administration of the schools—the National Education Association (particularly its administrative branches), state departments of education, departments and schools of education in colleges and universities, educational

---

[3] Keith Goldhammer, *et al., Issues and Problems in Contemporary Educational Administration* (Eugene: University of Oregon Center for the Advanced Study of Educational Administration, 1967), pp. 3–4.

[4] James D. Koerner, *Who Controls American Education?* (Boston: Beacon Press, 1968), p. 155.

A local builder took ten minutes of a board meeting to present a proposal that local residents build the three million dollar high school with their own labors—"the old church raising type of idea."

Hundreds of residents claimed vociferously that a two-story school building was cheaper than a one-story building, despite public testimony to the contrary by architects, and evidence from studies made by building experts throughout the nation.

The editor of a local newspaper editorialized for months in opposition to home economics before he discovered that it was required by State law. It was the superintendent who finally told him.

A local builder attacked the school board for securing property at exorbitant prices, and had to be informed in detail about the requirements of terrain for school buildings, and of the real estate practice of marking-up the property which was being considered by the board.

Several residents confessed that they did not know what a bond issue was, although a community-wide campaign had been conducted for a number of weeks, which included daily coverage on the front pages of most local papers.

A woman threatened to go straight to the board of education if she could not get satisfaction from the school board.

Norman D. Kerr, "The School Board as an Agency of Legitimation," in Rosenthal, *Governing Education*, p. 164.

accrediting organizations and other groups such as school administrators. A more detailed discussion of the NEA and the American Federation of Teachers follows in Chapter Nine.

Koerner argues that the people most directly involved—classroom teachers, parents and other laymen, and academic specialists in departments other than education—have for too long been dominated by the professional education "fraternity." For instance, the state board of education is entitled to do nearly anything it chooses, within the limit of the law, affecting education in the state. However, Koerner asserts, it rarely governs in any but the most general way. The board of education usually allows the state department of education to make policy, or yields its power to local school authorities. State departments of education and the superintendencies of local school districts are staffed by professional educators, and as a result the influence and power wielded by this group is much greater than Koerner believes it should be.

Looking at the local scene, Koerner argues that the power of local school boards is greatly overestimated, and that local control is largely a myth. He attributes the school board's weakness to three sources: its preoccupation with housekeeping details, its failure to assert authority and external controls forced on it by other bodies. The board's preoccupation with trivia instead of policy-making and its failure to assert its authority is seen by Koerner as the result of the superintendent's increased power. Although in theory the superintendent is the servant of the board, in recent years he has increasingly become its leader.[5] Because local school boards often lack adequate staff to do their own research, they must rely on professional educators (primarily the superintendent and his staff) for such services. As a result the superintendent has become the major policy-maker in the public schools.

In many school districts, for example, the school board agenda is prepared by the superintendent, with occasional suggestions from the board members. Matters relevant to the educational program are often conspicuously absent from the agenda. When someone remarked that the school board in one particular district seemed to devote very little time to education, the superintendent replied, "They don't know anything about it; but the things they know they talk about, like sidewalks, sites, and so forth. I let them go on sometimes because I don't want them to talk about curriculum."[6]

The outside controls exerted on the local board are numerous and strong. Koerner cites a hypothetical example of a board which wishes to make changes in the vocational training curriculum. Realizing that vocational training no longer serves the needs of the students, the board decides to cut back on its programs. This is, theoretically, one of the local school board's sovereign rights, but a number of events are likely to occur to change the board's mind. First, the vocational education lobby might exert pressure on other members of the local government and on the state legislature or state department of education to protect the interests of vocational education teachers. Second, the regional accrediting association might come to the aid of the status quo, threatening possible disaccreditation of the schools involved if the board does not rescind its decision.[7] Third, the National Education Association state affiliate might "investigate," and through its power "persuade," the board to a different view. Does the board, then, in fact have the power to control the curriculum?

This example illustrates how various educational groups and associations protect vested interests in the continuation of, or opposition to, certain programs or practices, and can exert pressure on the legally-constituted

---

[5] Roscoe C. Martin, "School Government," in Rosenthal, *Governing Education*, p. 279.

[6] Norman D. Kerr, "The School Board as an Agency of Legitimation," in Rosenthal, *Governing Education*, p. 159.

[7] While accreditation does not bring distinction to a school, the lack of it is a stigma. Its graduates will have trouble gaining entrance to certain colleges and universities, and teacher organizations may discourage their members from teaching there.

body responsible for making such decisions. It is appropriate at this point to discuss the role of superintendent, since he is quite often the direct recipient of these pressures.

INFORMAL GROUP POWER

Outside Pressures on the Superintendent. In a 1965 study sponsored by the New York Board of Regents, Ralph B. Kimbrough interviewed a large number of school board members and superintendents in the state of New York. Among other questions, he asked: "In actual practice, whose views carry the greatest weight in the important decisions in each of these areas (such as the curriculum and staff selection)?" The responses indicated that the superintendent was allowed to make all such decisions.[8]

The superintendent thus has almost complete control over the internal operations of the school district, an area in which the informal power structure takes little interest. However, Kimbrough's findings indicate that decisions pertaining to economics which might have great impact on the community are not made by the superintendent but by the informal power structure in the community.

The superintendent is subjected to pressure by a number of different groups and individuals which impinges on his decision-making power. Table 8.1 identifies the pressures to which superintendents and school board members say they are exposed and the percentage of superintendents and school board members who report being subjected to each form of pressure. Table 8.2 identifies the various interest groups which superintendents and school board members think are responsible for attempts to pressure them.[9] As might be expected, parents and PTAs are the most frequent source of pressure on superintendents and school board members. As you examine both tables, think about these questions: Who applies what pressures? Who wants more money for the schools? Who wants less? Are politicians more interested in getting their friends hired or in reducing the tax rate? What interest groups object to the use of particular textbooks? What kinds of pressures do members of the press apply? And does the most frequent source of pressure have the most clout?

Gross's survey indicates that parents, followed by teachers and school board members, are most likely to demand money for the schools, and that the town finance committee or city council is most likely to apply pressure to reduce expenditures. Because local and municipal officials fear that the

---

[8] *School Boards and School Board Membership; Report of the New York State Regents Advisory Committee on Educational Leadership,* 1965, pp. 58–59, as cited in Koerner, *Who Controls American Education?,* p. 141.

[9] Tables 8.1 and 8.2 represent the results of a study conducted among over 100 superintendents and 500 school board members in Massachusetts. Neal Gross, *Who Runs Our Schools?* (New York: John Wiley & Sons, 1958), pp. 49–50.

Table 8.1 *Percentage of superintendents and school board members exposed to specified pressures*

		SUPERINTENDENTS (N = 105)	SCHOOL BOARD MEMBERS (N = 508)
PRESSURE	1. Demands that the schools should place more emphasis on the three R's.	59%	53%
	2. Demands that the schools should teach more courses and subjects.	64	47
	3. Protests about the use of particular textbooks.	19	19
	4. Protests about the views expressed by teachers.	49	41
	5. Demands that teachers should express certain views.	13	12
	6. Protesting school tax increases or bond proposals.	73	70
	7. Demanding more money for the general school program.	66	52
	8. Protesting the introduction of new services (in addition to academic instruction) for pupils.	39	35
	9. Demanding the introduction of new services (in addition to academic instruction) for pupils.	63	49
	10. Demands that school contracts be given to certain firms.	46	24
	11. Demands that teachers be appointed or dismissed for reasons other than competence.	46	24
	12. Demanding the introduction of new teaching methods.	29	35
	13. Protesting the introduction of new teaching methods.	43	28
	14. Demanding that greater emphasis be placed on the athletic program.	58	52
	15. Demanding that less emphasis be placed on the athletic program.	40	38

Neal Gross, *Who Runs Our Schools?* (New York: John Wiley & Sons, 1958), p. 49. Reprinted by permission of the publisher.

Table 8.2 *Percentage of superintendents and school board members who said they were exposed to pressures from the specified individuals and groups*

		SUPERINTENDENTS (N = 105)	SCHOOL BOARD MEMBERS (N = 508)
INDIVIDUALS OR GROUPS WHO EXERT PRESSURE	1. Parents or PTA	92%	74%
	2. Individual school board members	75	51
	3. Teachers	65	44
	4. Taxpayers' association	49	31
	5. Town finance committee or city council	48	38
	6. Politicians	46	29
	7. Business or commercial organizations	45	19
	8. Individuals influential for economic reasons	44	25
	9. Personal friends	37	37
	10. The press	36	19
	11. Old-line families	30	26
	12. Church or religious groups	28	18
	13. Veterans organizations	27	10
	14. Labor unions	27	5
	15. Chamber of commerce	23	5
	16. Service clubs	20	11
	17. Fraternal organizations	13	9
	18. Farm organizations	12	4
	19. Welfare organizations	3	1

Neal Gross, *Who Runs Our Schools?* (New York: John Wiley & Sons, 1958), p. 50. Reprinted by permission of the publisher.

voters will consider them responsible for all local taxes, including school levies, they use whatever means they can to reduce taxes, including pressuring the superintendent and the school board to limit school expenditures.

Superintendents reveal that school board members and parents often apply pressure to have friends hired by the school district or to have teachers they dislike fired. Interestingly, although newspapers are not normally a source of pressure, they do at times try to promote greater emphasis on school athletics. Local businessmen are likewise interested in promoting athletic competitions.[10]

One superintendent related an incident about the chairman of the school board who called to inquire about the bus contract. The usual complaints had been received about the bus service, and the chairman argued that a friend of his, the owner of a local taxi service, could do a better job. The superintendent replied that the company which presently held the contract cost less than would the chairman's friend's company, and also provided better equipment and more experienced drivers than could be obtained locally. "That's all very well and good," the chairman responded, "but you've got to learn to support the local community if you're going to stick around."

One hour later the superintendent received a telephone call from another school board member, who usually supported him on crucial issues. The school board member explained that he knew what he was about to ask was against the rules, but that he thought he would ask anyway. His niece had applied for a teaching job—was there anything the superintendent could do to help her? He knew that she didn't have as much experience as some of the other applicants, but he felt sure she would make a pretty good teacher. After all, he had known her all her life. The conversation ended with the board member asking the superintendent to do what he could.

The pressures brought to bear on both superintendents and school boards are tremendous. The superintendent's job is particularly vulnerable to pressure, since his livelihood depends on community support, and inability to reconcile the conflicting pressures of different groups is a major reason for the short job span of the average superintendent. These pressures may also influence how he administers the public schools. As Gross says, "If he must spend much of his time placating certain pressure groups, anticipating threats, and developing strategies to deal with them, he will not have much time left to administer the schools efficiently and work with his staff to develop and carry out an effective educational program. He may not have time to do these things at all."[11] Thus, while the superintendent possesses considerable power, he maintains it only so long as he is effectively able to handle outside pressures.

[10] Neal Gross, "Who Applies What Kind of Pressures," in Rosenthal, *Governing Education,* pp. 91–99.

[11] *Ibid.,* pp. 103–104.

How Is Such Pressure Exercised? The influence of informal groups on decision-making in school districts has only recently been explored, but data from a number of case studies indicate that an informal power structure exists in many, and probably most, school districts.[12] These data further indicate that the pressure of informal groups of power elites, such as middle-class businessmen or key influentials, has a telling influence upon decisions; this important power is exercised in most local school districts by a relatively few persons who hold top positions of influence in the informal power structure of the school district. In fact, these informal groups tend to exert far more influence than do formal organizations on basic decisions affecting the public schools.

Evidence from case studies of many school districts reveals that the composition of these power-wielding informal groups varies; however, businessmen are the largest single occupational group represented. Kimbrough states that, "as a consequence of their superior status, businessmen exercise the greatest effect upon, and often dominate, educational policies in the nation."[13] In contrast to Koerner's assertions, Kimbrough found that educators are poorly represented at the top levels of the power structure, with the occasional exception of the superintendent. Kimbrough agrees with Koerner that most school board members are not part of the informal power structure.

How do these influential members of informal groups actually exercise their power? Kimbrough cites an example from a medium-sized district. First, let us assume that an educational project costing several million dollars is proposed for the local school system and that there exists an informal group of community leaders who will be positively affected by the project if it is approved. The project may have been proposed by one of the leaders of this group, by an organization or public official, or it may have evolved through some combination of circumstances. Kimbrough's studies indicate that the following activities may be expected:

There will be an increase in interactions among the leaders of the power group. These interactions to discuss the proposal may occur at civic occasions, on the telephone or at social gatherings. Small groups of leaders may get together for personal discussions. Thus, definite action is preceded by considerable informal talk.

Because of the project's importance, a meeting of the top power-wielders in the group is held to resolve differences of opinion and to make a decision, for which the preliminary informal interaction has provided a framework. A decision is reached, and plans for action are drawn up.

A fanning-out process then occurs—key persons not at the meeting are drawn into the group and numerous others are alerted about the decision. This process involves the use of persuasion and reasoning to convince

---

[12] Kimbrough, "An Informal Arrangement," pp. 105–136.

[13] *Ibid.,* p. 119.

OFF BASE

others of the logic of the decision. The public officials who will formalize the decision may, at this point, experience some form of subtle anticipatory coercion. The "Big Men" rarely make direct threats but will, if necessary, later resort to threats, bribes, coercion and political deals.

If for some reason formal action on the project does not proceed according to the wishes of the power brokers, key supporting personnel are induced to resort to parliamentary roadblocks, such as appointing a study committee or referring the issue to a standing committee established for such emergencies. This maneuver allows time to exert heavier pressure for a favorable decision.

Power or control is exercised on a different level by other individuals and groups outside the formal decision-making structure, including the Parent-Teachers Association, taxpayers' associations, and teachers' organizations. Some individuals who influence decisions informally through group membership also occupy positions within the formal organization; teachers are a notable example.

Informal interpersonal relationships are often used to achieve desired objectives, as in the case of a certain principal who managed to get for his school materials and privileges denied other principals.[14] A casual observer might have attributed his success to his aggressive personality. However, the real explanation was that he usually sat by the assistant superintendent

---

[14] Kimbrough, "An Informal Arrangement," pp. 128–129.

An in-depth study of modern DANCE BAND STAGING which I researched PERSONALLY in ACAPULCO and LAS VEGAS and TAHITI!   What's YOURS O Principal?

Some new BARBER SHEARS, a revised HEM LINE CODE and a system of BELLS, WHISTLES and LIGHTS that'll REVOLUTIONIZE BETWEEN PERIOD TRAFFIC FLOW in the HALLS!

Good! Anyone see the STAR we're supposed to be following?

There's a GLOW up ahead but I think it's just a BONFIRE at a STUDENT RIOT!

Cartoon by Barry Base.

in charge of administration at Rotary Club meetings. Whenever he wanted something he simply told the assistant superintendent at the meeting. Try to trace that decision-making process on a formal organizational chart!

In many school districts there exist two administrative networks: one formal and legally-recognized; the other informal, friendly and, in many instances, far more efficient than the official one. Consider the situation which permits the following kinds of occurrences in one large school district. A university professor, speaking at an in-service workshop for teachers, utters some uncomplimentary remarks about the school board's attitude toward segregation. While the professor is still talking, the remark is reported to a member of the school board, who calls the professor at the end of his speech to tell him that the city will no longer participate in the workshop. A teacher who has received good reports from her superiors is not rehired because she does not believe in filing lesson plans. When the dismissal is announced, there is no dissent; the favorable reports have been forgotten. A principal who has refused to let a child transfer into his school under the open-enrollment regulation, because there is no more space, receives a call from a legislator or school board member and suddenly discovers that he does have an empty seat and will be glad to accommodate the child.

PARENTS AND TEACHERS

The local parent-teacher organization serves as a communications link between parents and the formal school organization, with teachers usually

The politics of education is complex and ever changing. At various times and places it can appear to be an asset or a liability. But it is real. Only through understanding and making proper use of politics can education be improved. Wendell H. Pierce, What's New In Education.

acting as representatives of the schools. The formal school system ordinarily operates by means of down-the-line communications. When the formal hierarchy does not respond to up-the-line communications from parents or teachers in a manner satisfactory to them, the informal system can be resorted to in an attempt to get a more favorable response.

An instance of this occurred when the energetic principal of a New Haven, Connecticut, school in a low-income neighborhood organized the PTA in an attempt to improve the school's facilities. He began by going to an important neighborhood leader and persuading her that the children in the school needed help. Convinced, the woman and the principal went to work on the PTA. In order to arouse parent involvement, they convinced the PTA to endorse a hot lunch program; this required the PTA to raise funds and hire kitchen help. As the PTA became more active, the principal began a campaign for a new school to replace the old one. When the city administration raised obstacles, the principal called together the PTA members and other neighborhood leaders to ask their support for a new school. Within twenty-four hours they were exerting pressure on the administration. Needless to say, the problem was solved.

However, teachers have become increasingly frustrated by the impotence of most parent-teacher organizations and their ineffectiveness as a means of implementing teachers' educational aims. Consequently, the role of teachers' organizations in determining educational policy is ever-increasing. Largely as a result of collective bargaining techniques, including strikes and the threat of strikes, teacher organizations are winning more and more power over educational policy.

As recently as 1956 one expert succinctly characterized teacher influence thus: "Teachers as a group have little or no say in the formulation of school policy."[15] Today, however, many teacher organizations have won recognition as the official bargaining representatives of their members, while in the past, boards of education insisted on dealing with teachers as individuals. Teacher organizations are also demanding that issues previously considered the prerogatives of school boards and superintendents be subject to collective bargaining. Among these issues are teacher and paraprofessional salaries, clerical and secretarial assistance, curriculum development, fringe benefits, in-service training, class size determination, textbook selection

---

[15] Daniel Griffiths, *Human Relations in School Administration* (New York: Appleton-Century-Crofts, 1956), p. 106.

Jim: We haven't given much attention in this chapter to one of the key figures in the business of governing and controlling schools.

Kevin: Who's that?

Jim: The principal. He's the one whose influence the teacher feels most. No other person influences school environment, faculty and student morale, curriculum and instruction as much as the principal.

Kevin: I tend to agree, but one study I know of found that in the primary grades 63 percent of the students didn't know the principal's name, and 86 percent had never spoken to him. And the 14 percent who had spoken to him had done so in a negative situation. That study doesn't indicate much impact.

Jim: Oh, but it does! I would say that the principal was influencing the students tremendously. His absence from their daily life was having an impact on them.

Kevin: Well, in that sense, yes.

Jim: The critical factor, as far as I'm concerned, is that the principal see himself as the school's leader rather than its administrator. If he is skillful and adept at human relations, decision-making, and facilitating staff wishes, he can enhance the conditions in which he, his staff and the students work.

Kevin: I think that his attitude toward children is the single most significant factor in determining or changing the school's climate. He can set the tone of the entire school through his actions.

Jim: My advice to young teachers who are looking for their first jobs is to find out as much as they can about their prospective principal's beliefs about children and about how learning should occur. I'd also talk to other teachers in the school about his leadership ability. Does the school reflect his beliefs about children and learning? If the teachers can't tell what his beliefs are, he can't be much of a leader.

and even the appointment of department heads and other school administrators. As one commentator has put it, "They want to negotiate everything." In an increasing number of school districts, teacher organizations are winning the right to negotiate these issues with school boards. As another observer has remarked, "It is not at all difficult to foresee a time when virtually all American teachers will be employed under collective bargaining contracts that cover not only salaries but a long list of other items."[16]

---

[16] Koerner, *Who Controls American Education?*, p. 42. A more detailed discussion of teacher organizations follows in Chapter Nine.

Collective bargaining is one of many procedures which educators are borrowing from the business world. But the impact of business on education is not a new phenomenon. Industrial growth in the United States was paralleled historically by the application of industrial principles in the schools. At the height of an industrially-inspired "efficiency movement" in the Twenties, a number of business techniques of dubious educational merit were introduced into the schools. Schools were compared to factories whose products were students; dollar values were assigned to parts of the curriculum; the size of classes and teacher loads were increased for the sake of efficiency, and detailed clerical records were kept. Education was, in effect, confined to cost-saving and mechanical functions to reduce "overhead." The public then demanded a profitable return on money "invested" in schools. Some teachers and educators fought the trend, but so powerful and far-reaching was the movement that their voices were not heard. It was later recognized that educators had gone overboard in applying commercial principles, unscientifically, to a social institution. But the damage had been done, and many such practices of questionable educational value are still used in countless schools across the country.

Increasing attention has been given in recent years to the amount of control business exercises over education. In one recent study, Grace Graham shows that the great prestige of the business world has enabled it to have significant influence on American education.[17] Today's schools by and large endorse and teach the values of business. The dominant theme of the "business creed" consciously and unconsciously disseminated by businessmen is praise for the achievements of American capitalism; the fundamentals of this creed are being absorbed by most students throughout the school day.[18]

In general, teachers seemingly stress many of the values that businessmen praise highly. For example, teachers struggle to inculcate respect for hard work, punctuality, neatness, a sense of duty, and acceptance of the sanctity of private property.

Teachers usually grade their pupils at least partly on the basis of how hard they try. They emphasize the importance of education as preparation to get a job. "This emphasis by educators on the economic rather than on the intellectual and aesthetic contributions of education to a full life indicates the extent to which teachers themselves accept the businessmen's creed."[19]

Charles Reich argues in *The Greening of America* that the young are rejecting the values of business. He asserts that a new consciousness is emerging which will impel the young to try to humanize the institutions of the corporate state and to transform their goals from profits to the public good.

---

[17] Grace Graham, *The Public Schools in the New Society* (New York: Harper and Row, 1969), Chs. 2, 6 and 8.

[18] *Ibid.,* p. 27.

[19] *Ibid.,* p. 28.

Control by business
Perhaps a little more flagrant in 1952, but no less influential today.

Photo courtesy of Dow Chemical Co.

If Reich's controversial thesis proves correct, we should expect the business values which currently prevail in American education to give way to humanitarian principles.

Both the school board and the superintendent are vulnerable to influence from the business community. In most school districts, the superintendent resembles an executive or business manager more then he does an educational philosopher. Knowledge of budgeting and finance is essential for hiring and success as a superintendent. Most school boards are also likely to have a business orientation, since businessmen have continually been well-represented on local boards. As a result, school boards tend to be economy-minded and to stress the elimination of frills and the reduction of overhead—approaches which may be sound in business but are unlikely to encourage educational experimentation.

The National Association of Manufacturers, the public-relations arm of the business community, runs a comprehensive and far-reaching public relations program directed at the schools which consciously disseminates the "business creed."[20] The NAM exerts influence to try to eliminate from the

---

[20] Graham, *The Public Schools*, p. 18.

The public knows more about potato prices, the number of hogs slaught-
ered, and the status of bank loans than it knows about its schools. Davereux
Josephs, Chairman of President Eisenhower's Committee on Education
Beyond High School, quoted in Alma S. Wittlin, "The Teacher," in The Professions in America, ed. Kenneth S. Lynn (Boston: Houghton Mifflin, 1965),
p. 96.

Just as war is too important to be left to the generals, education is too im-
portant to be left to the educators. Paul Woodring, A Fourth of a Nation
(New York: McGraw-Hill, 1957), p. 1.

curriculum and from textbooks any tendency toward "creeping collectiv-
ism," and promotes "pro-American" doctrines. Local manufacturers are
urged to investigate what is being taught their own children and to find out
how much money is being spent by taxpayers to spread doctrines abhor-
rent to the business community.[21] Another NAM public-relations project is
Business Education Day, when teachers and local business leaders exchange roles. Its purpose is to show educators how our economic system
functions, and the exchanges provide a channel of communication between
schools and the community. However, the project also tends to promote a
pro-management slant on business issues, and the American Federation of
Teachers, a union organization, has taken a strong stand against closing the
schools at taxpayers' expense for the advantage of a particular interest
group. Business corporations also give the schools free products, such as
films, pamphlets, records, graphs and slides, to promote their images. It
is estimated that the cost of free instructional material entering the nation's
schools from private sources is greater even than the cost of textbooks.[22]

During the Sixties, the relationship of business to education underwent a
change. While business had always courted and asserted its influence on
education, the lines between the two remained distinct; during the last
decade, however, the boundaries between public education and private
industry have become blurred. People now speak of the "partnership" of
business and education. A number of mergers between manufacturers of
educational hardware and the communications media reflect the ever-in-

---

[21] S. A. Rippa, *Education in a Free Society, An American History* (New York: David McKay, 1967),
p. 156.

[22] William O. Stanley, *Education and Social Integration* (New York: Columbia University Press,
1953), pp. 6–9.

creasing scope of the "education industry": big business has entered the educational market. Businesses have offered direct assistance to schools, particularly in the large cities; in some instances businesses have even "adopted" particular schools, offering technical, managerial and financial aid. Performance contracting, an arrangement long employed in industry whereby the contracting business guarantees to produce certain results or not be paid, is becoming more common in education. Business firms are contracting with school districts on this basis to raise the reading and mathematical skills of students. School management and budgeting processes are being revitalized by the "systems" approach, borrowed from private industry.

The concept of "accountability," or responsibility for producing certain growth outcomes on the part of students, will have significant implications for education. It is probable that teachers' functions and roles will be redefined in terms of accountability. Private companies will offer schooling in competition with local school boards, and contracts will be drawn on a performance basis. The involvement of big business could bring about far-reaching changes in school finance. It is one thing for the PTA to lobby for state or federal legislation; it is quite another when the combined forces of, say, IBM and GE support a bill.

Big business is directly challenging educators for control of education. Many educators feel threatened by big business in general, and by the computer in particular. But any discussion of control of education, now or in the future, would be incomplete without a review of the federal government's role, to which we now turn.

CONTROL BY THE FEDERAL GOVERNMENT

It could be argued that the most powerful educational decision-making body in the United States is the Supreme Court, several of whose decisions in recent years have had a profound effect on education. A prime example is *Brown* v. *Board of Education of Topeka,* the 1954 desegregation decision which struck down the doctrine of separate but equal educational facilities. Because some of the Court's decisions have reduced the power of state and local educational authorities, deep resentment has been generated among those who abhor this "federal intrusion" into state rights. Many people, of course, applaud the Court's decisions as steps to make American education more responsive to democratic principles.

The federal government also exerts powerful influence on education through legislation providing monetary aid to local and state authorities and through the administration of these monies by federal offices and departments. Congressional acts apportioning federal funds to education have increased in number and scope in recent years. They have provided funds to selected schools, colleges, cities, states, school boards and agencies to finance a wide variety of projects, including construction of buildings and other educational facilities; improvement of instruction or administration;

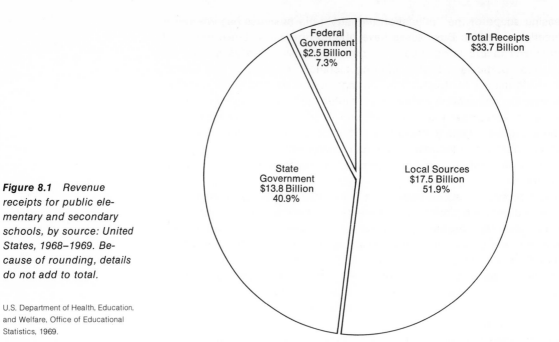

Figure 8.1 *Revenue receipts for public elementary and secondary schools, by source: United States, 1968–1969. Because of rounding, details do not add to total.*

U.S. Department of Health, Education, and Welfare, Office of Educational Statistics, 1969.

development of educational personnel, including teachers and paraprofessionals, particularly for poverty areas; loans for prospective teachers, and educational research. In 1969 the federal government provided for about 7 percent of the total cost of public elementary and secondary education.[23]

Because most federal aid is categorical—that is, the money must be spent for purposes which are specified generally in the legislation and more precisely by the federal agency administering the funds—the federal government is able to exert influence on school districts and institutions that accept or seek this aid. For example, in order to qualify for federal funds to improve its reading program, a school district must conform to the guidelines and restrictions which accompany the money. Many financially-stricken school districts are grateful for funds regardless of the restrictions on their use.

There is a danger inherent in this situation that a school district might be tempted to divert its own resources from a much-needed program to a less important project which the federal government would be willing to help finance. Thus, the prospect of federal money may encourage neglect of a local district's particular needs. Despite these potential dangers, the majority of educators support the federal government's role in education and

---

[23] *Digest of Educational Statistics, 1969* (Washington, D.C.: U.S. Government Printing Office, 1969), p. 49.

it is probable that its power in education will continue to increase. The long-range effect of federal participation in education, both judicial and financial, is probably to make schools more uniform nationwide.

EDUCATIONAL BUREAUCRACIES

Up to this point we have focused on distinctions between governance and control and on the individuals, groups and units of government involved in each. There is another aspect of governance and control of education which deserves special attention: the powerful educational bureaucracies.

Bureaucracies are not all bad. They develop as systems of rules and regulations to insure equality of treatment, to prevent graft and to protect the organization from idiosyncratic behavior by its employees. Bureaucracies also permit specialization, with particular employees performing only particular specified functions, in order to increase efficiency. But these procedures inevitably tend to rigidify, and individuals unfamiliar with the bureaucracy's operations often find that its rules are impenetrable and encourage the avoidance of decision-making responsibility.

Have you ever tried to get a bureaucracy to make a decision which deviated slightly from the established rules and regulations? Frustrating, isn't it? Buckpassing and reluctance to accept responsibility for decisions which do not conform to standard procedures are notoriously common among bureaucrats. As the institution gets larger, so does the bureaucracy. The result, almost inevitably, is impersonalization, which is becoming common in colleges and universities.

It is precisely this impersonalization which students are rebelling against. As a teacher, you may find yourself working in a school district which has so centralized the decision-making power that the teacher and the child are both restricted, and their creativity denied. This section will explore the issues surrounding such educational bureaucratic structures.

THE EFFECTS OF BUREAUCRACY

Most schools and school systems are organized and run to facilitate order. There is, of course, nothing wrong with order *per se.* Order becomes objectionable when schools, administrators and teachers give it a higher priority than creativity or empathy and concern for individuals and their problems. When that kind of misalignment of priorities takes place, the schools become guilty of dehumanization. Emphasis on keeping the organization running smoothly without concomitant concern for the individual, and unwillingness to allow exceptions to the rules even when they are warranted, are symptoms of a sick organization. In Chapter Two we discussed classroom practices which tend to dehumanize. This section will examine how school districts' administrative and bureaucratic practices tend to dehumanize.

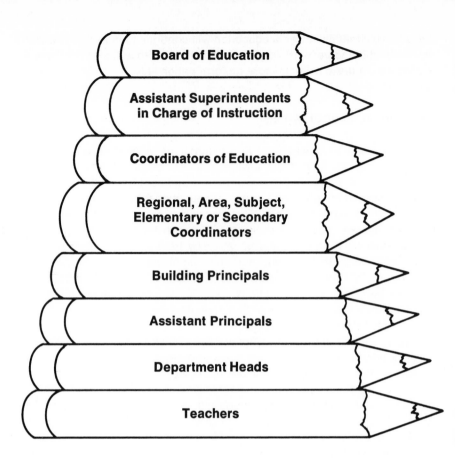

Figure 8.2 *Tall school administrative organization*

The labels within the figure, from top to bottom, read:

- Board of Education
- Assistant Superintendents in Charge of Instruction
- Coordinators of Education
- Regional, Area, Subject, Elementary or Secondary Coordinators
- Building Principals
- Assistant Principals
- Department Heads
- Teachers

First, virtually all schools are bureaucracies. What does that mean? They are characterized by a hierarchy of authority, rules specifying how individuals who work within the bureaucracy should behave and the sense of impersonalization which these conditions tend to generate. Schools differ, however, in the degree to which they manifest bureaucratic characteristics.

TALL ORGANIZATIONS

The growing militancy among teachers today can be traced, at least in part, to their isolation from the decision-making process in most school districts. This is a result of the way most school systems are organized. Public school systems, particularly those in metropolitan areas, are what is known as "tall organizations," characterized by complex hierarchies of command within which each official has a minimal range of control. The hierarchical arrangement illustrated in Figure 8.2 is typical. A building principal, for example,

THE REAL WORLD

might have responsibility for only fifteen or twenty teachers, while one with a wider range of control might be responsible for forty or fifty teachers.

The assumptions which underlie tall organizations have been discussed by sociologists, notably Talcott Parsons, Robert L. Peabody and James D. Thompson.[24] Two of these assumptions are worth noting here. The first is that the most capable people in an organization are those at or near the top of the hierarchy. As a result of this belief, the organization expects them to provide most of the leadership and make all of the important decisions. The second assumption is that those persons at the bottom of hierarchy are often, if not usually, incompetent and unreliable. As a consequence, little is expected of them and the organization operates on the premise that they will function best under close supervision. Hence the short span of control. As one observer has remarked, "Little wonder, then, that teachers in tall institutional structures, since they are at the bottom of the hierarchy, find themselves with little real authority, with minor decision making roles, and with little opportunity to exert leadership."[25]

As an example, imagine yourself as a more-than-competent elementary school teacher with some specific ideas about new ways of organizing the curriculum. If you are lucky and your principal has faith in his teachers and does not feel restricted by guidelines and rules imposed on him by his superiors, he might give you the go-ahead to experiment with the curriculum. If you are not so lucky, you may find yourself restricted to teaching a prescribed curriculum using prescribed instructional materials selected by a regional coordinator totally unfamiliar with the needs of the children you are teaching.

One of the major defects of tall school bureaucracies is that most decisions regarding curriculum and instruction are not made by the persons most competent to make them—the teachers. Teachers today are more competent and more highly trained than ever before, but bureaucratic school systems still have an investment in considering teachers incapable of making intelligent decisions. In practice, this means that others do the planning for the teachers. School boards, administrators or outside experts often prescribe curriculum guides, texts and even learning outcomes or objectives. These activities are usually followed by evaluation tasks also prescribed by those outside the classroom. Thus, teachers often cannot exercise decisive influence over the major circumstances and nature of their work. Is it any wonder that teachers are frustrated and feel that their creativity is stifled?

---

[24] Talcott Parsons, "Suggestions for a Sociological Approach to the Theory of Organizations," *Administrative Science Quarterly* 1 (September 1956): 225–239; Robert L. Peabody, *Organizational Authority* (New York: Atherton Press, 1964); James D. Thompson, ed., *Approaches to Organizational Design* (Pittsburgh: University of Pittsburgh Press, 1966).

[25] J. Michael Palardy, "Needed: Requiem for a Structure," *The Clearing House* 44 (February 1970), p. 361.

One observer has described this system as operating on an assumption of distrust:

The school board has no faith in the central administration, the central administration has no faith in the principals, the principals have no faith in the teachers, and the teachers have no faith in the students. In such a system it seems natural not to give the principal of a school control over his budget, not to give the teachers control over their syllabus, and not to give the students control over anything. Distrust is the order of the day.[26]

A Case in Point: New York City.   The New York City school system has suffered from many of the defects of a tall bureaucracy. In a study of the political and social forces that have affected the New York public schools, David Rogers closely examined the professional bureaucracy of the district.[27] He concludes that the New York City school system is a "sick" bureaucracy—a term for organizations whose traditions, structure and operations subvert their stated missions and prevent any flexible accommodation to changing client demands. Among the symptoms of the sickness he cites:

1. overcentralization, the development of many levels in the chain of command, and an upward orientation of anxious subordinates;

2. vertical and horizontal fragmentation, isolating units from one another and limiting communication and coordination of functions;

3. the consequent development of chauvinism within particular units, reflected in actions to protect and expand their power;

4. the exercise of strong, informal pressure from peers within units to conform to their codes, geared toward political protection and expansion and ignoring the organization's wider goals;

5. compulsive rule following and rule enforcing;

6. the rebellion of lower-level supervisors against headquarters' directives, alternating at times with over-conformity, as they develop concerns about ratings and promotions;

7. increasing insulation from clients, as internal politics and personal career interests override interests in serving various publics; and

8. the tendency to make decisions in committees, making it difficult to pinpoint responsibility and authority are the institution's main pathologies.[28]

---

[26] Christopher Jencks, as quoted in Charles E. Silberman, "How the Public Schools Kill Dreams and Mutilate Minds," *The Atlantic* (June 1970), p. 88.

[27] David Rogers, *110 Livingston Street* (New York: Random House, 1969), pp. 266–323. Copyright © 1968 by David Rogers.

[28] *Ibid.*, pp. 267–268.

THE PETER PRINCIPLE

"In a hierarchy, each employee tends to rise to his level of incompetence: Every post tends to be occupied by an employee incompetent to execute its duties."

In The Peter Principle *(New York: William Morrow, 1968), Laurence J. Peter expounds a principle which he believes helps explain incompetence in bureaucratic hierarchies. Simply put, a person who is competent at a particular job will be rewarded with promotions to new and different jobs until he is appointed to a job in which he is incompetent, and in which he will remain. Thus, for example, a bright teacher at a large secondary school who gets along with the other teachers, parents and students may be promoted to principal. The new job may require social sensitivities and skills to work well with the school board and superintendent that the new principal has never developed, and as a result his relationships with them may be very poor. This principal has moved upward in the hierarchy from a job in which he was very competent to one for which he is unsuitable. Laurence J. Peter would predict that this man would remain at his job as principal until he retired. Have you ever come across examples of the Peter Principle in action?*

Rogers indicates that these administrative patterns are not necessarily bad if they are not carried too far. But in the New York City school system they are so extreme as to paralyze the system at a time when rapid social change demands new administrative arrangements.

Rogers cites Dr. Mortimer Kreuter of the Center for Urban Education, who says that teachers become "infantilized" by a system whose functionaries grade and inspect them like children. "They literally have no time to go to the toilet," Kreuter reports, "and when they must, they are obliged to summon a next door teacher to keep an eye on the classroom. They must punch time clocks daily and file affidavits when ill."[29]

Rogers quotes another administrative study on the New York system which states, "The greatest failing of the schools today is the failure to use the creative ability of teachers. Too often little or no opportunity is given teachers to contribute to the development of the educational program or to the management of the school. Supervision is never creative unless the people being supervised are given responsibility commensurate with their professional competence."[30]

One of the reasons for bureaucratic ineptitude is that most of the decision-

---

[29] *Ibid.,* p. 283.

[30] *Ibid.,* p. 283.

makers and staff personnel have been trained as teachers and supervisors, rather than as administrators. "There are teachers in auditing, zoning, human relations, demographic research, programming and data processing, and guidance counselling, who have little or no technical training."[31] The result is inefficiency.

Lest it seem that we are singling out the New York City school system for criticism, we want to mention that within the last few years major efforts have been made there to decentralize many decision-making and administrative functions and to cope with the other problems which develop in large inefficient bureaucracies.

SOME ALTERNATIVE STRUCTURES

Although New York City's case is one of the most dramatic, many large cities' school districts suffer from a similar form of arteriosclerosis caused by the congenital weaknesses of tall organizations. One educational writer has suggested that there should exist a dual chain of command in which teachers and administrators have separate areas of responsibility; administrators would make purely administrative decisions, related to such matters as scheduling, and teachers would have the right to make decisions about professional matters, such as curriculum and instruction.[32] To some extent this is what has occurred in the Temple City, California, school district (see Chapter Eleven) with its differentiated staffing plan.

Differentiated Staffing. Temple City is a small district, with approximately 175 teachers, where much of the decision-making has been decentralized by allowing classroom teachers to make important decisions which affect curriculum and instruction. Each school has an Academic Senate, which is its policy-making body. It is directly responsible to the superintendent. The school principal is a member of the Academic Senate, and has a vote equal to that of any teacher. The authority that previously belonged to the principal is now vested in the Academic Senate as a body. The Senate possesses broad and comprehensive powers to determine dollar priorities, develop school policies, initiate change and innovation at the building level and recruit and retain staff. The principal administers decisions and interprets policies established by the Senate, while the mundane chores are relegated to the school manager. Two student representatives, elected by the Executive Committee of the high school student body, are members of the Academic Senate. A District Senate, comprised of the school principals and an equal number of teachers selected from within the school Senates, recommends for School Board approval policies and programs related to instruction

---

[31] *Ibid.,* p. 326.

[32] Ronald G. Corwin, *A Sociology of Education* (New York: Appleton-Century-Crofts, 1965).

and curriculum. Temple City's efforts to decentralize and return decision-making power to its teachers seems to us to be a step in the right direction.

Flat Organizations.   Another alternative to the present bureaucratic structure, advocated by some educators, is to replace the tall organization with a *flat* one, as illustrated in Figure 8.3. A flat institutional structure is characterized by short chains of command and broad spans of control. Thus a teacher, instead of being seven steps removed from the board of education (as is the case in the tall organizational structure diagrammed on page 344), would be only three or four steps away. Also, each person in authority would be responsible for a larger number of subordinates.

In advocating a flat organizational structure J. Michael Palardy argues that the more subordinates a person in authority has reporting to him, the less closely he can supervise them; as a consequence, they are freer to exercise their own judgment in performing their jobs.[33] Superiors will also lack specific information about the challenges and problems their subordinates face and the materials they need. In order for superiors to make decisions on the basis of factual information, they must first consult their subordinates to obtain that information. As a result, communication would be increased. The danger, however, is that decisions would simply be made without the necessary information, a situation which would be no improvement over a tall organization.

Another advantage of a flat organization is the greater possibility of emergent leadership among teachers. If they are not closely supervised, teachers

[33] Palardy, "Needed: Requiem," pp. 361–362.

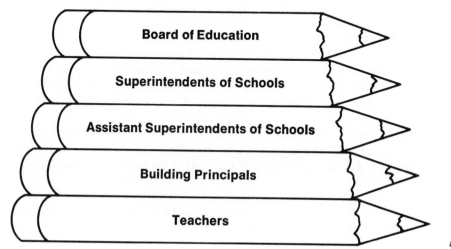

Figure 8.3 *Flat school administrative organization*

can assume more individual responsibility. Leadership positions among the teachers would then develop.

What Is a Successful Alternative?　Any successful alternative to the existing bureaucracy must have three identifiable characteristics. First, the school system must be responsive to the demands and needs of its clients and employees. Parents, students and teachers must have access to the system's decision-makers so that their needs can be made known. Second, decision-making regarding curriculum and instruction must be decentralized. Teachers, who have responsibility for implementing the curriculum, should have the final say in the choice of books and materials. Third, the system must operate on trust rather than distrust. As long as people are treated as though they are not trusted, they will be resentful, their creativity will be stifled and they will work to "beat the system." A school or school district which puts faith in its teachers' ability to make good decisions will be rewarded more often than it will be disappointed. Teachers who operate in such a school or school district cannot help reflecting its humanistic outlook in their own classrooms. Conversely, it is virtually impossible for a teacher to "humanize" his classroom if he and his students operate in an environment which systematically dehumanizes through distrust and impersonality. To humanize the classroom, the system must be made humane.

DISCUSSION QUESTIONS

1. Can you offer any examples from your experience of the distinction between governance and control? How do you suppose the persons in control obtained their power? What were the advantages and disadvantages of this state of affairs in the situations you are familiar with?
2. What do you see as the advantages and disadvantages of the public schools being a branch of the federal government? Are you familiar with any country where this is the case? What is its school system like? How does it compare to the system you are a product of?
3. How were the interests and values of business reflected in your education? Were you aware of the influence of commercial values and methods on your schooling at the time? What is your opinion of this state of affairs?
4. Do you think the PTA is a potentially effective means of influencing school policy? Where do you think the interests of teachers and parents coincide? Where do they diverge? In what areas do you think informal influence might be more effective than collective bargaining?
5. What do you see as the advantages and disadvantages of collective bargaining? of accreditation? of accountability? Would you teach in an unaccredited school? Would you be willing to be held accountable for the learning of your students?

6. In the light of what you have learned from this chapter, what do you think of Paul Woodring's statement that "education is too important to be left to the educators"?

7. What do you see as the advantages and disadvantages of the dual chain of command system suggested on pages 348–349? Do you think the Temple City plan would work in a huge urban school district? Why or why not? How might it be modified for use in a big city?

8. What current happenings are affecting the power of teachers to implement their own desires? In what issues are teachers most interested? How involved in these issues do you see yourself five years from now? Through what channels do you foresee yourself working?

FOR FURTHER READING

Barnes, Melvin W. "The Administrator's Role in Humanizing the School." *The National Elementary Principal* 49 (February 1970): 37–40. Deals with ways the principal can establish and maintain a humanistic atmosphere of trust and respect in his school.

Bishop, Lloyd K. "Bureaucracy and Educational Change." *The Clearing House* 44 (January 1970): 305–310. Reports the results of a study designed to determine what effect the bureaucratic structure of school systems has upon a system's capacity to make significant educational changes. Bishop's findings indicate that a stable (bureaucratic) school system seems better able to enhance change than a less structured organizational system.

Koerner, James D. *Who Controls American Education?* Boston: Beacon Press, 1968. Koerner's major thesis is that professional educators and their organizations exert major control over American education. Koerner deplores this, and urges that changes be made to reduce the power of superintendents, professors of education, state departments of education and the professional organizations.

Leles, Sam. "Educational Structure: Is It Capable of Innovation?" *The Clearing House* 44 (February 1970): 368–372. Argues that organization is an integral part of the educational system, and examines it as a determinant of the curriculum.

McLure, William P. "Major Issues in School Finance." *Educational Administration Quarterly* 5 (Autumn 1969): 2–14. Interprets contemporary issues in school finance as functions of three phenomena: 1) the educational needs of individuals and society, 2) governance, and 3) ecological characteristics of the population. Emphasizes the logical order of issues and the necessity to resolve them as a total complex.

Palardy, J. Michael. "Needed: Requiem for a Structure." *The Clearing House* 44 (February 1970): 360–362. Advocates a different administrative approach designed to reduce the hierarchical structure of a school system, and thereby increase the leadership potential and effectiveness of the teacher.

Rogers, David. *110 Livingston Street.* New York: Random House, 1969. 110 Livingston Street is the address of the New York City school district administration offices. The author examines the operation of the city schools, with particular emphasis on the bureaucratic structure. His is not a book favorable to the school system.

Rosenthal, Alan, ed. *Governing Education.* New York: Doubleday, 1969. A compilation of readings on the politics of education. Case studies, as well as expository articles, demonstrate how educational decisions are made and who makes them. Chapters by Kimbrough and Gross are particularly interesting.

Saxe, Richard W. "Toward a Feary of Administration." *The National Elementary Principal* 49 (April 1970): 26–30. A humorous article that attempts to explain administrative behavior as a function of fear. Saxe believes that bizarre administrative behavior results from a corruption of the ideal form of bureaucracy, and that this corruption is based on fear. Fun to read.

FILMS

A Chance to Learn (NBC Educational Enterprises, Code #006C1, 16mm, color, 16 min.) Daniel Moynihan and Charles Hamilton discuss some of the basic issues underlying the confrontations taking place in schools across the country: Who shall control the schools? Who shall decide who teaches in them? Who shall decide what is taught? The public school system in Rochester, New York, is used as an example.

Community Control (Boston Newsreel, 16mm, 50 min.) Documents the struggle of the black and Puerto Rican communities to control their own schools. The forces they are working against: the police who enforce the political decisions of the municipal bureaucracy and the teachers' union which is striking against the demands of the community.

I Ain't Playin' No More (EDC Film Library, 16mm, b&w, 61 min.) Filmed at the Morgan Community School in Washington, D.C., this film documents the efforts of the community to become more conscious of its needs and goals, so that it can more effectively formulate an educational program.

No Little Hope (Center for Urban Education, 16mm, color, 28 min.) Documents the meaning of education to various people in New York City. Through the words of the people interviewed, many of them parents, it becomes clear that "the process of education" cannot be fully understood without taking into account parents, the community, mass media—and, of course, the schools.

The Teacher Gap (Indiana University Audio-Visual Center, 16mm, b&w, 60 min., 1965, NET) Compares the efforts of two communities to provide quality education to large numbers of students. The less successful approach of Bay City, Michigan, in relation to the success of Newton, Massachusetts, is attributed to a difference in the community's attitude toward education.

AUDIOTAPES

Public Education as a Business Enterprise (The Center for the Study of Democratic Institutions, 3.75 ips, reel, ½ track, 20:44 min.) A highly-charged discussion on the proposition that private corporations replace, or at least supplement, the public schools. The concept of "public education as a business enterprise" is examined, denounced and finally conditionally supported.

Religion in the Schools (The Center for the Study of Democratic Institutions, 3.75 ips, reel, ½ track, 59:10 min.) John Cogley, editor of *The Center* magazine, leads a staff discussion of the Supreme Court decision on prayers in public schools.

The System (National Education Association, 3.75 ips, reel or cassette, 55:45 min. total) This hour-long audiotape is divided into seven short sections, each intended to serve as the basis for a complete discussion. The topics are:

A CALL TO ACTION (3:20 min.),

TOWARD COOPERATIVE GOVERNANCE (17:10 min.),

PUBLIC SCHOOLS OF CHOICE (7:10 min.),

THE TEACHER AS DECISION MAKER (6:40 min.),

PARENT POWER (5:20 min.),

THE NORTH DAKOTA STORY: SYSTEM REFORM THROUGH
  TEACHER EDUCATION (8:20 min.)

THE NORTH DAKOTA STORY: PARENTS AS PARTNERS (8:25 min.).

Refer to Appendix for distributors' addresses.

Where Have Schools Been?

Do these pictures make your school experience look better or worse to you, in comparison? Would you have preferred to use good old Dick and Jane? To learn biology in a sex-segregated seminar? How about the idea of kittens as teaching aids?

9   Where Have Teachers Been and Where Are They Going?

The essence of a career in teaching is work and involvement with the young. When someone is thinking about becoming a teacher, his thoughts and daydreams usually revolve around interaction with students. Rarely does he bother with hypothetical issues beyond the scope of the classroom. This is both natural and appropriate, since the teacher's success or failure depends on his effectiveness with children. Nevertheless, there is more to being a teacher than this. Teachers work within a system which subjects them to pressures from many quarters. Frequently the prospective teacher is somewhat naïve about the pressures and forces which will impinge upon him, and naïveté can be dangerous, in terms both of making a career decision and of making a successful career.

To help you see this point, we would like you to indulge in a different set of daydreams for a few moments. We will offer you a series of vignettes and, after reading each one, you should reflect on how you might react. As you read each one, imagine yourself teaching in that ideal classroom you carry around in your head. Assume that all indications are that you are doing a fine job. You are really enjoying it. Your students are making nice progress. They seem to be interested in their work. A few parents have indicated that although they were initially worried that their precious child was to have a new (read "untested") teacher, they are thrilled with his progress in your class. Okay. Things are going very well . . .

AND

1. Two mothers ask for a conference with you. You haven't met them, and know only that they are parents of two girls who act very quiet and cliquish in class. At the conference, the mothers come right to the point. They claim you favor the boys in your class and systematically ignore the girls—not just their girls, but all the girls. They say you teach only to the boys. The mothers become quite emotional and suggest that since you are a young unmarried woman you are working out your preoccupation with boys on the class. [If you are a male, reverse the situation. The mothers are parents of boys and are accusing you of excessive interest in little girls. Fiend!!] They say they have talked to some of the other mothers of girls in the class and claim that these mothers agree. They came to warn you that they "intend to take action!" On that note, they raise eyebrows, pick up purses and huff out.

2. Four days in a row representatives of the Yearbook Committee burst into your classroom unannounced and literally take over. They claim they are signing up subscribers for the Yearbook, but they take a good ten minutes each time, most of which is devoted to wisecracking, showing off and putting you down in various ways. Their attitude is something on the order of, "Look, teach. You're new in this school and you've got a lot to learn. We've been here four years and we know our way around. Don't try to pull rank on us." When they finally leave, it takes a long time to get your students back in a mood to do some serious work. You complain to the principal (who

happens to be a former Yearbook adviser) and he tells you, "Yearbook is one of the biggest things in this school. It is a student-run activity in which everyone takes great pride. Last year the Yearbook won Honorable Mention in the South-Southwestern Regional Yearbook Conference for high schools with over 2,000 and under 2,500 students with a lower middle-class socio-economic population. All of us who were here last year were very proud of the kids and what they did for the school. I know once you're here with us a little longer, you'll get into the swing of things. I'll send you a few copies of past yearbooks. I know you're going to help this year's Yearbook staff in every way you can. They're really great, live-wire kids and come from some of our best families."

You ask around and find out that you should expect visits from the Yearbook Staff three or four times a week for the next two months. They have pictures to take, workers to enlist, advertisements to sell . . . and new teachers to break in.

3. You get a special-delivery letter from a group called PAP (Patriotic American Parents). You have heard that they are very active in your area and are especially interested in schools. Their letter informs you that their lawyer is preparing a case against you for using books which are on their disapproved list. (You didn't know there was such a list but, sure enough, there is and you have.) They claim they have evidence that you are waging a subtle but nevertheless vicious war against the cause of justice and liberty and have succeeded in temporarily deflecting the minds of some of your students from the truth. Furthermore, they want to know why you display the UN flag. Finally, you are said to recite the Pledge of Allegiance in an indecorously hasty fashion, which is clearly a sign of your disrespect for country. This is the first you have heard of these charges or even of the Patriots' interest in you. They have requested that you respond in writing by next week or they will begin legal proceedings.

4. In late January, the superintendent—who holds a conference with each new teacher—told you he thought you were doing a fine job and that he wanted you to return next year. In passing, he remarked that he would be getting a contract to you in the spring. Toward the end of April, you got a little nervous and called him. You spoke to his executive secretary, who said not to worry, that you were on the list and that a contract would be coming before long. You stopped worrying. Today is the last day of school, and you find a very nice personal note from the principal in your school mailbox. He thanks you for your fine work during the year and says he is sorry you will not be back next year. You call the superintendent's office. He is in conference, and his executive secretary says that they are not renewing your contract. She cannot remember speaking to you in April. She knows nothing about the case. She does know, however, that the Board of Education has put on a lot of pressure for cuts in next year's personnel budget. She ends by telling you, "You must be very disappointed, dear. I know how you feel."

Jim: *Reciting the Pledge of Allegiance too fast!!? Aren't we going a bit overboard here?*

Kevin: *Maybe so. But . . .*

Jim: *But what?*

Kevin: *But not too many years ago Gordon Lish, an English teacher at Mills High School in Burlingame, California, was fired. Although he was a distinguished scholar and edited an important literary quarterly, he was found guilty of reciting the pledge too rapidly and of telling his students that they didn't have to crouch under their desks during nuclear attack drills!*

Jim: *Wow! Hard to believe.*

5. You noticed something peculiar when you sat down at the faculty dining table one lunch hour. Conversations stopped, and you had the distinct impression your colleagues had been talking about you. A few days later, an older teacher stopped you in the hall after school and said, "I don't want to butt in, but you really are upsetting Mrs. Pruitt and Mrs. Wise." Mrs. P. and Mrs. W. have the classrooms on either side of yours. Apparently, they claim your class makes so much noise that they can't get anything done. Both are very conservative teachers in the tradition of the school. You believe in a more open approach to education. Although your class is somewhat noisy occasionally, it is never chaotic and its noise is usually a by-product of involvement and concentration. Twice Mrs. Wise has sent messengers with notes asking that your class be a bit more quiet. You have always complied. You hardly know either teacher. You have never really talked to Mrs. Wise except to say hello. Mrs. Pruitt, with whom you've chatted, prides herself on being a disciplinarian. What she means, you have inferred, is that she is able to keep the children quiet. You know Mrs. Wise is chummy with Mrs. Pruitt. You go to the vice-principal for advice. He seems to know all about the case, but only from the Wise-Pruitt angle. Inexplicably, he gets quite angry and claims that until you came along the faculty got along beautifully. Further, you are being very unprofessional to make complaints against experienced teachers. You feel as if you are trapped in a Kafka novel.

6. You had been teaching Industrial Arts for two months when you met another new teacher at a faculty meeting. A few weeks later you chaperoned a dance together. Then you began going out on "real dates." By Christmas you knew you were over the edge. On New Year's Eve you proposed. Forty-eight sleepless hours later she accepted. On Valentine's Day you both announced it to your students (none of whom were surprised) and to your

faculty colleagues (who didn't have a clue). You have both been doing well and want to stay on at your jobs next year. On Washington's Birthday, you get a notice from the personnel director calling your attention to the Board ruling against hiring couples. You know that there are no openings in any nearby schools. You plan to get married on the first Saturday in June after school ends. Your fiancée is crying.

These little horror stories are designed to provoke the realization that you can be an effective teacher and still have trouble keeping your job. What is the common theme running through each of these anecdotes? You, the teacher, were succeeding in your work with children, but forces outside the classroom began to impinge on you. A parents' vigilante group accused you of prejudice. The Patriots wanted to make a target case of you. When the Yearbook wise-guys start playing havoc with your class, the principal failed to back you up. On two occasions the school system bureaucracy was ready to put you on the unemployed rolls. Two of your colleagues damaged your reputation with the faculty and administration. Other than that, it's been a super year.

While you may feel confident that you could handle some of these situations, it is doubtful you could cope with all of them. In some cases you would be powerless to respond effectively to your adversaries, and might end up a helpless victim of circumstances. Fortunately, a teacher is not alone. Like many other occupational groups, teachers have organizations which protect them from such indignities and injustices. These organizations function on several levels, from the local to the national, and their very existence can keep situations like those described above from occurring, except in rare instances. But when they do occur, these organizations are committed to supporting the teacher.

In becoming a teacher, you are doing more than committing yourself to work with children. You are joining an occupational group composed of other individuals with similar responsibilities, concerns and pressures whose help you need and who in turn will need your help.

TEACHERS AS A POWERLESS GROUP

Having confronted the individual teacher's potential powerlessness against impinging pressures, let us turn to the occupational group or profession of teaching. Just as individuals can have different degrees of power, so it is with groups of people. A great deal has been written lately about the power of the military-industrial complex to shape the policy of our government both at home and abroad. Charles Reich's *The Greening of America* and John Kenneth Galbraith's *The New Industrial State* describe the power of the giant corporations to affect the texture of our lives. We are becoming increasingly aware of the power of labor unions to affect the nation's economic health, and the power of the American Medical Association to influence the quality

YOU'VE COME A LONG WAY, TEACH!

I. The Colonial Period

In 1647 a law was passed in New England which required towns of fifty or more families to establish elementary schools and towns of 100 or more families to establish Latin grammar schools at the secondary level. Religious instruction was the mainstay of these Colonial schools, but the character of many of the teachers was hardly exemplary. Many were drunkards. Some were sadists and swindlers. Some ran up debts and then skipped town, occasionally with the school's meager funds. This behavior is at least partially explained by the fact that teachers were held in very low esteem and paid pitifully meager salaries. The Colonial teacher received wages equivalent to those of a farmhand.

Teaching was hardly a profession in Colonial America. Schools were poorly equipped, and students attended irregularly. The school term was short, making teaching in many cases a part-time occupation. And along with his teaching and janitorial responsibilities, the teacher had a number of "extracurricular duties." Take the example of a New York schoolmaster, Johannes von Edkellen, who contracted to teach in the town of Flatbush, Long Island, in 1682.

> He had to agree to clean the church, ring the assembly bell, read portions of the Bible, hear the children recite questions and answers out of the catechism, give them religious instruction, provide a basin of water for baptismal purposes, furnish bread and wine for the communion, act as messenger for the consistory, give funeral invitations, ring the funeral bell and dig graves. (Reprinted by permission of Coward-McCann, Inc., from *What's Happened to Teacher?* by Myron Brenton [p. 67]. Copyright © 1970 by Myron Brenton. Much of the information in this chapter about the history of teaching in America has been adapted from Brenton's very lively account.)

To keep the teacher in an itinerant status, he was "boarded round," living with a different family each week in order to stretch out meager school funds. These and other indignities kept the turnover rate high and contributed to keeping the status of teachers low.

and nature of health service. Rarely, however, do people consider teachers to be in the same league as these power groups. Teachers are extolled rhetorically for having the future of the country—its youth—in their hands, but they have rarely tested their immediate power even to affect the conditions of their own employment. Though in recent years teachers have struck (or, more euphemistically, "withheld their services"), by and large we have been a quiet, unmilitant profession.[1] Think back for a moment to Chapter

---

[1] The issue of teacher power is discussed more fully in Chapter Ten.

Eight. Teacher power did not loom large in the discussion of who controls the schools. The important decisions about a community's educational programs are not made by teachers, either individually or in groups.

While teacher groups are becoming increasingly aggressive about salaries and welfare benefits, they have no firm place in the formal governance of the schools and little impact on educational decision-making. In the previous chapter, a distinction was made between governance and control of the schools. It seems logical that teachers, because they outnumber administrators and work full-time in the schools, should have gained a good deal of control of what actually goes on there, but this does not appear to be the case. Of course, they have control over a good deal of what happens in their own classrooms. In fact, however, what happens in a teacher's classroom is severely limited by forces outside the classroom over which she and teachers' organizations have very little control. The major curriculum decisions—what should be taught—are not made by teachers. Hiring and tenure decisions are neither made by nor, in fact, much influenced by teachers or teacher groups. If a new school is to be built, the teachers who will work in

```
┌────────────────────────────────────────────────────────────────┐
│                   Memos From the Main Office                   │
│                                                                │
│   To the faculty:                                              │
│                                                                │
│        The following teachers are to be commended on achieving 100% │
│   attendance yesterday:  NONE.                                 │
│   ───────────────────────────────                             │
│                                                                │
│        There will be a fire drill at the end of the fourth period │
│   today; please do not give any tests.                         │
│   ───────────────────────────────                             │
│                                                                │
│        Circulars on open school day have been placed in your letter- │
│   boxes.  Please read them carefully and follow instructions.  │
│   ───────────────────────────────                             │
│                                                                │
│        Teachers who line up in front of the time clock waiting to punch │
│   out in the afternoon create a crowded condition in the doorway.  Please │
│   wait until dismissal bell rings before coming down.          │
│   ───────────────────────────────                             │
│                                                                │
│        The office telephone is not to be used for personal calls.  Please │
│   use the pay-telephone in the basement.                       │
│   ───────────────────────────────                             │
│                                                                │
│        Teachers' interest committee meeting today during lunch period in │
│   room 404.  Please come promptly with your lunch:  last month no one │
│   showed up!                                                   │
│   ───────────────────────────────                             │
└────────────────────────────────────────────────────────────────┘
```

From the book *Up the Down Staircase* by Bel Kaufman. © 1964 by Bel Kaufman. Published by Prentice-Hall, Inc., Englewood Cliffs, New Jersey. Pp. 197–198.

the new building are rarely, if ever, consulted about the kind of environment they would consider most suitable and conducive to learning. When a new principal is chosen, the teachers are not asked to participate in the decision-making. Rarely are they even asked what they think the new principal's qualifications should be. As one Arkansas teacher stated, "I've been teaching in this same school and living in this same community for twenty-six years. I've had all sorts of commendations and good teaching awards. But in twenty-six years not once has anyone on the school board or any of the administrators asked my advice on an educational matter. I haven't been asked about one darned thing."

Discouraging as this picture may seem to some of you, not all teachers are dissatisfied with the existing state of affairs. Some are quite content to "simply teach and leave all the squabbling to the high mucky-mucks." They think teachers have come a long way in recent years and that they should be satisfied with what they have gained. The more militant teachers, however, feel that this attitude is itself the problem, and that this kind of passivity has kept teachers oppressed and the quality of their service low. They assert that teaching will not truly become a profession until their colleagues take a more vigorous, independent position. And this leads us directly to the question, "Is teaching a profession?"

TEACHING: A PROFESSION OR A TRADE?

A profession is more than a group of individuals all engaged in the same line of work. Professions have a more-or-less recognizable set of characteristics[2] which distinguish them from nonprofessions. As you read the list of characteristics of a profession, check whether or not you think teaching qualifies on each premise.

Does teaching qualify?

First, a profession renders a unique, definite and essential social service. Only the people in the particular profession render the service. For instance, only lawyers practice law. The service rendered must be considered so important that it is available to all the people in a society.   Yes ☐   No ☐

Second, a profession relies upon intellectual skills in the performance of its service. This does not mean that physical actions and skills are not needed, but rather that the

---

[2] We have drawn heavily on an excellent book by Myron Lieberman entitled *Education as a Profession* (Englewood Cliffs, N.J.: Prentice-Hall, 1956). For a fuller discussion of whether or not teaching is a profession, we recommend this book to you.

emphasis in carrying on the work is on intellectual skills and techniques.

Yes ☐ No ☐

Third, a profession has a long period of specialized training. Because professional work requires special intellectual skills, specialized intellectual training is needed. General education, such as that represented by a bachelor's degree, is valued, but not considered adequate. The specialized training must cover a substantial period of time and not be obtained in cram courses or correspondence schools.

Yes ☐ No ☐

Fourth, both individual members of the profession and the professional group enjoy a considerable degree of autonomy and decision-making authority. Whereas factory workers have very limited decision-making powers and are closely supervised in the performance of their work, professionals are expected to make most of their own decisions and be free of close supervision by superiors. Also, professional groups regulate their own activities rather than having outsiders set policies and enforce adherence to standards.

Yes ☐ No ☐

Fifth, a profession requires its members to accept personal responsibility for their actions and decisions. Along with having a high degree of freedom and autonomy, the professional must shoulder a large measure of responsibility for his performance. Since the professional's service is usually related to the human welfare of individuals, this responsibility is an especially serious one.

Yes ☐ No ☐

Sixth, a profession emphasizes the services rendered by its practitioners more than their financial rewards. While the personal motives of any individual professional are not necessarily any higher than any other worker's, the professional group's public emphasis is on service.

Yes ☐ No ☐

Seventh, a profession is self-governing and responsible for policing its own ranks. This means there are professional groups who perform a number of activities aimed at keeping the quality of their services high and looking out for the social and economic well-being of the professional members. Also, these self-governing organizations set standards of admission and exclusion to the profession.

Yes ☐ No ☐

Eighth, a profession has a code of ethics which sets out the acceptable standards of conduct of its members. In order for a professional group to regulate the quality and standards of service, it needs a code of ethics to aid it in enforcing these high standards.   Yes ☐   No ☐

These, then, are the major requirements of a profession. Few professions satisfy all of them fully. However, the list does serve as a benchmark by which occupational groups can measure themselves and direct their development if they wish to enjoy professional status.

The question "Is teaching a profession?" probably arouses little interest in many of you. Most people thinking about a career in teaching are more interested in whether it will be a personally rewarding way to spend their time than in whether or not it is a profession. Will teaching bring me personal satisfactions? Will it provide an outlet for my talents and energies? Will I be effective with kids? These questions are, we suspect, closer to your skin. Whether or not teaching fits the specifications of a profession appears to have very little bearing on these issues. The question may seem to reek of someone else's (the authors'?) status hangups. We agree on both counts. However, one of this book's major aims is to help prospective teachers get to know the woods, lest they get lost amid the trees. Examining the argu-

---

CIRCULAR #59

Please keep all circulars on file, in their order.

TOPIC: TEACHERS' WELFARE

   The president of the United Federation of Teachers has asked the Board of Education to support legislation for higher death benefits and pensions for teachers who die or are hurt in the line of duty. Your support of this measure is needed.

FROM: James J. McHabe, Adm. Asst.

TO: All teachers

   Since school aides have relieved teachers of many non-teaching assignments, teachers are requested to report to the office for further assignments.
                                   JJMcH

From the book *Up the Down Staircase* by Bel Kaufman. © 1964 by Bel Kaufman. Published by Prentice-Hall, Inc., Englewood Cliffs, New Jersey. P. 152.

ments for and against teaching as a profession should help you learn your way around. Trust us!

TWO SIDES OF THE ISSUE

The Case For *Teaching as a Profession.* The very nobility of the teacher's work is evidence in favor of its status as a profession. Society has entrusted teachers with its most important responsibility—the education of the young. Although teachers have never received the respect that is their due, through the course of history great minds have acknowledged their worth. Martin Luther asserted that the teacher's vocation was second only to that of the ministry. Thomas Carlyle in *Sartor Resartus* calls teachers "fashioners of souls," who ought to be "world-honored dignitaries" like generals and field marshals. As more and more people recognize how crucial education is to the fulfillment of our personal and national goals, the lot of the teacher will improve.

Although children learn from many people—from mothers to TV entertainers—teachers are the specialists who pass on to the young the key skills necessary to participate in the culture. They aid the young to acquire the most difficult, if not the most important, skills: those that involve thinking and manipulating ideas. Neither reading nor geometry is often learned on the street. Although teachers do not undergo a particularly lengthy period of specialized training, they are in a sense continually training. Teachers are expected (and, in some states, required by law) to continuously upgrade their teaching skills.

The autonomy of the teacher, like that of every professional, is somewhat limited. Unlike lawyers and doctors, who can reject clients, a teacher's students are assigned to him. He also has a supervisor, his principal or department chairman. He teaches a curriculum which has been chosen or developed largely by others. However, within these limits, the teacher has an immense area of personal control. He normally determines the method of instruction. He decides which aspects of the curriculum he will highlight and which he will cover quickly. The limits on his creativity are few or nonexistent. After the initial few years of teaching, he is seldom, if ever, supervised. The teacher's classroom is his castle. And if a teacher feels that he does not have enough autonomy or does not agree with his administrator, he is free to move to another school. However, a teacher's autonomy is accompanied by a responsibility to teach effectively. Like any professional, he must be able to justify the manner in which he renders his social services. He must be able to justify his grading policy and his evaluations of student work. The teacher is expected to claim responsibility for his actions and to be open to criticisms of his teaching performance.

Teachers are represented by organizations, such as the National Education Association and the American Federation of Teachers, whose major function is improving education by improving the teaching profession. They provide

In 1967 there were 2,100,000 school teachers in the country.

90 percent of them were in the public schools, the rest in private, mostly Roman Catholic, institutions

60 percent of them were elementary school teachers

69 percent of them were female

93 percent of them held at least a bachelor's degree in education or some other subject

24 percent of them held the master's degree in education or some other subject

65 percent of them had been teaching for less than ten years

Their average age was 36

Their average salary was $7,000, slightly higher for secondary school teachers, slightly lower for elementary

There was one teacher for every 27 students in the elementary schools

There was one teacher for every 21.4 students in the secondary schools.

James D. Koerner, *Who Controls American Education* (Boston: Beacon Press, 1968), pp. 25–26.

information and aid to the classroom teacher; they support him against unjust pressures from members of the public or the school board; they set standards and censor teachers who violate these standards; finally, they attempt to influence legislation and public opinion about education and teaching. Also, they have established codes of ethics by which teachers guide their professional activities.

Some argue that teaching is not a profession because teachers lack the autonomy of, say, a small-town lawyer, or because they have not achieved the economic status of dentists and doctors. These arguments are superficial. So, too, is the assertion that teaching is not a profession because many teachers do not act like professionals. Neither do many ministers, architects and lawyers. Certainly the crucial nature of the teacher's work and the self-less spirit of service of the best teachers raises teaching to the level of a profession.

The Case Against *Teaching as a Profession.*   The roots of the teaching "profession" go back to ancient Greece, where slaves called *paidagogos,* or pedagogues, taught children to read and write and helped them memorize passages of poetic history. Recently teachers, along with such other occu-

II. The Nineteenth Century

The nineteenth century was a period of immense growth and development for the country as a whole and for education. Schooling gradually became compulsory, and new and better schools were established, with improved curriculum and equipment. Normal schools for the training of teachers came into being in many states. Special journals for teachers were published and professional associations formed. Conventions were even held for teachers, usually to deal with "practical" classroom concerns. Myron Brenton reports on a teacher institute held in Jamestown, Pennsylvania, on January 14, 1858:

. . . teachers gather to discuss these questions: Is it better for teachers to board around? Should the teachers encourage pupils to chew tobacco? Should teachers open their schools in the morning by reading a portion of the Scripture? Should the door be closed against pupils who are not present at 9 o'clock in the morning? Should the rod be used in school? Should the wages of females be equal to those of male teachers? (Brenton, *What's Happened to Teacher?*, p. 69.)

The place of females in teaching was a major issue in the nineteenth century. Industrialization and urban migration created new and attractive work opportunities, and schools could no longer compete for men's services. As a result, teaching became tagged as a "feminine" occupation by mid-century. A forerunner of the women's liberation movement, suffragette Susan B. Anthony, told a group of disgruntled male teachers why people held them in such low esteem:

It seems to me that you fail to comprehend the cause of the disrespect of which you complain. Do you not see that so long as society says that woman has not brains enough to be a doctor, lawyer or minister, but has plenty to be a teacher, every one of you who condescends to teach tacitly admits before Israel and the sun that he has no more brains than a woman? (Brenton, *What's Happened to Teacher?*, p. 69.)

The nation's general prosperity during the nineteenth century had no effect on the teaching profession. Teacher's salaries were wretchedly low. Teachers were among the worst trained, lowest paid and most shabbily treated of professional workers. They were continually subjected to verbal and even physical abuse from hostile parents and, occasionally, students themselves. They were constantly being evaluated and examined by capricious laymen who knew nothing about education and cared less.

Pay remained abysmally low and, on top of this, women were discriminated against in pay scales. In Massachusetts in 1874, men teachers received a monthly salary of $24.51; women were paid $8.07. In Connecticut, during the same period, men earned $16.00 and women earned $6.50 a month. Shoemakers, harnessmakers, blacksmiths and other skilled workers often earned twice the wage of men teachers. As for the image of the teacher, a bitter teacher described him in the August 1864 issue of *Illinois Teacher* as "someone who can parse and cypher; has little brains and less money; is feeble minded, unable to grapple with real men and women in the stirring employments of life, but on that account admirably fitted to associate with childish intellects. . . ."

Amidst major educational reform and the expansion of education, the teacher's personal life was still seriously restricted. In a typical New England school system, men were allowed one evening a week for courting; two evenings if they were regular churchgoers. Teachers were expected to vote in accordance with the sentiments of the majority of the community. Loyalty oaths of a political nature were common to insure "right thinking" in the teacher. This practice continued until after the Civil War. In fact, it has never quite died away.

pational groups as barbers, beauticians, chiropractors and taxidermists, have latched on to the term "professional" in an attempt to raise their salaries and their status. But a careful look reveals that teaching does not qualify as a profession. If education is a teacher's unique function, he has a great deal of competition. Ignoring for a moment the mounting criticism of compulsory miseducation, let us admit that teachers have no monopoly on education. Children today learn a tremendous amount from the media: *Sesame Street,* public-affairs specials, talk shows, Hugh Downs and Eric Sevareid, *Life, Time,* films, novels, Bob Dylan, Rod McKuen, *Seventeen, Popular Mechanics.* Then there are the nonteacher educators: parents, ministers, older friends, neighbors, employers, close friends, coaches, scout leaders, playground and camp counselors, grandparents. The world is bursting with teachers and those who hold forth in school buildings have only a small piece of the action.

While teaching has intellectual and theoretical foundations, and requires a rather short period of specialized training (considerably less than some of the skilled trades), entrance into the profession is not particularly competitive, particularly on intellectual grounds. If it is a profession, it is one composed of a large percentage of average folks.

Although there is a good deal of talk about teachers' autonomy and decision-making power, both exist at a very low level. Teachers are the second rung from the bottom (superior only to students) of the hierarchy commanded by the Board of Education. They teach whom they are told, what they are told and when they are told. If their supervisors do not like the results, teachers are not protected by their professional group from being fired (or, more gently, "not rehired") by the Board of Education. Most of the important decisions which affect teachers' daily lives, even those that bear directly on

OFF BASE

Ten forty-three.
In exactly TWO MINUTES
I'll ring the
FIRST BELL and
they'll all
stand still!

All, that is, except
your potential DEVIATE!
Your fledgling REBEL!
Your incipient BOAT-
ROCKER! THEY'LL try
to move alright!
THEY'LL have to
learn the HARD
way not to move!

So I'll SCREAM at 'em
and take their NAMES
and give them FIVE
DETENTIONS and EXTRA
HOMEWORK! NEXT time
they won't move
after the first
bell!

Cartoon by Barry Base.

the standards of their own profession, are made by nonteachers. Teachers do not evaluate other teachers. Administrators do that. Teachers do not have much to do with (and very little say in) the pre-service training of teachers. University professors do that. Teachers do not control licensing and certification of teachers. Laymen and bureaucrats do that. Some teachers, like factory workers, even have to punch a timeclock (more genteelly, they "sign in and sign out" . . . to the same effect). In sum, they have very little to say about what goes on.

The same is true of the teacher's responsibility. Teachers are rarely fired because Johnnie can't read or Samantha failed calculus. After a teacher achieves tenure, it takes something like a serious sexual offense for him to lose his job. As for the professional organizations policing their own ranks, there is much rhetoric but next to no action. The professional organizations exist primarily to protect teachers, increase their salaries and expand their welfare benefits. Most teachers are minimally involved and interested in professional organizations and their activities, except when they call a strike—an odd activity for a "profession." Most teachers claim they are too busy to take an active role in professional affairs. This lack of real involvement in professional activities might stem from the fact that so many teachers have

Because when they've
learned not to question
the FIRST BELL, they'll
learn not to question
their TEXTS! Their
TEACHERS! Their
COURSES!
EXAMINATIONS!

They'll grow up to accept
TAXES! HOUSING DEVELOP-
MENTS! INSURANCE! WAR!
MEN ON THE MOON! LIQUOR
LAWS! POLITICAL SPEECHES!
PARKING METERS!
TELEVISION!
FUNERALS!

Non-movement
after
the first
bell is
the
backbone
of Western
Civilization!

second jobs, either as housewives or in the labor market. They are unen-
thusiastic about working for higher standards because one of the first
sacrifices to professionalism would be their second jobs.

In actual fact, teachers work in circumstances very different from those of
other professionals. They are hired, like other public servants, rather than
operating as independent agents. They are on a fixed salary schedule and
protected by tenure laws, rather than having independently to find a market
for their services. Teaching is a low-pay, high-security job, rather than a
high-pay, low-security profession. Seniority as a teacher is more important
than competence. Talk about professionalism may be personally satisfying
to teachers, but it does not conform to the facts of the teacher's occupational
life.

A Third Possibility. Like most important questions, "Is teaching a profession?" cannot be answered satisfactorily with simple pro and con arguments
like those offered above. Also, teachers vary so much in knowledge, commitment and expertise that it is difficult to come up with a definitive answer. However, our view is that teaching is a semi-profession. In certain ways teaching
is clearly eligible for professional status and in certain others it deviates

sharply from accepted canons of professionalism. On the one hand, teachers provide an intellectual service to the community. They undergo specialized training to master the theoretical basis of their work. Ethical standards guide their work with students. On the other hand, they function like many other lower-level white collar workers and civil servants. Seniority and security are the rule, rather than excellence and independence. Like many other occupational groups that are called professional, teaching, at this moment in history, only partially qualifies.

Another way to look at the issue is to think of teaching as in the *process of becoming a profession.* As the historical descriptions of the work and living conditions of teachers which accompany this chapter show, things are improving at a dramatic rate. Nevertheless, "you've got a long way to go, teach!" Whether teaching becomes a profession in your career lifetime will depend on some of the following factors. First, teachers must take on a larger role in the governing of their career affairs. While the direction of education and the schools should be in the hands of many groups (parents, community leaders, students and teachers), control over the teaching profession *per se* should be in the hands of teachers. Up to now, the great mass of teachers has taken the attitude "Let George do it." As a result, outsiders make the major decisions about who should teach, how they should be trained and under what conditions they should render their services. In this sense, teachers are an oppressed minority group. While teachers are eating better these days, we still lack self-determination.

Second, teachers must demand better training. As long as the public feels that any reasonably intelligent person can walk in off the street and do a teacher's job, people will not treat teachers as professionals. We do not for a moment mean to imply that teachers should adopt artificial trappings, like a doctor's smock or a general's uniform, to seem more distinctive and im-

Cartoon by Brickman © 1970, King Features Syndicate, Inc.

THE REAL WORLD

III. The Early Twentieth Century

With the dawn of the twentieth century, America came into her own as a nation and as an international power. This new maturity brought about a broadened outlook and a general loosening of mores. Not so, however, for the teacher. Teachers remained more -or- less enslaved to Victorian decorum. As late as 1920, teachers who smoked cigarettes had a difficult time getting jobs in California, Tennessee and Illinois. In Mississippi and Kansas, teachers were not allowed to attend dances; if they did, it meant instant dismissal. A town in Louisiana required its teachers to stay around over weekends and be in bed by 10:00 p.m. In one Ohio county, teachers who dated other teachers faced the threat of immediate dismissal. School boards generally frowned on bobbed hair. Many contracts stipulated a long list of no-no's: no dates, no petting, no dancing, no smoking, no short skirts. We have all heard a great deal about the Roaring Twenties. If teachers took part in the fun, it was strictly on the quiet. What follows is an excerpt from the teacher's contract of one North Carolina town:

I promise to take a vital interest in all phases of Sunday school work, donating of my time, service and money without stint for the benefit and uplift of the community.

I promise to abstain from dancing, immodest dressing, and any other conduct unbecoming a teacher and lady.

I promise not to go out with any young man except as it may be necessary to stimulate Sunday-school work.

I promise not to fall in love, to become engaged or secretly married.

I promise to remain in the dormitory or on the school grounds when not actively engaged in school or church work elsewhere.

I promise not to encourage or tolerate the least familiarity on the part of any of my boy pupils.

I promise to sleep eight hours a night, eat carefully, etc., etc. (Brenton, *What's Happened to Teacher?*, p. 74.)

The nation enjoyed increased prosperity but, again, teachers did not share in it. In the early decades of the century teachers were barely paid a subsistence wage. One way that teachers could save money (and nosy school boards could keep an eye on them) was by living in community-owned boardinghouses, called "teacherages." While these houses were generally well-kept and inexpensive and provided the teacher with companionship, it was quite difficult for a teacher to have a private life.

A society's image of a group is mirrored in its popular culture. One researcher read sixty-two novels published since 1900 to discover fiction's image of the teacher. The male teacher, he found, was portrayed as solitary, effeminate and impractical. The female teacher was either young, single and frustrated or a tired sexless old maid. Another researcher looked at portraits of teachers in movies and books before 1950 and saw passive lives—monotonous, pedestrian, colorless—worthy of pity, but scarcely worthy of the respect granted to those who provide leadership and inspiration to the young.

pressive. Rather, we must *appear* better because we *are* better. Like architects and surgeons, we must know our craft, and our work must be imbued by a sense of high purpose. When that happens, the public will be able to tell the difference.

Third, we may have simply to recognize that all of the two-and-a-half million people working in the American schools are not interested in and, in some cases, not capable of measuring up to the standards of professionalism. At present, what we, the authors, are calling (and, incidentally, will continue to call) the teaching profession is a mixed bag, with large numbers of transients, "just passing through," large numbers of rather uncommitted teachers and large numbers of truly excellent, dedicated career teachers. "Let us define a career teacher as one who plans to, and actually does, make a life occupation of teaching; one who is philosophically, emotionally, and spiritually committed, that is, never satisfied with what he does and how well he's doing it, and who fully intends to keep on growing for the rest of his life."[3] In this description of the "career teacher," Walter Beggs of the University of Nebraska captures the essence of the professional teacher. He goes on to estimate that only about one out of four teachers presently practicing fit his definition. And herein lies the difficulty. Until the great majority of teachers qualifies by Beggs' definition, or until there is a qualitative regrouping of those presently identified as "teachers," teaching will not be called a profession.

The protection of teachers' freedom and the improvement of their working conditions and rewards will not just happen. In the words of J. Paul Getty, "Nobody gives you nothing for nothing."[4] Whatever advance teachers make will occur as a result of their hard work and readiness to fight for what they believe.

Our country has many troublesome problems and there is great competition for resources. For instance, it was clear during the Sixties that the space program and the war in Southeast Asia enjoyed a higher priority than did civil rights, pollution and education. In the rough-and-tumble of a democracy, teachers need someone or something to look out for their interests and the interests of the recipients of their services, children. This is the function of the teachers' associations. At present, there are two national organizations, the National Education Association and the American Federation of

---

[3] Quoted at 1963–64 convention of the National Commission on Teacher Education and Professional Standards (NEA), in Myron Brenton, *What's Happened to Teacher?* (New York: Coward-McCann, 1970), p. 242.

[4] The J. Paul Getty we have quoted is not to be confused with J. Paul Getty the oil baron and sometime writer for *Playboy*. Our J. Paul Getty was an English teacher in wealthy suburban St. Louis, Missouri. Parents claimed that Yale-educated Getty was teaching their offspring bad grammar. At a heated public hearing, Getty's students came to his defense with impassioned rhetoric and a sea of placards stating: "Up, Getty. He done good by us." "Getty teaches good, like a teacher should." They fired him. Getty is now a secretary for an Indian mystic and a mutual fund salesman on the side.

TWO VIEWS OF THE BIG CITY TEACHER

The status of the teacher as a professional is particularly precarious. New York City recruiting brochures paint a glowing picture of the teacher's professionalism, of the opportunities for professional development, and of the personal relationship between administrative staff and teachers:

The administrative staff is composed of men and women with a modern outlook. They realize the value of creativity in teaching, encourage innovation and new approaches, and understand the need for academic freedom within a professional atmosphere. But even more important, they know that the most effective teaching will result where the teacher is recognized as an individual and is given the opportunity to make full use of his abilities and specialties. The personal relationship established between the administration and the teachers has promoted the progress of education both in the schoolroom and at the level of professional development.

The picture painted by the report of the Mayor's Advisory Panel on Decentralization in the New York City Schools, commonly called the Bundy Report, is altogether different:

New York City teachers are isolated at the end of a long chain of command. They are not consulted regularly, if at all, about curriculum, or classroom surroundings, or the criteria on which colleagues, to say nothing of supervisors, are chosen. Initiative and innovation, if not discouraged, are administratively difficult because of the uniformity imposed perforce by a highly centralized system. Furthermore, the Panel has it on the word of teachers who appear to be dedicated to their profession that in too many schools teachers are fearful. They are said to be subject to overt and subtle reprisals (including, ironically, assignment to difficult classes) for any criticism of the school. The way to avoid reprisals, as one teacher put it, "is to take all directives from the supervisors at face value and never question, criticize, suggest, or file grievances."

Anthony G. Oettinger, *Run, Computer Run: The Mythology of Educational Innovation* (Cambridge: Harvard University Press, 1969), pp. 112–113.

Photos by Mark Silber.

Johann Pestalozzi (1746–1827)

Well into middle age, Johann Pestalozzi gave every sign of being a bungling failure. As a youth in Zurich he hated school, and afterward pursued a long series of abortive occupational ventures. Nor was he a success as a personality. Raised by his widowed mother and a maid, he developed great sensitivity but remained overly dependent on women and slightly effeminate. In later life, the fame he achieved reportedly went to his head. But despite all his personal failings, Pestalozzi is both a hero and a model for educators.

After attending the University of Switzerland, where he finally learned to enjoy studying and became active in social and political reform, Pestalozzi established an orphanage in his own home, where he taught neglected children the rudiments of agriculture and simple trades. But the orphanage failed in 1780 and Pestalozzi, in despair, went into seclusion to write *The Evening Hour of a Hermit,* a moving compendium of aphorisms and reflections.

Much later, at the age of fifty-two, he began a new career. When Napoleon's armies massacred the citizens of the town of Stans, he collected several dozen destitute children and cared for them under extremely difficult conditions. Pestalozzi made the Institute for the Poor an educational experiment, teaching the children to spin, weave and do farm work, as well as to study. But because he had accepted more students than he could accommodate, including retarded children, he was forced to close the school for lack of funds. This was one more failure in an uninterrupted series, but Pestalozzi was undaunted. He had found his vocation in teaching and his happiness among children.

In 1805 Pestalozzi founded a boarding school in an abandoned castle at Yverdon, which flourished for twenty years. It quickly became famous and attracted students from all over Europe. Its curriculum, which emphasized drawing, writing, singing, physical exercise, group recitations, map-making and field trips, was based on the principle of "sense impression"—the idea that we understand only what we observe clearly, and that words and ideas have meaning only when they are related to concrete objects. Pestalozzi thus put considerable stress on the importance of concrete situations in the child's learning.

The study of geography involved field trips and the construction of elaborate models of whole territories. Pestalozzi anticipated modern methods of math instruction by using concrete objects to develop number competence. Four students or four chairs, for instance, illustrated the concept "four." Students learned to read and write with slates, pencils and alphabet cards. Pestalozzi also emphasized the importance of art in the curriculum, not only as an emotional outlet for the children but also to encourage creativity and develop intellectual discipline.

Pestalozzi's educational theory was built on the assumption that human beings are motivated by three drives: primitive impulses, social needs and ethical yearnings. He conceived of education as the process by which ethics triumphed over animal impulses. His model of learning was the family, with the teacher acting like a father and serving as a model to be imitated. The ideal of love governed Pestalozzi's philosophy of education—love that should not be modified or withdrawn even if the student misbehaved. The teacher, he was convinced, should never punish or show disapproval, a very novel attitude in the early nineteenth century. The Yverdon curriculum offered carefully graded instruction, allowance for individual differences and ability grouping; in general, Pestalozzi was less concerned with "meeting standards" than with the integrity of the student and his work.

Misunderstood by his contemporaries, who considered him too radical and emotional and accused him of taking children too seriously, Pestalozzi nevertheless achieved fame and international influence within his lifetime. He came to be called the Christopher Columbus of elementary education because he opened up so much new territory in that field. Several foreign governments sent teachers to Yverdon for instruction—Pestalozzi's teacher-training department was unique at the time—and he was made an honorary citizen of the French Republic and knighted by the Czar. Such fame might make any man dizzy.

Advocates of love and acceptance in the educational process owe and acknowledge a heavy debt to Johann Pestalozzi.

Photos by Frank Siteman.

Teachers, which claim to speak for teachers. They represent teachers to the federal, state and local governments, to educational authorities at the state and local level and, finally, to the general public. It is important to know something about them, because if you become a teacher they will claim to be speaking for you.

Before discussing the two major organizations, we should point out that there are many different teacher organizations operating at a multiplicity of levels. Normally, each school district has professional associations which are linked to county, regional and state organizations. Of perhaps greater importance to the beginning teacher are organizations of teachers in particular specialties at these different levels. There are active organizations for teachers of reading, English, mathematics, home economics and all the established curricular areas. They play an important part in keeping the teacher informed about his field through journals, in-service training institutes and conferences and conventions. Because there are so many of these organizations and their activities are so varied, we will restrict our attention to the large umbrella organizations, the National Education Association and the American Federation of Teachers.

THE PROFESSIONAL ASSOCIATIONS

THE NATIONAL EDUCATION ASSOCIATION

The National Education Association, or NEA, is a complex institution difficult to describe briefly. Perhaps a metaphor might help. Think of the NEA as a huge department store which sells many kinds of goods and services to a very diverse clientele. Think of it, too, as an old established firm with deep traditions and a large, loyal clientele. In fact, the NEA has over one million members and directly affects almost as many more. It has thirty-three different departments, national affiliates and associated organizations (such as Classroom Teachers, Public School Adult Education and School Librarians), nineteen Headquarters Divisions (Research, Human Relations Council, International Relations), and twenty-five Commissions (NEA and American Textbook Publishers Institute, NEA and American Legion, Teacher Education and Professional Standards). It operates on the national, state and local school district levels. It provides a variety of services to its more than eight thousand local level affiliates. It has an annual operating budget of over fifteen million dollars.

The NEA was founded in 1857 as, significantly, the National Teachers Association. Shortly after the Civil War, its name was changed to the National Education Association and it became, generally speaking, the professional organization for school administrators. Up until World War II, the NEA had a small and relatively constant membership of about ten thousand. The

Jim: *Where was the NEA when Gordon Lisk was getting the ax for reciting the Pledge of Allegiance too fast?*

Kevin: *I don't know. Maybe he wasn't a member!?*

American Federation of Teachers had been founded in 1916, with the primary purpose of organizing classroom teachers, rather than anybody who could claim the label "educator." This competition was a strong incentive to the NEA to broaden its membership and its concerns. In the next fifty years the NEA grew tremendously, not only in membership but also in services and national influence.

The goals of the NEA, as declared in its Charter, are "to elevate the character and advance the interests of the profession of teaching and to promote the cause of education in the United States." In recent years it has been influential in improving the pre-service training of teachers and raising the entrance qualifications for teaching, largely through the establishment and activities of the National Commission on Teacher Education and Professional Standards. Much of the NEA's energies, however, are expended on services for its membership. The NEA conducts studies on practical issues of instruction in various teaching fields and with various types of children. It has an active research department which supplies data on teacher supply and demand, working conditions and salaries and a great variety of issues related to schooling. It makes these data and studies available to local and state associations for their efforts to improve conditions at their level. It engages in lobbying efforts at the national, state and local levels to influence legislation in accord with its vision of how public education should be conducted. Because of its lobbying efforts, the NEA can take a major share of the credit for various federal aid to education programs. Also, the NEA aids teachers whose legal rights are being violated or who are being treated unethically. In sum, it is attempting to move education and the profession of teaching forward on a very broad front.

The NEA has made mistakes, and it is frequently criticized for its slowness to take action on important issues and problems. It avoided taking a stand on the Supreme Court's important school desegregation decision of 1954. Recently, however, it has championed the black teachers in some southern states who have lost their jobs as a result of the consolidation of black and white schools. Only within the last few years has it begun to respond to the deteriorating state of education in the nation's urban centers. Critics claim that its size and broad representation—rural and urban, north and south, administrators and teachers—make it slow to respond to pressing social and educational problems. A more persistent criticism, particularly in the Sixties, came from classroom teachers, who make up the bulk of the dues-paying membership. They complained that the NEA was too busy with "broad front" educational issues to give adequate attention to the problems of teachers.

During the same period, by contrast, the American Federation of Teachers was acting quite militantly on behalf of teachers. Furthermore, teachers argued, the NEA was dominated by school administrators, who do not always have teachers' interests at heart. (A school administrator who can keep teachers' salaries and benefits at a low level is highly valued by some Boards of Education.)

More recently, the NEA has begun to move again. A transferral of power from the school administration groups to the Classroom Teachers' Association is said to be taking place. The Association is becoming more aggressive. It has dropped its former objections to strikes and now looks on the strike as a last-resort but legitimate weapon to attain its ends. What was once "the great big happy educational family" of NEA is beginning to show cracks and rifts. This is frequently the price of movement. The cause of its power shift and increasing militance is said to be the rise of the American Federation of Teachers.

THE AMERICAN FEDERATION OF TEACHERS

If the NEA can be compared to a large department store, then the American Federation of Teachers, or AFT, more closely resembles a small specialty store which aggressively promotes a few items. In contrast to the NEA, the AFT has traditionally been interested exclusively in representing teachers and other nonsupervisory school personnel.

John Dewey, the great American philosopher and educator, took out the first AFT membership card in 1916 and remained an active member throughout his entire life. Dewey thought there ought to be an organization exclusively for teachers. As we have indicated, this "teachers only" emphasis has been a major instrument in the AFT's struggle with the NEA for the allegiance of teachers. The AFT contends that in the NEA's broad efforts to improve education little has been done to improve the lot of the classroom teacher. "In the structure and successful operation of schools, the teacher is central. Good teachers make good schools. The professional teacher not only knows how to direct the educational and personal development of children in the classroom, he also joins with his colleagues in an effective organization to advance the interest of teachers, pupils, and the schools through collective bargaining."[5]

---

[5] Goals of the American Federation of Teachers AFL–CIO (Washington, D.C.: The Federation), p. 3.

WHERE HAVE TEACHERS BEEN AND WHERE ARE THEY GOING?

The AFT has a membership of 185,000, making it approximately one-sixth the size of the NEA. Although the AFT has only 850 local affiliates throughout the country, in recent years it has built up great strength in the major urban centers. The AFT won a big victory in 1960, when its affiliate, the United Federation of Teachers (UFT), became the sole bargaining agent for all New York City teachers. At present, the AFT represents teachers in New York City, Philadelphia, Washington, D.C., Baltimore, Cleveland, Chicago, Detroit and Boston.

The American Federation of Teachers considers itself part of the labor movement. The AFT itself is affiliated with the AFL-CIO, which in turn has a membership of over fourteen million. Much of the AFT's recent growth has been due to its success in introducing the collective bargaining process into the annual salary negotiations of teachers. Through the use of the strike, and the threat of strikes, it has been responsible for raising starting salaries for beginning teachers to around $10,000 in some cities. Although the AFT is noted for hard bargaining on bread-and-butter issues such as salaries, benefits and retirement after twenty-five years of service, it has also been a defender of academic freedom and of greater participation in decision-making by teachers. Although the AFT has been considered the more liberal of the two major teachers' organizations, it has recently been criticized for a growing protectionism. It has been charged with appearing unwilling at times to support the demands of urban communities seeking neighborhood control of schools. Also, the AFT's strong commitment to win more autonomy for classroom teachers in dismissing and disciplining "disruptive" children has been interpreted by some poor and minority-group people as against the interests of their children.

Although facts are hard to come by, there is persistent talk that representatives of the NEA and AFT are meeting to discuss merger. At present, both organizations are spending a great deal of time, money and talent competing with one another. A merger would eliminate that waste, and, for better or worse, create one giant organization which could speak authoritatively for all the nation's teachers.

DISSIDENT VOICES

Recently a new kind of teachers' group has sprung up around the country. These are grassroots groups, composed primarily of young, action-oriented teachers. The groups are independent, unconnected with one another and without a national superstructure. They are bound only by the commonality of their ideas and their goal—to humanize the schools. Their program, sometimes explicitly formulated and sometimes not, vary from radical to militant reformist.

These dissident teacher groups feel just as alienated from the official associations and unions as they do from the official school bureaucracy. In fact, they are frequently more disenchanted with the teachers' organizations, which they feel should be representing them and allege are failing to do so. They criticize the official groups for being too political and too concerned with bread-and-butter issues, instead of working on issues which affect the quality of life in the school. They also complain that the official teacher groups are becoming increasingly conservative, bureaucratic and remote from "where it's at," the classroom. Often their attitude toward the AFT and NEA can be characterized as "a plague on both your houses."

The dissident groups represent the avant garde in education. As the excerpt from The Guerilla Manual illustrates, their style is outrageous, creative, cunning, cavalier and egalitarian. However, behind the free style are teachers seriously bent on changing the public schools. They feel their natural allies are civil rights workers, peace activists and militant social workers and are more concerned with connection to "the movement" than to "the profession."

Their intellectual leaders are such people as John Holt, Herbert Kohl and George Dennison. They read journals like Toronto's *This Magazine is About Schools* and publish their own newspapers, like *The Red Pencil* in Boston. They have names like Teachers for Action Now! and The Radical Teachers Caucus. Besides providing a support system and a rallying point for like-minded teachers, these groups are a means of in-service training. Teachers

Photo courtesy of VISTA.

aid one another by sharing curriculum materials on socially relevant issues or ideas on how to make the traditional curriculum more meaningful to the immediate lives of their students. These groups are seriously concerned about developing more real and honest communication in the classroom between teacher and students. Especially in poor areas, they work to achieve closer relationships between the schools and the local community and between teachers and parents. Often they involve themselves in free schools for dropouts or adults.

It is impossible to predict the future impact of these dissident teacher groups. They differ markedly in seriousness and in strength. A few are simply momentary outlets for malcontents escaping from the hard work of schooling. The others must be taken more seriously. They appear to be an emerging third force at a time when the warring giants are talking merger. At their best, they represent the creative minority which breaks new ground, raises fresh issues and, in effect, shapes the future agenda of the established teacher organizations. What organizational form they will take is equally difficult to predict. They may get stronger and become much more widespread than at present, but remain organizationally unconnected. Or, they may begin to develop a tight network and, eventually, a national organization. A third alternative is merger—or infiltration—on the local level with the official organizations with the aim of working from the inside to redirect its priorities. Whatever form these dissident groups take, it is clear that teachers have a new and insistent voice speaking for them and at them.

POGO

"We has met
the enemy
and
he is us."

Drawing by Walt Kelly, © Simon and Schuster, 1968.

THE REAL WORLD

Preamble

The educator believes in the worth and dignity of man. He recognizes the supreme importance of the pursuit of truth, devotion to excellence, and the nurture of democratic citizenship. He regards as essential to these goals the protection of freedom to learn and to teach and the guarantee of equal educational opportunity for all. The educator accepts his responsibility to practice his profession according to the highest ethical standards.

The educator recognizes the magnitude of the responsibility he has accepted in choosing a career in education, and engages himself, individually and collectively with other educators, to judge his colleagues, and to be judged by them, in accordance with the provisions of this code.

Principle I—Commitment to the Student

· · · · ·

In fulfilling his obligation to the student, the educator—

1. Shall not without just cause restrain the student from independent action in his pursuit of learning, and shall not without just cause deny the student access to varying points of view.
2. Shall not deliberately suppress or distort subject matter for which he bears responsibility.
3. Shall make reasonable effort to protect the student from conditions harmful to learning or to health and safety.
4. Shall conduct professional business in such a way that he does not expose the student to unnecessary embarrassment or disparagement.
5. Shall not on the ground of race, color, creed, or national origin exclude any student from participation in or deny him benefits under any program, nor grant any discriminatory consideration or advantage.
6. Shall not use professional relationships with students for private advantage.
7. Shall keep in confidence information that has been obtained in the course of professional service, unless disclosure serves professional purposes or is required by law.
8. Shall not tutor for remuneration students assigned to his classes, unless

no other qualified teacher is reasonably available.

Principle II—Commitment to the Public

· · · · ·

In fulfilling his obligation to the public, the educator—

1. Shall not misrepresent an institution or organization with which he is affiliated, and shall take adequate precautions to distinguish between his personal and institutional or organizational views.
2. Shall not knowingly distort or misrepresent the facts concerning educational matters in direct and indirect public expressions.
3. Shall not interfere with a colleague's exercise of political and citizenship rights and responsibilities.
4. Shall not use institutional privileges for private gain or to promote political candidates or partisan political activities.
5. Shall accept no gratuities, gifts, or favors that might impair or appear to impair professional judgment, nor offer any favor, service, or thing of value to obtain special advantage.

Principle III—Commitment to the Profession

· · · · ·

In fulfilling his obligation to the profession, the educator—

1. Shall not discriminate on the ground of race, color, creed, or national origin for membership in professional organizations, nor interfere with the free participation of colleagues in the affairs of their association.
2. Shall accord just and equitable treatment to all members of the profession in the exercise of their professional rights and responsibilities.
3. Shall not use coercive means or promise special treatment in order to influence professional decisions of colleagues.
4. Shall withhold and safeguard information acquired about colleagues in the course of employment, unless disclosure serves professional purposes.
5. Shall not refuse to participate in a professional inquiry when requested by an appropriate professional association.

6. Shall provide upon the request of the aggrieved party a written statement of specific reason for recommendations that lead to the denial of increments, significant changes in employment, or termination of employment.
7. Shall not misrepresent his professional qualifications.
8. Shall not knowingly distort evaluations of colleagues.

Principle IV—Commitment to Professional Employment Practices

· · · · ·

In fulfilling his obligation to professional employment practices, the educator—

1. Shall apply for, accept, offer, or assign a position or responsibility on the basis of professional preparation and legal qualifications.
2. Shall apply for a specific position only when it is known to be vacant, and shall refrain from underbidding or commenting adversely about other candidates.
3. Shall not knowingly withhold information regarding a position from an applicant or misrepresent an assignment or conditions of employment.
4. Shall give prompt notice to the employing agency of any change in availability of service, and the employing agent shall give prompt notice of change in availability or nature of a position.
5. Shall adhere to the terms of a contract or appointment, unless these terms have been legally terminated, falsely represented, or substantially altered by unilateral action of the employing agency.
6. Shall conduct professional business through channels, when available, that have been jointly approved by the professional organization and the employing agency.
7. Shall not delegate assigned tasks to unqualified personnel.
8. Shall permit no commercial exploitation of his professional position.
9. Shall use time granted for the purpose for which it is intended.

National Education Association, *Code of Ethics of the Education Profession,* adopted by the NEA Representative Assembly, July, 1968; amended July, 1970. Reprinted by permission of the Association.

The teacher is entitled to a life of dignity equal to the high standard of service that is justly demanded of that profession. Therefore, we hold these truths to be self-evident:

I

Teachers have the right to think freely and to express themselves openly and without fear. This includes the right to hold views contrary to the majority.

II

They shall be entitled to the free exercise of their religion. No restraint shall be put upon them in the manner, time or place of their worship.

III

They shall have the right to take part in social, civil, and political affairs. They shall have the right, outside the classroom, to participate in political campaigns and to hold office. They may assemble peaceably and may petition any government agency, including their employers, for a redress of grievances. They shall have the same freedom in all things as other citizens.

IV

The right of teachers to live in places of their own choosing, to be free of restraints in their mode of living and the use of their leisure time shall not be abridged.

V

Teaching is a profession, the right to practice which is not subject to the surrender of other human rights. No one shall be deprived of professional status, or the right to practice it, or the practice thereof in any particular position, without due process of law.

VI

The right of teachers to be secure in their jobs, free from political influence or public clamor, shall be established by law. The right to teach after qualification in the manner prescribed by law is a property right, based upon the inalienable rights to life, liberty, and the pursuit of happiness.

VII

In all cases affecting the teacher's employment or professional status a full hearing by an impartial tribunal shall be afforded with the right to full judicial review. No teacher shall be deprived of employment or professional status but for specific causes established by law having a clear relation to the competence or qualification to teach, proved by the weight of the evidence. In all such cases the teacher shall enjoy the right to a speedy and public trial, to be informed of the nature and cause of the accusation, to be confronted with the accusing witnesses, to subpoena witnesses and papers, and to the assistance of counsel. No teacher shall be called upon to answer any charge affecting his employment or professional status but upon probable cause, supported by oath or affirmation.

VIII

It shall be the duty of the employer to provide culturally adequate salaries, security in illness and adequate retirement income. The teacher has the right to such a salary as will: a) Afford a family standard of living comparable to that enjoyed by other professional people in the community; b) To make possible freely chosen professional study; c) Afford the opportunity for leisure and recreation common to our heritage.

IX

Teachers shall not be required under penalty of reduction of salary to pursue studies beyond those required to obtain professional status. After serving a reasonable probationary period a teacher shall be entitled to permanent tenure terminable only for just cause. They shall be free as in other professions in the use of their own time. They shall not be required to perform extracurricular work against their will or without added compensation.

X

To equip people for modern life requires the most advanced educational methods. Therefore, the teacher is entitled to good classrooms, adequate teaching materials, teachable class size and administrative protection and assistance in maintaining discipline.

XI

These rights are based upon the proposition that the culture of a people can rise only as its teachers improve. A teaching force accorded the highest possible professional dignity is the surest guarantee that blessings of liberty will be preserved. Therefore, the possession of these rights imposes the challenge to be worthy of their enjoyment.

XII

Since teachers must be free in order to teach freedom, the right to be members of organizations of their own choosing must be guaranteed. In all matters pertaining to their salaries and working conditions they shall be entitled to bargain collectively through representatives of their own choosing. They are entitled to have the schools administered by superintendents, boards or committees which function in a democratic manner.

American Federation of Teachers, *Bill of Rights*. Reprinted by permission of the Federation.

The Guerilla Manual is serious. Very serious. Some tactics focus on generating support from parents whose kids are getting shafted by the schools. Others can serve to eliminate barriers isolating good teachers from one another. All are concerned with humanizing the schools. But since schools vary (mediocre-bad-terrible), applying any given tactic may prove a conservative, liberal, or radical act. If you want to find out where *you* and *your school* fit, just try No. 7 below. Or choose any tactic appropriate to your situation and discover, uncover, even recover the resources to take a second step . . . and then a third . . .

1. Stop the gossip about kids in faculty lounges.
2. Assist kids in setting up a curriculum evaluation committee.
3. Conduct free Saturday classes—open the school, invite the janitor.
4. Send the school board a bill for chaperone services—take it to small claims court if they don't pay.
5. Calculate and publicize the total man-hours wasted by bad jokes at faculty meetings, taking attendance, writing hall passes, counting lunch money, etc.
6. Help students draft a Students' Bill of Rights.
7. Post the Guerilla Manual on the faculty bulletin board.
8. Give students their choice of instructors.
9. Demand that doors be placed on the commodes in the student cans.
10. Set aside a blackboard for graffiti for students and/or teachers.
11. Start an argument at a faculty meeting early in the year and find out who has any guts and brains.
12. Bring in a community person at least once a week to teach, or watch, or take notes.
13. Let your kids sit where they want (floor not excepted).
14. Bring in doctors, carpenters, housewives, mechanics, engineers, cops, etc., and let your kids ask questions.
15. Run satiric ads in the local newspaper: "For sale—one school, 39 teachers (31 conservatives, two liberals, five middle-of-the-roaders, one radical . . .)" etc.
16. Bring EVERYTHING that's not being used in school to your room: pianos, AV equipment, sofas, books, magazines, typewriters, globes, maps, aquariums, statuary, brains. . . .
17. Encourage older students to teach younger ones.
18. Plaster the faculty bulletin board with mind-bending articles about schools, books, plays, politics, movies, meetings, pot parties, etc.
19. Attend school board meetings, take notes, ditto summaries, distribute.
20. Initiate public debates on education in your district.
21. Teach grammar for nine solid months and help speed up the revolution.
22. Teach evening mini-courses to parents in local history, city-county government, spelling, political action, art, dramatics, physical fitness, writing, video-taping, typing, community newsletters, and underground papers.
23. Telephone one parent every night to talk about his child, the schools, etc., for fifteen minutes.
24. Find a good idea your principal has and compliment him (her?) on it.
25. Use parent conferences to agitate for change.
26. Interview as a team—tell the board to take all of you or none.
27. Abandon the schedule one day a week and substitute films, games, athletics, dancing, open labs in shop, science, art. . . .
28. Invite the school board to visit your classes. Invite them to teach one.
29. Organize a spring festival of the Arts: music, art, writing, athletic events, etc., and ask the local talented adults to perform.
30. Buy your superintendent (a) a box of Uncle Sam cereal, (b) a dictionary, (c) a stuffed bunny, (d) a copy of *Elementary Logic*.

NOTE TO THE ADMINISTRATOR AND/OR TEACHER WHO REMOVES THIS POSTER FROM THE BULLETIN BOARD: You are the reason this manual even came into existence. Think about it.

PROFESSIONALISM: A MIXED BAG

Myron Lieberman, a long-time student of teacher professionalism, has said that the history of education shows very clearly that strong teacher organizations are required to prevent arbitrary, irresponsible action by school boards and officials.[6] The accounts in this chapter of the historical treatment of teachers underline the need for teachers to assert themselves. Teachers are choosing to do so by means of a drive for fuller professionalism which, in turn, will bring teachers greater autonomy and a large decision-making role. This evolution toward professionalism may be a great boon for teachers and for education in general.

Professionalism is not, however, desirable in itself. It may, indeed, work against the highest goals of education. When all the rhetoric is pruned away, professional groups, whether they be the American Medical Association, the American Bar Association or the National Education Association, appear to exist primarily for the benefit of their members. In the interest of protecting and expanding the rights of its members, a professional group may ride roughshod over the needs and rights of the client group. For instance, insisting on tenure rights makes it difficult to get rid of incompetents. In the big cities, basing eligibility for transfer to more congenial schools on seniority may be robbing the most difficult schools of exactly the experienced teacher talent those schools need. Behind the never-never-land jargon of professionalism, one often finds naked self-interest. Occasionally, teachers use their "professional status" as a barrier to protect themselves from criticism by children and parents. "How dare you question what I have done. *I am a professional!*"

The question of professionalism is a tricky one. It seems that it ultimately reduces to a need for balance. The teachers' right to be rewarded and safeguarded against unfair practices must be carefully balanced against the students' and the taxpayers' right to be served justly and well by the teacher. It is a constant struggle to strike an even balance. As Myron Brenton has said,

Every professional group closes ranks to protect its own; teachers are no exception. But teachers are the exception in that they seem to want—at this juncture, at least—the best of both worlds: the security of the civil servant and the prestige and rewards of the professional. More than that, they want a major say in matters of educational policy while getting tenure protection. In other words, they want power without accountability, which is basically an antidemocratic stance.[7]

At this moment in history, the direction the teaching profession will take is unclear. The struggle between the NEA and the AFT on the one hand, and

---

[6] Lieberman, *Education as a Profession*, p. 13.

[7] Brenton, *What's Happened to Teacher?*, p. 255.

the general uncertainty about the future course of the schools on the other, make the situation very fluid. The energy and ideals which the next generation of teachers brings to these issues may decide the outcome.

As important as these questions about the professional associations and their future directions are, a more important question is, "Will I be a professional?" In answering this question we must put aside codes, slogans and contracts. Fundamentally, professionalism is a state of mind. No one can make you a professional. Nor can you become a professional by demand. Being a professional is a matter of performance and determination—of working to live up to the standards of the best teachers and of continually striving to master the craft and invest it with a sense of high purpose.

DISCUSSION QUESTIONS

1. Do you think that teachers should devote themselves to becoming professionals? If so, what must you do? Are you willing to do it? How do you feel about Walter Beggs's description of the "career teacher" on page 376?

2. Do teachers need a professional organization? What are the essential functions performed by such a group?

3. Compare the NEA Code of Ethics and the AFT Bill of Rights. How do the assumptions and attitudes about teaching represented by the two documents differ? What seem to be the overriding concerns of the two organizations? How do the images of teachers they project differ? To what extent do you think a merger of the NEA and the AFT would solve the problems of each and end the competition between them? What new problems might such a merger create?

4. Do you think that discrimination or prejudice against women is still a factor in the working conditions or image of teachers today?

5. Our capsule reports on teaching in past centuries illustrate the immense amount of attention that was paid to teachers' conduct and personal lives. On what assumptions about the role of the teacher was this practice based? Do you think any such concern is justified? Do you think there is any kind of behavior outside the classroom that should be forbidden to teachers, or that should be cause for dismissal? To what extent is the teacher's personal life still subject to scrutiny by school officials?

6. How do you react to the general outlook and specific suggestions in The Guerilla Manual? Are there any with which you emphatically agree or disagree? Can you suggest any new tactics?

7. For you, right now, what seem the most important issues for teachers to concern themselves with—increased power? higher salaries? better training? something else? Be prepared to defend your choice. What can you do to work for the changes you consider most important?

8. What dangers or weaknesses seem to be endemic to professional organizations? Would you be willing to sacrifice security for professionalism? Will you be a professional? Why?

9. What is your opinion of tenure for teachers? What arguments for or against it can you suggest? Would you be willing to work in a school system that did not offer tenure?

10. How do people react when you tell them you are thinking of becoming a teacher? Why?

FOR FURTHER READING

American Federation of Teachers. *Goals of the American Federation of Teachers.* Washington, D.C.: The Federation, n.d. A statement of philosophy and priorities by the major labor-related professional association of teachers.

Brenton, Myron. *What's Happened to Teacher?* New York: Coward-McCann, 1970. A professional writer's view of the new mood among teachers, and why they have moved from passivity to militance. Highly readable journalistic account of the teaching profession.

Darland, David. "Preparation in the Governance of the Profession." In *Teachers for the Real World,* edited by B. Othaniel Smith, *et al.,* pp. 135–150. Washington, D.C.: American Association of Colleges for Teacher Education, 1969. The editor of the *Journal of Teacher Education* outlines how and why teachers must take over the governance of their own profession.

Lieberman, Myron. *Education as a Profession.* Englewood Cliffs, N.J.: Prentice-Hall, 1956. The occupation of teaching is carefully analyzed to determine how it "fits" the standard qualifications of a profession and how it does not.

Lindsay, Margaret, ed. *New Horizons for the Teaching Profession.* Washington, D.C.: National Education Association, 1961. Highly readable report of the "New Horizons" project, which examined the status of teaching and charted new goals for the profession.

National Education Association. *The NEA Handbook.* Washington, D.C.: The Association, 1965–1966. A yearly directory of the NEA and its component organizations. Outlines the Association's purpose, status, recent activities and achievements.

Stinnett, Timothy M., and Huggett, Albert J. *Professional Problems of Teachers.* New York: Macmillan, 1963. A study of the professional needs of teachers and the ways in which school systems normally try to meet them. A good introduction for people planning to teach.

Stuart, Jesse. *The Thread That Runs So True.* New York: Charles Scribner's Sons, 1948. An autobiographical account of the famous writer's experience as a teacher in a one-room school. Interesting description of the problems and successes of a beginning teacher, and also of life in rural America.

Vollmer, Howard M., and Mills, Donald L., eds. *Professionalization*. Englewood Cliffs, N.J.: Prentice-Hall, 1966. This collection of essays deals with several professions (including teaching) and the professionalization process. Highly specialized but interesting volume.

Waller, Willard. *The Sociology of Teaching*. New York: John Wiley & Sons, 1965. Originally written in 1932, this survey of what students and citizens thought of teachers and education thirty years ago still contains much of value. It is rich in incisive analyses of the teacher's role and suggestions for prospective teachers.

Woodring, Paul. *A Fourth of a Nation*. New York: McGraw-Hill, 1957. Presents a major program to improve American education. Although somewhat dated, it was influential in changing the direction of the American schools in the Fifties and Sixties.

FILMS

Quiet Too Long (Guggenheim Productions, 16mm, b&w, 29 min.) Presents scenes in the classroom, on the streets, in budget meetings and at a space center, reflecting the new militancy among teachers determined to persuade citizens and local politicians of the need for improved school facilities, better teaching conditions and adequate school budgets.

AUDIOTAPES

On Education (The Center for the Study of Democratic Institutions, 3.75 ips, reel, ½ track, 39:17 min.) Begins with an excerpt from Robert Hutchins' farewell address at the University of Chicago in 1951 and moves into a question-answer session on American education and educational institutions.

The Organized Profession (National Education Association, 3.75 ips, reel or cassette format, 53:39 min. total) This hour-long audiotape is divided into six short sections, each intended to serve as the basis for a complete discussion. The topics are:

A CALL TO ACTION (3:20 min.)
THE N.Y. STATE TEACHERS ASSOCIATION TACKLES PROFESSIONALISM (15:00 min.)
INSTRUCTIONAL COUNCILS: ONE WAY TO BEGIN (6:45 min.)
NEGOTIATION: MORE THAN BREAD AND BUTTER (10:23 min.)
THE TEACHER AS POLITICIAN (10:06 min.)
WANTED: A SECRETARY OF EDUCATION (8:05 min.)

Refer to Appendix for distributors' addresses.

10 What Are the Tension Points in American Education?

STUDENT POWER AND UNREST

TEACHER POWER

SEX EDUCATION

STUDENT DRUG USE

BLACK STUDIES

RELIGION AND THE SCHOOLS

ACCOUNTABILITY

Rarely a day goes by that educational issues fail to make headlines in news-papers across the country. Sex education, teacher strikes, student unrest, inequality of educational opportunity, decentralization, local control of schools and drug usage are only a few of the issues that we read about daily. Before you launch into the rest of the chapter, take a few moments to answer the following questions about the most controversial topics in American education in order to assess your own position. Compare your responses with those of your classmates.

1. How do you feel about the discipline in your local public schools? Is it too strict, not strict enough or just about right?
2. Is drug usage a serious problem in your local community? Are the schools doing a good job of teaching about the effects of drug use? Are they treating the subject honestly? Should this topic be taught in the schools?
3. Do you favor or oppose a system that would hold teachers and adminis-trators accountable for the progress of students?
4. Should teachers be paid on a standardized salary scale, or should each teacher be paid on the basis of the quality of his work?
5. Do teacher organizations have too much power? Should they have the right to strike for higher salaries and better working conditions?
6. Should junior and senior high school students have more say in such school affairs as curriculum? student dress? hiring and retention of teachers? school rules?

7. Do you believe that local control and financing of schools is desirable?
8. Should each public school student in the United States have an approximately equal amount of money spent on his education per year, or should the amount vary depending on each community's financial ability to support its schools?
9. Do you approve or disapprove of public schools offering courses in sex education? What if these courses discussed topics such as birth control?
10. Do you support or oppose giving public tax money to parochial schools?

Opinion on these issues is extremely diverse. Whatever your views, however, you and your classmates are probably short on data to support your opinions. This is not unusual, since even people who feel strongly about these topics have often not really investigated the arguments for the other side and weighed the issues in order to arrive at a reasoned, logical position. Because these topics touch on our religious, political or philosophical convictions, we usually respond to them emotionally rather than rationally.

The goal of this chapter is simple: to explore opposing positions on some of the most controversial topics in American education today in order to equip you, as a teacher, with understanding of, and sensitivity to, the exposed nerve endings of American education. Keep in mind the significance of these tension points: they are the result of an attempt to educate children in a pluralistic society. That is, our society is made up of diverse individuals and groups, each with different axes to grind and different ideas about what a school should be, what it should teach and what life in school should be like. Tension points are inevitable when diverse groups and individuals with different objectives for the schools attempt to achieve their objectives. As a teacher, you will certainly be involved. Since teachers have a deep responsibility to the schools, it is important that they provide leadership in seeking enlightened solutions to these complex and touchy issues.

One warning: our coverage of these tension points is like an iceberg, one-ninth of which is visible, while the other eight-ninths is submerged. We only skim the surface of these issues; you should not be satisfied to stop here. It is your responsibility to don the diving suit if you want to find out what those icebergs really look like.

INEQUALITY OF EDUCATIONAL OPPORTUNITY

There is probably no issue in education today more important or more emotionally loaded than the charge that children of the poor, blacks, Chicanos, Puerto Ricans and Indians are educationally discriminated against by the public schools. Statistics reveal, for example, that twelfth-grade Negroes in the urban northeast read at the ninth-grade level and do mathematics at the seventh-grade level, while southern Negroes, Mexican-Americans, Puerto Ricans and Indian Americans achieve at even lower levels. Dropout statistics

DIALOGUE

Jim: I think it's a little unfair to ask the reader to respond to our questions without giving him a chance to see how we would respond to them.

Kevin: All right, let's pick a few and respond. What about question 1, on discipline?

Jim: I think that discipline in the schools is generally too strict. Schools are organized for the teacher to set the goals for the children, decide what activities should take place and how long these activities should last. When one person tries to impose his will on others, regardless of their wishes, a control problem usually results. Therefore, I say that discipline is too strict mainly because classrooms are too teacher-dominated. Why don't you respond to question 3?

Kevin: In theory, I'm in favor of more accountability on the part of teachers and administrators, but I don't see how they can be held accountable for student progress when so many factors like class size, instructional materials and the like are beyond their control. Right now we're pretty unsophisticated about the whole question, but I suspect that procedures will be developed in the future which will make teacher accountability a reasonable process.

Jim: Questions 7 and 8 are interesting for me. I would like to see school districts organized so that gross inequalities in per pupil expenditures from district to district are remedied. Unless poor districts can pay salaries and obtain materials comparable to those of richer districts. we'll continue to perpetuate inequalities. Local control does allow for more experimentation than do the centralized systems typical of European countries. I guess I would like to see finances more centralized to even out per pupil expenditures, but I'd like local control over curriculum. How do you feel about public tax money going to help parochial schools?

Kevin: Thanks a lot for the hot potato. This is a terribly complex issue. A few things are clear, though. With the costs of education soaring every month, many parochial schools are going out of business and will continue to. A related point is that few parents who would like to send their children to parochial schools can afford to pay taxes for the public schools and pay tuition to a parochial school. Unless public tax money is used to support parochial schools—for instance, to support the nonreligious teaching and curriculum expenses—this question will just be academic because there will be only a handful of parochial schools left. This would tend to solidify what is called by some the public school monopoly on education in this country. Also, taxes would have to be increased to accommodate former parochial school students in the public schools.

attest to an even greater inequality between white middle-class children's education and that received by children of the poor and minority groups. There is ample evidence, notably the Coleman Report and the report on racial isolation prepared by the Commission on Civil Rights, that massive inequality exists in public school educational achievement along social-class and racial lines.[1] In other words, students of low socioeconomic status and minority group background score much lower than white middle-class students on a variety of verbal and numerical tests.

Whatever the reasons, large numbers of poor minority-group students are leaving school without the verbal and computational skills necessary to function effectively in American society. Who, if anyone, is to blame for this situation? the schools? teachers and administrators? Or is the responsibility that of society as a whole, and are the schools merely a scapegoat? Talk to five different people and you will probably hear five different opinions about where blame should be affixed. But assessing blame is not a particularly fruitful exercise. Better questions can be asked, such as: What is meant by equality of educational opportunity? How is it measured? What are school systems' responsibilities for providing equal educational opportunity? How can the achievement of poor and minority-group students be improved? Simple enough questions, but their answers are guaranteed to be controversial.

Equality of educational opportunity is hardly a new concept in American education, but its components have changed dramatically in the last two decades. For a long period in our history, the idea of equal educational opportunity involved the following elements:

1. Providing a *free education* up to the time when the majority of students entered the labor force;
2. Providing a *common curriculum* for all children, regardless of background;
3. Providing that children from diverse backgrounds attend the *same school;*
4. Providing equality within a given *locality,* since local taxes supported the school system.[2]

As a result of _Brown vs. Board of Education,_ the 1954 Supreme Court decision which held that segregated schools are inherently unequal because the *effects* of such separate schools are likely to be different, a new component was introduced into the concept of educational opportunity: that equality of educational opportunity is defined in terms of the effect, rather than the provisions, of schooling. In the *Brown* decision, the Supreme Court

---

[1] James S. Coleman *et al., Equality of Educational Opportunity* (Washington: U.S. Government Printing Office, 1966); and U.S. Commission on Civil Rights, *Racial Isolation in the Public Schools,* (Washington: U.S. Government Printing Office, 1967).

[2] James Coleman, "The Concept of Equality of Educational Opportunity," *Harvard Educational Review* 38 (Winter 1968): 11.

found that even when facilities and teacher salaries were identical, "equality of educational opportunity" did not exist.

Previous to *Brown,* the community and educational institution were expected only to provide equal resources—teachers, facilities, materials—and responsibility for advantageous use of those resources lay with the child and his family. Today many people have come to consider it the responsibility of the educational institution, not the child, to create achievement. As James Coleman states, "The difference in achievement at grade 12 between the average Negro and the average white is, in effect, the degree of inequality of opportunity, and the reduction of the inequality is a responsibility of the school. This shift in responsibility follows logically from the change in the concept of equality of educational opportunity from school resource inputs to effects of schooling."[3]

Others do not accept Coleman's assertion, arguing that the school should do its best to provide equal educational resources to all its students, but that it cannot be held accountable for differences in student learning. Although it is agreed that many poor minority children are not learning in our schools, opinions vary considerably as to the locus of the problem. At one extreme it is assumed that failure to learn is a result of the student's own deficiencies—physical, economic, mental, cultural or environmental. At the other extreme is the idea that if pupils are failing it is the school system that needs rehabilitation. This position assumes it is the school's obligation to diagnose the learner's needs, concerns and cognitive and affective style, and to adjust its program accordingly. As with most issues, the answer probably lies somewhere in between—the students do have certain deficiencies but the school needs to learn how to overcome them.

It is undeniable that the achievement of white middle-class children and poor lower-class minority children is unequal—the important question is how the achievement of poor and minority group children can be improved. As you are probably already aware, solutions to this problem are proposed from many quarters, and considerable friction exists between groups who advocate different approaches. The five most widely-advocated approaches to the reform of public education are compensatory education, desegregation, model subsystems, parallel systems and total system reform.[4]

COMPENSATORY EDUCATION

Compensatory education is an attempt to overcome deficiencies in the learner by grafting extra education onto the regular school program, or to avert potential learning problems through preschool programs such as

---

[3] *Ibid.,* p. 22.

[4] The authors wish to acknowledge Mario Fantini's identification and elaboration of these five approaches in his discussion of implementing equal educational opportunity, *Harvard Educational Review* 38 (Winter 1968): 160–175.

Project Headstart. It is the oldest and currently the most prevalent approach designed to raise pupils' academic achievement. Programs such as the Ford Foundation-supported Great Cities School Improvement Programs, Title I of the Elementary and Secondary Education Act, New York City's early Higher Horizons Program and the more recent More Effective Schools Program are all aimed at remedying specific learner defects, such as verbal retardation, lack of motivation and experiential and sensory deprivation, which prevent the student from participating effectively in the learning process.

A tremendous amount of money and energy has been spent attempting to develop special programs to improve the academic achievement of poor children. Unfortunately, evidence indicates that little headway has been made in even the most successful programs. Proponents of this approach argue that expenditures thus far are a mere drop in the bucket, considering the enormity of the problem. They also argue that a simultaneous attack must be made on external factors which contribute to low achievement, such as poor housing, family instability and low income.

The parents of children enrolled in these compensatory programs, whose expectations were initially very high, are becoming increasingly dissatisfied with their results.

Some observers of compensatory education programs criticize them for simply offering massive doses of methods that have not worked previously. They see little point in strengthening programs which have failed in the past. Mario Fantini says of the compensatory approach, "It builds layers onto the standard educational process in order to bring the strays into the fold and to fit them into the existing school mold. The assumption is that the schools need to do somewhat more for disadvantaged pupils, but it does not presume that the school itself is in need of wholesale re-examination."[5]

DESEGREGATION

Since 1954, one of the prime motivating forces in school integration efforts has been the assumption that Negro students' achievement will improve in an integrated school environment. Notably, the findings of the Coleman Report and the U.S. Commission on Civil Rights support this assumption. The latter asserts, "Negro children suffer serious harm when their education takes place in public schools which are racially segregated, whatever the source of such segregation may be. Negro children who attend predominantly Negro schools do not achieve as well as other children, Negro and white."[6]

From the late Fifties to the middle Sixties, efforts were made to desegregate schools, particularly in the South. Despite the time, energy and money expended, the nationwide results have been rather poor. One estimate indi-

---

[5] *Ibid.*, p. 164.

[6] U.S. Commission on Civil Rights, *Racial Isolation*, p. 1.

cates that only 23 percent of the more than six million Negro students in the United States attend integrated public schools.[7] In urban settings, integration has proven almost impossible to achieve, primarily because of the growing concentration of black and other nonwhite minorities in the inner cities. While in the Fifties and Sixties many blacks fought and demonstrated for integration, today many blacks and other minority group members are resisting integration at the option of the white majority. They are focusing instead on gaining control over the schools their children presently attend.

At least two other factors have contributed to integration's poor track record. First, blacks are resentful that the present power structure makes integration an option of the white community. Second, minority groups feel a strong need for racial identity and pride. Many parents fear that this sense of identity will be lost if integration takes place, and that the best way of insuring racial pride is to operate the schools under the control of the Negro community with a curriculum especially designed to foster a sense of identity among the children.

Community control over the schools is not perceived by blacks as a throwback to the old "separate but equal" situation which the 1954 Supreme Court decision overruled. They argue that when blacks achieve quality education under their own jurisdiction, they will be prepared to enter a society on a basis of parity rather than deficiency. Thus, they argue, equality of educational opportunity will best be achieved by concentrating more power and control over the schools in the hands of the parents and the community, and allowing them to hire teachers, develop curricula and govern their children's education.

Attempts to decentralize large city school districts are a direct outgrowth of inner-city minorities' dissatisfaction with unequal education and with the lack of response to their demands for change. In brief, decentralization in many large urban school systems is an attempt to redistribute administrative power from an unresponsive centralized bureaucracy to smaller "communities" within the large city. On the assumption that the local "community" knows better than the centralized school system what its children need, decentralization efforts such as the Ocean Hill-Brownsville experimental school district in New York City have been undertaken. Advocates of this program collided head-on with the Union of Federated Teachers, the largest teacher organization in New York City, when some white teachers were fired and black teachers were hired in their places by the experimental school district. In a showdown, the New York City teachers mounted a strike which lasted for weeks. A settlement was reached, and eventually the New York City school system was subdivided into thirty districts in an attempt to make the system more responsive; however, these districts are much larger than the original experimental districts.

---

[7] Alexander M. Bickel, "Desegregation: Where Do We Go From Here?" *Phi Delta Kappan* 51 (June 1970): 518–522.

Opponents of community control argue that decisions are made without consulting professional educators, that staff are chosen along racial lines and that professional competence is judged by unqualified people. Advocates of community control insist that teachers should be chosen for their positive attitudes toward students, rather than on the basis of longevity. They also argue that local control allows mothers and other community personnel to assist the teacher in the instructional process. Most of all, local community control allows for a responsiveness to the children's needs which, they insist, never existed under a centralized school system.

Whether integration or decentralized community control offers the best hope for equal educational opportunities for minority groups is a moot point. It is worth noting that integration efforts have been much more successful in small and middle-sized school districts than in the large urban areas.

MODEL SUBSYSTEMS

A model subsystem is an experimental program created within the existing school system to explore new and improved teacher training methods, curriculum development and community participation. If these experimental programs prove effective, their methods may be disseminated and adopted throughout the entire school system. A number of these experimental programs have been developed in cities such as Washington, New York, Boston and Syracuse.

Because these programs are experimental, they are frequently able to attract the participation of institutions and persons outside the educational establishment. For example, Howard University, Antioch College and Trinity College assisted an experimental subsystem in Washington, D.C., called the Cardozo Project in Urban Teaching. This project was one of the chief models for the legislation and operation of the national Teacher Corps. Other sources of talent and ideas for model subsystems are community agencies, U.S. Office of Education research and development centers, Peace Corps and Vista veterans, private industry and the professions.

It does not appear likely, however, that model subsystems will be able to exert enough influence to change bureaucracy-hardened school systems in more than a token way. For the most part, they receive only short-term funding, and tend to focus on isolated ways of improving learning rather than on system-wide reform.

PARALLEL SYSTEMS

There have always been alternatives to public education for those who could afford to send their children to private schools. For the children of the poor, there are no alternatives. Imagine the frustration of parents who see their children falling further and further behind in academic achievement,

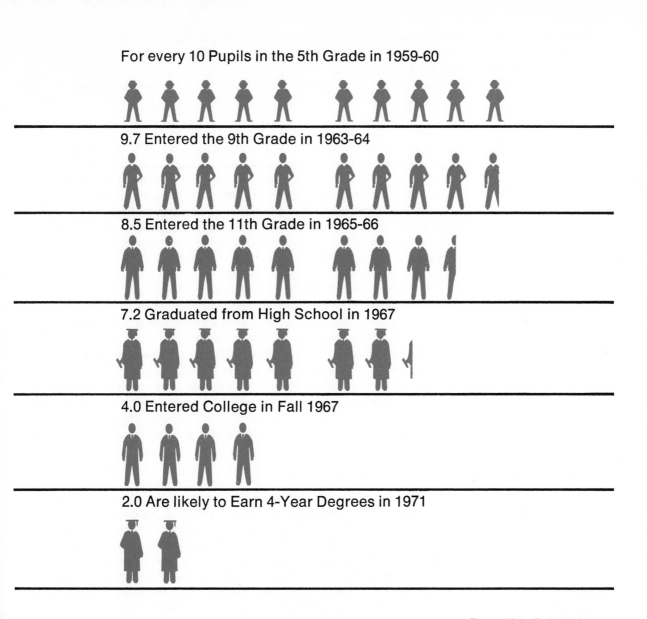

For every 10 Pupils in the 5th Grade in 1959-60

9.7 Entered the 9th Grade in 1963-64

8.5 Entered the 11th Grade in 1965-66

7.2 Graduated from High School in 1967

4.0 Entered College in Fall 1967

2.0 Are likely to Earn 4-Year Degrees in 1971

Figure 10.1 *Estimated school retention rates, fifth grade through college graduation: United States, 1969–1971.*

Courtesy of the U.S. Department of Health, Education and Welfare, Office of Education, *Digest of Educational Statistics 1967.*

Social reform is not to be secured by noise and shouting; by complaints and denunciation; . . . or the making of revolutions; but by the awakening of thought and the progress of ideas. Henry George.

but cannot afford to send them to private schools, and who are convinced that the system is unresponsive to their children's needs but lack the power to bring about change. In response to these frustrations, educational critics such as Christopher Jencks and Kenneth Clark propose that the poor should be offered options to the current public education systems. They propose a voucher system under which the government would grant vouchers to parents equal to the amount of public money spent each year for the child's education. The parents would be free to use the voucher to pay for their child's education at any school they chose.

Proponents of the parallel school system concept argue that the public schools have a monopoly on educational services, at least for poor children. If competing schools were created, they argue, the public schools would be forced to develop ways to deal effectively with poor children or suffer the consequences of diminishing financial support. The voucher system is discussed in more detail in Chapter Eleven.

The parallel system deserves experimental implementation, which it is receiving under a federal government grant. It is unlikely, however, that it could ever endanger the actual existence of the public schools, and doubtful that the public would support a private system of publicly-supported schools.

TOTAL SYSTEM REFORM

We can see deficiencies in each of the four basic approaches to equal educational opportunities. Compensatory education has thus far done little to raise the academic achievement level of children of the poor and minority groups. Desegregation has stalled in urban areas where blacks and other minority groups inhabit the inner city while the whites flee to the suburbs. Besides, many black people are demanding local community control which would, in effect, postpone integration efforts until parity in educational achievement is reached. Model subsystems have achieved only limited success in isolated situations and show little promise of initiating change of the magnitude necessary to deal with the problem effectively. The parallel system promises to create alternatives to the public schools, but avoids the challenge of reforming the schools where most children do, and will probably continue to, receive their education.

It appears, at least to our eyes, that reform of total school systems—structure, decision-making power, teacher training, curriculum and organization—offers the most promise of creating equal educational opportunity for poor children. Admittedly, the task is enormous, but some encouraging examples do exist. In Philadelphia, for instance, reform efforts have been undertaken to provide new leadership for the system as a whole, including the superintendent and central school board, while leaving the system's basic structure intact. The superintendent, with support from the school board, has attempted to infuse the system with new ideas, new staff and new styles. The Parkway Program discussed in Chapter Two is an example of the innovative approaches being attempted within the Philadelphia school system.

The decentralization of New York City into thirty smaller school districts is another attempt to change the operation of the school system to allow for innovation, development of curriculum suited for the students in each district, and general responsiveness to the community's needs. As we have mentioned, tension has already arisen in New York City between the local communities and professional teachers. Because many of the community residents are convinced the schools have failed to prepare their children to make it in society, they favor radical reform of the system, including the right to select their children's teachers. The parents are tired of traveling what they perceive as a one-way street where the school and its staff lay out their goods and the "consumer" either accepts them or goes hungry. They can no longer accept the schools' explanation that when their children fail, it is the children's fault. They can no longer tolerate a school system which pays no attention to consumer preferences, makes no provision for feedback from parents or pupils and does not respond to changing conditions and needs. Parents are demanding, and increasingly receiving, the right to make changes in the system. This movement is, of course, highly threatening to the professional teachers' organizations which see teachers' jobs being jeopardized. Because the interests of two powerful groups—the community and the professional teachers—are at stake, conflict is likely to be common in the foreseeable future.

Arguing for a total system approach to change, Mario Fantini summarizes our position very succinctly when he says,

In the subsystems, models of excellence must swim against the tide of the status quo system. The total approach has no such constraint; there is no boring from within, for everyone starts at the reform gate at the same time. In a federation of autonomous subsystems, each with an equitable share of resources, instructional practices would operate in an open, competitive market. The most successful models would be on display as a challenge to other school systems to adopt their approaches or surpass them in performance.[8]

---

[8] Fantini, p. 170.

STUDENT POWER AND UNREST

Compared to high school students in many countries, the American student has been remarkably docile. However, there are many signs that this pattern is changing. "A Profile of the Large-City High School," a 1970 study sponsored by the National Association of Secondary School Principals, reports that student strikes occurred in one-third of the 700 high schools surveyed between 1967 and 1969. These figures do not reflect minor disruptions which also occurred during the same time period. The issues which most frequently triggered strikes were matters of dress and style, such as the length of hair or skirts. Other provocative issues included demands for memorial services for black leaders, advocacy of national policies on the war or poverty, influence on the instructional programs, separate lounges for black students, soul food, and constitutional guarantees, such as the right to publish underground newspapers or to wear political insignia.

There can be no doubt that a distinctive teenage culture does exist. Adolescents express their strong feelings of ambiguity, boredom, love, anomie and conflict by differentiating themselves in language, dress and manners. Some are activists; others express their rebellion in passive resistance to adult suggestion, by sullenness and negativism—which may lead to underachievement or to dropping out.

The underlying issue in the majority of student strikes and disruptions is adult control over all decision-making, and the absence of democratic procedures in the high schools. It is easy to build a case that student unrest in the high schools is a result of the way students are treated. If questioned, a majority of students would probably describe their high schools as basically undemocratic. Students are barred from taking part in decisions which affect them as individuals and citizens. When their proposed innovations or complaints produce conflict, it is usually met with arbitrary action by teachers and administrators. Students are often not extended the rights of individuals in a democratic society. They usually have no say in what they are to learn or in how they are expected to dress. The typical student government has little or no real power in the governance of the school, and is readily recognized by the students as a sham. The student newspaper usually has a faculty advisor who censors articles which might offend certain elements of the community, but about which the students themselves may feel strongly. In short, there is little reason to expect high school students to form an allegiance to the democratic political system, because they do not experience democracy in their daily lives in school.

It is interesting to note that, at the same time students are demanding more freedom and less authoritarian dominance by school administrators and teachers, a Gallup poll indicates that the American public sees discipline as the greatest problem of the local schools. Asked "How do you feel about the discipline in the local public schools—is it too strict, not strict enough, or just about right?"[9] the sample of approximately 1600 adults responded:

Too strict	2%
Not strict enough	53%
Just about right	31%
Don't know/no answer	14%
	100%

[9] George Gallup, "Second Annual Survey of Public's Attitude Toward Public Schools," *Phi Delta Kappan* 52 (October 1970): 107.

Photo by D. Darrah through Stock, Boston

WHAT ARE THE TENSION POINTS IN AMERICAN EDUCATION?

The majority of adults interviewed would seem to favor stricter discipline in response to student unrest. We are convinced that it is this approach which is responsible for unrest in the first place! If it is true that we learn by experiencing—and there is considerable evidence in support of that notion—then students who experience arbitrary and one-sided decision-making by those in authority will learn to use the same nonnegotiable tactics to achieve their own goals.

The solution to most student demonstrations and strikes is, in our opinion, to allow students to experience democratic decision-making in those areas that are important to them—dress standards, school rules, curriculum and freedom of speech. One might expect this to be an approach to which few adults would object. But when George Gallup asked a sample of the American public "Should high school students have more say about school affairs such as curriculum? student dress? teachers? school rules?"[10] the response was:

	RESPONSE	NATIONAL TOTALS %
CURRICULUM	Yes	38
	No	53
	No opinion	9
		100
TEACHERS	Yes	22
	No	72
	No opinion	6
		100
SCHOOL RULES	Yes	36
	No	58
	No opinion	6
		100
STUDENT DRESS	Yes	37
	No	57
	No opinion	6
		100

If student decision-making in school affairs which concern and affect students is agreed to be desirable, then it is obvious that the communication gap between schools and the American public must be bridged. Teachers and administrators must take the lead in this process. High school students must be treated as citizens in a democracy if they are in fact to act like cit-

---

[10] Loc. cit.

izens in their schools and, later, on the college campus and in the community. Warning public school personnel of the consequences of excluding students from decision-making, Charles Silberman states, "In a war between faculty and students, the students are bound to win; there are more of them, and put to the test, they can be defiant in the most ingenious ways."[11] Forewarned is forearmed.

TEACHER POWER

Smaller classes, duty-free lunch periods, more planning time, more clerical and technical assistance, a clearly defined grievance procedure with binding arbitration, clearly described seniority rights, an improved transfer policy, more realistic teaching loads, more adequate counseling for students, curriculum provisions for potential dropouts, a more direct role in curriculum change, cultural enrichment programs for students, a larger school role in the development of values and morality, greater diversity of teaching materials, more teaching aids, a greater say in instructional budgets, provisions for usable curriculum guides—these are only some of the demands made by teacher organizations in contract negotiations with public school districts.

The day of meek Miss Dove is over. Teachers, through their professional organizations, are demanding both improved benefits for themselves and revised and updated instructional policies for the schools. Teachers are calling for administrators and school boards to relinquish some of their decision-making power to those whom they believe are most qualified to make instructional and curricular decisions.

Demands, of course, arouse conflict. As teachers demand higher salaries, more clerical assistance and improved personal benefits, all of which require additional funds, legislators must propose and the public must accept increased taxes. And as teachers demand greater decision-making power, those who now hold such power must be willing to relinquish it.

If such conflict does occur, and the teachers feel strongly about the issues in question, they increasingly resort to strikes or the threat of strikes to pressure the opposition into capitulating to their demands. In 1969–70, for example, there were 171 teacher strikes in the United States, involving 117,000 teachers. The comparable figures for 1968–69 were 131 strikes and 129,000 teachers.[12] Two of the largest walkouts were in 1968—one in New York City involving over 50,000 teachers for 36 school days, and one in Florida involving 25,000 teachers. In the Florida case, many of the striking teachers were not reemployed by their school districts when the strike ended.

Teacher strikes generate much ill will. As long as the actions of teacher

---

[11] Charles E. Silberman, *Crisis in the Classroom* (New York: Random House, 1970), p. 340.

[12] "Teacher Strikes Increase," *Phi Delta Kappan* 52 (October 1970): 132.

Teachers are demanding more and more decision making power. Power is never given to anyone. Power is taken, and it is taken from someone. Teachers, as one of society's powerless groups, are now starting to take power from supervisors and school boards. This is causing and will continue to cause a realignment of power relationships. Albert Shanker, "Teacher-Supervisory Relationships: A Symposium," Changing Education 1 (Spring 1966): 23.

associations or unions do not disrupt the education of their children, most parents are indifferent to the arrangements teachers make for dealing with their employers. Many parents support teachers' demands for salary increases and improved instructional programs, but do not sanction strikes as a means of obtaining desired results because such tactics disrupt their children's schooling. Parents also resent strikes because they undermine the climate of friendliness and cooperation in which children work best. Strikes often result in divisiveness between teachers, parents, pupils, school administrators and school board members. Parents and children are frequently pressured to take sides in the dispute.

It is almost always with great reluctance that teachers strike. Strikes can mean loss of pay, fines, loss of jobs and, possibly, jail terms in states where teacher strikes are illegal. Teachers usually do not resort to a strike unless they feel very strongly about the issues and are convinced they have exhausted all other alternatives.

"Perhaps the best way to avoid this whole problem," says Joseph W. Cassidy, Commissioner of the Education Commission of the States, "is to remove the causes of [teachers'] unrest. . . . This solution, however, may be as distasteful to the legislator and the school board member as a strike itself. It seems to me that we have these two choices: (1) strikes or sanctions; or (2) removal of the cause for strikes or sanctions."[13] The second option is, of course, the more desirable, but it is not always possible. As Cassidy indicates, some legislators and school board members see a teacher strike as a lesser evil than an increase in taxes, even if the additional tax funds are for improved instruction for children. When this is the case, teachers believe they must point out the school system's weaknesses as strongly as they can. As one striking teacher organization has stated:

We sincerely—and most firmly—believe that our efforts to become first-class citizens, under the law, will provide a better school system in Warren, for Warren school

---

[13] Elizabeth S. Hendryson, "Parent Reaction to Teacher Power," *The National Elementary Principal* 48 (January 1969): 18.

district children. Somehow, sometime, someone must call out the shortcomings of this school system and its operations and make it the kind of leading educational system that Warren citizens have long indicated they prefer. If not now, when? If not teachers, who?[14]

SEX EDUCATION

"What schools need to do is treat sex as they would digestion—no more, no less."

"Sex education is more than just knowledge of the mechanics of the sex act, and the development and birth of a baby. The physical aspect should not be emphasized at the expense of its psychological and social aspects."

"Sex education is a Communist conspiracy to corrupt youth."

"Sex, love, birth and family life are all one package and should be discussed in the reassuring warmth of the parents' presence."

Sex education is a headline-grabber in newspapers throughout the country, especially in smaller communities. The statements above represent four different positions on sex education, and give evidence of the controversy surrounding it. According to a Gallup poll taken in April, 1970, 72 percent of the parents interviewed expressed their approval of sex education in the

---

[14] Robert Kowalczyk, "The Teachers' Advocate," *N.E.A. Journal* (January 1969): 53.

Mutilated Books

The school authorities of the Mepham Central High School District on Long Island who cut forty pages on human sexuality out of four hundred copies of a textbook on health had in mind the protection of seventh-graders' morals. A little pedagogical sophistication might have told them that every pupil whose normal sense of curiosity has not yet been dulled by pedantry will rush to the nearest library to read the missing chapters. This is probably more than ordinary teaching could have accomplished. But such unintended increases in readership cannot offset the consequences of the barbaric example of book mutilation. A school that puts scissors to books slashes civilization and leaves it bleeding.

Courtesy of the New York Times.

public schools, while 22 percent were opposed.[15] But the minority is often very vocal in its opposition.

Most people agree that children should be given information about sex; the controversy centers around two subsidiary issues: 1) is the school the appropriate institution to offer such instruction? and 2) if so, should it limit instruction to strictly factual information, or should the psychological, social and ethical aspects of sex also be included in the curriculum?

[15] Gallup, "Second Annual Survey," p. 107.

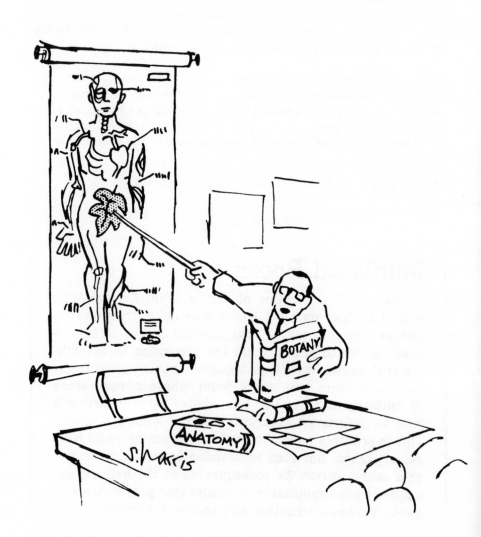

Cartoon by Sidney Harris.

With respect to the first issue, some people argue that because sex is such an intimate topic, and is closely related to religious and moral beliefs, sex education is the responsibility of the home and/or the church.

Advocates of sex education in the schools respond that they would agree with the above position if parents did, in fact, provide adequate sex information for their children. Unfortunately, they argue, this simply is not the case. The majority of parents fail to assume the responsibility to teach their children about sex because: 1) they don't know how to respond to their children's questions; 2) they cannot bridge the "conversation gap" between their own viewpoint and that of their children; 3) they overestimate the age at which sex information is most appropriate, and 4) they are inhibited and uncomfortable discussing sex. Many students complain that their parents either waited too long to give them information about sex, failed to give them any information at all or provided more misinformation than reliable facts. Advocates assert that the public school is the only institution which has access to most children over an extended period of time, and that the responsibility must fall to the school because of the demonstrated failure of the home, church, library and medical profession to provide effective sex education.

Argument among advocates over the kind of sex education the schools should offer is equally heated. One position can be succinctly summarized as: Sex Education, No! Sex Information, Yes! People who adhere to this position do not believe the school should impart attitudes or moral and ethical value judgments in relation to sex. They argue that it is not the schools' place to take stands on masturbation, petting and premarital sexual intercourse. Others agree that issues such as these should not be discussed from an ethical or moral standpoint, but are in favor of a curriculum which promotes respect for one's own body and acceptance of sex as a normal and basic aspect of human relationships.

While very few people want the schools to preach a particular ethical stance toward sexual issues, many people believe that the distribution of sexual knowledge alone is not enough. The role they propose for the schools is to teach students to analyze the range of value systems relating to sex, leaving decisions about sexual standards and behavior up to the students. They envision a sex education program which would help the student develop a moral code based on knowledge, responsibility and belief in the worth of individual fulfillment on a moral basis. This, they believe, can best be accomplished not by avoiding value issues, but by exploring them without favoritism or prejudice.

STUDENT DRUG USE

Is student drug use a serious problem in the public schools? Interestingly enough, a Gallup poll survey indicates that 64 percent of the adults seem to

Anselmo Garza (1944–   )

When Anselmo Garza resigned his position as a Spanish teacher in a Texas high school after two-and-a-half months, his superintendent called him a "complete failure." As a sixth-grade teacher in the same school system the year before, he had been a hero.

The oldest of seven Mexican-American children, Anselmo was born and went to school in Harlingen, Texas, a town about twenty miles from the Mexican border. The Garza family lives in the Mexican section, called the *barrio,* and is supported by Anselmo's father, who works as a migrant farm laborer. The children joined their father in the cotton fields each summer until picking machines took their jobs away. Since then Mr. Garza has migrated to Michigan in the summer to harvest strawberries and cucumbers.

Anselmo made the highest marks in his class at Harlingen High School and went on to Pan American College, a small state liberal arts school in Edinburg, Texas, on scholarship. Although trained as a secondary-school teacher, on returning to his hometown Anselmo was offered a position teaching in the all-Chicano elementary school he had attended. Before he began his first day at the school, the principal told him, "These sixth graders are three years behind in reading. Don't feel bad if you don't last a whole year with them. These kids will probably drop out next year. Oh, by the way, make sure they don't speak Spanish anywhere and don't check out any books to them because they can't read."

On the first day of school Anselmo spoke to his pupils in Spanish and told them that the principal had said they couldn't read. "I know better," he told them. "I was in this same room and I graduated from college with honors." The rapport was instantaneous. Anselmo knew enough about self-fulfilling prophecies to understand that children won't learn if they're expected not to learn. He threw out the workbooks and taught spontaneously. He filled the classroom with books and told the children they could read whenever they wanted to. Dusty, unused film strips were retrieved from the stockroom and the pupils learned to read from the scripts. The principal stopped in one day and left in amazement. "I wouldn't have believed it if I hadn't seen it," he remarked. "Those kids were asking thoughtful questions and were really engaged in learning!"

After a successful first year of teaching, Anselmo was assigned to teach high-school Spanish, which was more in keeping with his preparation. Ironically, he replaced his own former Spanish teacher. As a result of segregation by tracking, Anselmo's classes were either all-Chicano or all-Anglo. While all the Chicanos did well on a standardized test, scoring in the 80's and 90's, and while most of the Anglo students failed, the Chicano class was labeled as a lower track. But Anselmo's real problem was with his second-year class of Anglos. Their motivation and achievement were low. For weeks he adhered to the grammar and drills in the syllabus. Realizing that the students were not making progress, he attempted to motivate them by asking why they were taking Spanish. This quickly led to broader discussions about education and its relation to life. "Some started to see that there is something wrong with a system that makes them work only for a grade and prevents Chicanos from getting into high average classes. They had believed that theirs was the best of all possible educational systems, but I was questioning and getting a few others to question the whole structure."

In 1968 the Chicano movement was just beginning to gain momentum and support. The Chicanos wanted the schools to stop spanking children for speaking Spanish on the playground, and they wanted their place in history respectfully taught. The school's textbooks were full of stories about American heroes killing Mexicans. The Anglo students were upset by the Chicano protests, but Anselmo told them he supported the demands. He later explained: "I'm going to get in trouble with my views on education, politics, the Vietnam war, racism and bigotry." He felt he had to make them see that they had only one point of view—one that begged for elaboration.

The parents of some Anglo students complained about Anselmo's unorthodox ideas. He was asking the students to open their minds and to think about their educations and their lives—subjects ordinarily not mentioned in school. The principal called Anselmo into his office five times in response to parents' complaints. Each time the principal told him he was in trouble. Finally, on the fifth visit, both the principal and the superintendent told Anselmo that he was in deep trouble and that they would not support him. Anselmo resigned. On the day he submitted his resignation, the bilingual newspaper put out by the high school Spanish classes was dedicated "to Anselmo Garza, the greatest teacher we have ever had."

In Harlingen some say it is un-American to speak Spanish; children who speak it on the school grounds have had tissues stuffed in their mouths. The widely-repeated slogan of this viewpoint is: "Be smart. Be right. Speak English." Anselmo was called a Communist for advocating a bilingual policy for the school and for quietly encouraging Chicanos to support protests. He says, "I think the only way to change the dominant Anglo culture is to reach the high school students and get them thinking."

Anselmo is currently a student at the Harvard Graduate School of Education. He came to Harvard to tell people concerned about education what is happening "off the beaten path" in American schools. When he completes his work for an advanced degree he plans to return to Harlingen to work with and educate Chicanos.

think so, while only 29 percent of the high school juniors and seniors concur.[16] It is clear that the use of drugs by high school students and younger children is on the increase, but estimates of the proportion of drug users in the student population range from 3 percent to 50 percent. The discrepancy between parental and student opinion on the Gallup poll is probably due to disagreement about what constitutes a serious problem. Many students do not view marijuana as a serious problem, while their parents usually do. If we agree that drug use by public school students is fairly common, what, if anything, should the schools be doing about it?

Recognizing that ignorance and misinformation are major complicating factors surrounding drug usage, many communities and states—and even the federal government—have initiated drug education programs. These programs are designed to teach students, teachers, administrators and parents the abuse potential of specific drugs, their pharmacological properties, the meaning of drugs to the individual and the legal ramifications of drug usage. The federal government appropriated $12.4 million—a sixfold increase—for drug education during fiscal year 1971, including a training program for 150,000 teachers and 75,000 students and community leaders. Evidence of the need for such a program is the tendency of many adults to lump all drugs into the same category. To equate the risks of pot with those of LSD or heroin —as many adults do—is akin to ignoring the differences between beer, hard liquor and straight wood alcohol. Many of the programs also attempt to explore the question of *why*. Why would kids of all ages and backgrounds be tempted to try drugs in the first place? Attempting to answer this kind of question helps adults and adolescents cope with the underlying problems rather than limiting their attention to the symptom—drug usage.

Although the need for drug education is widely recognized, what is taught, how it is taught and official approaches to student drug use vary markedly. In New York City policemen pose as students in order to gather evidence against drug users, while in San Francisco four high schools have no-questions-asked crash pads staffed by nurses, psychiatrists, technicians and student aides.

How does all this affect you? Particularly if you teach in high school, it is quite possible that some of your students may be using drugs. If you suspect this to be the case, what should you do? Talk to them? If so, what would you say? Seek advice from an older teacher or the principal? Report them to the police? Call the parents? Mind your own business? Obviously, we cannot answer these questions for you. We can, however, urge several approaches.

First, become familiar with the signs of drug use. Know the differences between various types of drugs and the signs of their use. Second, avoid sermonizing; try instead to present objective facts about drugs and their known effects. Third, if a student indicates that he wants to talk to you about

---

[16] *Ibid.*, p. 105.

a drug problem, talk to him and ask him what you can do to help. His answer may range from just providing him a listening outlet to arranging for him to see a specialist in a drug clinic. However, if you do not know anything about drugs, don't pretend you do. Fourth, know and understand the legal implications of drug usage. Fifth, don't just ignore obviously heavy users with the rationale that it is none of your business. The course of action you choose to take is up to you, but you can't just hide your head in the sand and expect the problem to disappear.

BLACK STUDIES

In the late Sixties, a movement began to introduce into the curricula of the public schools and universities a previously-neglected field of study—black studies. Black students and scholars initiated these programs in an effort to define the historical experience of blacks in this country and to reevaluate both black culture and the dominant white culture in terms of the black experience. Some black studies courses take an historical perspective; others investigate and try to define the values and attitudes which have grown out of the black experience. In any case, black studies rejects the facile assumption of European cultural superiority. Black studies also represents an attempt to correct the ethnocentricity of the standard curriculum, which has by and large failed to acknowledge either the role of black people in American history or black accomplishments in literature, music, the arts and the economic development of the nation.

Many schools now recognize the need for white students to become familiar with black culture and history, just as blacks have been expected to learn about the dominant white culture. If students are to live in a multiracial society, they must know and respect each other's backgrounds. Until very recently, standard textbooks at best ignored blacks and at worst contained grossly misinformed and condescending statements. Neither whites nor blacks can afford that kind of "education"; the black studies movement is an effort toward redress.

There was much initial opposition to the idea of teaching minority studies (there still is in some parts of the country), but for the most part the public schools are no longer debating the inclusion of black studies in the curriculum. The major question now is whether to offer separate courses or to integrate the material into traditional classes.

Most educators believe that the best way to present material on blacks and other ethnic groups is to incorporate it into the regular curriculum from kindergarten to grade 12. However, in order to compensate for years of neglect, many school systems, especially in large cities, are providing separate courses in junior and senior high schools. Some educators, on the other hand, fear that unless separate black studies courses are offered, the schools will give only token or negligible attention to such material within the regular curriculum.

The two major obstacles to the inclusion of black history and culture in the curricula have been a lack of adequate materials and insufficient teacher preparation. Since about 1966, however, the schools and textbook manufacturers have almost overcome the problem of inadequate materials. Inadequate teacher preparation is still a major issue. As colleges and universities increasingly offer black studies programs, we can expect that more and more teachers will have been exposed to these courses as part of their college education.

A number of state legislatures have signaled their support for minority group studies by passing laws requiring or recommending that they be included in the regular curriculum. Other states are trying to accomplish the same thing through policy statements issued by the state boards or departments of education.

If you are planning to teach history, literature, art, music, or economics, an understanding of black contributions in these areas would be highly valuable to your preparation as a teacher. In the years to come, America will depend heavily on its teachers to educate a new generation in an understanding and appreciation of cultural diversity.

RELIGION AND THE SCHOOLS

May public tax money be spent for the support of parochial schools?

What religious observances, if any, are permitted in public school classrooms?

May religious holidays be observed in public schools, and if so, which ones?

From what public school activities may an individual be excused for religious reasons?

May public school authorities rent or lease space to or from religious institutions for school purposes?

"Congress shall make no law respecting an establishment of religion, or prohibiting the free exercise thereof . . . ." During the past two centuries, the American judicial system has interpreted the First Amendment to the Constitution inconsistently with respect to religion and the public schools. The controversy surrounding this issue is not new; it has been a bone of contention since the beginning of public education in the United States. Where do we stand today?

Until the middle of the twentieth century, religious observances, including Bible reading and prayers, were common in the public schools. In fact, Bible reading and the recitation of the Lord's Prayer were required by the constitutions or by statutes in a number of states. In a 1963 decision, however, the Supreme Court ruled both unconstitutional. In an earlier decision, the Court had ruled against the recitation of a nondenominational prayer, holding that Bible reading and prayer violate both clauses of the First Amendment. The Court recognized that the schools did not compel a child to join in religious activities if his parents objected, but held that the social pressures exerted on pupils to participate were excessive. In essence, no distinction was felt to exist between voluntary and compulsory participation in religious activities.

The court did note in its decision that the study of comparative religion, the history of religion and the relationship of religion to civilization were not prohibited by this decision. It would also appear that, although the Bible may not be used to teach religion, it may, if objectively presented, be used in such areas of study as history, civics and literature.

In another recent case, the Supreme Court approved the right of public school pupils who so desire to say prayers and read scriptures of their choice in the morning before school starts or after the regular school day has terminated. If prayers are said during lunch period they must be silent. Needless to say, the Court has also ruled that direct religious instruction is not permitted in the public schools. Nor may public school teachers place religious pamphlets in schoolrooms.

A related issue is "released time." In a series of decisions, the Court ruled that a state could not allow teachers employed by specific denominations to conduct religion classes in public school buildings during the regular school day. However, the Court did rule constitutional a New York City program which permitted students to leave the school grounds during the school day to receive religious instruction elsewhere. Its reasoning was that the state must be neutral in regard to religion and, since no public funds were involved, the schools should cooperate with religious institutions by adjusting students' schedules.

The real controversy, however, centers around the use of public tax revenues to aid private and parochial schools. The Supreme Court has already ruled that public money can be used to provide textbooks to private school students; but what other kinds of aid can, or should, the public provide? This question is currently generating considerable heat, smoke, and even fire.

The major breakthrough for private and religious schools was the passage of the Elementary-Secondary Education Act of 1965, which funneled millions of dollars into parochial schools through federal programs. In addition, parochial schools in many states have been receiving assistance ranging from pupil transportation, textbooks, health services and general auxiliary services to salary supplements for teachers. In general, state assistance in areas other than transportation, milk, school lunch programs and textbooks is attacked in the courts. People oppose the use of tax money to support non-public or parochial schools for reasons ranging from outright prejudice to fear that such assistance will undermine the public school system. The National Education Association and the American Federation of Teachers have consistently opposed the allocation of public money to private schools on the grounds that the public schools are not adequately funded now and that the situation would worsen if tax money went to private schools.

The other side of the argument is that the private schools, which provide education for approximately six million students a year, are lightening the burden of the public schools. For financial reasons, many of these schools are being forced to close. If, for example, the Catholic school system should collapse, five million new students would enroll in the public schools, creating a massive shortage of space, teachers and money. Advocates of private school aid argue that, by partially subsidizing private schools to keep them in operation, the public schools can avoid a deluge of students whom they would be unable to assimilate readily. Some sources estimate that if the Catholic schools were shut down the public school system would cost an additional $4 billion a year to operate.

In his 1970 education message, President Nixon revealed that private schools are closing at the rate of one a day. He added: "This Government cannot be indifferent to the potential collapse of such private-parochial schools." None of the supporters of private school aid urges support for religious instruction; they do advocate state and federal aid for school lunches, buses, secular textbooks and the purchase of secular services.

ACCOUNTABILITY

Earlier in this chapter, we discussed the way in which the legal definition of equality changed from an emphasis on resources to a focus on *results*. A related development is the growing insistence by parents and other concerned adults that if children fail to learn in school how to read, write and perform computations, the school must be held accountable for their failures.

The accountability movement is insisting that the public schools can no longer measure success in terms of the number of dollars spent on each child's education, the teacher-pupil ratio or the educational level of the teachers. Advocates of accountability argue that these measures are at best indirect, and that the only real test of a school is its students' achievement of knowledge, skills and attitudes the school is attempting to teach. Only by looking at the results of students' schooling, they argue, can we ascertain the schools' worth.

Another source of support for accountability is primarily financial. As schools become increasingly expensive to operate, inflation erodes the buying power of the dollar and property taxes—which support much of public education—reach their tolerable limits, the public is demanding that the schools demonstrate what they are accomplishing. The public is no longer willing to vote for increased taxes until they see what they are getting for their money. In fiscal year 1969, the U.S. Office of Education reports, school bond issues were defeated at a record rate. The voters approved only 44 percent of the $3.9 billion requested. Ten years earlier, 80 percent of such bond issues were approved.[17]

Few would deny that the schools should be held accountable for their performance, but the definition and nature of accountability are matters of controversy. Should the schools be held accountable only for improvement in reading and arithmetic, skills which are easily measured? Or are the schools also responsible for the personal and humane outcomes of education, which are not so easily measured? If school personnel are held accountable only for improving easily-measurable skills, might they not neglect other equally important educational outcomes? In any given year, is the student's improvement in reading more important than strengthening his self-concept and his ability to work and play with other children? Clearly, there are no pat answers to these questions. Many public school personnel who support accountability in theory are concerned about how it might work in practice.

Who is to be held accountable for any given child's progress? the superintendent? the principal? the teacher? How reasonable is it, for example, to hold a given teacher accountable for the progress of her students if she is teaching in a dilapidated building, using books that are fifteen years out of date and trying to cope with 50 percent more children than should be there? How democratic would it be to allow teachers no control over the standards to which they are expected to perform?

While the notion of accountability is appealing to many people, several fundamental questions must be answered before it can be put into practice:

To what extent should teachers, principals, superintendents and the community itself be held responsible for results?

If school personnel are to be held accountable, to whom should they be answerable? the school board? the community? And how are results to be defined and measured?

How will each participant's contribution to a child's learning be determined and distinguished from that of other participants?

The issue of accountability is one of the most complicated problems facing education in the near future. One thing appears certain: even if specific accountability proposals are not adopted, the debate over its merits and drawbacks is bound to help school personnel think more precisely about their goals, methods and measures of achievement.

---

[17] Gallup, "Second Annual Survey," p. 100.

DISCUSSION QUESTIONS

1. Do you agree that equality of educational opportunity should be defined by its effects rather than its provisions? Can you think of an analogy to support your case for or against this position?
2. In view of compensatory education's lack of success at combating the problems of inequality in educational opportunity, why do you suppose it is so popular?
3. Why is it so difficult to integrate public schools?
4. How do you feel about our statement that total system reform alone will solve the problem of unequal educational opportunity? Do you envision yourself as active in that kind of reform movement?
5. Do you agree with our analysis of the causes of student unrest or with the solution we propose? Why or why not?
6. What do you see as the advantages and disadvantages of teachers' strikes, from the point of view of teachers and from that of parents and students? Over what issues would you be willing to strike? Would you jeopardize your job? Would you go to jail?
7. Where do you stand in the controversy over sex education in the schools? On what assumptions do you base your stand? Is the issue important enough to you to cause you to make your stance public, at the risk of community criticism?
8. What kind of drug educational program do you think would have been most appropriate in the high school you attended? (Pretend you are an outside consultant hired to make recommendations concerning drug use and drug education in your high school.)
9. Do you think minority studies should be offered as a separate course or integrated into the curriculum? What do you think will be the long- and short-range effects of minority studies on minorities and on the total society?
10. Where do you stand on the issue of public support for parochial schools? If your view prevails, what will be the effects on private education—and on society as a whole?
11. What do you, as a prospective teacher, feel is your responsibility concerning your students' performance? For what are you willing to be held accountable? skills acquired? facts remembered? personal growth? What factors would you insist on controlling before you accept responsibility? What dangers do you foresee?

FOR FURTHER READING

Black Studies

Henshel, A. M., and Henshel, R. L. "Black Studies Programs: Promise and Pitfalls." *Journal of Negro Education* 38 (Fall 1969): 423–429. Discusses the psychological and social implications of black studies programs.

Wilson, C. E. "The Case for Black Studies." *Educational Leadership* 27 (December 1969): 218–221. The author argues for black studies programs, citing a need for American culture to accept human difference without implying inferiority. An argument for cultural pluralism.

Decentralization and Community Control

Cohen, David. "The Price of Community Control." *Theory Into Practice* 8 (October 1969): 231–246. Cohen examines the arguments for decentralization and notes that, while some political peace may be obtained by decentralization, the fundamental ills of society which produced tensions will not thus be solved.

Cohen, S. Alan. "Local Control and the Cultural Deprivation Fallacy." *Phi Delta Kappan* 50 (January 1969): 255–259. An argument that local control is necessary in New York City because of the demonstrated failure of the present system.

Fantini, Mario D. "Participation, Decentralization and Community Control." *National Elementary School Principal* 48 (April 1969): 25–31. An argument for decentralization of control in large cities.

Shanker, Albert. "The Real Meaning of the New York City Teachers' Strike." *Phi Delta Kappan* 50 (April 1969): 434–441. An article expressing the union leader's point of view on the New York City teachers' strike.

Drug Education

Demos, George. "Drug Abuse and the New Generation." *Phi Delta Kappan* 50 (December 1968): 214–217. An argument for offering objective study of drugs as part of the curriculum.

Drug Abuse: Escape to Nowhere. Philadelphia: Smith, Kline & French Laboratories and National Education Association, 1967. Sponsored by a pharmaceutical company, this booklet offers suggestions to teachers on how to prepare for the drug problem in schools.

Fort, Joel. *The Pleasure Seekers.* Indianapolis: Bobbs-Merrill, 1969. Written by an M.D., this book is one of the better treatments of the topic.

Inequality of Educational Opportunity

Bowles, Samuel. "Towards Equality of Educational Opportunity?" *Harvard Educational Review* 38 (Winter 1968): 89–99. The author argues that a number of changes are necessary if equality of educational opportunity is to be achieved, including reallocation of funds for educating poor children and a redistribution of political power within our society.

Clark, Kenneth B. "Alternative Public School Systems." *Harvard Educational Review* 38 (Winter 1968): 100–113. Argues strongly for the need to find viable competitors to the present public schools.

Cohen, David K. "Policy for the Public Schools: Compensation and Integration." *Harvard Educational Review* 38 (Winter 1968): 114–137. The author argues that the sources of racial inequality in educational opportunity are deeply embedded in the social structures of cities and their school systems. The remedy, he suggests, lies in changing those structural features of urban education which produce and sustain inequity.

Coleman, James S., et al. *Equality of Educational Opportunity.* Washington, D.C.: U.S. Department of Health, Education, and Welfare, 1966. The major sociological study of the Sixties which examined the inequalities which exist in our educational system.

Levine, Daniel U. "Unequal Opportunities in the Large Inner-City High School." *National Association of Secondary School Principals Bulletin* 52 (November 1968): 46–55. Examines how students in large inner-city high schools are deprived of equal opportunities by the sheer size of the schools and the resultant conditions.

Religion

Duker, Sam. *The Public Schools and Religion: The Legal Context.* New York: Harper & Row, 1966. Examines the major controversies over the relationship of public schools and religion.

Peterson, LeRoy; Rossmiller, Richard A.; and Volz, Marlin M. "The Law, Religion, and Public Education." *School and Society* 96 (December 7–21, 1968): 466–471. Examines the major court decisions regarding religious issues and the public schools.

Sizer, Theodore, ed. *Religion and Public Schools.* Boston: Houghton Mifflin, 1967. A book of readings on religion and the public schools which presents different perspectives from a broad ideological spectrum.

Sex Education

Donaldson, J. L. "Innovative Programs in Sex Education." *The PTA Magazine* 64 (January 1970): 26–28. Reviews several sex education programs across the country and their major goals and methods.

Fehrle, Carl C. "The Natural Birth of Sex Education." *Educational Leadership* 27 (March 1970): 573–577. Looks at the need for sex education and argues for instilling attitudes as well as presenting information about the sex act and the development and birth of a baby.

Karmel, Louis J. "Sex Education No! Sex Information Yes!" *Phi Delta Kappan* 52 (October 1970): 95–96. Argues that the schools should provide information about sex, but not instill attitudes and values.

Weinstock, H. R. "Issues in Sex Education." *Educational Forum* 34 (January 1970): 189–196. The author states that the schools are the most qualified institution to teach sex education since the home, church, library and medical profession have demonstrated their inability to do so.

Student Power and Unrest

Brammer, Lawrence M. "The Coming Revolt of High School Students," *National Association of Secondary School Principals Bulletin* 52 (September 1968): 13–21. The author posits that much student rebellion is in reaction to oppressive rules imposed by the schools. He believes that the answer lies in delegating more power to students.

Gorton, Richard A. "Militant Student Activism in the High Schools: Analysis and Recommendations." *Phi Delta Kappan* 51 (June 1970): 545–549. Gorton sees the recent strikes in high schools as stemming from different causes. He makes recommendations to channel or ameliorate student unrest.

Nystrand, Raphael O., ed. *Student Unrest in Public Schools.* Worthington, Ohio: Charles A. Jones, 1969. A book of readings dealing with causes of student unrest in public schools.

Pileggi, Nicholas. "Revolutionaries Who Have to Be Home by 7:30." *Phi Delta Kappan* 50 (June 1969): 561–569. An article on student unrest, with several case studies and interviews of students.

Williams, Sylvia. *Hassling.* Boston: Little, Brown, 1970. An excellent case study of a suburban high school and its problems with student unrest. Also includes excellent chapters on high school drug problems and black power.

Teacher Power

Hendryson, Elizabeth S. "Parent Reaction to Teacher Power." *National Elementary Principal* 48 (January 1969): 14–20. A past president of the National Congress of Parents and Teachers voices her perceptions of parental reactions to displays of teacher power.

Norton, Gayle. "The Florida Story." *Phi Delta Kappan* 49 (June 1968): 555–560. A case study of the extensive statewide Florida teachers' strike of 1968.

Theory Into Practice 7 (April 1968). The whole issue is devoted to articles on teacher power.

FILMS

A Chance for Change (Contemporary/McGraw-Hill, 16mm, b&w, 39 min., 1965) Follows the classroom and playground activities of children in the Head Start program in Durant, Mississippi. The film also reveals how the efforts of parents were instrumental in bringing about the development of the Head Start center.

A Chance to Learn (NBC Educational Enterprises Code #006C1, 16mm, color, 17 min.) Daniel Moynihan and Charles Hamilton discuss some of the basic issues underlying the confrontations taking place in schools across the country: Who shall control the schools? Who shall decide who teaches in them? Who shall decide what is taught? The public school system in Rochester, New York, is used as an example.

Cloud 9 (EDC Film Library, 16mm, 25 min.) Documents the reactions of fifth-graders in the Cardozo Model School District in Washington, D.C., to the death of Martin Luther King.

Community Control (Boston Newsreel, 16mm, 50 min.) Documents the struggle of the black and Puerto Rican communities to control their own schools. The forces they are working against: the police who enforce the political decisions of the municipal bureaucracy and the teachers' union which is striking against the demands of the community.

The Frustrated Campus (Indiana University Audio-Visual Center, 16mm, b&w, 47 min.) This film, produced for NET, presents students, faculty and administrators of several universities as they debate some of the issues confronting higher education, i.e., infringement of others' rights by student militants and the university's role in solving social problems such as racism and war.

The Game (Mass Media Ministries, 16mm, b&w, 28 min., 1967) Explores the emotional conflicts which arise in sexual relations, from the viewpoint of a teenage boy. Few adults are seen or heard from and no moralizing mars the impact of viewing this personal event.

Grooving (Benchmark Films, 16 mm, color, 31 min., 1970) Produced for the New York State Narcotics Addiction Commission, this film is remarkably honest and reasonable. Although the message is clearly antidrug, it is presented through unscripted rap sessions about drugs among kids ranging in age from fourteen to eighteen.

Hear Us O Lord (Indiana University Audio-Visual Center, 16mm, b&w or color, 51 min., NET) School District 151 in Cook County, Illinois, was the first incorporated suburb in the United States to desegregate its schools by means of busing. The experimental programing division of NET wanted to present on film the responses of the community and spent a great deal of time with many of the families involved.

Hooked (Churchill Films, 16mm, b&w, 1966) A film which assumes that you have already read the statistics and heard the "lectures." There is no narration, no charts, no interviews with doctors or other professionals, no newsreels of arrests—just honest conversation with former drug addicts as they look back on their addiction.

Kenneth Keniston: This Student Generation: Conflict and Commitment Part II (APGA Film Sales, 16 mm, b&w, 35 min., 1968) An Associate Professor of Psychology at Yale and author of *Young Radicals* and *The Uncommitted,* Kenneth Keniston discusses "alienated" students, radicals, black militancy, violence and drug use on campus.

Marked For Failure (Indiana University Audio-Visual Center, 16mm, b&w, 59 min., NET) Focuses on the problems facing educators and children from depressed areas. A number of solutions are proposed and described through the use of documentary film footage.

AUDIOTAPES

Reading, Writing, . . . and Race (Center for the Study of Democratic Institutions, 3.75 ips, reel, ½ track, 39:52 min.) An interesting panel, including former Berkeley, California, superintendent Neil Sullivan, Senator Robert Kennedy, anthropologist Oscar Lewis and sociologist Kenneth Clark, discusses "How do we make the public schools function for our children? Integration or compensation? Money or commitment or more of each?"

Campus Unrest—What is it About? (Center for the Study of Democratic Institutions, 3.75 ips, reel, $\frac{1}{4}$ track, 44:25 min.) This tape was made at a three-day conference on Students and Society attended by twenty-two students from eighteen schools and colleges. The discussion revolves around the question, "Is reform of the university any longer possible?" There is no consensus among the students.

The End of Schooling: A Strategy for Revolt (Noumedia #7005, 3.75 ips, reel, $\frac{1}{4}$ track, mono or stereo, 1.5 hours, 1970) In the third of three lectures given at Yale University, Ivan Illich discusses possible solutions to the destructiveness and illusory goals of institutionalized schooling.

The 1970 Spring Crisis of Violence (Noumedia, 3.75 ips, reel, $\frac{1}{4}$ track, mono or stereo 1.3 hours, 1970) A public talk by Margaret Mead at Mountain High School, in West Orange, New Jersey, on the roots of the 1970 spring crisis of violence, the peculiar conditions of our time, an historical review of crisis, education and the need to listen. A dialogue evolves between Dr. Mead and the parents and students in the audience.

VIDEOTAPES

Political (Videofreex, $\frac{1}{2}$", Sony, Old and New Generation tapes) A videotape on political issues in high schools called "High School Confidential."

BIBLIOGRAPHY OF FILMS

99 Films on Drugs + (University of California, 38 pages, free) In response to the large number of 16mm films on drugs which have appeared recently, the Extension Media Center at the University of California, Berkeley, has assembled a comprehensive listing of drug film titles, including a description of the contents and a critical analysis of each film mentioned.

Refer to Appendix for distributors' addresses.

Photo by Paul Conklin.

Where Are Schools Going?

Same question: do these pictures make your own school experience look better or worse? How about the impersonality of teaching machines and the coldness of some modern architecture? The increasing creative and scientific opportunities and use of audiovisual aids?

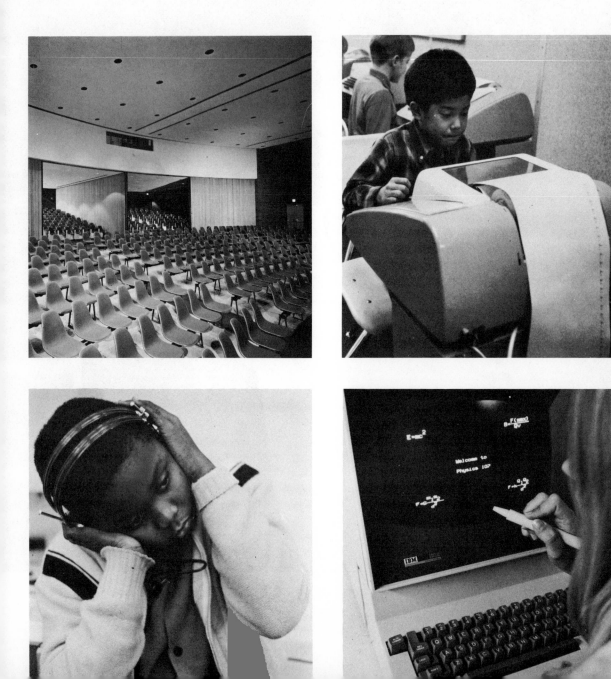

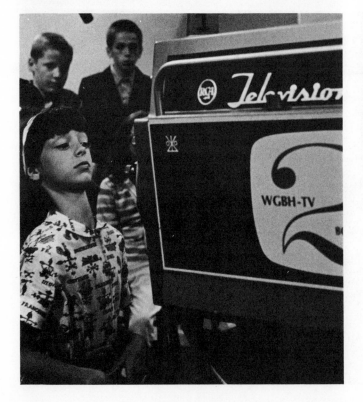

11 What's New in Education?

KEY POINTS

CLASSIFICATIONS
Horizontal and vertical advancement
Hierarchical and egalitarian leadership
Vertical and horizontal differentiation
Linear and branching programming

STUDIES
Brody's study of achievement in graded and nongraded programs

CONCEPTS
Uniqueness of individual learning rates and styles
Differentiation
Stimulus-response
Behavioral objectives
Architectural authoritarianism

CHAPTER CONTENTS

ORGANIZATIONAL INNOVATIONS
Nongraded schools
Team teaching
Differentiated staffing
Flexible scheduling
Middle schools

Competitive education and accountability
Performance contracting

INSTRUCTIONAL INNOVATIONS
Programmed instruction
Computer-Assisted Instruction (CAI)
Individually Prescribed Instruction (IPI)
The open classroom

INNOVATIONS IN SCHOOL DESIGN
Schools without walls
Individualized learning and school facilities

Education, as we have seen, is a fairly stable institution. How will it prepare people to face an unstable world—one which sometimes seems to be spinning apart or falling apart, or even blowing itself apart? Will we become victims of "future shock," unable to cope with rapid change and information overload?

Can existing educational institutions prepare youngsters for this new world? Does education itself offer sufficient diversity in response to this changing world? And if educators don't meet this challenge, what will be the result? Some would agree with Peter Drucker, who considers education too important to be left to educators who ". . . still talk of minor changes, or adjustments and improvements. Few of them see much reason for radical changes. Yet education will in all likelihood be transformed within the next decade *by giant forces from without.*"[1] Others predict that if education doesn't change sufficiently, people will seek alternatives outside the system; they will either create their own schools or entirely reject the validity of schools. In a sense, the institution of education is like a car. Despite frequent lubrication and constant maintenance, worn-out parts must be replaced; eventually it might become necessary to abandon the model entirely and shop for a new set of wheels.

Educators are now working on replacing the worn-out parts, and better communications systems are spreading new ideas more rapidly than ever

---

[1] Peter Drucker, *The Age of Discontinuity* (New York: Harper and Row, 1969), p. 334.

We must understand that a totally new society is coming into being, one that rejects all our old values, conditioned responses, attitudes and institutions. Marshall McLuhan.

before. But none of these new ideas represents *the* answer. The only adequate response to diversity is continuously to reflect it in action. We need to guard against letting our innovations become as inflexible and embedded in tradition as the methods they have replaced.

Innovations are rarely isolated in their effect. A new educational movement which deals principally with a reorganization of school staffing is sure to affect curriculum and instruction as well. It is very rare that a new procedure is simply "tacked on" to one area of a system without affecting its other parts or the system as a whole. Considering nongraded schools without simultaneously examining curriculum and teacher instruction is futile. In a sense, then, any innovation is as "instructional" as it is "organizational," or vice versa.

New ideas in education reflect a growing concern with individualization of instruction; students themselves are diverse, and attempts to reach them must involve a recognition that they learn at different rates and through different modes of instruction. When you read or hear about a specific proposal or innovations—or if you have the opportunity to implement change in the classroom—ask yourself how it can improve the quality of the individual student's learning situation.

ORGANIZATIONAL INNOVATIONS

NONGRADED SCHOOLS

Do you remember descriptions of the old one-room country schoolhouse? Students ranging in age from five to fourteen or fifteen were all taught by the same teacher in the same room, each studying material appropriate to his own learning level? We normally think of this scene as pretty old-fashioned. In many respects it is, but one aspect of it is extremely modern: the nongraded character of the school. Grade levels made no sense in a one-room schoolhouse because there was no way to separate the students accordingly. In effect, the teacher was forced to treat each student differently; each was at a different level of achievement in reading, 'riting and 'rithmetic. Grouping of the students made sense only when several were at the same level of achievement for a particular learning task.

Schools in America were ordinarily ungraded until 1848, when the Quincy Grammar School in Boston introduced graded levels. By 1860 the graded system had been widely adopted, especially in the cities, and was rapidly becoming standard practice in elementary schools.

Although graded classes were originally advocated as a means of individualizing instruction, it eventually became apparent that in practice this was not the case. As Joseph Shea says:

The graded school did not markedly alter the lock-step teaching of the monitorial school which preceded it. Instead, by specifying precisely what was to be covered each day in each subject area and by rigidly adhering to the textbook presentation a program resulted which was sterile, uninteresting and forbidding for all of the pupils. Moreover, those who could not attain the predetermined levels of mastery were

"I'M IN THE NON-GRADED THIRD GRADE."

Cartoon by Short and Weaver.

doomed to failure and the unhappy prospects of retardation and non-promotion. Lock-step teaching can best be described as everyone doing the same thing, in the same way, at the same time. Soon this regimen became the model style for elementary teachers.[2]

One of the characteristics of the grade-level system is that for each level and subject there is a standard curriculum which is taught to each child. This practice assumes that there is such a thing as fifth-grade social studies," or "third-grade science." In other words, the grade-level system operates on the premise that all children within a certain age group should have mastered a certain body of knowledge and set of skills by the end of a school year. If a student is able to exceed these institutional expectations, he is said to be working "above grade level"; if he cannot meet official expectations he is said to be "below grade level" in that particular skill.

The grade-level system is an organizational convenience which allows the biological, psychological and physiological differences among children to be ignored. That students at any given age level possess individual differences which influence both their ability to learn and their rate of learning has been common knowledge for many years. But teachers and administrators have persisted in organizing the public schools according to age level and a lock-step curriculum.

A number of educators have recently advocated the establishment (or reestablishment) of nongraded schools as a way of forcing schools and teachers to treat students as individuals. John I. Goodlad and Robert H. Anderson point out that the nongraded school is designed to allow continuous pupil progress. By abolishing grade barriers, each child, whatever his ability, is enabled to move forward in his learning as rapidly and smoothly as possible.[3] Thus, in a nongraded school some pupils will require a longer period of time than others to achieve certain kinds of understanding or attain certain developmental levels.

Goodlad and Anderson note that the realities of child development defy the rigorous ordering of children's abilities into a conventionally graded structure. Children entering first grade, for example, may differ in mental age by as much as four full years. Thus, to reach most children, work levels must be aimed for two years below grade expectancies as well as for two years above. This spread of mental age increases as the children advance through the various grade levels. Grouping by grade level, which in essence amounts to grouping by age level, thus makes little sense educationally. Teachers are asked, first, to ignore the emotional and intellectual differences that exist among children at any given age level, and, second, to act

---

[2] Joseph Shea, "Organizational Patterns for the Elementary School," in *The Elementary School— Principles and Problems,* ed. Joe Frost and G. Thomas Rowland (Boston: Houghton Mifflin, 1969), p. 310.

[3] John I. Goodlad and Robert H. Anderson, *The Nongraded Elementary School* (New York: Harcourt, Brace & World, 1963), p. 21.

as if there were objectively such a thing as fifth-grade social studies, which all fifth-graders could be expected to master.

The pupil in a nongraded school is encouraged to progress in the various aspects of his development at rates appropriate to his own unique traits. As Goodlad and Anderson say, "The job of elementary education is not to convert the low horsepower child into a high horsepower machine, nor is it to promote senseless races between the two. The real job is to keep both tuned and operating at top level efficiency and then to clear the road blocks so that each may proceed at his unique and appropriate pace."[4]

Another argument against the grade-level system is the fear of failure which it generates. At the end of each year in the traditional system, the teacher must decide whether to promote each student to the next grade. Students who are not promoted bear the stigma of failure in the eyes of parents, peers, teachers and, more importantly, themselves. Children who experience such failure feel degraded or inferior—they are made to believe there is something wrong with them. In fact, they may be unable to keep up with the pace set for the rest of class, but perfectly capable of learning all the material if allowed to work at their own pace. In a nongraded school, the question of promotion or failure never comes up. Instead, each student moves through the curriculum as rapidly as he is able, with each member of the class likely to be at a different point at any given time.

Goodlad and Anderson's comparison of graded and nongraded structures will help highlight some of the differences between the two systems.[5]

Graded Structure	*Nongraded Structure*
A year of progress in subject matter is roughly comparable with a child's year in school.	A year of school life may mean much more or much less than a year of progress in subject matter.
Each successive year of progress is comparable to each past year or each year to come.	Progress is irregular; a child may progress much more rapidly in one year and quite slowly in another.
A child's progress is unified: advancing in rather regular fashion in all areas of development; probably working close to grade level in most subject areas.	A child's progress is not unified. He spurts ahead in one area of progress and lags behind in others; may be working at three or four levels in as many subjects.
Specific bodies of content are appropriate for successive grade levels and so labeled; subject matter packaged grade by grade.	Bodies of content are appropriate over a wide span of years. Learning viewed vertically or longitudinally rather than horizontally.

[4] *Ibid.*, pp. 28–29.

[5] *Ibid.*, pp. 58–59.

Adequacy of progress determined by comparing child's attainment to coverage deemed appropriate to the grade.	Adequacy of progress determined by comparing child's attainment to his ability and both to long-term view of ultimate accomplishment desired.
Inadequate progress made up by repeating the work of a given grade: grade failure the ultimate penalty for slow progress.	Slow progress provided for by permitting longer time to do given blocks of work; no repetitions but recognition of basic differences in learning rate.
Rapid progress provided for through enrichment: encouragement of horizontal expansion rather than vertical advancement in work; attempt to avoid moving to domain of teacher above.	Rapid progress provided for both vertically and horizontally: bright children encouraged to move ahead regardless of the grade label of the work; no fear of encroaching on work of next teacher.
Rather inflexible grade-to-grade movement of pupils, usually at end of year.	Flexible pupil movement; pupil may shift to another class at almost any time: some trend toward controlling shifts on a quarter or semester basis.

How successful are nongraded schools? Are they really working? Do students learn better in a nongraded system than a graded one? These are legitimate questions but, unfortunately, clearcut answers are not yet available. Individual nongraded schools are so different in aim and organization that it is extremely difficult to generalize about nongradedness as a whole. Furthermore, it is very difficult to prove a direct relationship between broad organizational changes and changes in pupil achievement.

A number of attempts have been made to ascertain how nongradedness affects pupil learnings, but the results are mixed. In most of these studies, nongraded students performed as well as or better than students in graded classrooms on standardized achievement measures. One study involved 362 boys and girls in their first and second years at two nongraded public elementary schools in Pennsylvania, and 241 students in the first and second grades of a graded school in the same school system.[6] The nongraded pupils achieved higher mean scores on all five subtests of the Stanford Achievement Test: paragraph meaning, word meaning, spelling, arithmetic reasoning and arithmetic computation. The results indicate that, after one year in the program, pupils of low ability benefit most from nongrading. However, after two years in the nongraded program the reverse is true, pupils of high ability benefiting more than those with low ability. The in-

---

[6] Ernest Brody, "Achievement of First and Second Year Pupils in Graded and Nongraded Classrooms," *Elementary School Journal* 70 (April 1970): 391–394.

DIALOGUE

Kevin: As far as I'm concerned, the nongraded approach to school organization is definitely superior to a graded approach.

Jim: I feel the same way, but I'd be interested in your reasons.

Kevin: I think we let time influence the curriculum far more than it should. If we're really interested in helping students acquire new knowledge, skills and attitudes, we should organize our curriculum so they can achieve mastery rather than automatically promoting them to a higher grade level that assumes prior knowledge and skills which they may or may not have actually acquired.

Jim: In other words, you think that if we arranged the curriculum so students could spend as long as they need to master basic skills and knowledge, we wouldn't have so many high school students who can barely read or perform simple arithmetic.

Kevin: Right. But nongradedness by itself won't do the job. We'd need new curricular materials that allow students to work at their own pace; teachers would have to change their style from teaching to groups to working more with individuals, and generally, a new philosophical approach to learning and instruction would have to be adopted by many teachers.

vestigator comments that the results of this study accord with those of previously-reported studies comparing achievement in nongraded and graded programs. Pupils in nongraded schools usually, but not invariably, perform better on standardized tests.

The popularity of the nongraded approach is increasing rapidly, particularly at the early elementary school level. Anderson reports that by 1967 approximately one school system in four was experimenting with nongradedness.[7] In a 1966–67 survey of elementary principals conducted by the Department of Elementary School Principals of the National Education Association, 55.4 percent of those principals who had used a nongraded plan in the primary (K-3) grades rated it as very valuable, while 5.6 percent considered it of no value and 39.1 percent were not sure of its value. Of those who had used a nongraded plan in the upper (4–6) grades, 35.6 percent rated it as very valuable, 9.0 percent as of no value and 55.3 percent were not sure of its value.[8] Although its popularity is greatest at the elemen-

---

[7] Robert H. Anderson, "The Nongraded School: An Overview," *National Elementary Principal* 47 (November 1967): 7.

[8] "Nongraded Schools—Some Findings," *National Elementary Principal* 47 (November 1967): 10.

442   *THE REAL WORLD*

tary level, there is no reason why the concept should not be applicable to the secondary school, though problems will occur because of the entrenchment of particular courses of study at certain grade levels.

School systems currently experimenting with nongraded schools are finding curricular reform and teacher education activities necessary. The existing curriculum was developed for incremental grade levels, not for longitudinal organization spanning several years. Goodlad and Anderson confront this problem by visualizing a nongraded curriculum which allows for continuous pupil progress from kindergarten through college, with each learner proceeding at a different rate of speed along various curriculum threads running the entire length of the school's program.

Nongraded schools are designed to individualize instruction and treat each child's learning as unique. But in many instances these modifications haven't had the desired results. As long as teachers are forced to teach students in groups, the quicker will be held up by the slower, different levels of readiness will have to be accommodated and instruction cannot be truly individualized. Lack of appropriate materials has been a basic problem; another is a shortage of sufficient personnel to allow students to be working on different tasks at different times. Group instruction should be utilized only when it is the form of instruction most beneficial for the students. Until teachers are able to treat students as individuals with unique learning rates and styles, and until they receive support through training and appropriate materials, individualized instruction will remain largely a myth.

Fortunately, a number of other instructional and organizational processes are currently being tested in an attempt to personalize instruction. Let's look now at one designed to maximize staff utilization in order to provide for more effective instruction—team teaching.

TEAM TEACHING

At some time during your public school education you were probably exposed to team teaching. It is not a new idea, but still merits discussion because of its potential. Basically, team teaching is an organizational arrangement allowing a group of teachers, possibly including interns and teacher aides, to assume reponsibility for planning, executing and evaluating the instructional program for a group of students. Its major aim is to improve the quality of instruction and to individualize it by making possible more flexible arrangements of staff, time and curriculum. Team teaching is an attempt to abandon the self-contained classroom, in which the teacher shares responsibility with no one and has minimal communication with other adults about curriculum and instruction. The teachers on a team jointly diagnose student difficulties, plan and carry out instructional processes and share insights about students and their learning problems.

The team teaching approach makes a number of assumptions about students, teachers, administrators and learning. Initially, it assumes that increased learning can result if teachers pool their strengths and areas of expertise. For example, if one teacher is particularly effective at leading small group discussions, it is more sensible to allow many students to benefit from that teacher's expertise than either to make each teacher a discussion leader regardless of competence, or, alternatively, to forego small groups because of teacher reluctance.

For team teaching to work effectively, the school administration must cooperate in dealing with scheduling and evaluation needs. Team teaching requires sufficient flexibility in the schedule to permit dividing students into large and small groups, as well as allotting time for both individual student instruction and teacher preparation. The standard forty-five to fifty-minute class schedule severely inhibits such flexibility. Thus, if the school administration does not support and encourage team teaching efforts, the success of the venture is doubtful.

Teachers' inability to work together in harmony has been one of the main causes of the failure of team teaching experiments in some schools. Teachers who have taught for years in self-contained classrooms often have difficulty adjusting to an approach which requires them to cooperate with other teachers in planning objectives, designing learning experiences and evaluating the program. Many teachers are insecure in their teaching methods and hence reluctant to perform in front of their peers. Fears, insecurities and apparent jealousies have made team teaching less than successful in some settings. One survey indicates that, among twenty-seven different innovations, team teaching had the fourth highest abandonment rate. Slightly over 4 percent of all secondary schools that had at one time attempted team teaching later abandoned it.[9]

Because of the difficulties encountered in implementing team teaching, studies have been made to facilitate its effectiveness. Robert H. Anderson has listed a number of criteria for an ideal team teaching program, all founded on the principle of sharing; successful team teaching requires full participation by all team members in formulating objectives, planning, sharing ideas and instructional techniques and evaluation. Involvement and openness to evaluation of one another's teaching are essential in each team member.[10]

One of the most unfortunate characteristics of the self-contained classroom is that when the classroom door closes behind the teacher, his authority and instruction are virtually unquestioned. If another teacher should ask to observe their teaching, most teachers would probably feel threatened by the implied comparison with other teachers. But even teachers who feel secure in their teaching techniques are unaccustomed to being observed and feel threatened by another adult in the classroom. A doctor who hesi-

[9] James Meyer, "Salvaging Team Teaching," *The Clearing House* 44 (December 1969): 203–205.

[10] Robert H. Anderson, *Teaching in a World of Change* (New York: Harcourt, Brace & World, 1966), pp. 91–92.

tated to consult others for a diagnosis or felt threatened by observation or evaluations would not be respected or tolerated in the medical profession. Yet self-contained classroom organization encourages isolationist teacher behavior and often protects grossly incompetent teachers. Education can simply no longer afford to shelter its incompetents. We need to make teaching an open process, one which encourages evaluation and seeks what is best for the student, rather than the teacher. One of the most worthwhile objectives of a school is open and sustained communication among the staff, and team teaching is a deliberate attempt to achieve just that. It also provides a unique opportunity for teachers to share news and impressions of the students, thereby fostering the development of each child.

Despite the difficulties inherent in team teaching, a number of arguments in its favor have been advanced by educators. One advocate, Bruce Joyce, proposes that teachers need a rich laboratory of books, audiovisual media and other technological resources so that they can create at least three basic types of learning situations.[11] One is *personal inquiry,* in which the child pursues his own interests. To facilitate this, the student should meet several times each week with a teacher who functions as his academic counselor, personal guide and friend. In *independent study,* the student uses materials geared to his development to teach himself the skills and knowledge his teachers think are important to him. Teachers in this situation function as diagnosticians and prescribers. *Group inquiry* allows the student and his peers to develop study problems which are important to them and appear significant to the teacher. Joyce recommends that part of each child's day be spent working in a small group of five to ten students. The child would also join a large group for lectures and films.

To make these varied learning situations possible, Joyce advocates an instructional team and support centers. The instructional team would be composed of a leader, assistant leader, teachers and paraprofessionals. The flexibility provided by the instructional team and the learning support centers would allow the child to lead a balanced life as a learner.

There are several other significant arguments for the team teaching approach. The majority of teachers in the United States are females, especially in elementary schools. Evidence indicates, however, that young boys need male roles models with whom they can identify. Team teaching would allow more than the usual thirty students to benefit from contact with a male teacher.

Also, teachers working with one another on a team serve as models of adult-to-adult interaction for the students. The way teachers work together should provide the students excellent examples of cooperation.

Team teaching also encourages more child-to-adult interaction. It is important for a child to learn to interact with many different adult personalities.

---

[11] Bruce Joyce, *The Teacher and His Staff: Man, Media, and Machines* (Washington, D.C.: National Commission on Teacher Education and Professional Standards, NEA, 1967), p. 7.

If a child and a teacher do not hit it off in a self-contained classroom, there is no recourse for either one. The flexibility of the team approach allows both child and teacher more interpersonal contacts, and thus less chance for severe personality conflict.

Team teaching offers abundant possibilities for improving classroom instruction. Its success depends on cooperative relationships among team members, but in those cases where the conditions are right, the personalities compatible and the administration supportive, a team approach to instruction can be much more rewarding to both teachers and students. At the present time there is inconclusive evidence that a team teaching approach does, in fact, result in increased pupil learning. As with the nongraded system, team teaching is such a massive organizational arrangement that it is very difficult to prove that it is directly responsible for any increase or decrease in pupil learning. Also, team teaching takes so many different forms—hierarchical team leadership, egalitarian leadership, use of paraprofessional help on some teams and not on others, interdisciplinary teams, teams from the same subject matter area—that evaluating it can be like comparing apples and oranges. Studies show that the numerous variables in team teaching make it currently impossible to conclude that it is any more effective than the self-contained classroom approach.

DIFFERENTIATED STAFFING

"A teacher is a teacher is a teacher—a sum of interchangeable parts."

"A teacher with twenty years experience does essentially the same job as a beginning teacher, and that's what a beginning teacher can look forward to."

"Teachers are rewarded for endurance, not competence."

"A beginning teacher, the experienced professional, and the tired old war horse have the same responsibility—thirty students to a class, five classes a day—regardless of their competencies."

"There is no such thing as a career in teaching because there are no promotions except away from children."

"If a male teacher wants to support his family adequately he must either moonlight on another job or leave teaching for administration or another field altogether."

These charges by prominent educators have prompted a rethinking of the teacher's role in the public schools. What we need, according to the proponents of differentiated staffing, is a way of keeping good teachers in the classroom, increasing their responsibilities and decision-making power, paying them salaries as great as or greater than those of principals and more effectively utilizing the school staff. This could be done, they argue, by differentiating the functions performed in the school. Differentiated staffing

THE REAL WORLD

implies subdividing the all-encompassing role of the teacher into several professional and paraprofessional subroles, in keeping with the specific tasks required by the schools and the talents and strengths represented in the human resources of any given school community. Staff differentiation requires concurrent changes in scheduling, curriculum, decision-making power and individualization of instruction; without them staff differentiation is ineffective.

There are many explanations for the current interest in staff differentiation. First, there is increasing recognition that a single teacher cannot adequately perform all of the necessary classroom tasks.

Second, the financial crisis facing many school districts has led many taxpayers to conclude that all teachers should not be paid equally regardless of their degree of competence. Most school districts employ a salary schedule which provides for a teacher to receive additional remuneration for each year of teaching, up to a limit, and for additional graduate work, also to a limit, usually between sixty and ninety semester hours beyond the B.A. Taxpayers are becoming reluctant to pay two teachers equally simply because both have been employed for the same amount of time and have amassed the same number of graduate credits; one may be an excellent teacher and the other mediocre. In some systems, merit pay is awarded to particularly good teachers. The difficulty with merit pay is that it differentiates among teachers who are doing essentially similar jobs. Rewards are bestowed as a result of someone's subjective judgments, whereas a differentiated staffing plan remunerates teachers according to their performance of different functions at very different levels of responsibility. Because differentiated staffing offers an alternative to automatic raises of all teachers' salaries, regardless of competence or function, it is also of interest to a growing number of school boards.

Third, many educators see the traditional classroom organization as antiquated, since it does not recognize individual differences among students or teachers. The stultifying atmosphere of the self-contained classroom is probably responsible for the decisions of many potential career teachers to go into administration or to leave education entirely. Differentiated staffing is an alternative to the irrational system which forces out of the classroom talented teachers who want to earn more money.

Fourth, as teacher militants have pressed for more real authority in the governance of schools, differentiated staffing plans have incorporated the concept of greater teacher decision-making power. As teachers become more professional, some of them start making more money than many principals and all are relieved of certain menial tasks, the image and status of teaching is bound to be enhanced. Allowing the most qualified person—in many cases the teacher—to make decisions will also result in an upgrading of the teacher's role.

There are potentially as many varieties of differentiated staffs as there are imaginations to invent them. Like different types of team teaching, some will work well and others will not. Differentiated staffing cannot be judged generically; only specific models can be evaluated. To understand more clearly the concept of differentiated staffing, let's examine one version which is presently being implemented in Temple City, California.

The Temple City model differentiates teachers both vertically and horizontally (see Table 11.1). The horizontal differentiation is along subject matter lines, while the vertical axis represents a hierarchy of teachers, accompanied by variation in pay, status and authority. This hierarchy is composed of four professional levels—associate teacher, staff teacher, senior teacher and master teacher. All of the personnel must teach, and teaching is organized on a flexible schedule permitting increased student contact. Classroom teaching duties vary from 100 percent for associate and staff teachers to 60 percent for senior teachers and 40 percent for master teachers.

An associate teacher conducts large or small group instruction in his area of expertise, is a member of a teaching team and is responsible for the application of staff and senior teacher-developed curriculum units. The beginning teacher is not expected to function like an experienced and tenured staff teacher. He is not assigned markedly diverse pupils, and his workload is not as great as are those of staff teachers.

The staff teacher is the backbone of the instructional team. He is assigned more diverse pupils, and is expected to function well within varying instructional modes (large group, small group, individualized instruction). The staff teacher participates more deeply in the development of curriculum and the professional evaluation process. Staff teachers generally are experienced teachers who do not desire additional responsibilities.

Table 11.1   *Temple City differentiated staffing plan 1969–71*

POSITION	REQUIREMENTS	TENURE	RESPONSIBILITIES	WORK PERIOD	SALARY
master teacher	doctorate or equivalent expertise	no	40% staff teaching responsibilities	12 months	$15,646–25,000
senior teacher	M.A. or equivalent expertise	no	60% staff teaching responsibilities	10–11 months	$14,500–17,500
staff teacher	B.A. and California credential	yes	100% teaching responsibilities	10 months	$7,500–11,000
associate teacher	B.A. or intern	yes	100% teaching responsibilities	10 months	$6,500–9,000

The senior teacher's role represents a major break with the traditional functions and responsibilities of the teacher. His responsibilities extend into curriculum development, colleague evaluation, instructional specialization and increased coordination and responsibility for what students collectively learn in his area of expertise. In the Temple City model the senior teacher is also a member of the Academic Senate, the decision-making body for the school. The senior teacher is selected and evaluated by associate and staff teachers, and has tenure as a member of the staff but not as a senior teacher. A senior teacher continues to occupy that role only as long as his colleagues are satisfied with his performance and vote him these responsibilities.

The senior teacher is primarily responsible for implementing and adapting curricular innovations to the classroom. He is considered the master practitioner in his area and is knowledgeable about recent developments in teaching. He conducts in-service workshops for teachers in exemplary techniques and methods in subject or skill areas. He is also responsible for the assignment of student teachers.

The master teacher's title is misleading, for in the Temple City model it does not designate the teacher *par excellence,* but the teacher who has the broadest range of responsibilities directly connected to classroom teaching. The master teacher is the key to the school's "self-renewal": he is responsible for maintaining the vitality and pertinence of subject matter content, form and related teaching strategies to each area of the curriculum. He must be an expert in his subject matter, and is also responsible for initiating research programs of purely local interest, which may entail forming liaisons with universities, research centers, industry and business. He works with senior and staff teachers to determine the school program, schedule, utilization of resources, educational objectives and organization of new courses.

The role of the principal has changed as a result of the changes in teacher responsibilities and decision-making power. The principal is now viewed as a human relations manager—skilled in group dynamics, sensitivity and human engineering—rather than an administrator of paper and pencils. Nonacademic administrative duties are assigned to a school manager, whose role is completely subordinate to the instructional program. Detailed job descriptions have been written for each of these different roles so that the criteria for performance are clearly understood.

It is anticipated that by 1972–73 the staffing pattern in Temple City will be distributed thus: master teacher, four positions; senior teacher, twenty positions; staff teacher, eighty-five positions; associate teacher, sixty-six positions. In addition, there will be a number of instructional aides and clerks.

Many school districts are experimenting with other types of differentiated staffing. The U.S. Office of Education has funded a number of districts to develop different ways of utilizing school personnel; many are moving toward a differentiated staffing pattern. Florida, for example, has set up pilot programs in three different counties. There is opposition to the concept, however, particularly from teacher organizations and unions. One argument against differentiated staffing is that the establishment of a teacher hierarchy will weaken teacher solidarity and prevent collective bargaining. Some fear that teachers may become even less involved with students, while others say that the establishment of a hierarchy will create a new elite in teaching. Others argue that hierarchical organization is still too much like merit pay (which has been almost universally rejected by teacher organizations), and that it provides a legal means to use "unqualified personnel" at reduced salaries in an effort to economize on personnel costs. Rather than encouraging a spirit of cooperation among equals, they predict that it would foster rivalry among teachers as they compete for the more highly-paid positions.

Some of these objections are certainly valid and deserve consideration. Others, however, appear to be attempts to stifle reforms which might make teaching a well-paid career and at the same time improve instruction. It appears to us that efforts to raise teachers' salaries regardless of competence will meet increased opposition from overtaxed property-owners. If teacher organizations insist that all teachers be compensated strictly on the basis of experience and academic credit, they may be opposed by determined taxpayers who refuse to reward bad teachers and demand that alternatives be found. Perhaps teachers should start looking at alternatives before confrontations occur.

Differentiated staffing is still largely untested. There are many undeveloped models yet to be tested, and we hope that such a promising idea will be given a chance to succeed before being rejected.

FLEXIBLE SCHEDULING

Most young people feel that our institutions have become ossified. High schools, typified by excessively rigid schedules, are certainly no exception. While we can't hope to eradicate all the regimentation in mass society, it has been suggested that computers can be used to eliminate some of the rigidity of high school scheduling.

No matter what part of the country you visit, traditional high school schedules are the same. North, south, east or west, you'll find a standard system of units and credits, a schedule which requires every course to meet the same amount of time every day and the same number of days every week, a high level of control over students whose time is accounted for in formal classes and instructional activities limited to what the teacher can accomplish in one class period.

Advocates of flexible scheduling argue that the traditional school schedule is designed more for administrative convenience than for instructional benefit. It is much easier to schedule all subjects as if they were equal and to require each student to spend an equal amount of time mastering each course than to admit that proper instruction in different subjects may vary in time and in instructional mode. For these reasons advocates of flexible scheduling feel that a better instructional program would result if the traditional schedule were discarded.

Flexible scheduling is based on several assumptions about instruction and learning. First, in each subject area several groups of students can be identified whose needs are sufficiently distinct to require discrete programs of study. Second, most subjects, when properly taught, involve four types of instruction—independent and individual study, small-group instruction and discussion, laboratory instruction and large-group instruction. Third, class size, length of class meeting and the spacing of classes should vary accord-

"HOW'S THE FLEXIBLE SCHEDULING COMING ALONG?"

Cartoon by Short and Weaver.

ing to the nature of the subject, the type of instruction and the level of ability and interest of pupils. Fourth, students should not be restricted to formal classes or study halls for all of their learning experiences. And, finally, modern data processing equipment and high speed computers can be used to implement a high degree of schedule flexibility in order to provide for more individualized instruction and a better use of latent staff talent. These assumptions are the basis on which a new system of flexible scheduling is constructed.

To design a flexible or modular schedule for a particular school, the curriculum of the school is perceived as a totality composed of subparts, called modular units, which correspond to units of time. The modular unit should be the smallest amount of time which, when combined with other modular units, will form the varying period lengths desired for all instructional purposes. In other words, if classes of 40, 60 and 120 minutes are desired, a 20-minute module would be appropriate. The smaller the modular unit, the greater the flexibility and the complexity of scheduling. When the curriculum is considered a function of the time available, rather than vice versa, it is easier to consider altering the portion of time allocated to any one course. Some courses may meet for ten modules a week, some for sixteen and some for three. Table 11.2 is a model of a teacher's schedule on a 30-minute module system.

The flexible schedule not only allows the student a greater variety of learning experiences but also gives the teacher freedom to vary his mode of instruction. Within a traditional schedule, a biology teacher would teach five periods of biology a day, five days a week. The total amount of time any student spent on biology, assuming each class period to be 50 minutes long, would be 250 minutes per week. Because laboratory experience is an integral part of biology, the teacher would incorporate laboratory work into the class schedule. However, allowing time to set up the equipment, and afterward to clean up and put it away, there would remain only 15–30 minutes for actual laboratory work. The teacher is thus limited in the type of experiences he can offer his students.

With flexible scheduling, the same biology teacher could plan for a longer laboratory session. If the school had selected a time module of 20 minutes, the teacher could request a laboratory period of five modules, or 100 minutes, to be incorporated into the schedule. The teacher might also decide that he wanted to meet all of his students in a group once a week to give a demonstration, show a film or deliver a lecture. He might decide to schedule this large-group activity for two modules, or 40 minutes. The rest of the students' time might be scheduled for individual study and assignment, with the teacher available to meet individually with students who have questions. The amount of time allocated for such independent study might be five modules, or 100 minutes, for each student. The schedule of each student taking biology would then consist of five consecutive modules of laboratory work, two modules of large-group instruction and five modules of independent work, for a total of 240 minutes a week.

TIME	MONDAY	TUESDAY	WEDNESDAY	THURSDAY	FRIDAY
8:30	World History (Assembly Group)	World History (Assembly Group)	World History (Assembly Group)	World History (Assembly Group)	Instructional Materials Center Consultation
9:00	Planning	Planning	Planning	Planning	
9:30					World History (Inquiry Gr. Seminar A)
10:00	World History (Inquiry Group A)	Instructional Materials Center Consultation	World History (Inquiry Group A)	Instructional Materials Center Consultation	
10:30					
11:00	World History (Inquiry Group B)		World History (Inquiry Group B)		
11:30					Planning
12:00	Team Meeting	Special Projects	Special Projects	Team Meeting	
12:30	L	U	N	C	H
1:00	World History (Inquiry Group C)	Planning	World History (Inquiry Group C)	Planning	World History (Inquiry Gr. Seminar B)
1:30					
2:00	World History (Inquiry Group D)	World History (Inquiry Group E)	World History (Inquiry Group D)	World History (Inquiry Group E)	
2:30					
3:00	Planning	World History (Inquiry Group F)	Planning	World History (Inquiry Group F)	Planning
3:30					

Table 11.2 *A tenth-grade world history teacher's schedule with IndiFlexS. This teacher is responsible for the assembly-group instruction and serves as the teaching team chairman.*

From *Flexible Scheduling* by Donald C. Manlove and David W. Beggs. Copyright © 1965 by Indiana University Press. Reprinted by permission of the publisher.

A perfect schedule would be one in which each teacher's wishes were fulfilled and students had no scheduling conflicts. Unfortunately, this rarely if ever happens. The schedule usually represents a compromise, and is the result of several computer trial runs.

Evaluation of flexible scheduling is very difficult because of the huge variety of schools attempting it, the difference in educational organizations which schedule schools and the types of computer programs used for scheduling. Most evaluation to date has been anecdotal rather than empirical. Some problems have been reported by schools attempting to schedule flexibly by computer. One problem is the lack of adequate or appropriate physical facilities. Since flexible scheduling usually results in more unscheduled student time than does a traditional schedule, there must be proper study or resource centers available to facilitate independent study. Schools with inadequate facilities find that large numbers of students may wander about unsupervised, unable to utilize unscheduled time constructively.

A second problem lies, ironically, in the inflexibility of the schedule. Because the school schedule is usually developed and formalized during the summer, teachers and students are stuck with it for at least a semester. If a student wants to substitute a new course for one he has been scheduled for, their meeting times seldom dovetail. And if a large-group session must be canceled for some reason, the sequence of events can be disrupted for several weeks.

A third problem concerns the necessity for developing new teaching skills. One of the most frequently-voiced complaints regarding flexibly-scheduled schools is that new instructional patterns do not prevent teachers from teaching the same way they did to twenty-five or thirty students. This is particularly true of small-group instruction; often the teacher does most of the talking instead of allowing the students to discuss and develop their own ideas. Clearly, schools adopting flexible schedules must incorporate staff training in new instructional techniques if they are to maximize the potential of the new schedule.

On the positive side, many teachers have reported that they perceive themselves more involved in decision-making as a result of designing their own schedules. Students have reported that they feel flexibly-scheduled schools to be much less regimented than traditional schools.

Although flexible scheduling is a new way of organizing learning, it does not assure that a different kind of teaching will occur. Although it was designed to help individualize instruction, most schools have not yet developed the self-instructive curricular materials necessary when large groups of students are made responsible for their own learning. Implemented in isolation, flexible scheduling will do little to change instruction and learning. Combined with such other changes as nongradedness, differentiated staffing and team teaching, new curricular materials and new teaching techniques, flexible scheduling becomes part of a team of innovations designed to restructure the school and the nature of teaching and learning.

MIDDLE SCHOOLS

The middle school is an alternative to the junior high school; it generally encompasses grades 5–8 or 6–8, while junior high schools ordinarily comprise grades 7–9. During the last decade there has been a remarkable increase in the number of middle schools in the United States. Present estimates run to over 1100 schools, most built since 1960.

There are a number of significant advantages to the concept of a middle school. First of all, it offers a better environment for early adolescents than does the junior high school. Critics of the traditional junior high charge that it has been too imitative of the high school, with its graduation ceremonies, cheerleaders and dances. This kind of atmosphere is not appropriate for early adolescents. Why should they be subjected to the pressures of a high school milieu? The middle school offers a unique environment where eleven to fourteen year olds are free to grow up at their own rates, and where attention is focused on the needs of this age group rather than on competition at a "junior" level.

Middle schools also offer a major opportunity for curricular experimentation. Core curricular experiences and electives could be designed which focus on the identity and maturation problems of the early adolescent, thus providing learning experiences best suited to the child's needs. A variety of instructional procedures could be adopted to match the varied learning styles of students of this age. A core curriculum based on different learning rates and the abolition of grade levels would lead naturally to the implementation of nongraded experiences and classrooms. By giving the ninth grade —which is still considered the first year in the college entrance sequence— to the high school, middle schools would be free to try new programs and new approaches without having to make them specifically applicable to college preparation.

In addition, middle schools are uniquely suited to perform an enlarged guidance function for children. Because of the earlier onset of puberty in today's children, sixth-graders may be better served in a school designed for early adolescents in grades 6, 7 and 8 than in an elementary school. This grouping of children who are just becoming conscious of their potential roles as high-school students and as adults offers an opportunity to provide meaningful guidance when children need it most. Often the high-school student finds himself assigned to a "track" or grouping of classes which, as Talcott Parsons reported in Chapter Two, in large part determines his future role in life; guidance and counseling at or before this crucial juncture are ordinarily scanty or nonexistent. Theodore Moss, a leading advocate of the middle school, considers teachers the key element in the middle school, and urges that guidance-oriented teachers be specifically recruited to teach ten to fourteen year olds.[12]

---

[12] Theodore Moss, *Middle School* (Boston: Houghton Mifflin, 1969).

Middle schools have as yet not taken advantage of these opportunities; a unique program for early adolescents is more a dream than a reality. Clearly-defined purposes have not yet been developed to serve as guidelines for middle schools. If the rationale of the emergent middle school is not clearly distinguished from that of the junior high movement earlier in the century, the results will be no different. Merely subtracting the ninth grade and adding the sixth won't change much.

Secondly, though the middle-school movement may challenge junior highs to change their approaches or at least adopt some new concepts and techniques, there is still too great a disparity between the theory and the reality of what is occurring in existing middle schools. A 1967–68 survey indicates that relatively few of the middle schools operating at that time had curricula that differed significantly from those of the junior high schools they were designed to replace.[13] Few had adopted team teaching, few varied the types of instructional procedures used and only about 10 percent had abandoned the traditional marking system.

Middle schools must be truly new; newly-designed buildings alone are not enough. If the real problem is inadequate educational treatment of early adolescents, effective methods must be designed. As of yet, most middle schools have not produced answers.

COMPETITIVE EDUCATION AND ACCOUNTABILITY

Teachers are commonly held responsible for what their students learn, principals are judged in part by the performance of students in their school and superintendents are accountable to school boards for the progress of their districts. But the public is increasingly demanding that the public schools as a whole be held accountable for producing demonstrable learning in children. The poor, minority groups, disillusioned students and education critics cite the frequency with which schools fail to achieve their goals, and as consumers they are demanding alternatives to the public school system. Critics charge that for the poor there are few feasible alternatives to the public schools, and yet the schools are not really held responsible for children's learning. Statistics indicate that the children of the poor receive an education inferior to that of middle-class children. When large groups of children fail—even if there is strong evidence that the responsibility lies primarily with the school—the poor lack the alternative of moving to another district or sending their children to expensive private schools. They must continue sending their children to the same school to warm seats for another semester.

However, the urban poor are becoming increasingly vocal about the

---

[13] W. Alexander and R. Kealy, "From Junior High School To Middle School," *High School Journal* 53 (December 1969): 154–155.

Daring ideas are like chessmen moved forward; they may be beaten, but they may start a winning game. Goethe.

quality of public education, and "storefront schools" have been created in a number of urban communities to meet the needs of students which the public school isn't filling. And the poor are not the only group decrying the quality of public education. Throughout the country, "para-schools" have been established in churches and communes by people who find the public educational system too stifling and homogeneous.

Sociologist Kenneth Clark believes that the public educational system needs more competition. He argues that competitive education would make schools accountable for their performances, and cause them to take pride in their work. If we accept, and even take pride in, competition and free enterprise as the basis of our economic system, there is no reason to fear it in our educational system.

Christopher Jencks, director of Harvard's Center for the Study of Public Policy, says that private schools can and should be made an alternative to the public schools for the poor. People should, he declares, be free to send their children to the schools which best suit their needs, whether student-centered schools patterned after A. S. Neill's Summerhill or Montessori schools with their special approaches to teaching young children. Since there aren't at present enough private schools to handle large numbers of transfers from the public schools, Jencks proposes two ways of encouraging private initiative in educating the poor.[14] The first is to provide tuition grants equal to the cost of public education to students who opt out of publicly-controlled schools. One of these grants, or vouchers, could be taken to any "participating" school—public, parochial or private—in which a child enrolled, and the local government would reimburse the school for the amount of the voucher. In effect, the "voucher plan" would allow competing publicly-financed schools to coexist. Jencks also proposes that a university, a local business group or a group of teachers might contract to manage a school. Existing school districts would rent facilities to these various groups, with contracts subject to renewal each year.

Jencks's two proposals are aimed at radical decentralization of both power and responsibility. The private schools he envisions would not be subject to the central school administration, but would be directly accountable to the parents who send their children there. If the parents are dissatisfied with the education their children are receiving, they are free to transfer them to another school.

---

[14] Christopher Jencks, "Is the Public School Obsolete?" *Public Interest* (Winter 1966): 18–27.

Controversy surrounds the idea of the voucher system. The major objections seem to be that it could encourage the creation of all-black or all-white schools. Opponents point out that this is, in effect, the case today in areas where federally-enforced integration has been subverted by the creation of state-supported white private schools. It would also lead to direct public support of church-related schools. The parent's lack of knowledge about each school's qualifications could lead, critics claim, to a spate of fly-by-night schools. But the most serious objection to the voucher system is that it diverts attention and energy from the real task: improving the public school system, rather than seeking alternatives to it.

At any rate, in the fall of 1971 the U.S. Office of Economic Opportunity began testing the viability of Jencks's proposal in several demonstration communities. The OEO plan will attempt to meet the objections of opponents of the voucher plan by including specific safeguards against each of the dangers they envision.

There seem to be many reasons to try the voucher plan on an experimental basis. If it works, the voucher plan may do more to shake up the public schools than any other method of reform. The competitive school approach won't divert attention from the task of public school improvement: instead, it will force public school educators to respond to new societal demands.

PERFORMANCE CONTRACTING

Another manifestation of the accountability movement in public education is "performance contracting," in which private educational companies contract with a school district to assume at least part of the teaching load. The company is paid on the basis of improvement in students' performance: if there is no improvement, as measured by preselected standardized tests, the contractor is not paid; if there is improvement, he is paid on a sliding scale based on how quickly, how effectively and how much improvement has taken place.

The whole notion of accountability is a radical reversal of the traditional view of education. Education has tended to be concerned with the "inputs" of the system—instructional materials, teachers' training, new buildings—while accountability is concerned with the "output"—student learning. No matter how good the inputs, if there is no output of student learning the schools have failed. In other words, it's not how you play the game, but whether you win or lose.

As might be expected, accountability and performance contracting are extremely controversial. Many public school educators feel threatened by the idea; private educational companies welcome the chance to demonstrate their ability to design and operate learning systems; and the public welcomes the opportunity to judge what they are receiving for their money. However, leading advocates of accountability and performance contracting acknowledge that some aspects of education cannot be measured and that only those which can be operationally defined and reliably assessed should be eligible for performance contracting. For instance, we can't assess how well a student assimilates faith in a democracy—even though the fostering of democratic ideals is an objective of almost all schools. Skills such as reading and mathematics appear to be the most amenable to performance contracting.

The first school system to attempt performance contracting on a wide basis was the Texarkana School Districts on the Arkansas-Texas border. In an attempt to prevent dropouts, the districts solicited bids from ten educational companies to raise the reading and mathematics achievement levels of identified potential dropouts. The assumption behind this federally-funded Texarkana program was that a private contractor would have greater freedom to innovate and thus would motivate students more successfully than the regular school system. The Dorsett Educational Systems of Oklahoma won the contract, with the understanding that they could use whatever approaches and techniques they wished to raise the students' achievement levels.

Dorsett spared no effort, hiring teachers at good wages and constructing "rapid-learning centers" which were carpeted, air-conditioned, sound-proofed and attractive. Teaching was conducted primarily through programmed instruction; the teachers acted as instructional managers, programming each daily assignment. A variety of incentives was offered to students; those who successfully completed the lessons were granted free time and the equivalent of trading stamps which they could exchange for merchandise like magazines and transistor radios.

Preliminary findings indicated that Dorsett had had substantial success in raising the achievement levels of the students. However, outside evaluators discovered that many of the test questions had been pretaught to the students, thus invalidating the results and a portion of Dorsett's claim for remuneration. This charge embarrassed Texarkana school officials, the Office of Economic Opportunity, which was funding the project, and numerous schoolmen, researchers and contractors who see great potential in performance contracting.

However, a number of lessons were learned from the Texarkana experience, including the need for thorough preparation, outside evaluation and a respect for the power of the profit motive. Since then, several performance-contracting ventures have been initiated in Dallas, Gary and other cities; they resemble the Texarkana approach but with provisions to overcome the difficulties experienced in the first project. The Office of Economic Opportunity in September, 1970, began operation of a $6.5-million one-year experiment involving 28,000 disadvantaged students, eighteen different centers and six private contractors. If the results are favorable, it is likely that performance contracting will become more widespread; as a result, the tax-

DIALOGUE

Jim: *Here we are more than halfway through this chapter and the reader is probably wondering about the significance of all these innovations in education.*

Kevin: *It's really hard to say. Some, like flexible scheduling and nongradedness, have been tried out in many schools and have helped create a new spirit and excitement in some of them.*

Jim: *Sometimes I wonder whether all or most of these innovations aren't just fluff that occupies people's attention and energy while the real problems are ignored. In other words, how much effect are these new developments actually having, and how many of them are just being tried because the school district wants to tell the taxpayers that they are hip and up-to-date?*

Kevin: *I know what you mean, and I think that the "bandwagon effect" does motivate some school districts. But some schools try them because they really believe they will improve learning and instruction. Whether they do or not is difficult to prove.*

Jim: *I have another theory. I think many school districts try them because they are manageable, might make a difference and provide a sense of direction and accomplishment for those involved. The larger problems—like racial prejudice, equality of educational opportunity and survival in a changing society—are so huge and amorphous that many educators label them insoluble, and concentrate instead on problems of a lower order of magnitude.*

Kevin: *You may be right. Certainly the purposes of new developments must be questioned and fitted into a larger picture based on one's own philosophy of education and what learning and schooling is, and should be, all about. What worries me, though, is that innovations in education may just be minor variations on a bad theme—at a time when we need thorough reform in education.*

paying public may begin to demand the same kind of accountability from public schools. This pressure could force many school districts to discard old methods of instruction and adopt some new, more individualized approaches. If this occurs, the beneficial effects of performance contracting will be manifold. One potential danger—that the teacher who is not given adequate materials and facilities to utilize an individualized approach will be held accountable for things over which he has no control—will certainly be of concern to teacher organizations as accountability becomes more widespread.

INSTRUCTIONAL INNOVATIONS

New developments in school organization have been paralleled during the last ten years by new methods of instruction, whose outstanding characteristic is their emphasis on individualizing instruction. An individualized approach allows students to learn at their own rate, to receive instruction on an individual basis and to evaluate their own progress. Clearly, this type of instruction calls for new materials and different tasks for the teacher to perform. Let's look at some of them.

PROGRAMMED INSTRUCTION

Look at the sample of programmed instruction below. The material to be learned is broken down into a series of small, discrete steps known as *frames.* Each frame presented to the learner contains a piece of information (called the *stimulus*) and a question to be answered (the *response*). The correct answer (the *confirmation*), against which the student may check his response, is presented in the next frame. In other words, each frame demands a response from the learner, who can immediately check its correctness.

---

1. In his article Skinner states "there is a constant exchange between program and student," and "the machine does not simply present something to be learned; it induces sustained activity."

In these and other statements, Skinner makes clear his position on one of the main necessities governing learning. In order for learning to occur, the student must _____ .

---

respond, or do something, or be active, etc.

---

2. From what Skinner says about "lectures, textbooks, and their mechanized equivalents" (refer to Panel 1-1 if you wish), would you say that *listening, reading,* and *watching* a film or TV presentation are responses of the sort that Skinner intends to have the student make?

The question asks what you would say. If you find yourself tending to say "yes," reread the first paragraph of Skinner's article. Note the emphasis on making sure that the student understands before he is allowed to go on.

---

3. A basic principle derived from the learning theory on which linear programing is based is:

In order for learning to occur, a response must be made by the learner. It follows that if we give a student two bits of information, both of which

---

we expect him to learn, he should respond to
  (a) either of them
  (b) both of them.

(b) both of them.

> **4.** Suppose a student has been led to respond correctly to the question "What is the capital of France?" In psychological terms, we can say:
>   In the presence of the stimulus "capital of France," the student responds "Paris."
> Is this the same situation as that represented by the following?
>   In the presence of "Paris is the capital of what country?" the student will respond "France." ____.

If your answer is "yes," go to item 4a.
If your answer is "no," go to item 4c.

> **4a.** Your answer was "yes." When the sentence "Paris is the capital of France" is broken into a *stimulus* part and a *response* part, it can be made into several different combinations of stimulus and response:
>   "What country is Paris the capital of?" is one question to which the correct response is "France."
>   "What is the capital of France?" is another question to which the correct response is "Paris."
> According to the principle of active responding, the student who has learned the answer to the first question has *not necessarily* learned the answer to the second question. The principle has been supported—often to the chagrin of program authors who assume that reading is an adequate response—by data drawn from all levels of student age and ability.
>   Minor wording changes (what we call "synonymous" phrasing) may be made without changing the stimulus–response relationship. One item is different from another whenever the stimulus is changed and a different response is asked for.
>
>   Are the following questions the same or are they different?
> Q1. "What do we call the meaningful unit that goes in front of a root?"
> A. "A prefix."
> Q2. "When a meaningful unit precedes a root, it is a ____."'
> A2. "prefix."

For any student for whom "precedes" = "goes in front of," the items are the same.

> **4b.** In the presence of the stimulus "The particles that circle the nucleus are called . . . ," the student responds "electrons."

> Is this the same situation as when in the presence of "Electrons circle around the . . . ," the student responds "nucleus"?

4c. Answer to 4 and 4b: No.

Note. Although the question may seem obvious to you, the failure to discriminate that such situations are different has led to criticisms of linear programs as being too repetitive (i.e., asking the student to do the same thing over and over again), when in fact they might not be. Go on to item 5.[15]

Programming is designed to individualize instruction and to give the student a sense of accomplishment. It is based on two widely-accepted psychological principles: 1) instruction should actively involve the learner, and 2) it should provide him with feedback on his performance. The material to be learned is purposely broken down into small steps in order to insure that few mistakes are made. One of the most powerful arguments for programmed instruction is that the learner will make few errors, and thus will experience a sense of accomplishment rather than failure. A good program will initially provide the learner many cues to help him make the correct response, and will gradually reduce the cues until the learner has demonstrated mastery of the material without cues. Programs are often but not always written for use with a teaching machine.

The type of programming developed by Harvard psychology professor B. F. Skinner has been called *linear* programming; the learner progresses through the program sequentially, responding in writing and receiving immediate feedback on his response on the next frame. Various points of entry into the program allow for differences in prior learning. Another type of programming is called *branching* programming. Branching programs make use of multiple choice questions which are diagnostic in nature. If the learner's response is correct, he moves on to more advanced material. If it is incorrect, it will be corrected by the next frame and the learner will be directed to a branch of remedial frames. In this manner, branching programs allow for differences in learner responses, while linear programs are limited to a fixed sequence of items. Frame 4 above is an example of branching programming. Most programs today are moving away from a strictly linear sequence toward multiple paths and increments between frames in an attempt to adapt to the individual learner's needs.

Although the concept of programmed instruction is relatively simple, the actual writing of a program is a difficult process. During the early days of its development, programmed instruction suffered from hastily- and poorly-written programs. Good programs undergo extensive field testing and are

---

[15] Susan Meyer Markle, *Good Frames and Bad: A Grammar of Frame Writing* (New York: John Wiley & Sons, 1964), 2–5. Reprinted by permission of the publisher.

I HAD TO STAY AFTER SCHOOL. THEY CAUGHT ME WITH A TEXTBOOK HIDDEN BEHIND MY TEACHING MACHINE.

Cartoon by Tony Saltzman for Education Technology Magazine.

revised when frames prove too ambiguous, or when the error rate for a frame is too high. Because program-writing is a difficult and time-consuming process, there is presently a shortage of good programmed materials in the public schools. But as more and more schools and teachers begin to concern themselves with individualizing instruction, the incidence and quality of programmed materials in the schools will become higher.

Programmed instruction's potential for individualizing instruction is considerable, because it allows individual pacing, active responses and immediate feedback. It can be used either for independent study, or to present courses or material not otherwise available. Because it is immediately available upon request, programmed instruction offers great flexibility in its use. It is most suitable for mastering certain facts, concepts and principles, and to free the teacher for the more creative aspects of teaching. The kinds of material to which it is suited are limited but, when integrated with other modes of teaching, programmed instruction is an extremely useful learning aid.

COMPUTER-ASSISTED INSTRUCTION (CAI)

A number of prominent educators and computer technologists predict that within the next two decades the direct use of the computer for instructional purposes will become widespread in both elementary and secondary schools. Patrick Suppes, a leading figure in the CAI field, has predicted that by 1973 between 200,000 and 800,000 students throughout the country will receive

CAI daily, and that in ten years that number could be between one and ten million.[16]

The most important aspect of computer-assisted instruction is its potential for individualizing instruction. There are currently three possible levels of interaction between the student and the computer program. At the first level, individualized drill-and-practice systems supplement the regular curriculum taught by the teacher. These exercises can be presented to students on an individual basis, the advanced students receiving the more difficult exercises and the slower students receiving the easier problems. At the second level, tutorial systems assume the main responsibility both for presenting a concept and for developing skill in its use. This level is analogous to the interaction between a patient tutor and a single student. At the third level, dialogue systems permit the student to engage in genuine interchange with the computer. At present, such dialogue systems are more conceptual than they are operational. Suppes predicts that within the next decade many children will use individualized drill-and-practice in elementary school; by the time they reach high school, tutorial systems will be available on a broad basis. And the children of these children may use dialogue systems throughout their school experience.

Present computers can handle simultaneously over 200 students, each of whom is at a different point in the curriculum. The simplest mode of operation involves a terminal device, similar to an electric typewriter, at which the student sits. Messages are typed out by the computer and the student in turn records his responses on the keyboard. At the Brentwood Elementary School in East Palo Alto, California, where an experimental CAI program was developed by Patrick Suppes and Richard Atkinson, there were, in addition to the keyboard, sixteen terminals similar to television screens used to show letters, numerals, pictures or symbols, an image projector for color pictures from a 16mm film strip and earphones to enable the child to hear oral instruction. Students received instructions for drill-and-practice by digitized audio message. A vocabulary of 3,000 words was recorded and stored in digital form on the computer's magnetic disc. When the student made his response, it was typed out by teletype. He could then compare his response with the correct answer, which appeared on the screen, and could at the end of the session have a printed record of his work. First and second graders at Brentwood received much of their reading and mathematics instruction by computer.

The computer program is essentially a sophisticated version of branching programming. By adding an instructional display screen, head sets, an image projector and a computer, the program is made far more versatile than a programmed instruction booklet.

As computer technology costs are reduced and educational industries

---

[16] Patrick Suppes, "How Far Have We Come? What's Just Ahead?" *Nation's Schools* 82 (October 1968): 53.

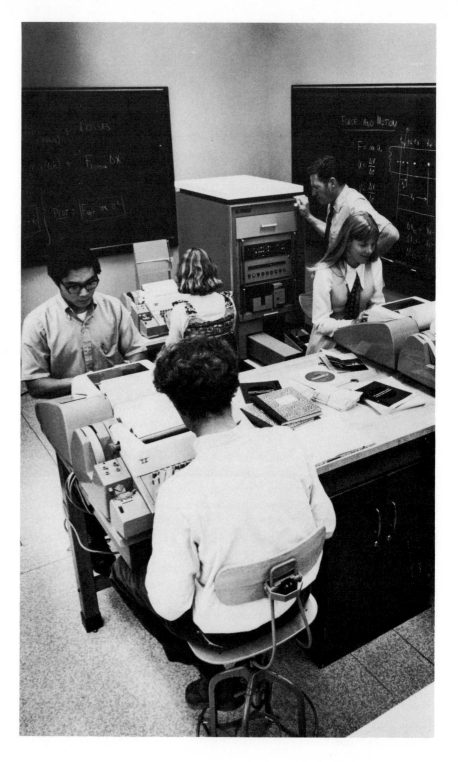

start producing computer programs, the computer will become a standard form of instruction in the public schools. Some educators fear that CAI will impose a rigid system of impersonalized teaching and lead to excessive standardization of education, but Suppes believes the opposite. He argues that CAI will make teaching even more personalized by increasing individualized instruction and freeing the teacher from routine tasks. He also believes that the wide use of computers will permit the introduction of an almost unlimited diversity of curriculum.

One thing is clear, though: if the computer does become commonplace in schools, the role of the teacher will change drastically. The computer, not the teacher, will impart facts and concepts to the students. The teacher will diagnose student learning difficulties and prescribe appropriate instruction. Many students will be working by themselves while the teacher works with small groups or individuals. It is also likely that many of the routine tasks the teacher now performs will be assumed by paraprofessional assistants.

INDIVIDUALLY PRESCRIBED INSTRUCTION (IPI)

Individualizing instruction means different things to different people. Some people use the term to suggest that all of the students proceed through the same curriculum but at different rates. To others, it means that the same curriculum is presented to all students but by different instructional methods, depending on the learning style of the students. For still others, it means that different curricula are offered to meet individual needs, allowing each student to choose the instructional objectives which best fit his unique interests and needs.

IPI is an instructional system which uses an approach originally developed at the University of Pittsburgh's Learning and Research Center. The essential characteristics of the IPI system are: the student's freedom to move through the curriculum at his own rate of progress; behavioral objectives—that is, objectives stated in terms of what the learner should be able to *do* when he has mastered the lesson, arranged sequentially in order of complexity (see pages 468–469 for further explanation of behavioral objectives); the intention that the student work on objectives until he achieves them, thus emphasizing accomplishment rather than failure; emphasis on self-direction, self-initiation and self-evaluation on the part of the learner; individualized techniques and materials providing a variety of instructional alternatives; the organization and management of the total school environment to facilitate individual instruction; provision for continuous feedback on the effectiveness of the program.

IPI is currently available in four areas: language arts, mathematics, social studies and science. Because its objectives are so clearly stated, teacher direction is at a minimum. Instead, diagnosis is a crucial aspect of IPI; placement tests are administered to students to determine the instructional program appropriate for each child. Before each unit, a pretest is administered

"Behavioral objectives identify goals and describe outcomes or perfor-mances learners should have as a result of participation in an activity." (H. H. McAshan, Writing Behavioral Objectives *[New York: Harper & Row, 1970], p. 8.) The behavioral objective specifies not only the goal but also the behavior the learner will have to manifest as a means of determining his success in achieving the goal.*

Objectives are often stated so ambiguously that they are subject to differ-ent interpretations. Consider the following general objective: "The stu-dents should know the difference between a revenue tariff and a protective tariff." Does the teacher who chose this objective want the student to be able to write definitions of the two terms? Or does he want the student to identify correctly written descriptions of the two terms? Or, given a de-scription of a specific tariff, does the teacher want the student to identify orally what kind of tariff it is?

You can see that the objective as stated above is too vague for a student to determine exactly what he is supposed to know about tariffs. Here is the same objective written behaviorally: "Given written definitions of both revenue and protective tariffs, the student will be able to correctly identify orally to the instructor the name of each type of tariff on his first attempt." The clarity and specificity of this objective are the advantages of behavioral objectives. Programmed instruction, computer-assisted instruction and systems for individualizing instruction are dependent on the translation of their goals into behavioral objectives.

The following fable is an eloquent argument for the need for behavioral objectives in the instructional process:

Once upon a time a Sea Horse gathered up his seven pieces of eight and cantered out to find his fortune. Before he had traveled very far he met an Eel, who said,

"Psst. Hey, bud. Where 'ya goin'?"

"I'm going out to find my fortune," replied the Sea Horse, proudly.

"You're in luck," said the Eel. "For four pieces of eight you can have this speedy flipper, and then you'll be able to get there a lot faster."

"Gee, that's swell," said the Sea Horse, and paid the money and put on the flipper and slithered off at twice the speed. Soon he came upon a Sponge, who said,

"Psst. Hey, bud. Where 'ya goin'?"

"I'm going out to find my fortune," replied the Sea Horse.

"You're in luck," said the Sponge. "For a small fee I will let you have this jet-pro-pelled scooter so that you will be able to travel a lot faster."

So the Sea Horse bought the scooter with his remaining money and went zooming through the sea five times as fast. Soon he came upon a Shark, who said,

"Psst. Hey, bud. Where 'ya goin'?"

"I'm going out to find my fortune," replied the Sea Horse.

"You're in luck. If you'll take this short cut," said the Shark, pointing to his open mouth, "you'll save yourself a lot of time."

to the child to determine the point within the unit where he should begin, or whether he has already mastered the material. At the end of the unit, a post-test is administered to see if the child has in fact achieved the behavioral objectives. If the student has not done so, the teacher notes where he has fallen short and prescribes additional instruction. There are also curriculum-embedded tests, taken while the student is progressing through the curriculum, designed to provide data on the mastery of each behavioral objective and to determine whether he needs additional work.

The instructional materials used in IPI programs include worksheets, tape and disc recordings, programmed materials, individual readers and manipulative devices. As computer-assisted instruction becomes more widespread and cheaper, IPI programs will undoubtedly incorporate it as an instructional alternative. Since no two students learn in quite the same way, IPI attempts to present a variety of instructional materials.

Although the evidence is not conclusive, preliminary results indicate that both teachers and students are enthusiastic about IPI. At the Oakleaf Elementary School in Pittsburgh, where IPI was initially piloted, students are strongly motivated since learning is highly personal. The students keep records of their own progress, and by grade 4 some children are writing their own prescriptions. Instead of telling students what and how to learn, the IPI system encourages them to assume responsibility for their own learning. If this objective can be achieved, it will be an accomplishment of monumental proportions which could revolutionize American education. Interviews indicate that IPI pupils like school better than non-IPI pupils. On standard achievement tests, IPI pupils do as well as non-IPI pupils. By 1970 IPI was endorsed by 175 schools in 32 states, involving 47,000 students and 1,160 teachers.[17]

A number of other individualized programs, with characteristics similar to those of IPI, have been developed. Project PLAN has reached almost 20,000 students in more than 40 different schools; this IPI-like approach was developed by the American Institute for Research and the Westinghouse Learning Corporation with cooperating school districts in California, New York, Pennsylvania, Massachusetts and West Virginia. In this program, the emphasis is on making the academic program relevant to the students by giving

---

[17] "On the Growth of IPI," *Phi Delta Kappan* 51 (June 1970): 539.

them an important voice in what and how they learn, for which the skills of appropriate decision-making are essential. During the first week of school the student goes through an orientation program to familiarize him with the instructional materials and equipment, and counseling sessions to help him develop his own objectives and learning program. Studies so far indicate that the approach is quite successful.

Public schools in the next two decades will increasingly assume characteristics similar to those of the IPI program. Behaviorally-stated objectives, self-pacing, self-direction, self-evaluation and alternative modes of instruction will become commonplace in our schools. Students will no longer be considered in groups, but individually. This does not mean that students will no longer participate in instructional groups, but that they will do so only as part of their own individually-prescribed learning. Peer interaction is an important part of the instructional process, and care must be taken not to isolate students from each other in an attempt to individualize instruction.

THE OPEN CLASSROOM

One of the most exciting recent imports from Great Britain is a new approach to teaching in primary schools. Known by a variety of names—"the open classroom," "the integrated day," "the Leicestershire model," "the British infant school"—it represents less a new teaching style than it does a set of shared attitudes and beliefs about learning, schooling and the nature of childhood. The traditional elementary school classroom situation and the usual roles of teacher and student are rejected. It is a highly individualized, child-centered learning experience based on the assumption that learning will be more effective if it develops from what interests the learner, rather than what interests the teacher. The teacher does not abdicate her position and authority in the classroom; instead, she facilitates learning by structuring the environment to respond optimally to each child's needs and interests. The child, rather than the teacher, is the source of learning.

There are four basic principles operating in an open classroom. First, the classroom is decentralized; open space is divided into flexible "interest areas'' according to function. The room does not look like a classroom. Second, the children are free to explore the room and choose their own activities. Third, the environment is rich in learning resources—books, rulers, measuring tape, tinkertoys, tape recorders and dozens of other instructional materials. And, finally, the teacher and the aides spend most of their time with individual children or small groups, and rarely present the material to the class as a whole.[18]

Respect and trust in the child are perhaps the most basic underlying principles of the open classroom. An American visiting an open classroom for the first time is usually surprised by what he sees—the room has no identifiable front or back, the children are all doing different things at different times and the teacher may be working with an individual child or observing. There is a beehive of activity, yet discipline problems are almost nonexistent. When it is no longer the teacher's responsibility to maintain order and control and the children are not required to sit still and be quiet, discipline problems seem to disappear.

The theoretical rationale for the open classroom is the work of the Swiss child psychologist, Jean Piaget. Piaget's lifetime has been spent studying children and their developmental stages. He believes that it is a waste of time to tell a child things that he can't experience through his senses. The child must be allowed to manipulate objects, try different experiments, pose questions and test his findings against other children's perceptions. Communication among peers is an essential part of a child's learning. Only after a child has had a great deal of sensory experience is he ready to comprehend abstract concepts. Piaget is critical of the traditional classroom approach for emphasizing conceptualization without offering the child the opportunity to experience through his senses.

The open classroom approach received widespread publicity in Great Britain in 1967 when a Parliamentary Commission, now referred to as the Plowden Committee, urged its adoption by all English primary schools. American schools are also increasingly adopting this approach. The state of North Dakota, for instance, is remodeling its elementary schools along the lines of the open classroom, in conjunction with the University of North Dakota's New School for Behavioral Studies in Education. Although the results of tests evaluating the students' progress in reading and mathematics are not available at this time, there are indications that the children are enjoying this new approach. Charles E. Silberman reports the following anecdotal accounts of interviews conducted in North Dakota:

"Last year we had to work all the time. Now we can play all the time," one little boy volunteers to the visitor, as he "plays" with a complicated mathematical game.

"The children won't stay home even when they're sick," a Minot teacher reports.

---

[18] Ronald and Beatrice Gross, "A Little Bit of Chaos," *Saturday Review* (May 16, 1970): 71–73, 84–85.

Ivan Illich (1926–   )

Aristocrat, intellectual, social revolutionary, shepherd of the dispossessed, enemy of schooling—no handful of descriptive phrases can begin to describe Ivan Illich.

Illich was born in Vienna to a titled Dalmatian family; his father had been a wealthy landowner and engineer in pre-World War II Germany. Young Illich was educated by governesses and tutors, and by the time he was twenty-four had been ordained a priest, earned masters' degrees in theology and philosophy from Rome's Gregorian University and a doctorate in the philosophy of history from the University of Salzburg. He also completed doctoral studies in natural science at the University of Florence. Illich's family was friendly with European intellectuals, and Ivan became close to philosopher Jacques Maritain, whom he considers a central influence on his life.

Illich came to the United States in 1953 as a young recently-ordained Benedictine to work in a New York City church inundated with newly-arrived Puerto Ricans. He learned to speak Spanish but, realizing that fluency in the language was not enough, Illich visited the island homeland of his parishioners and spent months walking the hills and living in the urban slums of Puerto Rico. When he returned to New York, he became a champion of the culture and organized a huge feast day for Puerto Ricans. By helping the archdiocese respond to the alienation of the people, Illich became a hero; he was their Babe Ruth.

Illich's involvement in education began when he was assigned to help the clergy become more responsive to their Spanish-speaking parishioners. To do so, he set up a "de-Yankification center" in Cuernavaca, Mexico, in 1961. Called the Center for International Documentation, it is a kind of secular monastery where North Americans and Europeans come for rebirth into Latin-American culture. The Center also hosts educational seminars. More recently, it has become a progressive university and think-tank deeply concerned with reform in education. In the summer of 1971 it was the site of a conference involving North American educationists such as George Dennison and John Holt, and Paulo Freire from South America.

A flamboyant exhibitionist and a profoundly modest man, Illich can be described only in contradictions. He is as radical in some domains as he is traditional in others. He is an arrogant aristocrat with a militant dedication to the poor. He enjoys teaching by puzzlement and answers questions in cryptic aphorisms worthy of a Zen master. Illich has given up his priestly duties, but asked to keep two religious obligations: celibacy and his daily breviary.

Passionately interested in education, Illich indicts existing schools for confusing "teaching with learning, grade advancement with education, a diploma with competence, and fluency with the ability to say something new." He proposes the abolition of schools as institutions, and the development of "opportunity webs" which would provide access to educational objects, skill exchanges and teachers to people of all ages. Illich considers night school and adult education to be solutions to many social problems. He points out that all traditional school systems favor the privileged middle classes at the expense of marginal groups, and believes that only through a radically-reformed adult educational system can the poverty-stricken attain self-determination.

The proper way to force renewal in society, he argues, is through a revolution in educational process. Teach a million Brazilian peasants to read in six weeks of night school and rid a few thousand missionaries of their Yankee hangups: such adult education, in Illich's view, is far more radical than training guerillas.

Illich believes that consumer resistance is growing in the knowledge industry and that we can depend on self-motivated learning instead of hiring teachers to bribe students to learn. In Illich's plan, the student is the center of focus. He determines his own goals; the teacher and administrators act only as facilitators and resource people. Instead of building expensive new schools, Illich would send students to apprentice with practitioners who have mastered the art or skill the student wishes to learn. Traditional teachers' roles would be severely diminished under this system; classrooms would seldom be used.

Illich envisions schooling being restricted to two months per year and spread over the first thirty years of a person's life. Noting that adults can be taught to read in six weeks of evening classes at one-tenth the cost of teaching reading to children, Illich argues that the education dollar would be more profitably used to make education widely available to people of all ages. The money now spent on the "sacred paraphernalia" of the school ritual could be used to provide all citizens with greater access to the real life of the city or community.

And a woman teaching in a wooden two-room schoolhouse wrote, in her self-evaluation, "I have had several mothers tell me that this is the first year they haven't had to fight every morning to get their youngsters to school. I think this is perhaps my greatest accomplishment."

From a father's letter to an elementary school principal: "May my son come to school earlier? There's so much he wants to do and he can't seem to fit it all in during the regular hours."

· · · · · · · ·

The science area in a second- and third-grade room in Starkweather. A small group of eight-year-olds guide their visitor through a display of seashells and rocks, talking knowledgeably as they go. Next they come to a section containing a snakeskin, jars of pickled frogs, pickled deer brains, pickled pig brains, and the pride of their display, a pair of pig's eyes rolling wildly in a jar of formaldehyde. Oblivious to the visitor's queasy stomach, the boy who had performed the surgery on the pig calmly discusses the procedure he used. He goes on to point out the toughness of the white of the eye: how he discovered the toughness while trying to pierce it, why the white of the eye has to be tough, and how it compares to the toughness of the white of the human eye. The visitor is relieved when the group moves on to a display of brilliantly colored photographs of dinosaurs, fossils, even insects, and then to a map of the moon, a microscope, slides, and other more familiar material.[19]

Some educators are concerned that essential skills such as reading and mathematics may be left up to chance in an open classroom. Teachers who have worked in open classrooms dismiss their concern on the grounds that their experience indicates children want to learn to read and solve mathematical problems, but do not want to be governed by a set timetable ("All right, children, put away the reading books—it's time to do math."). These teachers believe the children will learn to read when they are ready to do so.

An open classroom does not require an exceptional teacher. But the teacher does need alertness and readiness to respond to and help individual students in their various activities. Since the curriculum is not restricted to the teacher's lesson plans but is literally everything that is going on in the room, it can be as unpredictable and as broad as the children's interests. However, the teacher need not be afraid to admit ignorance in certain areas. In fact, the teacher can seize such opportunities to help the student by designing experiments or research problems himself. In this way, the teacher functions as a model and demonstrates to the child that ignorance is a problem to be solved, rather than a source of shame.

There is no doubt that the open classroom approach will become increasingly popular in the Seventies. Although similar to IPI in its emphasis on individualized instruction, it differs in its openness and in the child's almost total responsibility for what and when he wants to learn. IPI's behavioral

---

[19] Charles E. Silberman, *Crisis in the Classroom* (New York: Random House, 1970), pp. 289, 294. Copyright © 1970 by Charles E. Silberman.

objectives largely predetermine the scope of the curriculum, leaving the child free to move through it at his own rate. Whereas IPI gradually allows the student more responsibility for designing his own curriculum, the open classroom gives the child that responsibility at the outset. Both approaches promise tremendous improvement over current practices in most schools, and both deserve to be tried on a large scale. We are at a stage in education when alternatives are needed, not final answers. The answers will come only after extensive testing of the alternatives, and both IPI and the open classroom promise significant results.

INNOVATIONS IN SCHOOL DESIGN

The need for a fresh approach to school design is clear if we ask why, in any community in this country, a school building is instantly recognizable as such to a stranger. A school built in 1968 usually has more characteristics in common with a school built in 1898 than it does differences. Even schools that have received awards for their design seem to offer only slightly different ways of distributing space and people.

Educators are beginning to ask why school buildings are being designed to be isolated from the rest of the community and the natural environment. The answer is that education, like all institutions, has developed organized structures for the achievement of preestablished goals, and tends to permit and encourage only those experiences which contribute to the attainment of those goals. The public schools limit contacts and educational experiences in an attempt to preserve for themselves the transmission of the accumulated knowledge and values of the society.

The schools' attempt to circumscribe experience is reflected in the architectural nature of school buildings, which are almost invariably characterized by closed organizational structures and monumental architectural forms. Schools tend to be "eggcrates," or large groupings of small boxes of equal size and shape. Despite differences in appearance, the organizational structure of a school building is based on the principle of authority and characterized by a hierarchy of spaces, absence of osmosis between the different parts and interruption and control of internal and external communications. As the noted architect and urban designer Giancarlo DeCarlo has explained, organizational structures in architecture are defined as authoritarian when the articulation of the spaces does not stimulate the community (in this case, the school) to exchange communications at any time at a level of complete equality.[20] By this definition, virtually all public school buildings must be termed authoritarian.

---

[20] Giancarlo DeCarlo, "Why/How to Build School Buildings," *Harvard Educational Review* 39 (1969): 18.

DeCarlo also states, "School buildings built especially to house educational activity can house, therefore, only that part of this activity which is in the interest of the institutions which construct the school buildings. The rest of education—the richest and most active part—goes on elsewhere and has no need of buildings; or perhaps it has not yet found the appropriate spaces in which it would take place as a whole, becoming a part of a sphere of total experiences."[21] In this paragraph, DeCarlo expresses one of the most dramatic and imaginative views currently being advocated by some educators and school designers: that the city and its streets provide a richer and more diversified experience than that offered by the school system, and that the school as an established and codified institution may no longer have any reason for being.

Before you dismiss this idea as too extreme or idealistic, remember our discussion in Chapter Two of Philadelphia's Parkway Program, which utilizes the entire city of Philadelphia and its resources as a campus. Although there are designated meeting-places where students and teachers gather on a regular basis, this is only one aspect of the educational program of Parkway. The rest of the program is designed by the students and teachers to take advantage of the resources of the city itself, so the program is not confined to a single building.

Any building, no matter how "flexible" it is designed to be, has definite limitations. It can house only a certain number of people, some meaningful learning activities cannot occur within its walls and, as the interests of the children change and grow, the school building imposes definite limits on their expression. Educators who espouse the "school without walls" concept argue that the school cannot be a closed structure, but must encompass a network of social activities and be capable of continual variations. The entire environment must be the school if the school is to be relevant to society. Isolating the school from the rest of society is the best way possible to insure irrelevance.

In a sense, then, one of the new types of school design is no design at all, but a plan to utilize the existing community as an "open laboratory." In the next decade or two many more "schools without walls" will appear, particularly in large metropolitan areas where the community offers myriad resources. Teachers and students will continue to meet in buildings for certain purposes, but those buildings will not be considered the school. It is likely, however, that "schools without walls" will continue to be the exception rather than the rule. For one thing, smaller towns and cities do not have sufficient resources to support such a program. But the "schools without walls" concept will definitely affect the education that occurs within traditional school buildings by legitimizing the idea that all formal schooling

---

[21] *Ibid.,* p. 19.

Photo by Robert Perron.

THE REAL WORLD

need not take place within four walls. Even within traditional schools, formal credit will be given for informal educational experiences like the mini-courses described in Chapter Three.

INDIVIDUALIZED LEARNING AND SCHOOL FACILITIES

The traditional school is designed for the instruction of children in groups; the class, the primary unit of instruction, takes place in a classroom containing twenty-five to thirty desks, all facing the teacher. When the teacher serves as the dispenser of information, the traffic controller and the focal point of the classroom, this physical arrangement is probably appropriate. But as students begin to assume more self-direction and self-pacing responsibilities, a new physical arrangement is necessary to facilitate independent study and small-group discussion.

The major obstacle to be overcome in designing such facilities is the rigidity of spaces. It is difficult to adapt to a new purpose rooms which were designed for another. Consequently, either separate rooms must be designed for each specific purpose or spaces must be available which can be adapted to a variety of uses. Some designers believe that a space designed exclusively for one purpose suppresses the individual by dictating to him exactly how it should be used. Instead, they believe, spaces should be created which each individual can make relevant to his own needs. They advocate the use of large open spaces which are adaptable to many purposes.

School designers are attempting to individualize instruction with a variety of facilities. Learning laboratories which include several "how to" areas are being designed for a variety of student groupings—individual, tutorial, team discussion, small groups and large groups. A learning laboratory might include an art area where students working on particular projects could go any time they were free, a stand-up work area, scientific laboratories and the like.

Instructional materials centers would house instructional materials and tools for independent student or small group use. Individual student carrels would be available, perhaps with audiovisual tools such as cassettes and portable videotape playback units for special instruction. The recently-developed television cassette is a type of video phonograph which converts any TV set into a movie projector and screen. Video cartridges make a variety of programs, ranging from Shakespearean plays to carefully controlled science experiments, available to students at any time. In the future, schools will be able to develop video cartridge libraries similar to libraries which house books, enormously enhancing the teacher's ability to individualize instruction for his students. More importantly, such a center could provide all the materials necessary to the truly self-educating person.

An electronic information center would house modern equipment for assistance in seeking information. Students could engage in computer-based independent study and store their own computer programs in the

Photo by David Worts.

center. This equipment possibly could be made available to students at home via television, so that learning could become a continuous process.

Many new schools are including teacher studios, where teachers can collect and store materials and information, and can prepare lessons or counsel individual students. Some schools have built student recreational facilities where students can listen to records, dance, play games and buy food and beverages. Students need to unwind, too, and this kind of facility can be extremely beneficial.

The school designed to individualize instruction will contain many of these facilities. Square pegs will not fit into round holes—new schools must be developed to facilitate new approaches.

Perhaps we should ask ourselves, when we discuss the future of innovations in education, who is going to pay for it. The property-tax dollar which supports local schools will stretch only so far; most school districts can't afford to implement nationally-acclaimed innovations in education or experiment on their own without outside financial support. In large part, the future of educational innovation depends on government support, particularly at the federal level. Without such support, there would be no Head Start, day-care centers, open classroom implementation, performance contracting experiments or studies of the effectiveness of the voucher plan. Government

funds are also needed by university research centers, where innovations such as IPI are developed. In addition, financial support from private foundations must continue; without private aid research on variations in class size and scheduling would not have been undertaken, and new approaches in teacher education, urban education and differentiated staffing would not have been developed. Business and industry have contributed both financial and personnel aid to the development of performance contracting, CAI, IPI, Project PLAN and the voucher system.

If educators seek outside help for the development and implementation of new ideas in education, they must inevitably respond to outside influence and direction. Yet, without this aid, education would be hopelessly stuck in its pre-space-age rut. One of the crucial questions of the Seventies will be how educators handle the issue of influence through financial assistance for innovation.

DISCUSSION QUESTIONS

1. What problems might be anticipated by a school making a transition from graded to nongraded organization? What does the cartoon on page 437

imply about such a transition? Try to remember yourself at, say, eight years old—do you think you would have been capable of taking major responsibility for your own learning? Why or why not?

2. What is your personal reaction to the differentiated staffing model currently being implemented in Temple City? Which, if any, of the arguments against differentiated staffing do you consider valid? Would you want to work on a differentiated staff?

3. How do you feel about private companies contracting to raise achievement levels within the school system which employs you? Why can't accountability and performance contracting be considered panaceas for the problems of our educational system?

4. Will you welcome or deplore the changes in teacher roles which will be brought about by the widespread use of computers in schools?

5. Are you more in sympathy with the principles of the open classroom or those of IPI? Why?

6. Does it make sense to you that the style of a school's architecture can be authoritarian? Did your high school building have an authoritarian effect on students? Can you think of ways other than those we described to counteract this effect? Can you think of any inexpensive ways to do so?

7. Do you plan to become a teacher? Why or why not?

FOR FURTHER READING

Anderson, G. Ernest. "Computer Assisted Instruction: State of the Art." *Nation's Schools* 82 (October 1968): 49–51. Details the capabilities and potential of computer-assisted instruction.

Anderson, Robert H. "How Organization Can Make the School More Humanistic." *National Elementary Principal* 49 (January 1970): 6–13. A good article discussing essential components of school organization, including the absence of gradedness, abandonment of the self-contained classroom and the need for a more open, larger and more heterogeneous pupil family.

Brody, Ernest B. "Achievement of First and Second Year Pupils in Graded and Nongraded Classrooms." *Elementary School Journal* 70 (April 1970): 391–394. A research study comparing findings on first and second year pupils in graded and nongraded classrooms.

Cawelti, Gordon. "Does Innovation Make Any Difference?" *Nation's Schools* 82 (November 1968): 60–63. A report of a study comparing eleven flexibly scheduled high schools and eleven traditional schools.

Cooper, James M., ed. *Differentiated Staffing.* Philadelphia: W. B. Saunders, 1972. A collection of readings on differentiated staffing and its implications for paraprofessionals, administrators and in-service teacher education. Also included are case studies of differentiated staffing plans in Temple City, California, and in Florida.

Featherstone, Joseph. "The Primary School Revolution in Britain." Washington: The New Republic, 1967. A compilation of three articles which originally appeared in *The New Republic* of August 10, September 2, and September 9, 1967.

Goodlad, John, and Anderson, Robert H. *The Nongraded Elementary School,* rev. ed. New York: Harcourt, Brace & World, 1963. A strong argument for the nongraded elementary school.

Gross, Beatrice, and Gross, Ronald. "A Little Bit of Chaos." *Saturday Review* (May 16, 1970): 71–73, 84–85. An easy-to-read article describing the British infant school.

Harvard Educational Review 39 (1969), "Architecture and Education." The whole issue is devoted to exploring the relationship of architectural values to significant human experience and, in particular, to basic educational goals.

Jencks, Christopher. "Is the Public School Obsolete?" *Public Interest* (Winter 1966): 18–27. A strong argument for alternative school systems to compete with the public schools.

Joyce, Bruce. *The Teacher and His Staff: Man, Media and Machines.* Washington, D.C.: National Commission of Standards and Center for the Study of Instruction, NEA, 1967. In this booklet the author outlines a team approach to instruction and the kinds of media necessary to carry it out.

Kornegay, William. "The Open Market: A New Model for Our Schools?" *Phi Delta Kappan* 49 (June 1968): 583–586. An argument against the voucher system, detailing the problems the author sees it creating.

Lessinger, Leon. "Engineering Accountability for Results in Public Education." *Phi Delta Kappan* 52 (December 1970): 217–225. An article on performance contracting for the public schools.

Suppes, Patrick. "Computer Technology and the Future of Education." *Phi Delta Kappan* 49 (April 1968): 420–423. Asserts that computer-assisted instruction will make teaching more, rather than less, personalized by increasing individualized instruction and freeing the teacher from routine tasks. Also describes possible uses· of the computer for instructional purposes.

Wiley, W. Deane, and Bishop, Lloyd K. *The Flexibly Scheduled High School.* New York: Parker, 1968. Details the advantages of a flexible schedule as compared to a traditional one, and describes how schools are scheduled using computer programs.

FILMS

The Child of the Future: How He Might Learn (Contemporary/McGraw-Hill, 16mm, b&w, 58:06 min., 1965) Jerome Bruner of Harvard University and Marshall McLuhan draw conclusions about the effects of new mechanical and electronic teaching aids on the learning process.

Children as People (Polymorph Films, 16mm, b&w, 35 min.) Made at the Fayerweather Street School, in Cambridge, Massachusetts, this film portrays an "alternative" school in which kids are free to move about and to plan and direct their own activities.

Deeps and Highs (Negative Entropy/Allegra May, 16mm, b&w, 35 min.) This film uses Trout Fishing in America, a new free school in Cambridge, Massachusetts, as a vehicle to depict the hopes of children for a different way of being. Focuses on kids who are alienated from everything, even "radical society," and who begin to find a sense of comfort and community at Trout Fishing.

Education Under a Thatched Roof (Indiana University Audio-Visual Center, 16mm, b&w, 19 min.) The preparation and implementation of a unit team-teaching approach at a secondary school in Bangkok, Thailand, are illustrated in this film. Innovative resources such as media, team teaching, field trips and student-made materials are used to teach a unit on food sanitation.

Four Years Old and Ready to Grow (Center for Urban Education, 16mm, color, 27 min.) Documents some of the main features of a new approach to the teaching of young inner-city children. The goal of this program is continuous skill development in such language areas as vocabulary, syntax, listening, speaking, writing and reading.

I Am Here Today (EDC Film Library, 16mm, b&w, 43:30 min.) Presents an open classroom of five-, six- and seven-year-olds at the Shady Hill School in Cambridge, Massachusetts.

Infants School; Battling Brook Primary School; Medbourne Primary School (EDC Film Library, 16mm, b&w, 1st film, 31:30 min.; 2nd film, 23 min.; 3rd film, 12 min.) Three films on English educational instruction. *Infants School* presents a day in the Gordonbrook Infant School in London, where the nongraded approach is successfully being practiced.

Knowing to Learn (National Film Board of Canada, 16mm, b&w, 71:29 min.) A provocative look at the technological revolution in education—demonstrating the effects of computers, tape recorders, television, etc. on the learning process. The film was produced with the assistance of many institutions and individuals engaged in experiment and research into all forms of education.

The Remarkable Schoolhouse (Contemporary/McGraw-Hill, 16mm, color, 25 min., 1967) Originally produced for CBS television, this film examines the educational problems which have led to the introduction of technological innovations in elementary and junior high instruction. In addition, it defines the role of "new hardware," such as computers, television and educational games, in the educational system.

The Way It Is (Indiana University Audio-Visual Center, 16mm, b&w, 60 min., 1967) Depicts the chaos of the New York City schools, focusing on what is being done in one school in the Bedford-Stuyvesant section of Brooklyn to improve the situation. Participants in a New York University special learning project are shown visiting with parents, teachers and students.

AUDIOTAPES

The Person of Tomorrow (Big Sur Recordings, 3.75 ips, reel or cassette, mono or stereo, 90 min., 1970) Carl Rogers presents his views on rock music, violence on campus and the encounter group movement, and in so doing discusses some changes necessary in education.

The Curriculum (National Education Association, 3.75 ips, reel or cassette, 56:30 min.) This hour-long audiotape is divided into seven short sections, each intended to serve as the basis for a complete discussion session. Three of the sections discuss the Parkway Program in which the entire Philadelphia community has become the school campus. Another section describes a one-week Experiment in Free Form Education at a suburban high school and other programs in "affective education."

George Leonard: Steps Toward Utopia (60 min.); *Predictions for Education* (60 min.) (Big Sur Recordings, 3.75 ips, reel, mono) George Leonard, author of *Education and Ecstasy,* discusses some experimental programs currently in progress, as well as educational programs for the future.

Gestalt Training Tapes (Big Sur Recordings, 3.75 ips, reel, mono or stereo) Tape recordings of Frederick S. Perls discussing his approach to Gestalt Therapy: *Dream Theory and Demonstration*—a concise one-hour Gestalt Awareness presentation. *Lecture Demonstrations*—a full series of confrontations and self-encounter demonstrations (6 hours). *The Perls Encounter*—A complete weekend seminar of demonstrations of Gestalt Awareness with a wide variety of participants (9 hours).

John Holt and George Dennison: Alternatives in Education (Big Sur Recordings, reel or cassette, mono or stereo, 2½ hours, 1970) A sound collage made at a large gathering of people interested in experimental education. Both John Holt and George Dennison actively discuss the problems and possibilities of the new school movement.

VIDEOTAPES

Alternative 70's (People's Video Theatre, ½", Sony, Old Generation) A survey on videotape of people in culture, science, politics, education, media and government service about their views of the coming decade.

California Experimental High School (Videofreex, ½", Sony, 1969) A videotape made at an experimental high school in California.

Clinton Project (Raindance, ½", Sony, 1 hour) One hour of edited tapes made by junior high school students, tracing their video class from the first session to the last.

System of Teaching Reading by Coloring Coding Words (Electric Eye, $\frac{1}{2}$",
several hours) This tape, produced by a group whose motto is "tell a vision,
not sell a vision," presents the work of Dr. Caleb Gattegno at San Jose
State.

MULTIMEDIA

Living and Learning Schools (Living and Learning Schools, 140 frs., record,
15 min., automatic synchronization when used on a Dukane filmstrip
projector) A document on the "open classroom" program at the Living and
Learning Day Care Center in Braintree, Massachusetts. The sounds and
images are intended to show that a community-oriented, privately-owned
day care center can be "an educational program and not just custodial
care."

The Building of a School as a Learning Experience (Harvard Graduate School
of Education Library, films, slides, cassettes, tapes) This illustrated paper
by William Coperthwaite explains the building of a school in New Hampshire by twelve students and two teachers who found that a more conventional institution did not serve their needs. They built the school from a
design based on the shelter of nomadic Mongol tribes. Constructed of
wood, these round structures, called "yurts," provide "classrooms without
corners."

Refer to Appendix for distributors' addresses.

THE REAL WORLD

An Invitation to Respond

We would appreciate knowing your reaction to *Those Who Can, Teach.* We'd be grateful if you'd take a moment to complete the following questionnaire, tear it out of the book, fold, seal and mail it. **Kevin Ryan** and **James Cooper.**

1. Were there any chapters or features that you particularly liked or disliked? If so, why?

_____

_____

2. How did you respond to the attempted informality of the book?

_____ I liked it very much.

_____ I generally liked it but sometimes it didn't come off.

_____ I didn't like it.

_____ Other.

3. How would you rate the cartoons and illustrations?

_____ Excellent   _____ Good   _____ Fair   _____ Poor

Were there any that you particularly liked or disliked? Why?

_____

_____

4. If you were to revise the book, what changes would you suggest we make?

_____

_____

5. Other comments:

_____

_____

First Class
Permit No. 2166
Boston, Mass.

BUSINESS REPLY MAIL
No postage stamp necessary if mailed in the United States

Postage will be paid by

HOUGHTON MIFFLIN COMPANY
110 Tremont Street
Boston, Massachusetts 02107

EDUCATION EDITOR, COLLEGE DEPARTMENT

Appendix

American Documentary Films, Inc.
336 West 84th Street
New York, New York 10024
  or
379 Bay Street
San Francisco, California 94133

APGA Film Sales
1607 New Hampshire Avenue, N.W.
Washington, D.C. 20009

Audiofilm Center/Brandon Films
34 MacQuesten Parkway South
Mount Vernon, New York 10550

Benchmark Films, Inc.
516 Fifth Avenue
New York, New York 10036

Big Sur Recordings
117 Mitchell Boulevard
San Rafael, California 94903

Board of Public Education
Division of Instructional Materials
Audiovisual Office Room 328
Parkway, South of 21st Street
Philadelphia, Pennsylvania 19103

Boston Newsreel
595 Massachusetts Avenue
Cambridge, Mass. 02139

Boston University
Krasker Memorial Film Library
School of Education
765 Commonwealth Avenue
Boston, Mass. 02215

Center for the Study of
Democratic Institutions
P.O. Box 4068
Santa Barbara, California 93103

Center for Urban Education
105 Madison Avenue
New York, New York 10016

Churchill Films
622 North Robertson Boulevard
Los Angeles, California 90060

Columbia Cinemathèque
711 Fifth Avenue
New York, New York 10022

Commonwealth of Massachusetts
Department of Education
Office of Audio Visual Services
182 Tremont Street
Boston, Mass. 02111

Contemporary Films/McGraw-Hill
330 West 42nd Street
New York, New York 10036

EDC Film Library
Education Development Center
55 Chapel Street
Newton, Mass. 02160

Electric Eye
584 Park Court
Santa Clara, California 95059

Films Incorporated
35–01 Queens Boulevard
Long Island City, New York 11101

Grove Press Film Library
80 University Place
New York, New York 10003

Guggenheim Production, Inc.
815 Seventeenth Street, N.W.
Washington, D.C. 20006

Harvard University Graduate School of
Education Library
Longfellow Hall, Appian Way
Cambridge, Mass. 02138

Audio-Visual Center
Indiana University
Bloomington, Indiana 47401

Liane Brandon
2½ Douglas Street
Cambridge, Mass. 02138

Living and Learning Schools
764 Main Street
Waltham, Mass. 02154

Mass Media Ministries
2116 North Charles Street
Baltimore, Maryland 21218
  or
1714 Stockton Street
San Francisco, California 94133

The Moving Image
WNYE-TV
Channel 25
112 Tillary Street
Brooklyn, New York 11201

National Education Association
Publication-Sales Section 131
1201 Sixteenth Street, N.W.
Washington, D.C. 20036

National Film Board of Canada
Suite 819
680 Fifth Avenue
New York, New York 10019

NBC Educational Enterprise
Room 1040
30 Rockefeller Plaza
New York, New York 10020

Negative Entropy Allegra May
20 Cogswell Avenue
Cambridge, Mass. 02140

Noumedia Co.
P.O. Box 750
Port Chester, New York 10573

People's Video Theatre
544 Avenue of the Americas
New York, New York 10011

Polymorph Films, Inc.
331 Newbury Street
Boston, Massachusetts 02116

Project Inc.
Attention: Ruth Wilson
141 Huron Avenue
Cambridge, Mass. 02138

Raindance
24 East 22nd Street
New York, New York 10010

Teaching Film Custodians
25 West 43rd Street
New York, New York 10036

Time-Life Films
43 West 16th Street
New York, New York 10011

Twyman Films, Inc.
329 Salem Avenue
Dayton, Ohio 45401

University-at-Large
70 West 40th Street
New York, New York 10018

University of California
Extension Media Center
Berkeley, California 94720

Videofreex, Inc.
98 Prince Street
New York, New York 10012

Warner Bros., Inc.
Non Theatrical Division
400 Warner Boulevard
Burbank, California 91505

Zipporah Films, Inc.
54 Lewis Wharf
Boston, Mass. 02110

Index

Ford Foundation, 121, 184, 400
foreign language curriculum: elementary school, 101; secondary school, 101–102
foundation aid to education, 121, 122, 400, 479
Fuchs, Estelle, 258–306 *passim*

Galbraith, John Kenneth, 362
Gallagher, James, 49–50
Galloway, Charles, 51–53, 54–55
Gallup polls: on discipline, 406–407; on sex education, 411–412; on student decision-making, 408; on student drug use, 413, 415
Gardner, John, 9–10, 23, 25
Garza, Anselmo, 414
George, Henry, 404
Getting Straight, 224
Getty, J. Paul, 376
Getzels, J. W., 196
Gibran, Kahlil, 285
Glasser, William, 42
Goethe, Johann, 457
Goldhammer, Robert, 20, 61, 63, 64, 117
Goodbye, Mr. Chips, 140
Goodlad, John I., 438, 439–440, 443
Good Morning, Miss Dove, 224
Graham, Grace, 338–339
Grambs, Jean, 118
Great Cities School Improvement Programs, 400
Greater Cleveland Mathematics Program, 97
Greening of America, 338–339, 362
Gross, Neal, 329–332
group study, 250
Guerilla Manual, 385, 389
guidance and counseling, 455
Gwynn, Minor J., 90, 122–123

Haberman, Martin, 207–208
Hall, Edward, 50
Harvard University Center for Cognitive Studies, 92
Hassling, 140
Hedgecock, Laurie, 295–299
Henry, Jules, 65–66
Herndon, James, 140
Hersey, John, 114
high school(s): Computer-Assisted Instruction in, 465; flexible scheduling in, 450–454; mini-courses in, 125; student drug use in, 413, 415–416

Hilton, James, 140
Holt, John, 385
human tendency, teaching as, 222–223, 229–230
Hunter, Evan, 140
Hunt, Maurice, 109–110

If, 141
Illich, Ivan, 472
independent study, 249, 467–470, 473, 474
Individually Prescribed Instruction (IPI), 467–470, 473, 474
individualized instruction: CAI, 465–467; IPI, 467–470, 473, 474; in nongraded schools, 436–441, 443; in open classroom, 470–471; programmed, 459, 461–464; school facilities for, 477–479
in-service teacher training, 336, 385–386, 449
instruction: group, 443; individualized, 436–441, 443, 459, 461–474, 477–479; new methods of, 461–474; types of, 451–452
instructional materials centers, 477
integration, school, 401, 458. *See also* desegregation
Interaction Analysis, 46–47, 52–55, 75
Intern Teaching Program, 208
interviews, as classroom observational method, 77–78
IPI. *See* Individually Prescribed Instruction

Jackson, Philip W., 42–45, 70, 196
Jencks, Christopher, 346, 404, 457
Jersild, Arthur, 190, 198, 199
John Birch Society, 120, 124
Josephs, Davereux, 340
Joyce, Bruce, 445
junior high schools, 455, 456
Justman, Joseph, 166

Kandell, I. L., 227
Kaufman, Bel, 140, 273, 364, 367
Kerr, Norman D., 327, 328
Kes, 141, 224
Kilgo, Reese Danley, 141
Kimbrough, Ralph B., 329, 333–334
King, Martin Luther, Jr., 136
Koerner, James D., 326–329, 333, 337, 369
Kohl, Herbert, 140, 198, 262, 293, 385
Kozol, Jonathan, 39, 140, 209
Kramer, Rita, 294–295

theoretical knowledge, teacher's, 185–191
36 Children, 140, 198
This Magazine Is About Schools, 385
Thompson, James D., 345
Thoreau, Henry David, 212
Thorndike, E. L., 232–233
Time, 371
To Sir, With Love, 141, 224
turnover rate, high school teacher, 238
Twain, Mark, 325

United Daughters of the Confederacy, 124
United Federation of Teachers (UFT), 384, 401
universities, black studies in, 416–417
University of Illinois Committee on School Mathematics (UICSM), 97
University of Maryland Mathematics Project, 97
University of North Dakota New School for Behavioral Studies in Education, 417
University of Pittsburgh Learning and Research Center, 467
University of Wisconsin Intern Teaching Program, 208
Up the Down Staircase, 140, 141, 224, 273, 364, 367
U.S. Office of Economic Opportunity, 458
U.S. Office of Education, 102, 119, 121, 342, 402, 403, 420, 449; English Program, 99

U.S. Supreme Court: *Brown v. Board of Education,* 398–399, 401; effect of, on education, 341; on religion in the schools, 418

values and social policies, studying, 109–110
Veterans of Foreign Wars, 124
video- and audiotapes, use of, in teacher education, 78–81, 246–247
Vista, 402
vocational course curriculum, 102–103
"voucher plan," 404, 457–458

Walden, 212
Washington (D.C.) school system, 402
Watson, Goodwin, 187
Watson, James D., 108
Why It Spozed To Be, 140
Webster College Madison Project, 97
Weinstein, Gerald, 116
Westinghouse Learning Corporation, 469
What's Happened to Teacher?, 210, 363, 370, 375, 376, 390
Williams, Emlyn, 140
Williams, Sylvia, 140
Woodring, Paul, 340
World and the American Teacher, 235

Photo Credits

It's very interesting but is it relevant?

There are no poor students, only poor teachers.

A little learning is a dangerous thing.

To get a good job, get a good education.

Show me a troubled child, and I'll show you a troubled home.

I don't teach history. I teach children.

The kids were just great—not a sound out of them.

Teachers are born, not made.